SMITHSONIAN INSTITUTION
BUREAU OF AMERICAN ETHNOLOGY
BULLETIN 120

BASIN-PLATEAU ABORIGINAL SOCIOPOLITICAL GROUPS

By JULIAN H. STEWARD

UNITED STATES
GOVERNMENT PRINTING OFFICE
WASHINGTON : 1938

Reprint 1997
THE UNIVERSITY OF UTAH PRESS
Salt Lake City

CONTENTS

CONTENTS

ILLUSTRATIONS

EXPLANATION OF PLATES

1. *a*, Owens Valley and the Sierra Nevada Mountains. The valley, elevation 4,000 feet, lies in the arid artemisia belt but is well watered by streams issuing from the mountains. These summits exceed 14,000 feet and extend into the arctic zone. *b*, A typical formation of scattered pinyons (*Pinus monophylla*) and junipers in the White Mountains east of Owens Valley, elevation 7,200 feet. Winter camps were often made near pine-nut caches in such localities, snow perhaps being used for water. *c*, Death Valley. This gravel-covered and alkaline valley lies below sea level and supports little vegetation.

2. *a*, Joshua trees in the lower portion of the Silver Peak Range, Fish Lake Valley. Buds of these trees could be eaten before any seeds had ripened. *b*, An unusually dense grove of screw-bean trees at Ash Meadows. Screw beans, like Joshua trees, occur only in the southern portion of the area. *c*, The light, fluffy plants are sand bunch grass (*Oryzopsis hymenoides*) near Walker Lake, one of the most important seed plants in Nevada and eastern California. Although this was an unusually good crop caused by an abnormally wet year, it will be noted that the individual plants are widely spaced.

3. *a*, Spring Valley and the eastern face of the Snake Range. The valley is entirely arid except where a few dots running out from the base of the mountains indicate the course of streams which flow but a short distance before sinking into the sands. Winter villages were located on such streams. The lower portion of the mountains is speckled with juniper and pinyon trees, the upper portion with larger pines. Wheeler Peak, 13,058 feet elevation, may be seen rising above timber line into the arctic zone. Valleys like this had a few antelope and jack rabbits while the mountains sheltered deer and mountain sheep. *b*, Deep Springs Valley, elevation 5,000 feet, with its alkaline lake at the base of the mountains. The mountains, rising to 7,000 and 8,000 feet elevation, are speckled with pinyon and juniper trees. *c*, The canyon of the Colorado River in southeastern Utah, near the Escalante River. This rugged topography of sandstone mesas and deep canyons afforded few natural resources or habitable sites and was a barrier to communication through this region.

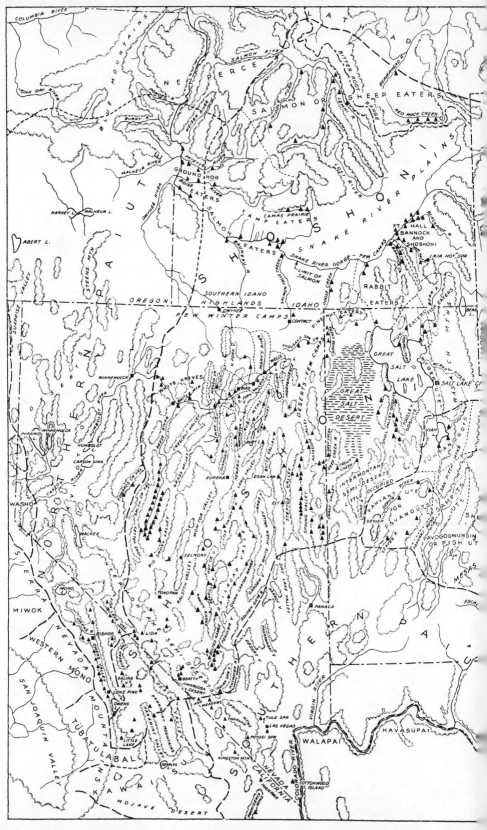

FIGURE 1.—Map of the Basin-Plateau area.

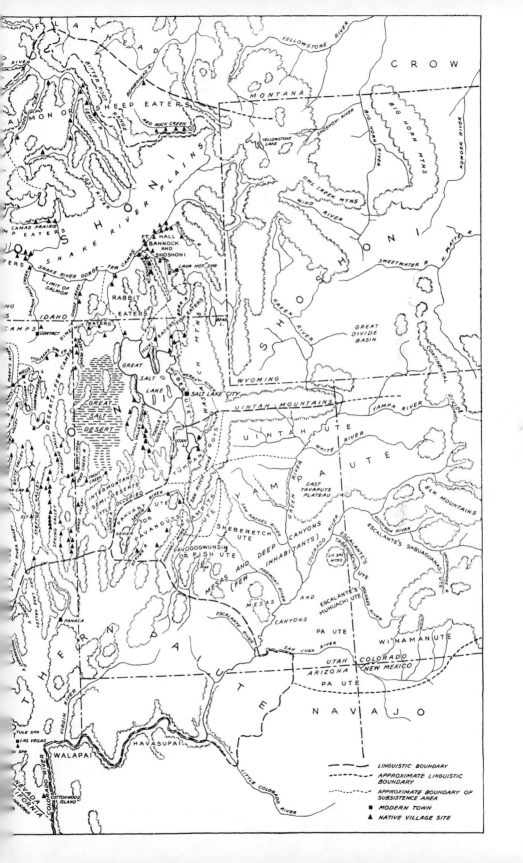

F L A T H E A D

CROW

BITTER ROOT RANGE

MONTANA

YELLOWSTONE RIVER

SHEEP EATERS

SALMON OR

RED ROCK CREEK

YELLOWSTONE LAKE

SHOSHONI R.

BIG HORN RIVER

BIG HORN MTNS

POWDER RIVER

LEMHI RIVER

SNAKE RIVER PLAINS

OWL CREEK MTNS

WIND RIVER

SWEETWATER R

N. PLATTE R

CAMAS PRAIRIE SHEEP EATERS

FT. HALL
BANNOCK AND SHOSHONI

LAVA HOT SPR.

SNAKE RIVER GORGE—FEW CAMPS

LIMIT OR SALMON

RABBIT EATERS

BEAR R

BEAR L.

GREEN RIVER

GREAT DIVIDE BASIN

S H O S H O N I

IDAHO

WYOMING

CONTACT

PINE NUT EATERS

FEW CAMPS

GREAT SALT LAKE

WEBER R

SALT LAKE CITY

WASATCH MTNS

UINTAH MOUNTAINS

YAMPA RIVER

CONTINENTAL DIVIDE

GREAT SALT DESERT

INTERMONTANE SEMI DESERTS

LITTLE OCCUPIED

UTAH

UINTAH UTE

WHITE RIVER

U T E

EAST TAVAPUTS PLATEAU

ELK MOUNTAINS

P A I U T E

UNCOMPAHGRE UTE

ESCALANTE'S SABUAGANAS UTE

PAVANT UTE

SEVIER UTE

PAVANDUTS

SAN PITCH UTE

SAMPITS

SHEBERETCH UTE

SAN RAFAEL RIVER

GREEN RIVER

COLORADO RIVER

LA SAL MTNS

ESCALANTE'S TABEHACHIS UTE

GUNNISON RIVER

DOLORES RIVER

ESCALANTE'S MUHUACHI UTE

PAVOGOGWUNSIN OR FISH UTE

MESAS AND DEEP CANYONS

(FEW INHABITANTS)

FREMONT RIVER

AND

CANYONS

PA UTE

WI'NAMANUTE

PANACA

MESAS

ESCALANTE RIVER

UTAH COLORADO

ARIZONA NEW MEXICO

PA UTE

S O U T H E R N   P A I U T E

SAN JUAN RIVER

N A V A J O

VIRGIN RIVER

TULE SPR

LAS VEGAS

WALAPAI

HAVASUPAI

LITTLE COLORADO RIVER

NEVADA CALIFORNIA

COLORADO RIVER

COTTONWOOD ISLAND

LEGEND:

— — — LINGUISTIC BOUNDARY

- - - - APPROXIMATE LINGUISTIC BOUNDARY

········· APPROXIMATE BOUNDARY OF SUBSISTENCE AREA

■ MODERN TOWN

▲ NATIVE VILLAGE SITE

PREFACE

This paper is based largely upon data collected during 6 months in 1935 on a field trip financed by the University of California and a grant-in-aid from the Social Science Research Council, and during a trip of 4 months in 1936 for the Bureau of American Ethnology. Other trips to the Great Basin area (fig. 1) had been made from time to time during the previous 9 years.

The research had several objectives. The first was to make an ethnographic reconnaissance of the Western Shoshoni and some of their Northern Paiute, Ute, and Southern Paiute neighbors. Most of the Shoshoni had not, to my knowledge, been previously studied and many had not even been visited by an ethnologist. The reconnaissance was made by means of element lists, of which 25 were procured from as many localities—3 from Northern Paiute, 1 from Bannock, 1 from Southern Paiute, 18 from Western Shoshoni of Idaho, Nevada, and Utah (2 of these being from Gosiute in Utah), and 2 from Northern Shoshoni of Idaho and Utah.

The second objective was to analyze the functional relationship of the different parts of the culture to one another and to the local environment. This analysis will be published with the element lists elsewhere.

The third aim was to ascertain the types of Shoshonean sociopolitical groups and to discover their ecological and social determinants. This is the subject of this paper.

Orthography used for native words will be found on page 273.

Initials in parentheses are informants.

English words in parentheses are translations of the native names which they follow.

A list of informants is given with the element lists elsewhere. The knowledge of each informant was, of course, greatest for his own village. It decreased for neighboring villages more or less in proportion to their remoteness from his own. These villages or the valleys in which they are located are shown on map (fig. 2). They are abbreviated as follows, those at which element lists were taken being starred:

NP–FSp,* Northern Paiute of Fish Springs in Owens Valley.

NP–FLk,* Northern Paiute of Fish Lake Valley, eastern California.

NP–LnPn, Northern Paiute of Lone Pine, Owens Valley.

NP–GeoCr, Northern Paiute of Georges Creek, Owens Valley.

NP–MC,* Northern Paiute of Mill City, near Winnemucca, Nevada.

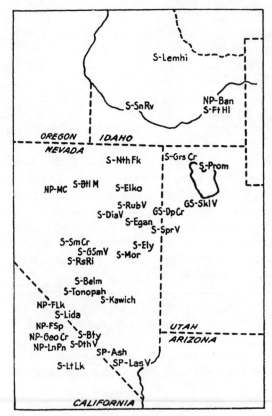

NP–B a n,* Bannock of Fort Hall, Idaho.

SP–A s h,* Southern Paiute of Ash Meadows, Nevada.

SP–LV, S o u t h e r n Paiute of Las Vegas, Nevada.

S–LtLk, Shoshoni of L i t t l e Lake, eastern California.

S–DthV,* Shoshoni of Death Valley, eastern California.

S–Bty.* Shoshoni of Beatty, Nevada.

S–Lida,* Shoshoni of Lida, Nevada.

S–GSmV,* Shoshoni of Great (Big) Smoky Valley, Nevada.

S–RsRi,* Shoshoni of Reese River Valley, Nevada.

S–SmCr,* Shoshoni of Smith Creek Valley, Nevada.

FIGURE 2.—Map of key to locations.

S–Tonopah, Shoshoni near Tonopah, Nevada.

S–Belm, Shoshoni of Belmont, Nevada.

S–Kawich, Shoshoni of the Kawich Mountains, Nevada.

S–Mor,* Shoshoni of Morey, Nevada.

S–Hmlt,* Shoshoni of Hamilton, in Railroad Valley, Nevada.

S–Ely,* Shoshoni of Ely in Steptoe Valley, Nevada.

S–SprV,* Shoshoni of Spring Valley, eastern Nevada and western Utah; sometimes called Gosiute.

S–Egan,* Shoshoni of Egan Canyon, near Steptoe Valley, eastern Nevada.

GS–DpCr,* Gosiute (i. e., Shoshoni) of Deep Creek, Utah.

GS–SklV,* Gosiute (i. e., Shoshoni) of Skull Valley, Utah.

S–DiaV, Shoshoni of Diamond Valley, Nevada.

S–RubV,* Shoshoni of Ruby Valley, Nevada.

S–Elko,* Shoshoni of Elko on the Humboldt River, Nevada.

S–BtlM,* Shoshoni of Battle Mountain on the Humboldt River, Nevada.

S–NthFk, Shoshoni of North Fork of the Humboldt River, south of Owyhee, in Nevada.

S–SnRv,* Shoshoni of the vicinity of Bruneau on the Snake River, Idaho.

S–GrsCr,* Shoshoni of Grouse Creek, northwest of Great Salt Lake, Utah and Nevada.

S–Prom,* Shoshoni of Promontory Point and vicinity, northern shore of Great Salt Lake, Utah.

S–FtHl,* Shoshoni of Fort Hall on the Snake River, Idaho.

S–Lemhi,* Shoshoni of the Lemhi River and adjoining mountains, Idaho.

Nomenclature for this area and the groups in it involves considerable difficulty. Linguistic terms are not satisfactory. Most often, all of the inhabitants except the Washo have been classed together as Shoshone or Shoshonean. But Kroeber (1907, 1909, and 1925) classed the languages with those of southern California as Shoshonean. More recently Whorf (1935) has suggested that each division of "Shoshonean," such as Shoshoni-Comanche and Ute-Chemehuevi, is really a separate branch of Uto-Aztecan. Thus, Kroeber's classification would make "Shoshonean" too inclusive; Whorf's would eliminate it. Moreover, Ute-Chemehuevi speaking peoples occur outside the area in southern California, Shoshoni-Comanche occur outside it in the Plains, while the Washo, with a different language, occupy a corner of Nevada. Linguistic terms would therefore seem to be eliminated.

Cultural terms have rarely been satisfactory unless some outstanding culture pattern is limited to an area, for example, "Pueblo." In this area a term descriptive of culture would be too long and unwieldy.

A geographical term would appear more satisfactory. The important feature of the entire area is its semiarid or steppe character. But "steppe" seems too vague and too unlikely to be understood. The area embraces all of the Great Basin but also includes portions of the Columbia Plateau to the north and the Colorado Plateau to the south. On both plateaus are other peoples with cultures unlike those treated here.

Apparently a somewhat arbitrary choice is necessary. I shall use Basin-Plateau peoples for the Mono-Bannock, Shoshoni-Comanche, and Ute-Chemehuevi speaking inhabitants of the two plateaus and the Great Basin.

The question of designating subdivisions of these groups is equally difficult. Inhabitants of portions of the areas of each linguistic group have been named according to culture (e. g., Digger, Walker), geographical location (e. g., Owens Valley Paiute, Surprise Valley Paiute), or some assumed political grouping (e. g., White Knives, Tümok's band, Southern Paiute bands). I shall not attempt here to settle the question for the Mono-Bannock or Ute-Chemehuevi. The Shoshoni-Comanche, though having very slight linguistic variation, divide into several distinct cultural groups. One is the Comanche with whom we are not concerned. Another is the Shoshoni occupying eastern Idaho, northeastern Utah, and Wyoming. Though divided into several bands, they had in common the horse, bison hunting, and a large number of Plains traits. Following Lowie, I shall call these Northern Shoshoni. The third group is the Shoshoni who occupied western Idaho and Utah and a large portion of Nevada. They lacked horses, had no bands, and possessed a remarkably simple culture which was relatively uniform throughout the area. I shall call these Western Shoshoni, a term previously used especially for the Shoshoni on the Western Shoshone Reservation at Owyhee, northern Nevada.

BASIN-PLATEAU ABORIGINAL SOCIOPOLITICAL GROUPS

By Julian H. Steward

INTRODUCTION

Objectives of the Study

Analysis of the factors or determinants which, in complex interplay, have produced any society is ordinarily forbidding. Most societies are manifestly the end result of a long history of internal development, borrowing, and adaptation to a particular environment. Greatest success should attend analyses of societies which evince a less complicated history, whose structure is simpler in content and form, and whose institutions were most extensively patterned by subsistence activities. Such societies usually exist among the simple hunters and gatherers in areas of low population density. All of the institutions of these peoples are not, of course, either primordial or the product of the environment, but they are ordinarily structurally simple and show minimal borrowing and conspicuous environmental conditioning.

A previous review of hunters and gatherers in low population areas—Bushmen, Australians, Tasmanians, Negritos, Fuegians, Athabascans, Algonkians, certain Shoshoneans, and others—indicated that despite the occasional presence of clans, moieties, and marriage classes, certain essentially simple sociopolitical patterns occurred repeatedly and were largely explainable in terms of human ecology (Steward, 1936 c).

The Basin-Plateau peoples were also simple hunters and gatherers with a sparse and scattered population, but data permitting either a description of their sociopolitical forms or an analysis of the factors producing them were not available. The present survey aimed to supply and interpret such data.

Most of the Basin-Plateau people lived at a bare subsistence level. Their culture was meager in content and simple in structure. Pursuits concerned with the problems of daily existence dominated their activities to an extraordinary degree and limited· and conditioned

1

their institutions. It was inevitable, therefore, that considerable study should be given to subsistence activities in the different natural areas. This, however, must not be construed as "environmental determinism," which is generally understood to postulate some kind of automatic and inevitable effect of environment upon culture. It is human ecology or the modes of behavior by which human beings adapt themselves to their environment. Any adaptation necessarily involves an interaction of two elements: The natural environment and the particular cultural devices, invented and borrowed, by which the environment is exploited. The kinds of activities entailed in this exploitation affect the different phases of the culture to varying degrees. The present problem, therefore, is partly to ascertain the effect of ecology upon the sociopolitical institutions.

Many modes of behavior were, of course, partly or entirely noneconomic, but the latitude permitted them was often partly established by the framework of ecology. Some noneconomic behavior, moreover, overlapped or somewhat merged with economic behavior. The problem, then, is also to ascertain the role of purely social factors.

Analysis of human ecology in the Basin-Plateau area requires consideration first of certain features of the natural landscape or environment; second, of cultural devices by which the environment was exploited; and third, of resulting adaptations of human behavior and institutions. The important features of the natural environment were topography, climate, distribution and nature of plant and animal species, and, as the area is very arid, occurrence of water. These are described in the first part of the paper. The devices for exploiting the environment were certain hunting and gathering techniques and transportational facilities, which are also described in the first section. The adaptation of certain behavior patterns to the general ecology requires consideration of the density and distribution of the population, of the role of the sexes, the family and communal groups in hunting, fishing, and seed gathering, of the territory covered and the time required for different economic pursuits, and of the size, composition, distribution, and degree of permanency of villages. As the ecology varied with both natural regions and local cultural devices, each region was visited when it was possible to do so and food areas, village sites, sources of water, topography, natural barriers, and other features relevant to the local subsistence problems were noted.

It is found that some ecological factors made the biological or bilateral family the most stable sociopolitical group. Sexual division of labor prevented the economic unit from being smaller than the family, while the expediency of families working alone in seed gathering, which was the most important activity, prevented it from exceeding the family during much of the year. Other factors, however, brought families into association in larger groups: location of winter residences with reference to food resources, water, and other natural advantages; communal hunting and fishing enterprises and some communal irrigation; unusually dense population; possession of the horse; and abnormal abundance of certain foods in small localities.

Within the limits imposed by ecology, social features—some borrowed, some developed locally—contributed to the sociopolitical groups. Some of these were integrative and gave cohesion to small, usually village groups. These include marriage and extended kinship bonds, dances, gambling, death and burial ceremonies, shamanistic activities, and occasional warfare. Factors tending to unite larger groups were intervillage marriage, festivals, annual mourning ceremonies, communal sweat lodges, and large-scale warfare. On the other hand, group solidarity was disrupted by frequent shifts of residence, wife abduction, witchcraft, and crime.

The combined effect of these ecological and social factors produced the observed sociopolitical types, with their varying size, composition, structure, unity, and political controls. But not all of the factors are universal in the Basin-Plateau area and some vary in strength. The second and largest portion of the paper is devoted to a description of these sociopolitical types.

In order to segregate fact and theory as far as possible, a synthesis and interpretation of the data are relegated to a third section of the paper. A concluding part suggests the broader and more theoretical implications of the findings.

The data pertinent to the problems of this investigation are admittedly unequal in completeness and reliability. The essential facts are, however, repeated with such monotonous similarity in locality after locality that there can be no question of their correctness.

As certain interpretations of culture process in this study involve acculturation both in the late prehistoric and historic periods, a brief history of the area follows.

HISTORY OF THE BASIN-PLATEAU AREA

At present there is little historical depth in the picture of Basin-Plateau cultures. Archeological evidence of ancient cultures is almost negligible. Gypsum Cave in present Southern Paiute territory in southern Nevada (Harrington, 1933), Lovelock Cave in northern Paiute territory in western Nevada (Loud and Harrington, 1929), and caves at Black Rock and Promontory Point in Shoshoni territory around Great Salt Lake (Steward, 1937) have yielded evidence to show that the area was occupied probably for a very long period by simple hunting and gathering peoples. The old cultures cannot, however, be adequately characterized until more research has been carried on.

Of pure classical Basket Maker culture there is no certain evidence outside the Colorado Plateau and perhaps southern Nevada. Contemporary with Pueblo I or Pueblo II of the San Juan area, a blended Basket Maker-Pueblo culture spread, probably with some rapidity, northward throughout all of Utah and most of the eastern half of Nevada. It was not uniform in this area, but showed many local adaptations and inventions. Nor was horticulture uniformly important. Sites in the northern portion are small and contain abundant evidence indicating great reliance upon hunting and presumably also upon gathering. Southern sites—those in central and southern Utah and southern Nevada—are larger and were evidently more permanent, and more dependent upon cultivation.

None of the Northern Periphery sites, however, contain positive evidence of San Juan Pueblo III elements, with the possible exception of some in southern Nevada and along the lower Colorado Plateau. Occupation of them must have ceased with the collapse of Pueblo III in the south, if not before. The most probable explanation of their abandonment is inroads by hostile tribes. Adaptation of horticulture to local conditions, while apparently not precisely like that of the modern Pueblo, seems to have been reasonably successful in at least central and southern Utah, where it probably involved irrigation with perennial mountain streams. There is no obvious reason to postulate economic failure (Steward, 1936 b).

There is at present no means of identifying either the pre-Puebloan or Puebloan inhabitants of the Northern Periphery. Perhaps some spoke Hopi, but as neither the modern Hopi cultures nor cultures of prehistoric sites in the Hopi area correspond in any important way with either Northern Peripheral Puebloan or modern Paiute or Shoshoni culture, there is no reason to postulate a specific connection between them. That the Ute-Chemehuevi, Shoshoni-Comanche, or Mono-Paviotso had more than contact with the Northern Periphery Puebloan peoples is doubtful. There are important specific cultural resemblances between the modern and ancient people, but these do not necessarily prove genetic relationship, for there are equally important dissimilarities.[1]

Sometime in the post-Puebloan period there was probably a rapid expansion of the recent peoples. Evidence which must be interpreted

[1] The question of the relationship of modern Shoshoneans to Basket Makers and Puebloans is too complex and insufficiently relevant to this study to be taken up here. It will be developed in a future paper, based on the writer's archeological and ethnological studies in Utah, Idaho, and Nevada.

in this way is their modern distribution and language. They are now distributed where the cultures of Pueblo sites, Lovelock Cave, and probably other peoples once existed. But they must have been new-comers to these places, because their culture is too unlike that of the previous occupants to postulate radical alteration in a few centuries. The Shoshonean dialects, though perhaps inherently slow to change, are similar over an enormous area. Shoshoni of Death Valley, California, of Nevada, Idaho, and Wyoming, and Comanche can understand one another with no great trouble.

But at sometime in the post-Puebloan period a culture unlike that of the Shoshoneans, the Promontory Cave culture, existed in the Great Salt Lake area. This was based upon hunting and gathering, with particular reliance upon the bison and other large game which must have been very abundant in the region at that time (Steward, 1937 b). The correspondence of this culture with that of the modern Shoshoni is slight and insufficient to link the two. The Promontory pottery is neither Shoshonean nor Puebloan. It is possible that the Promontory people were temporary residents in the area; they may even have been Athapascans then on their way south.

Shoshonean archeology so far has been unrevealing. Known camp sites have only assorted flints and occasional pottery scattered thinly over large areas. House remains are extremely rare. Cave sites are more promising than open-air sites but have not yet been studied to any great extent. The most profitable archeological research in the area will be the excavation of caves and the systematic study of flints.

When the white man arrived in the West the Basin-Plateau peoples seem to have had very nearly their present location. (See Appendix A, Tribal Distributions.)

For the purpose of this study, the Indian's contact with the white man may be divided into four periods: (1) Exploration and penetration of the territory by trappers, approximately 1776 to 1840; (2) immigration which usually passed on through the country to more fertile lands on the coast, but settled Utah and the Humboldt Valley, 1840 to 1860; (3) settlement by miners and agriculturists and the climax of strife between whites and Indians, 1860 to 1870; (4) removal of many Indians to reservations where they still remain.

Although several major expeditions were made into the Shoshonean area by early explorers, their records contain little of ethnographic interest. The first traveler was Escalante, who, in 1776, journeyed northward through western Colorado and eastern Utah to Utah Lake, thence southward through western Utah (Harris, 1909), but left scant record of tribes visited. Lewis and Clark described the Shoshoni on the Lemhi River, Idaho, visited by them in 1806, with their usual completeness. But from the Lemhi River they turned northward and saw little more of the Basin-Plateau peoples in question. The Astoria party went down the Snake River in 1811, making records which Irving compiled (1897). Observations by Ross (1849, 1855) in this region during the next 15 years are of doubtful accuracy. Wyeth, who founded Fort Hall in 1834, made valuable observations in Schoolcraft (1851, vol. I, pp. 205-228). Most other accounts are uninformative or inaccurate.

By 1825 trappers were fairly numerous in western Wyoming and southern Idaho. They extended their activities into northern Utah and somewhat into Nevada, though accounts of these trips are extremely rare. Peter Skene Ogden made several journeys into eastern Oregon and probably visited the Humboldt River in northern Nevada between 1826 and 1828, but said little about the natives. Journeys across Nevada were made in 1825 by Jedediah Smith, perhaps even earlier by Old Greenwood (Kelly, 1936), in 1833 by Walker, and subsequently by a large number of parties. The journals of these trips, however, manifest a striking lack of interest in the Indians. Some dubious information may be gleaned only from the narrative of Zenas Leonard (1904) who accompanied Walker and from Russell (1921) who traveled from 1834 to 1843. The most important contemporary account of southern Idaho is that of Bonneville, 1832-34 (Irving, 1898).

This early period of contact seems to have had little cultural or economic effect on the Indians, except in the East where they traded with the whites. There was slight strife but it did not reach serious proportions for many years. Even the obstreperous Bannock maintained peace with the white man much of the time.

The period of immigration which began about 1840 initiated changes that were to have an important effect on the Indians. Except in Utah, where the Mormons settled in 1847, however, the stream of immigrants poured down the Humboldt River across Nevada or along the Oregon trail to more fertile lands on the coast. Clashes of increasing seriousness occurred along the line of travel but the many Indians in remote valleys were untouched by the first real impact of the white man.

Despite the large number of travelers, which included many ambitious chroniclers, records of the Indians continue to be disappointing. The natives between the Rocky Mountains and the Sierra Nevada Mountains were generally dismissed with the remark that they were only miserable "Diggers." The only important sources for Nevada and Utah are Remy and Brenchley (1861). Frémont who traveled from 1843 to 1854 (1887), Simpson (1876), Stansbury (1852), and Egan (1917). There is more information about the

"Snake" to the north, but as this name was applied indiscriminately to Shoshoni of Wyoming, Idaho, and Utah, sometimes to Nevada Shoshoni, and even to Oregon Paiute, most of it is worthless.

The decade following 1860 brought the crisis for most of the Basin-Plateau peoples. In 1857 the great Comstock lode at Virginia City had been discovered in western Nevada. Within 10 years prospectors penetrated the remotest parts of the territory and boom towns sprang up in the midst of sheer desert. Shoshoni, who had previously had little contact with the white man, congregated at many of these towns. Meanwhile, immigrants had begun to settle at oases in the desert and soon live stock grazed the hills, decimating native food plants, and white men cut down pinyon trees for fuel.[1a]

Friction which had first developed along the immigration trails now became open and widespread warfare. Indians by this time had horses, which so increased their mobility that formerly independent groups could unite under new war leaders and traverse a wide territory in large groups. They had, moreover, guns with which to fight. The first serious clashes were between the white men and Northern Paiute in about 1860, but by 1865 Shoshoni of Battle Mountain and Austin were involved. Meanwhile, south of the Great Salt Lake Desert in Utah and in eastern California, Shoshoni, especially those known as Gosiute, were committing depredations against immigrants, raiding the pony express and attacking the stage line which ran through this territory. Pahvant Ute had some hand in this (Egan, pp. 256–265). For protection, Fort Ruby in Ruby Valley was built in 1862. This was the only fort in eastern Nevada, whereas there were several in western Nevada at this time. An army unit massacred a large number of Shoshoni in Steptoe Valley in 1862, but by 1865 the strife was ended. In 1869 the railroad across the continent was completed and the native period was at an end.

Shoshoni of central Nevada and of the more remote valleys seem to have kept pretty well out of the conflict. The treaty of 1863 included all the Shoshoni of northern Nevada. They were given the Western Shoshone or Duck Valley Reservation in 1877, but by no means all Shoshoni went to it. A few of the more westerly Shoshoni joined Paiute on reservations in western Nevada, but most Shoshoni remained near their native haunts, gradually abandoning their native economy and attaching themselves to ranches or mining towns.

Conflict had reached Owens Valley Paiute about the same time. The loss of lands and food resources brought amalgamation of the native bands and wars in the early sixties.

[1a] See, for example, Rept. Com. Ind. Affairs, 1864, pp. 145, 148.

Events in Utah had followed a similar course. The climax came in 1860, the Army in 1862, several overwhelming defeats and slaughter of Indians with subsequent treaties in 1863. The Uintah Ute Reservation was founded in 1865, but no lasting provision was made for Shoshoni.

In Idaho there had been intermittent strife since the period of the trappers, but it became most serious about 1860. Though Fort Hall was set aside as a reservation in 1868, the prosperous and well-organized Bannock and Shoshoni did not cease all struggle until 1878.[2]

Since 1870, then, the Shoshoneans have been rapidly dislodged from their native habitat, though Douglas (1870, p. 95) reported that only 10 percent of Nevada Shoshoni and 12 percent of western Nevada Paiute were then working for white people, the remainder living off the country as previously. Many of them went to reservations within the next few decades to attempt a new life based on cattle raising and farming. Others remained near home but were gradually forced off the native economy. Left largely to their own devices, small groups and colonies of them have attached themselves to ranches and towns, where, on a very low standard of living, they maintain a kind of symbiotic relationship with the white man.

The following quotations from early observers, though often gross exaggerations, are representative of the impression created by the aborigines of this area.

Frémont (1887, vol. 1, pp. 391–392) said that the Great Basin is "peopled . . . but miserably and sparsely. From all that I heard and saw, I should say that humanity here appeared in its lowest form and in its most elementary state. Dispersed in single families; without firearms; eating seeds and insects; digging roots (and hence their name)—such is the condition of the greater part. Others are of a higher degree, and live in communities upon some lake or river that supplies fish, and from which they repulse the miserable *Digger*. The rabbit is the largest animal known in this desert [not literally true]; its flesh affords a little meat; and their baglike covering is made of its skins. The wild sage is their only wood [in valleys only], and . . . serves for fuel, for building material, for shelter to the rabbits, and for some sort of covering for the feet and legs in cold weather," and (p. 438) "In the Great Basin, where nearly naked he traveled on foot and lived in the sagebrush, I found him in the most elementary form; the men living alone, the women living alone, but all after food. Sometimes one man cooking by his solitary fire in the sagebrush which was his home, his bows and arrows and bunch of squirrels by his side; sometimes on the shore of a lake or river where food was more abundant a little band of men might be found occupied in fishing; miles away a few women would be met gathering seeds and insects, or huddled up in a shelter of sagebrush to keep off the snow."

[2] For summaries of these Indian wars, see Bancroft, vol. 25, pp. 205–223; vol. 31, pp. 410–413, 514–526; Mack, pp. 301–334.

Leonard, 1831–36 (1904, p. 127), said the "Diggers or Root eaters" Shoshoni or Snake "keep in the most retired recesses of the mountains and streams, subsisting on the most unwholesome food, and living the most like animals of any race of beings."

Parker, 1835 (1842, p. 83) : "These are probably the most destitute of the necessities of life of any Indians west of the mountains . . . They are often called Snakes and Root Diggers, from being driven to these resorts to sustain life ; and parts of the year they suffer greatly from hunger and cold. They are more squalid than any Indians I have seen . . ."

Farnham (1843, pp. 248–249), speaking of "Paiute" and "Land Pitches" whom he erroneously placed on the Sevier River, said, "They wear no clothing of any description—build no shelters. They eat roots, lizards, and snails . . . They provide nothing for future wants. And when the lizard and snail and wild roots are buried in the snows of winter, they are said to retire to the vicinity of tim- ber, dig holes in the form of ovens in the steep sides of the sand hills, and having heated them to a certain degree, deposit themselves in them, and sleep and fast till the weather permits them to go abroad again for food. Persons who have visited their haunts after a severe winter have found the ground around these family ovens strewn with the unburied bodies of the dead, and others crawling among them, who have various degrees of strength, from a bare sufficiency to gasp in death, to those that crawl upon their hands and feet, eating grass like cattle. It is said that they have no weapons of defense except the club, and that in the use of that they are very unskilled. These poor creatures are hunted in the spring of the year, when weak and helpless . . . and when taken, are fat- tened, carried to Santa Fe and sold as slaves . . ." The last reference is to slave trade, carried on by the Ute of western Utah.

Ogden, the first visitor to write of the northern portion of this country, traveled the Humboldt River in 1827–28 and wrote that the Indians were numerous, wretched, and wild (vol. 11, p. 383). Near Malheur Lake, Oregon, he met Indians (probably Northern Paiute) who were leading a wandering life, and were wild and starving (vol. 11, p. 208), and on the plains somewhere between the Raft River and Owyhee River he met Indians moving on foot, loaded with baggage (vol. 11, p. 362).

Campbell (1866, p. 120) says of Nevada Shoshoni and other desert tribes that "suffering and scarcity at times forms a part of their history from time immemorial."

Domenech said, "The Indians who inhabit [the Great Basin] live solitarily, either in families or in little societies. According to the season, they emigrate from one place to another to seek miserable roots, which form their only nourish- ment ; even animals are seldom to be found there" (1860, vol. 1, p. 242). The "Digger" Shoshoni are "compelled to spend two-thirds of the year among the mountains, with no other resource than a little fish and roots. When both these provisions fail, or become scarce, it is impossible to picture the wretched state of these pariahs of the wilderness . . . The Snakes are less unhappy than the Shoshonees, properly so called. They are rather cleanly in their persons and never eat horse or dog flesh. They have good horses, and are admirable riders and skillful hunters . . . The Shoshonees who possess horses sometimes join the Flatheads in making incursions into their ancient territory . . .," i. e., east of the Rocky Mountains, for buffalo (vol. 2, p. 61). "The Indians of Utah are the most miserable, if not the most degraded, beings of all the vast American wilderness. They belong to the Shoshonees, properly so called, to the Snakes and Utahs, or Pan-Utahs, called Payuches by the Spaniards.

They live almost always on roots, seeds of indigenous plants, lizards, and field crickets; at certain seasons they have fish in abundance; this period of plenty once past, they remain in dreadful destitution" (vol. 2, p. 64).

GEOGRAPHICAL ENVIRONMENT AND SUBSISTENCE

Basin-Plateau activities were related in certain ways to the flora and fauna, topography, climate, and distribution of sources of water. As hunting and gathering was the basis of subsistence, certain material devices, seasonal movements of families, population density, and the location and nature of cooperative enterprises were adjusted to the kind and distribution of plant and animal species. The last, in turn, are intimately related to topography and precipitation. Topography also directly affected the population where mountain ranges offered slight barriers to population movements and gave a partial predisposition to group affiliation. As the area is generally extremely arid, the location of springs and streams which made habitation possible was of paramount importance. Water supply, in turn, depended upon altitude, topography, and mountain structure.

These salient features of the natural landscape are so interrelated with one another and with the cultural landscape that great altitude, heavy rainfall, relative abundance of edible foods, sources of water, and consequently population concentration largely coincide.

THE PHYSICAL LANDSCAPE

A large portion of the Shoshoni area lies in the Great Basin. This extends from the Wasatch Mountains on the east to the Sierra Nevada Mountains on the west, from southeastern Oregon and the uplands of southern Idaho on the north to all but the southern portion of Nevada and southwestern Utah. This area is high throughout, the valleys and lesser basins ranging from 4,000 to 6,000 feet altitude, the mountains from 6,000 to 11,000 and even to 12,000 feet. None of the streams find egress to the sea; instead, they drain into vast aggraded valley plains, either to be absorbed by the hot sands or to empty into shallow alkaline lakes, where they evaporate. An alkaline lake with marshy borders or an alkaline playa or dry lake, the relic of a true lake of a former moister period, occurs in nearly every valley.

Extreme northern Nevada and the adjoining portion of southern Idaho falls within the Columbia drainage. Streams originating in the highlands of northern Nevada and southern Idaho traverse the Columbia lava plateau to feed the Snake River, part of which is deeply entrenched in the lava. The Snake River plains slope gradually from 2,125 feet at Weiser on the west to 5,000 feet near Yellowstone on the east and are punctuated only by occasional buttes which rise up conspicuously. Ranges of the Rocky Mountains, especially the Bitterroot Mountains, form a massive boundary to the plateau in eastern and central Idaho. In central Idaho these ranges are dissected by the Salmon River and are exceptionally rugged, attaining altitudes of 6,000 to 12,000 feet.

Extreme southern Nevada, adjoining portions of Arizona, southwestern Utah, and eastern Utah, are drained by tributaries of the Colorado River. Northern Arizona and eastern Utah form part of the Colorado Plateau, an area of horizontally bedded sandstones elaborately and deeply dissected by canyons. Southern Nevada, like the Great Basin, is an area of broad valleys separated by mountain ranges which run north and south. But it is lower than the Great Basin, the valleys lying generally below 3,000 feet.

Topography determined the flora, fauna, and location of encampments, largely through its effect upon precipitation and temperature, which are closely correlated. Altitude is more important in this respect than latitude.

The lofty Sierra Nevada Range of California, which continues northward as the Cascade Range of Oregon, intercepts moisture from the west, leaving the interior basins and plateaus with low precipitation and extremely dry air. The valleys rarely enjoy more than 5 or 10 inches of annual rainfall, some of which falls in thunderstorms. In the low altitudes of southern Nevada, the lake basins of western Nevada (Carson, Pyramid, and Walker Lakes), the Salt Desert south and west of Great Salt Lake, the Sevier Lake desert, and the Snake River plains, the annual rainfall is less than 5 inches. The air, moreover, is so extremely dry that annual evaporation is in excess of precipitation. The annual evaporation is, for example, 141 inches at Clay City, Nevada, 60 at Fallon, 40 near Elko, and 80 at Pahrump and in the Great Salt Desert, as compared with 22 over Lake Michigan.[3]

Precipitation increases rapidly with altitude, however. The western portion of the Snake River plains receive 5 to 10 inches, the extreme eastern portion over 15 inches, and some of the higher ranges to the north over 30 inches. Most of Nevada receives 5 to 10 inches, but the high central area receives over 10 and mountain ranges over 20 inches. In Utah, Wendover, on the western edge of the Salt Desert, receives 4.2, the Wasatch piedmont 15 to 20, and some mountain stations even 50 to 70, the maximum recorded being 83.80 at 8,750 feet, though 20 to 30 inches is more common. The low

---

[3] These data from Summary of the Climatological Data for the United States by Sections, U. S. Department of Agriculture, Weather Bureau.

deserts of the Colorado drainage in southern Nevada receive under 5 inches (4.51 at Las Vegas). (See map, fig. 3.)

Mountain ranges not only capture but retain greater precipitation. As more than half of the annual precipitation generally falls in winter throughout most of the area, it is retained as snow on high mountain summits until well into summer (the Sierra of California even have small glaciers) and is released gradually in springs and streams.

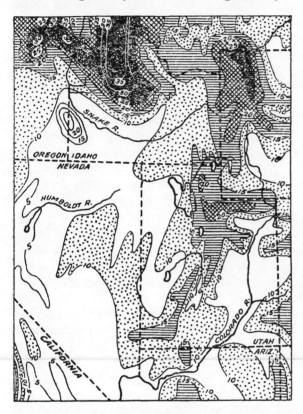

The run-off of moisture, however, depends upon mountain structure. A range which is a balanced anticline has equal run-off on opposite sides. Many ranges, however, are monoclines, having one steep escarpment, one gradual dip. On the escarpment the drainage area is small and the moisture flows down the steep rock face, much of it sinking under the thick alluvial deposits which form valley floors without emerging as springs. The opposite side not only has a gentler slope and hence greater drainage area, but the moisture runs along the surface of the strata to emerge here and there as springs. Consequently, one side of these long axial ranges in Nevada may be favored with many sources of water, while the opposite side is comparatively arid. As water is essential for location of camps, the population tends to cluster predominantly along one side of a range. Thus, the Toyabe Range drains predominantly into Reese River Valley, where the population was relatively dense, while Great Smoky Valley was arid, with few villages. Valleys which are bounded on both sides by escarpments may have a very sparse population.

FIGURE 3.—Map of rainfall distribution.

Despite the great number of mountain ranges, there are few whose height and greater rainfall give important streams to the valleys. Most streams flow but a few miles to sink in the alkaline sands. The only localities in the area under consideration where flow maintained perennial rivers of any size are the Owens River in California fed by the Sierra, Reese River, the Humboldt River, and a few large tributaries of the latter, made possible by the great general elevation and several high ranges of northern Nevada, the Salmon and Snake Rivers in Idaho originating largely in the Rocky Mountains, and the Sevier, Weber, and Bear Rivers in Utah fed by the Wasatch Mountains. These were generally areas of abnormally dense population. There are, of course, other rivers in the Great Basin lying outside our area.

Temperature also has some effect upon population. The entire area has a large number of days of bright sunshine and extreme diurnal temperature range. Summer heats reach 100° and more everywhere except in the high mountains. It well surpasses 100° in certain of the lower valleys in the south, especially in Death Valley where, reaching 135° to 140°, it made summer habitation impossible. In most of the region, however, maximum temperatures are not too great for human beings, and nights are cool.

Winter temperatures are mild in the lower valleys, especially those in the south, and on the lower Snake River. Above 4,000 feet, however, zero or subzero weather is not uncommon, and high mountain ranges are often impossibly cold. Despite the fact, therefore, that the principal foods occurred in mountains, often at some altitude, winter villages were preferably located at the foot of ranges. 4,000 to 6,000 feet was the choice elevation, for juniper and pinyon trees provided ample timber for houses and for fuel.

In summary, interrelated physical features of the landscape affected the population as follows. Water was essential. Its absence prevented permanent occupation of vast areas, for example, the Salt Desert, much of the Snake River plains, and many valleys of the Great Basin and Colorado Plateau. Furthermore, except where a few perennial streams flowed out from unusually high mountains, settlements were forced back to springs and small streams against the mountain sides. But altitude and consequently temperature restricted the inhabitable portions of mountains. High summits were too cold. The southern Idaho uplands, the bulk of the Wasatch, and the Sierra harbored no winter encampments. Consequently, where there were no rivers, permanent winter settlements were restricted to a comparatively narrow zone near the foot of mountain ranges. Excursions into arid valleys were temporary and for special purposes. Occupation of higher altitudes was possible only during summer. And finally, to a minor extent, ranges served as barriers to travel and therefore slightly demarked natural areas. The last, however, could easily be overestimated except in the case of truly massive and high ranges like the Sierra Nevada, Wasatch, or Ruby Mountains.

PLANT FOODS

The physical landscape further affected the human population through its influence on flora and fauna. The area has a large range of life zones (see map, fig. 4), each of which contributed to human existence in a very different way and consequently predetermined to a large degree not only population distribution but seasonal movements. The flora was most important, for the Shoshonean economy was essentially based on gathering. Moreover, distribution of food animals also depended somewhat upon flora. The native flora, however, was quickly altered by the introduction of cattle and sheep. Hamblin (1881, pp. 87–89) observed that by 1862, only 15 years after the Mormons entered Utah, grazing had so reduced native seeds that the Indians were starving.

The floristic zones are correlated primarily with altitude, secondarily with latitude. Any zone is 1,000 to 1,500 feet lower in the north than in the south.

The floristic zones and belts below are adapted from data by Tidestrom, Shantz, and Sampson (in Tidestrom, pp. 7–31) and Wooton (1932). The floral content of the zones above the pinyon-juniper belt, having apparently been established mainly for the Wasatch Mountains of Utah, are only partially applicable to the Nevada zones, but approximate their types.

Arctic-alpine: above timberline, usually above 11,000 feet. Flora restricted; mainly grass; unimportant to man except as it supports animal species.

Canadian: spruce-fir belt. Usually 9,000 to 11,000 feet, and therefore including only small areas in Nevada. Trees are fir (*Abies lasiocarpa*), Engelmann spruce (*Picea engelmanni*), whitebark pine (*Pinfus albicaulis*) in northern Utah and perhaps elswhere, and several willows (*Salix*).

Characteristic herbaceous plants include 16 species of grass, the seeds of most of which probably served as food. Food grasses collected by the writer and others came from lower altitudes and though they belong to genera found in this belt (wheat grass, *Agropyron*, which has 4 species here; redtop grass, *Agrostis*, which has 1; blue grass, *Poa*, which has 3; needlegrass, *Stipa*, which has 2; *Trisetum*, which has 1), they are, excepting *Poa nevadensis*, of different species.

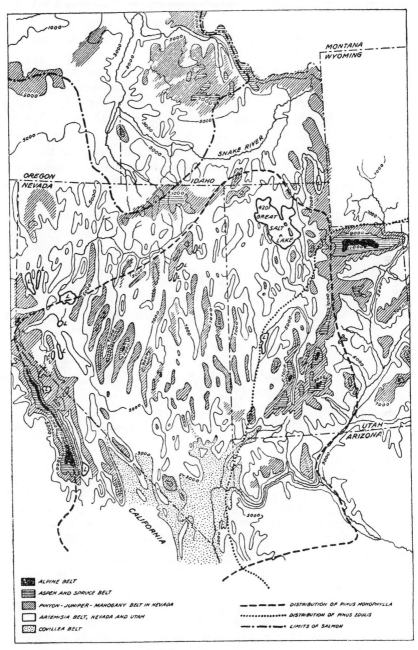

FIGURE 4.—Map of life zones.

Of 9 other characteristic plants of this belt, 3 probably served as food: Wine gooseberry, *Grossularia inermis* (none of this genus collected); wax currant, *Ribes cereum* (*R. aureum* was collected in lower altitudes); and elderberry, *Sambucus microgotrys* (same species as collected).

The abundant grasses which today make this an important grazing zone formerly supported many deer and mountain sheep.

Canadian zone: aspen-fir belt. In Utah, 7,400 to 9,500 feet. Trees are Douglas fir (*Pseudotsuga mucronata*), aspen (*Populus aurea*), some limber pine (*Pinus flexilis*) and yellow pine (*P. ponderosa*).

Characteristic herbaceous plants include 23 species. Of these, 11 may have served as food: 2 species of *Agropyron*, 1 of *Agrostis*, 2 of *Poa*, 1 of *Stipa*, and possibly the strawberry, *Fragaria*. The species in these zones, however, though belonging to the same genera, differ from those collected in the lower zones. Of 8 shrubs, those providing food were: Service berry (*Amelanchier alnifolia*), chokecherry (*Prunus melanocarpa*), rose (*Rosa fenleri*), elder (*Sambucus melancarpa* and *S. microbotrys*).

Transitional zone: mahogany belt in Nevada (elsewhere, yellow pine belt). Intermediate between pinyon-juniper and aspen-fir belts. Characteristic tree, mountain mahogany (*Cercocarpus ledifolius*). On the eastern and western fringes of Great Basin some oak brush enters this belt (*Quercus gambelii* in the east).

Of 24 species listed as characteristic and most abundant in this belt, only 11 probably served as food: *Amelanchier*, *Rosa*, 3 species of *Agropyron*, 2 of *Poa*, perhaps junegrass (*Koeleria cristata*), 2 of *Stipa*, and possibly raspberry (*Rubus parviflorus*).

Upper Sonoran zone: pinyon-juniper belt. Roughly, 5,000 to 7,000 feet, occupying the greater part of most mountain ranges, but rarely descending into valleys which are too low (pl. 1, *b*). Trees are: Pinyon (*Pinus monophylla* in Nevada; *P. edulis* in Utah); juniper or "cedar" (*Juniperus utahensis* and *J. scopulorum*). Junipers have a greater range, sometimes straggling into high valleys. Practically all mountainsides above 6,000 feet in the south and 5,000 feet in the north are speckled with pinyons and junipers. The former occasionally form fairly dense and extensive groves, supplying the chief source of food of the area.

Many other edible plants occur in this area, most of them, however, being those of higher zones which range downward under favorable moisture conditions. Species characteristic of the lower belts which range upward into this zone supply little food.

In many localities the lower part of this zone was favored for winter villages.

a, Owens Valley and Sierra Nevada Mountains.

b, Pinyon and juniper trees, White Mountains, Calif.

c, Death Valley, Calif.

a, Joshua trees, Fish Lake Valley, Calif.

b, Screw-bean trees, Ash Meadows.

c, Sand bunch grass and sagebrush.

a, Spring Valley and the Snake Range, Nev.

b, Deep Springs Valley and alkaline lake, Calif.

c, Colorado River Canyon, Utah.

Upper Sonoran zone: artemisia belt. Occupies most of the valleys and many foothills and consequently the bulk of the area north of the thirty-seventh parallel (pls. 2, *c;* 3, *a, b*). Flora is xerophytic, adapted to aridity and generally excludes grasses and herbaceous forms. It is subdivided into two formations, which are adapted to soil conditions: Northern desert shrubs and salt desert shrubs. Dominant species of different formations of the first are: Sagebrush (*Artemisia tridentata*), small sagebrush (*Artemisia nova*), little rabbitbrush (*Chrysothamnus puberulus*), shadscale (*Atriplex confertifolia*), winter-fat (*Eurotia lanata*), hop-sage and coleogyne (*Grayia spinosa* and *Coleogyne ramosissima*), bud sagebrush (*Artemisia spinescens*), malt saltbrush (*Atriplex corrugata*), gray molly (*Kochia vestita*). Probably none of these were of real importance for food. *Artemisia tridentata* and *A. nova* served only in a minor degree at times of food shortage. Occurrence of grasses and other food plants listed below in this area was either limited to the narrow moist border of streams or was sporadic in moist years, growing in restricted parts of the valleys and hills. The greater part is without any food plants. However, Indian testimony indicates that many areas now occupied especially by rabbitbrush had much grass before the introduction of cattle and sheep.

Over vast areas, especially in and near salt lakes and playas, where the soil has been left alkaline by evaporation, the salt desert shrub or greasewood formation flourishes. Practically all of its genera and species are worthless for food: Greasewood (*Sarcobatus vermiculatus*), shadscale (*Atriplex confertifolia*), seepweed (*Dondia torreyana*), pickleweed (*Allenrolfea occidentalis*), samphire (*Salicornia utahensis* and *S. rubra*), saltgrass (*Distichlis spicata*), alkali sacaton (*Sporobolus airoides*), rabbitbrush (*Chrysothamnus graveolens*).

Winter villages often were located in the upper portion of this belt, against mountain ranges where streams and springs emerged, or along rivers, for example, Owens, Humboldt, and Snake Rivers, which flowed through it (pl. 3, *a*).

Lower Sonoran zone: creosote-bush or Covillea belt; southern desert shrub. This comprises warm, low valleys, mainly south of the thirty-seventh parallel. "It differs from the northern desert shrub largely in that there are within its borders a larger number of yucca and cactus forms" (pl. 2, *a*). Principal plants dominating formations are: Desert saltbrush (*Atriplex polycarpa*), creosote-bush (*Covillea tridentata*), bur-sage (*Franseria dumosa*), joshua-tree (*Clistoyucca brevifolia*), hop-sage (*Grayia spinosa*), and coleogyne (*Coleogyne ramosissima*). Of these, only the joshua-tree

afforded food. However, mesquite (*Prosopis glandulosa*), screw
bean (*Strombocarpa odorata*), growing in moist places, and several
cacti and yucca growing scattered in hills and somewhat in valleys,
supplied food.

The areas of Nevada comprised by these different zones, however,
varied somewhat inversely in proportion to their importance to the
Indian. According to Wooton (1932, p. 11), the area of the forest
association (the mahogany, aspen-fir, and probably spruce-fir belts
above) covers only 0.8 percent of the State, yet these belts yielded
many of the important foods. The pinyon-juniper belt covers 12
percent. The artemisia belt, with large areas devoid of food plants,
covers 75.9 percent. The creosote-bush belt covers 5.8 percent, being
limited to the southern part of the area.

North of the Snake River plains the flora rapidly becomes less
xerophytic.[4] It contains a greater number of tubers, roots, grasses,
and berries, many of which were important food plants. The grasses
were also of great importance in affording grazing for buffalo and
other game and in making it possible for the Indians to keep horses.

The plateau along the Snake River is largely dominated, like the
valleys farther south, by *Artemisia, Atriplex*, and other xerophytic
plants. Along the upper reaches of the river, however, and on some
of its tributaries are flood plains supporting grasslands and a few
trees, especially willow (*Salix*) and cottonwood (*Populus*).

Increased precipitation at greater altitudes produced many "prairies" which abounded in food plants, especially *Quamasia quamash*
(Pursh) Cov. (camass), *Valeriana edulis* Nutt. (tobacco root or bitter
root), and species of *Agropyron* (wheat grass). Several such prairies
lie along the northern edge of the Snake River plains, the most important being Camas Prairie. Others occur in the mountains to the
north. In early historic times the distribution of horses among the
Shoshoni was restricted to the region of grasslands and prairies north
of the Snake River and along the upper course of the Snake River.

Passing upward toward the coniferous forest zone in Idaho, the
pinyon tree (*Pinus monophylla*) is found to be absent, but such edible
berries as service berry (*Amelanchier*) and wild cherry (*Prunus*)
grow in considerable abundance associated with other shrubby plants.

The coniferous forests include yellow pine (*Pinus ponderosa*),
Douglas fir (*Pseudotsuga*), white fir (*Abies grandis*), and larch
(*Larix occidentalis*).

Not only were many of the species of food plants different in the
northern and southern parts of our area, but the relative proportion

---

[4] No detailed study of the flora of southern Idaho is available. Weaver, 1917, however,
made a comprehensive study of the vegetation of southeastern Washington and adjacent
Idaho.

of roots or tubers and berries is greater in the north. This was of some advantage in food gathering as roots permit a longer harvesting period. The following tabulation, though not based upon a complete list of all edible plants, is a fair sampling of the relative numbers of different kinds of plants.

Locality	Seeds	Roots	Berries	Greens	Total species	Reference
Owens Valley_____	41	5	5	4	54	Steward, 1933.
Reese River_____	13	9	7	?	29	JF.
Gosiute_____	47	8	12	12	81	Chamberlin, 1911.
Lemhi_____	13	20	3	2	38	JP.

Gathering implements and methods of storing and preparing plant foods have been described previously. It remains here to sketch their effect upon seasonal subsistence activities.

In a very rough way, these activities divided the year into four periods. In early spring, when stored foods were running low, people eagerly awaited the first growth of new plants to stave off starvation. The first edible plants were those whose stems or leaves were cooked or eaten raw as "greens." They occurred along streams, near lakes and in low hills, where snow had first disappeared and warmth had come earliest.

By early summer, seeds of herbaceous and other plants had begun to ripen, some in the desert valleys, but most in the moist hills. These required that people leave their winter villages, if they had not already done so, and trek sometimes considerable distances. In a moist year a number of families might go into valleys to favored localities, but, as water had to be carried in ollas, their stay was limited to a few days or a couple of weeks at the most. When other seeds began to ripen in the mountains they moved back into the hills. Sometimes, if information reached them that certain species were abundant in another range, the entire family crossed one or more valleys, traveling 30 or 40 miles to procure the harvest. They preferred, however, to remain near their winter village so that any cached seeds would be within a convenient distance of it. The harvest period in any locality was delimited because the seeds of most species fell off the plants within a few days or weeks after ripening.

Later in the summer edible roots began to mature. These could be dug at leisure provided the stems did not wither beyond recognition. With a few berries, they provided foods during late summer. If roots were not available, however, stored seeds had to last the summer out.

By early fall pine nuts began to ripen. But the crops were extremely erratic. Some years there are virtually none in the entire area; in other years they are abundant in some places but not in others. As a good crop provided far more than could be harvested there was no competition for pine-nut lands except in the west where some idea of group rights to food areas generally prevailed. Families went in the fall to the nearest locality which offered an abundant crop. They usually stored the nuts in the mountains and wintered nearby. If the crop had failed, however, winter fare was extremely poor. And if, in addition, a drought had restricted other crops, winter usually brought great suffering, starvation, and even cannibalism.

Gathering, therefore, entailed erratic movements of the Indians. Individual families wandered from spring to fall as the promise of foods was greater in one locality or another. Though members of a winter village tended to go to the same localities, they often separated when foods were too scarce or foregathered, perhaps with people from other villages, at places of plenty. If foods near home were abundant they cached them in accessible locations in the mountains and returned home for winter. But often winter found them in distant ranges, associated with people from various localities.

Although the actual quantity of wild plant foods was probably often sufficient to have supported many times the population, several factors limited its availability. First, plants usually grew scattered, seldom occurring in dense patches, so that Shoshonean gathering techniques, which seem reasonably efficient, did not afford great quantities. Second, the seeds usually ripened and fell before many could be gathered. Third, they were unreliable, as seeds bear a close relationship to rainfall. One year might provide enough food, especially pine nuts, to support thousands, but the next 3 years have few seeds and no pine nuts. In poor years crops grew only in small quantities in limited areas and scarcely sufficed to support the sparse population.

Finally, all seed-gathering activities were carried on by family units. There was no feature whatever of the techniques that favored cooperation. A woman gathered as much, perhaps a little more, alone than she could in company with others; and once gathered, all seeds were the exclusive property of the gatherer and her family.

Details of food plant occurrence and of group and family seasonal movements are given under each district discussed subsequently.

The following list of food plants is not a complete ethnobotany. It is based upon plants collected by the writer and identified by Indians when opportunity presented itself and upon certain published works, especially Chamberlin's splendid ethnobotanical study of the Gosiute (1911) and the writer's previous work in Owens

Valley (1933). Attention should also be called to Chamberlin's list of Ute plant names and uses (1909). I am indebted to Dr. Walter P. Cottam, of the University of Utah, for identification of these plants. Data on their occurrence are taken from Tidestrom. A more detailed study of the Great Basin and especially of Idaho and Utah would greatly enlarge the list of edible plants. Present data on the known edible species, however, is a fair sampling and gives considerable insight into the relation of the flora to human activities.

Agrostis, redtop grass. Several species appear to have been utilized, though none was collected. It was probably a species of *Agrostis* that was called: sihū, S–DiaV, S–Ely, S–Hmlt, S–SprV, S–Elko; simu, S–RubV. Seeds eaten. NP–MC ate seeds of 2 species called paui'a and paso'pi.

Agropyron, blue joint or wheat grass. Species eaten by Gosiute, Chamberlin, 1911: 49, and Owens Valley Paiute, Steward, 1933: 243–244. Possibly hu: gwi, S–Bty, S–Eureka, S–GSmV and hugi, described as "wheat grass" but not collected, are species of *Agropyron*.

Allium acuminatum Hook., wild onion. Wet places artemisia to yellow pine belt. Called: gunk:, S–Elko, S–RubV; kunk, S–Lemhi; guŋga, S–DiaV, S–Ely, S–RsRi; giiŋga, S–SprV; possibly koxi', NP–MC. Eaten as greens, or S–Lemhi, bulb sometimes roasted in hot ashes. Never preserved. Gosiute used *A. bisceptrum* Watson and *A. acuminatum*, Chamberlin, 1911: 49.

Several other unidentified species of *Allium* which were eaten were called: ămu, S–Ely, S–Hmlt; amu, S–SprV; amuʰ or muh, S–Elko, S–RubV. Another larger species; bădusi, S–Ely, S–SprV, S–Elko, S–RubV, S–Hmlt, but unknown, S–Lemhi. NP–MC called two species sii and padü'nz.

Amaranthus hydridus L., weed, recently introduced to waste and cultivated ground around settlements. A: dzin, S–Elko; seeds probably eaten. Unknown, S–RubV.

Amelanchier alnifolia Nutt., service berry. Also, in some localities, *A. glabra* and probably other species. At considerable altitudes except in north; mountain sides and canyons, especially yellow pine and aspen-fir belt. Called: dühavi, S–Elko; düəm, S–RsRi; duambi, S–RubV; duəmb:, S–SprV, S–Elko; tüemb:, S–Lemhi, S–SnRv. Also, Gosiute, Chamberlin, 1911: 49; Idaho, Lewis and Clark, 3: 12, and Townsend (p. 249). Berry eaten. Seeds mashed and made into small cakes for drying and storing.

Amsinckia tessellata A. Gray. Gosiute, Chamberlin, 1911: 50, called kuhwa. But Nevada Shoshoni called *Mentzelia* kuhwa.

Anisocoma acaulis Torr. & Gray, desert portions of Covillea and artemisia belts. Tci'wi, S–LtLk; greens covered with hot rocks in small hole and cooked all day. Müigü'bump, SP–Ash; eat as greens. Unknown Lida and northward.

Aphyllon fasciculaton T. & G., cancer root. Gosiute, Chamberlin, 1911: 50.

Aplopappus. Ak: S–Lida. Perhaps ak:, is usually sunflower, wrongly applied here. Seeds eaten.

Artemisia biennis Willd., seeds; Chamberlin, 1911: 51.

Artemisia discolor Dougl. Gosiute ate seeds, Chamberlin, 1911: 52.

Artemisia dracunculoides Pursh. Gosiute ate seeds, Chamberlin, 1911: 52.

Artemisia nova A. Nels., "small sage brush". Pinyon, yellow pine, aspen and spruce belts. Kanapohovi, S–RubV; seeds eaten. Kanambi, "mountain sage", S–Elko; not used.

Artemisia tridentata Nutt., common sage. Dominates sage belt most places, ranging up to spruce belt. Called: sawava, etc., by Northern Paiute (Steward, 1933: 243); sawavu'hya, NP–LnPn; bohovi, etc., by Shoshoni; poo'vi, S–LtLk; pohovi or pagwinump, the plant, and bohombi, the seed, S–Lida. S–Elko, S–RubV, S–Ely, S–SprV, and elsewhere; bombi, seed, S–RS Ri; pagwin p:, the plant, S–Lemhi; sawa'bü, Sp–Ash. Seed eaten most places when other foods are scarce, but is bitter. Use of seeds denied only S–LtLk and S. Lemhi. S–RS Ri, parched in winnowing basket but not leached.

The wood was used for fire apparatus; bark for bags, clothing, etc.

Asclepiadora decumbens Gray. Used for chewing gum by Gosiute; Chamberlin, 1911: 52.

Asclepias speciosa Torr. and *A. mexicana* Cav., milkweed. Seeds eaten in Owens Valley; Steward, 1933: 242, 244.

Aster canescens, was called pawa'ziba, NP–LnPn, and used only medicinally. NP–FLk, however, said seeds of pawatsiva, perhaps the same or a related species, were eaten.

Atriplex. Remy and Brenchley (p. 129) state that northern Nevada Shoshoni gathered the seeds of an *Atriplex* and Burton (1862, p. 472) that they were important in Ruby Valley.

Atriplex argentea Nutt., salt brush. Alkaline plains and valleys. Lacking in south; it was probably this species that was frequently sown broadcast in north central Nevada. Sü'nu", S–SmCr; sunu, S–Elko, S–SprV, S–RubV (BM); su:na, S–RubV (RVJ). (Sunu, S–Ely, called "tickle grass.") Similar names elsewhere. A root also called sunu, S–Elko. Seeds eaten in Owens Valley, Steward, 1933: 243–4.

Atriplex canescens (Pursh) Nutt., fourwing saltbrush. Plains and foothills of the Covillea, artemisia and pinyon belts. Called: kosbadüp, S–SprV; seeds eaten. Not recognized S–Lida (PF). Not used S–RubV. Probably little used anywhere. Gosiute; Chamberlin, 1911: 52; Owens Valley, Steward, 1933: 244. *A. confertifolia* Watson and *A. truncata* Torr., seeds important to Gosiute; Chamberlin, 1911: 52, 53.

Balsamorhiza hookeri Nutt. Seeds eaten by Gosiute; Chamberlin, 1911: 53. *B. sagittata* Nutt., arrowroot, seeds and greens eaten by Gosiute; Chamberlin, 1911: 53; called kusiak, but this name given by Shoshoni to *Helianthus*.

Bidens levis, burr marigold. Seeds eaten in Owens Valley, Steward, 1933: 244.

Bigelovia douglasii Gray., rabbitbrush. Used for chewing gum by Gosiute; Chamberlin, 1911: 53.

Brodiaea capitata Bent., ground nut. Probably the irrigated plant, tüpüsi'[1], NP–Owens Valley; dübüs[1], NP–LnPn; Sego (?), S–Lida (JS).

Bromus breviaristatus Thurb., broom grass. Seeds eaten by Gosiute; Chamberlin, 1911: 54.

Cactus. Species of cactus, probably of different genera, used as foods were: a small, spherical cactus, called täsum, S–Ely; dasimb: S–SprV, S–Hmlt; tsin: (tsin:, however, is more probably a thistle; see *Cirsium*), S–RubV; a large, spherical cactus, eaten raw, called mütä', S–Ely, S–Hmlt; müts, S–Elko; absent, S–RubV. Müts, S–Lemhi, roots used, but cannot be stored. Tsin:, S–Lemhi, however, was said to be a thistle. Gosiute mutsa is cactus, possibly *Mammillaria*. Chamberlin, 1911: 85.

Calochortus gunnisonii Wats., gunnison mariposa lily. Called: sigo, S–Lida, S–RubV, S–Elko; bulb eaten except at S–Lida. *C. kennedyi* Porter, mariposa lily, growing in desert areas, canyons, and mountain sides of the Covillea belt, southern portion of area. Called: kogwi, S–LtLk, abundant in Koso Mountains;

kogi'ha, NP–FLk; bulb eaten. Probably *C. nuttallii* Torr. & Gray, in the northern part of the area is si:go, S–Ely, S–Elko, S–RubV, S–Hmlt; sigo, S–Lemhi; bulb eaten but not suitable for storage. See also its use by Gosiute, Chamberlin, 1911: 54.

Carum gairdneri Benth. & Hook., yampa, yamp. Mountain sides and canyons of the artemisia, pinyon, and yellow pine belts; important quantities for food occur only in northern portion of the area, especially at Camas Prairie, Idaho; some grows on Lemhi and Salmon Rivers. Frémont (1887, vol. 1, pp. 192–193) said of yamp (*Anethum graveolens*), "among the Indians along the Rocky Mountains, and more particularly among the Shoshonee or Snake Indians, in whose territory it is very abundant, this is considered the best among the roots used for food." It was encountered south to Reese River and Spring Valley. Called: yomba, S–DiaV; yümba, S–Ely, S–Hmlt, S–SprV, and S–RsRi; yümb:, S–Elko, S–RubV; yamba, NP–MC; yamp, NP–Ban, S–Lemhi. Roots used everywhere, including Gosiute, Chamberlin, 1911: 55. Frémont (1887, p. 220) says this was abundant along the Snake River. Hoffman (1878, p. 465) states that it was an important food among Nevada Shoshoni, calling it "yambi'-tsi," "yam-pa," or "yani'-pah." Large quantities were stored for winter use.

Caulanthus pilosus S. Wats., eaten as greens, S–DthV, Coville, 1892.

Chaetochloa, foxtail grass. Introduced; waste land around settlements. A species, probably of *Chaetochloa*, was called panodop, NP–MC; seeds eaten.

Chenopodium. Seeds of different species were important to Nevada Shoshoni. Remy and Brenchley mention this (p. 129), and Burton (1862, p. 472), speaking of Ruby Valley. *C. album* L., goosefoot or lambs quarters; introduced. Probably names given this species were natively applied to other species, which were sown broadcast by various central Nevada Shoshoni. *Chenopodium* called: üap:, S–RsRi, S–GSmV, S–Elko, S–Mor, S–Ely, S–SprV, S–RubV, S–Hmlt, NP–MC, S–Lemhi; üapi, S–Diav, S–SmCr. Probably üyüp; S–Lida, is same. Seeds eaten and young plants eaten as greens. Rare on Salmon River; more abundant on Snake River. Chamberlin says Gosiute utilized *C. capitatum* Watson, *C. rubrum* L. and *C. leptophyllum* Nutt., 1911: 55. Owens Valley Paiute used *C. fremonti*, Steward, 1933: 243–244.

Chrysothamnus, rabbitbrush. One or more species of rabbitbrush, probably including *C. stenophyllus* (Gray) Greene, were used widely for chewing gum. The bark of the lower stem and roots was chewed until gum formed. *C. stenophyllus* was called: tosa' mbi, S–LtLk, su:wap:, S–Hmlt (seeds said to form when pine nuts are ripe); siwap:, S–Elko, dubiciwap:, S–RubV (BM); pasawi': jab*, NP–FLk.

Cinna arundinacea var. *pendula* Gray., wood reed grass. Seeds eaten by Gosiute; Chamberlin, 1911: 56.

Cirsium, thistle. A species, perhaps *C. neomexicanum* Gray., was called: pazünü, S–Elko; roots and stem eaten; aiwabok:°, S–RubV, not used. Frémont says the large, carrot-like roots of *C. virginianum* were eaten by Shoshoni north of Great Salt Lake (1887, p. 256). Remy and Brenchley (p. 129) list *C. acaule* (probably same as *C. drummondii acaulescense* (Gray) Macbr. as important in Nevada; it was eaten raw or cooked. S-Lemhi called some thistle tsin: roots baked over night to prepare for drying and storing. Chamberlin records Gosiute dzina as *Claytonia caroliniana* var. *sessilifolia*, spring beauty, and also as potato (1911: 81) but Gosiute tsina, tsiŋgabogop, tsïŋga, tïntsiŋga is *Cirsium drummondii* Torr. & Gray or *Cnicus drummondi* Gray and *Cirsium undulatum* (Nutt.) or *Cnicus undulatus* Gray., plumed thistle (1911: 56). The latter also called pabogo. Probably the thistle called tiŋgambogo', S–Ely.

S–Hmlt, S–SprV; bambibogo, S–RubV, S Elko; tsinambogo, S–Lemhi, is also *Cirsium. Cirsium eatoni* (Gray) or *Cnicus eatoni* (Gray) was called by Gosiute, pogwo, pogo, aiwabogop, aigwabogop, Chamberlin, 1911: 56. A purple flowered species, tsin' was not eaten, S–GSmV, but young leaves of another species, tsüŋ', were eaten.

Claytonia caroliniana var. *sessilifolia* Torr. spring beauty. Gosiute ate bulb; Chamberlin, 1911: 56.

Claytonia lanceolata. Roots eaten by Shoshoni, Lewis and Clark (vol. 5, pp. 159–160).

Clistoyucca brevifolia (Englm.) or *Yucca brevifolia* or *Yucca arborescens,* Joshua tree (pl. 2, a). Upper Covillea belt, scattered or forming thin forests; ranging from 3,000 to 4,000 feet altitude; none north of Lida. Flower buds eaten in spring.

Cogswellia ambigua (Nutt.) Jones or *Eulophus ambiguus* Nutt., tuber. Used in Idaho (Townsend, p. 248), "dried, pulverized with stones, and after being moistened with water, is made into cakes and baked in the sun. Thwaites (Townsend, note 62), however, thinks this plant is *Psoralea esculenta,* or "pomme blanche" or "swan-apple."

Crepis glauca Torr. & Frem. Gosiute ate leaves, Chamberlin, 1911: 57.

Cymopterus longipes Watson leaves and *C. montanus* Torr. & Gray seeds and roots eaten by Gosiute, Chamberlin, 1911: 57.

Deschampsia caespitosa Beauv., hairgrass. Gosiute ate seeds, Chamberlin, 1911: 57.

Dondia erecta, seepweed. Called: wadzovi'¹, S–SmCr and probably S–RsRi; seeds eaten. Wadzovi, S–DiaV, S–Hmlt; use denied. Not recognized, S–RubV, S–Lida, S–Elko, and S–RubV.

Dracocephalum parviflorum Nutt., dragon head. Gosiute ate seeds; Chamberlin, 1911: 58.

Echinocactus polycephalus, devil's pin cushion. S–DthV pried out and ate seeds, Coville, 1892.

Echinochloa crusgalli L., water grass. Seeds eaten in Owens Valley, Steward, 1933: 243.

Eleagnus argentea. Seeds eaten in Owens Valley, Steward, 1933: 244.

Eleocharis, spike rush. Seeds eaten in Owens Valley, Steward, 1933: 245. Shoshoni plant called mahavit may be same.

Elymus condensatus Presl., wild-rye. Plains, mountain sides, and canyons up to 10,000 feet. Called: waiya⁽ᵃ, NP–FLK (Steward, 1933: 244); waya, NP–MC. The plant was called: pa (water) sonip (grass), S–Elko; bai (big) sonip, S–Elko S–RubV; wadunzip, S–RsRi, S–Lemhi. The seeds were called: wavi, S–Elko; waavi, S–SmCr; wahavi, S–Lemhi; wa: vi, S–Hmlt, S–RubV, S–Ely, S–SprV, S–DiaV, S–RsRi; wayabim:, S–Lida (PF), Wayiabi, S–Lida (JS). Wada, S–RubV and waduzip, S–SnRv, probably same; people of S–RubV sometimes called wada düka (eaters) because of abundance of this seed. Seed everywhere eaten.

Probably other species of *Elymus* were similarly named and eaten, but no specimens were collected. See also Owens Valley, Steward, 1933: 244. *E. canadensis* L. and *E. sibiricus* L., seeds eaten by Gosiute; Chamberlain, 1911: 58.

Ephedra. Two species of this were used for tea. *E. viridis* Cov., occurring in the pinyon belt up to 8,000 feet, was most commonly employed. This was called: tutəmb; or tutəmbi, S–Lida (PF), S–Ely, S–Elko, S–RubV, S–Mor. *E. nevadensis* Wats., occurring in the artemisia and lower pinyon belts, was sometimes used. It was called tutum'bip, S–LtLk; tutump:ᵃ, SP–Ash. This species was also used at S–Lida. Owens Valley also used *E. californica* Wats., Steward, 1933: 245. S–DthV also roasted seeds of *E. nevadensis*, Coville, 1892.

Eragrostis secundiflora Presl., love grass. Owens Valley Paiute ate seeds, Steward, 1933: 243. Called: mono, NP–FLk.

Festuca tenella Willd. Gosiute ate seeds; Chamberlin, 1911: 60.

Festuca ovina var. *brevifolia* Watson, fescue grass. Gosiute ate seeds; Chamberlin, 1911: 60.

Fritillaria pudica Spreng., buttercup. Gosiute ate bulb; Chamberlin, 1911; 61, called winago. S–Lemhi, winigo, may be same.

Gilia micromeria Gray. Valleys and mountains sides of the artemisia and yellow pine belts. Called: ovü'ha, NP–FSp and NP–FLk; seeds eaten. Not recognized SP–Ash and S–Lida.

Glyceria aeroides Thurber, manna grass, *G. aquatic* Smith, reed meadow grass, and *G. nervata* Trin. Seeds eaten by Gosiute, Chamberlin, 1911: 61.

Grossularia, gooseberry. Some species eaten S–RsRi and probably elsewhere.

Helianthus, sunflower. Seeds of several species, distinguished in native terminology but generically called ak:, were eaten. Species collected were not, however, consistently named everywhere. *H. annuus* L. and *H. aridus* Rydb., both common, especially in the moist parts of the artemisia, pinyon, and yellow pine belts, were the most important. The first was called akü'ü, S–SmCr; kusiak, S–Elko; ba: k or hiomb:, S–RubV; akü', NP–MC; woakü, S–Lida (PF); pak: (pa, water), S–Owyhee (TP). The second was called akü, S–SmCr; woakü, S–Lida (PF). S–Elko distinguished two species, usiakü and biakü (biap:, big); S–RubV, also two, kusiak: and biakü; NP–Ban, five pak:, ak:, kosi'ak:, yuhu'ak: bühü'ak:; S–Lemhi, also five, ak:, bühak:, biak, pa'ak:, kusiak:, all occurring on the Salmon River; S–SnRv, four, biak:, kusiak:, pü^hu (hairy) ak:, pa: k:; Owens Valley and NP–FLk, 3, akü', pak:, and påk. SP–Ash cultivated a species of wild sunflower called ak^ü. See also Chamberlin, 1911: 62, for Gosiute use of sunflowers; Steward, 1933: 243, for Owens Valley use, including *H. bolanderi* Gray.

Hilaria jamesii (Torr.), galleta grass. Dry deserts, canyons, and hillsides; lacking in northern portion of area. Sonip: (grass), S–RubV, not eaten. Absent, S–Elko. Sobi', NP–MC, seeds eaten. Eaten also S–Lida. S–RubV said a larger species was eaten.

Holodiscus dumosa, S–Elko, bauwuŋgop: (?), tea made from roots. S–RubV, kwütciani, not used.

Hookera sp., in most places in southern portion of the area. This may be *Broadiaea capitata*, grass nut or blue dicks (Steward, 1933: 245). Abundant in Koso Mountains and 1 mile east of Big Springs in Ash Meadows and Owens Valley. Called: sigo (same name applied to *Calochortus*), S–LtLk; a: nzi (?), NP–FSp. Eaten also S–Lida.

Humulus lupulus L., hop. Seeds eaten by Gosiute, Chamberlin, 1911: 63.

Juncus parous Rydb., rush. Meadows of the pinyon belt. Called: Saip:, S–GSmV; seeds eaten. S–SmCr said saip: applied to some other plant, probably tule, *Scirpus*. Owens Valley Paiute ate seeds of *Juncus balticus* Willd., wire rush, Steward, 1933: 243, 246.

Lactuca ludoviciana DC. Leaves eaten by Gosiute, Chamberlin, 1911: 64.

Lappula occidentalis (Wats.), stickseed. Plains, canyons, and mountain sides of artemisia and pinyon belts. Called sohna, S–Elko, S–Lemhi; suna, S–RubV; seeds eaten. S–Lemhi, root probably also eaten. Sünu'^w, S–RsRi, and sunu', S–Eureka is either this or *Atriplex*.

Lepargyrea, buffalo berry. See *Shepherdia*.

Lepidium tewanum Buckl., peppergrass. Plains and dry hillsides of the Covillea and artemisia belts. Called Ko:ga, S–SmCr, S–Ely, S–DiaV; ko:gᵃ, S–Hmlt; koga, S–Elko. Absent or not recognized, S–Lida, S–RubV.

Lilium parvum Kell., tiger lily. Bulbs eaten in Owens Valley, Steward, 1933: 244.

Lithospermum pilosum Nutt. and *L. multiflorum* Torr. Seeds eaten by Gosiute, Chamberlin, 1911: 65.

Lophanthus urticifolius Benth. Seeds eaten by Gosiute, Chamberlin, 1911: 66.

Lycium andersonii Gray., a small, red berry. One of the few berries growing in desert areas and hillsides of the Covillea and artemisia belts; northern limit is Cloverdale near Tonopah and Hot Creek, north of the Kawich Mountains. Called huʰpiʳya, NP–LnPn; hup:i, S–LtLk; hu:pi, S–DthV, S–Bty, S–Lida, S–RsRi, S–GSmV; Hu'u'piva, SP–Ash; hupuhya, NP–FLk. Beaten into a basket by means of a stick; dried and stored.

Mammillaria (?), cactus. Eaten by Gosiute, Chamberlin, 1911: 66.

Mentha, mint. Wet places, probably throughout area. Called baugona, S–Elko; bagwana, S–RubV. Boiled to make tea. Probably used everywhere. *M. arvensis* L., tule mint, used in Owens Valley, Steward, 1933: 245. *M. canadensis* L., used by Gosiute, Chamberlin, 1911: 66.

Mentzelia dispersa Wats. Covillea belt upward to the yellow pine belt. Seed was sometimes sown broadcast by central Nevada Shoshoni. Called kuha, NP–LnPn, NP–FLk; ku:ᵁ, ko', SP–Ash; kuha or kuhwa, S–LtLk and Nevada Shoshoni; kūha, S–RsRi.

Monolepis chenopodoidea. Seeds eaten by Gosiute, Chamberlin, 1911: 67.

Nasturtium palustre DC., watercress. Plant eaten by Gosiute, Chamberlin, 1911: 67 and Shoshoneans elsewhere.

Oenothera biennis L., evening primrose. Seeds eaten by Gosiute, Chamberlin; 1911: 67. *O. hookeri* T. & G., seeds eaten in Owens Valley, Steward, 1933: 243. S–DthV ate seeds of *O. brevipes* A. Gray and other species, Coville, 1892.

Opuntia basilaris Engelm. & Bigel., pricklypear. Desert areas and hillsides of the Covillea and artemisia belts in south. S–DthV, called nava (Coville, 1892).

Opuntia. Various species seem to have been used in different places, the stems and sometimes fruit being eaten. A species at S–Hmlt called huvi. Other names of pricklypear are ă:govi, S–Ely; agovi, wogavi, S–Elko, S–Lemhi; wo:gavi, S–SprV, S–Elko, S–Diav, S–RubV. Gosiute also used it, Chamberlin, 1911: 67. S–Lemhi, needles burned off, then baked in hot ashes in a hole, covered with earth and ashes; handled with sticks; not stored.

Orobanche, broomrape. Remy and Brenchley (pp. 129, 136) say that the enlarged root of a species of *Orobanche* was an important food to Nevada Shoshoni. This may be the *Aphyllon fasciculatum* T. & G. listed by Chamberlin; see above.

Oryzopsis hymenoides (Roem. & Schult.) Ricker, sand bunch grass or Indian mountain rice (pl. 2, c). Desert areas, plains, canyons, and mountain sides of the Covillea belt upward to about 9,000 feet. Scarce on the Snake River, unknown to the Salmon River, S–Lemhi. An important seed in the southern portion of the area, occurring in considerable quantities which were gathered in late spring or early summer for storage. But the harvest period was limited to only a few weeks, which restricted quantities which could be gathered. Called by Shoshoni and Northern Paiute everywhere wai, except S–Lida, where PF called it hugwi, and S–DthV, where BD called it huvi or wai. Used also by Gosiute, Chamberlin, 1911: 68 and in Owens Valley, Steward, 1933: 244. *O. miliacae* (L.) B. & H., also eaten in Owens Valley.

Parosela. Eaten in Owens Valley, Steward, 1923: 243.

Phragmites communis Trin., reed. Used througout the area for sugar. See also, Chamberlain, 1911: 69; Steward, 1933: 245; Colville, 1892: 355.

Pinus edulis Engelm., pinyon or pine nut. Occurs in eastern portion of area, extending but little west of Ute territory and only slightly overlapping *P. monophylla.* See Chamberlain, 1911: 69, on Gosiute use. Gathered by Pahvant Ute in a manner similar to Shoshoni gathering. Ute, however, preferred *P. monophylla,* requiring travel to west of Sevier Lake.

Pinus monophylla Torr. & Frém., pinyon or pine nut pine (pl. 1, *a*). Occurs throughout most of the Nevada Shoshoni area in important quantities to the Humboldt River and in western Utah to Grouse Creek near the Idaho border (fig. 4). In the south, it ranges from about 6,000 to 8,000 feet; in the north, about 5,000 to 7,000; grows scattered on mountain sides, usually associated with juniper, but has a more restricted range than the latter.

The nut called tuba everywhere; the tree, wakai, S–RsRi.

It is the most important single food species where it occurs, but harvests are unpredictable. Each tree yields but once in 3 or 4 years. In some years there is a good crop throughout the area, in some years virtually none. In other years, some localities yield nuts but others do not. When a good crop occurs, it is far more abundant than the local population can harvest. The cones begin to open in early fall, the nuts first being knocked from the cones with a pole or the cones knocked to the ground then opened by pounding or roasting. Within a few days nuts begin to drop from the cones. The period during which they can be harvested is consequently 2 to 3 weeks, rarely longer; Ruby Valley, it was only 10 days. Had crops been reliable each year, and per- mitted a longer harvesting period, the harvest would have supported many times the population. Actually, a family sometimes procured enough for 1 year, rarely for 2, and frequently passed two or three winters without pine nuts, living on scanty supplies of other seeds. Cooked nuts might keep 2 years, but usually spoiled after a year. When burned from the cones, nuts were thereby cooked. Those picked up from the ground were stored green, according to OD, because coyotes would eat cooked nuts.

The daily harvest per person varied considerably with the annual yield. Dutcher said 10 or 12 Shoshoni women gathering in the Panamint Mountains got 1 or 2 bushels a day. This would be about 100 to 150 pounds. Ruby Valley informants said a person could pick 200 pounds in 10 days. BG, S–Elko, thought a person could pick not over 50 pounds of pine nuts a day. (From the writer's experience this figure is substantially correct.) Four persons, in- cluding BG, once picked 300 pounds in a week, a rate of about 12½ pounds per person per day. At this rate, a family which included four pickers could gather not over 1,200 pounds in the probable maximum of 4 weeks during which they could be harvested. Even this figure is probably excessive. The quan- tity consumed during the winter depended upon use of other foods. If pine nuts were virtually the only food, a person could easily eat 2 pounds a day, or about 10 pounds for a family of five. In this case 1,200 pounds would last but 4 months. And 1,200 pounds is probably the maximum crop possible. Consequently, it is not difficult to see why starvation by early spring was very common.

Another feature of pine nut gathering is that the impossibility of harvesting the entire crop provided no motive for ownership of pinyon areas. Persons lacking crops in their own country were welcomed, even invited, *to harvest* elsewhere. Each family ordinarily traveled to a locality with a good crop, even if it were 50 miles away. This naturally threw different people into association in successive years. Once the crop was harvested, it was manifestly too heavy to carry any great distance. Consequently, people wintered near the pine nut caches, usually in the mountains where there was timber for houses and for fuel. If, however, they had gathered near their habitual winter village, they returned home and packed down nuts from the caches as needed.

For details of pine nut gathering, see Dutcher; Coville, 1892; Chamberlin, 1911: 69; Steward, 1933: 241–242.

Pinus. Seeds of another, unidentified species, occurring in the northern portion of the area were eaten. This was probably either *P. flexilis* James or *P. albicaulis* Engelm., the tree called woŋgovi, the nut called woŋgoduba, S–Elko, S–Lemhi, referred to as "white pine" (white bark pine?). This occurred on the higher altitudes in small quantities in the Ruby Mountains, and abundantly in the mountains around Jarbridge, which are consequently called woŋgogadudoyavi (woŋgo, pine+gada, sitting+toyavi, mountain). BG thought they were too small and "too greasy" and the trees too difficult to climb to make them profitable. S–Lemhi procured seeds in September, felling or climbing the tree, burning nuts from the cone in a large fire, cooking them at the same time, then storing them.

Poa nevadensis Vasey, bluegrass. In yellow pine, aspens, and spruce belts. Called nadü'mb:ⁱ, S–LtLk; siup:, S–Lida (JS); nadü'mp:a, SP–Ash; kwasina'b:ᵃ NP–FLk; seeds eaten everywhere except NP–FLk. Gosiute ate seeds of *P. californica* Munro and *P. tenuifolia* Nutt., Chamberlin, 1911: 69–70.

Polygonum, knotweed. Eaten in Owens Valley, Steward, 1933: 244.

Populus angustifolia James, cottonwood tree. Gosiute procured sugar from it; Chamberlin, 1911: 70. Suŋgavi, S–Mor, probably this species.

Prosopis glandulosa Torr., mesquite. Plains, desert areas, and dry canyons of the Covillea and lower artemisia belts; none north of Death Valley. Important food where occurs. Young beans gathered in April and eaten like string beans; mature beans gathered and cached in July. Young pods eaten whole; dry pods ground to eliminate seeds. Called ovi, S–DthV. (See Coville, 1892.)

Prunus, chokecherry or wild cherry. In moist canyons and mountains, pinyon to aspen belts; more abundant and in lower altitudes in northern part of area. Probably different species eaten. Called to'ocawi, NP–MC; doŋgwicǝp or donambi, S–RsRi; donombi, S–Ely, S–SprV, S–Elko, S–DiaV, S–Hmlt; do'nambi, S–GSmV; tonumbi, S–RubV; tonump:, S–Lemhi; do:nambe, S–SnRv. Gosiute used *P. demissa* Welpers, Chamberlin, 1911: 71. S–Lemhi and elsewhere pounded cherries on a metate to mash the seeds, squeezed out the juice, dried and stored the pulp, including the seeds.

Quamasia quamash (Pursh) Cov., common camas. Plains, meadows, and hillsides up to 8,000 feet. In important quantities especially in Idaho; rare south of Idaho, but used by Gosiute, Chamberlin, 1911: 54; Remy and Brenchley, p. 135, mention its use in Nevada. Townsend (p. 247) says Idaho Indians place it in a pit with hot stones for several days, and "when removed it is of a dark brown color about the consistency of softened glue, and sweet like molasses. It is made into large cakes, by being mashed, and pressed together, and slightly baked in the sun."

Quercus, oaks. Acorns were eaten in the vicinity of the Sierra Nevada Mountains of California (Steward, 1933: 246) and of the Wasatch Mountains of Utah (Chamberlin, 1911: 71) but not in most of the Nevada and Idaho area. Acorns called wiya, S–LtLk. *Q. kelloggii* Newb. called tcakicavü'ü, *Q. palmeri* (?) called wiya, Owens Valley. Wiya, NP–FLk, unidentified, is probably the same. This did not occur in important quantities if at all in Fish Lake Valley. Central Nevada was largely if not entirely devoid of oaks.

Radicula curvisiliqua Hook., western yellow cress. Seeds eaten in Owens Valley, Steward, 1933: 242.

Ranunculus aquatilis L. Greens eaten by Gosiute, Chamberlin, 1911: 71.

Rhamnus californica Esch., coffee berry. Eaten in Owens Valley, Steward, 1933: 245.

Rhus trilobata Nutt., sumac, squaw berry. Plains and mountain sides of Covillea, artemisia and pinyon belts. Called ütcüp, S-Ely; berry eaten. Gosiute, Chamberlin, 1911: 72, ate berries of *R. glabra* L.

Ribes aureum Pursh., golden or black currant. Hillsides and along creeks, artemisia to aspen belts. The plant called bagon p, S-Elko, E-RubV. The berry called bogombi, S-RsRi, S-Elko, S-GSmV, S-SprV, S-RubV, S-DiaV, S-Hmlt; bo:gümbi, S-Ely. Berries eaten. Owens Valley called paŋwavu'hia (Steward, 1933: 245); NP-FLk, panwabuih^{xx}, dried and stored. Gosiute also ate *R. divaricatum* Dougl., *R. lacustre* and *leptanthum* Gray var. *brachyanthum*, and *R. oxycanthoides* L., Chamberlin, 1911: 72.

Rosa ultramontana (Wats.) Heller and perhaps other species, wild rose. Canyons and water courses in the pinyon to aspen belts. Called tsiavi, S-Elko; tsiabi, S-RubV; tsiəmb, S-Lemhi; seed sometimes eaten. Also eaten by Gosiute, Chamberlin, 1911: 72. *R. pisocarpa* Grey, eaten in Owens Valley, Steward, 1933: 244.

Rubus leucodermis Dougl., raspberry. Eaten by Gosiute, Chamberlin, 1911: 73, and no doubt elsewhere.

Rumex crispus L., dock, sorrel. Introduced from Europe; occurs around settlements. Called pauwiya, S-SmCr, S-Elko, D-DiaV, NP-MC; bauwiya or tümü, S-Elko, S-RubV (RVJ), S-RsRi. Seeds eaten. S-Lida, leached seeds in cold water; this is among the few instances of leaching plants other than acorns. Also called nüwünoko, S-Elko; and S-RubV. The latter did not eat it. See also "Medicinal plants," appendix E. Unknown to S-SprV. Perhaps some of these names were formerly applied to native species of Rumex.

Salicornia herbacea L., glasswort. Gosiute ate seeds, Chamberlin, 1911: 73.

Salvia columbariae Benth., chia. Southern portion of area. Called pasida, Owens Valley, NP-FLk, S-LtLk, S-DthV, S-Bty, S-Lida. Seeds eaten. Owens Valley, Steward, 1933: 243.

Sambucus microbotrys Rydb., elderberry. Aspen to subalpine belts. Probably other species, which grew in moist canyons down to the artemisia belt, were also eaten. Called kunugi' (probably the plant), S-Ely, S-Hmlt; kunugip, S-Elko, S-RubV, S-Hmlt, S-Lemhi; duhiyumbu' (probably the berry), S-DiaV; tu:uyümba, S-RubV; gunu'vip (the plant) and tuhiumbi (tu, black+hiumbi, berry), S-RsRi. Berries ordinarily dried and stored, though S-Lemhi said they would not keep. Owens Valley used *S. mexicana*, Steward, 1933:245. Gosiute used *S. glauca* Nutt. and *S. racemosa* L., Chamberlin, 1911: 74.

Scirpus lacustris L., tule. Occurs in swampy areas of valleys which are not too alkaline. Lower stems and roots eaten. Gosiute ate *S. maritimus*, Chamberlin, 1911: 74. In the Humboldt sink, Indians gathered a "honeydew" exuded by tule, making balls of it for preservation (Bidwell, p. 52).

Shepherdia argentea Nutt., buffalo berry. Artemisia and pinyon belts, northern portion of the area. Called biawiyumbi, S-Elko; berry eaten. Absent, S-Ely, S-RubV. Gosiute also ate it, Chamberlin, 1911: 75.

Probably wi:yum^{b1}, S-DiaV; wi'yumb, S-GSmV; wiyumbi, S-RsRi, S-SprV and Star Valley; wiyup^{11} NP-MC ("buck berry") is a smaller variety or species of bia (big) wiyumbi. This was lacking S–Ely, S–Hmlt, S–Elko, S–RubV, according to informants' knowledge.

Sisymbrium canescens Nutt., hedge mustard. Seeds eaten by Gosiute, Chamberlin, 1911: 75.

Sitanion hystrix (Nutt.) Smith. Called wücitüp, S–Lida (PF), S–RubV (BM). Wüsitüp, S–DiaV; wü: sia, S–Ely, S–Hmlt, S–Elko, S–RubV (RVJ) S–LtLk; wacitüp:, S–Lida; kwasinab:, NP–FLk are probably the same. All except S–RubV (BM), S–LtLk and NPFLk ate the seeds. S–Lemhi did not know of it.

Solidago, golden rod. Seeds of various species eaten by Gosiute, Chamberlin, 1911: 76.

Sophia, tansymustard. Two species of this seem to have been similarly named. *S. parviflora* (Lam.) Standl., introduced and growing around settlements, was called poina, S–Tonopah (LJB). *S. sonnei* (Robins.) Greene, native and growing in the aspen and spruce belts, but collected in many lower altitudes in the artemisia belt, was called atsa, NP–FLk, NP–LnPn; ǎk, akǎ vü, SP–Ash; pōīa, S–LtLk; poina, pō a or poina, S–Lida (JS); boina, most Nevada Shoshoni; boi', S–Lemhi. Seeds were eaten.

Spiranthes. Root eaten in Owens Valley, Steward, 1933: 244.

Stachys palustris L., woundwort. Seeds eaten by Gosiute, Chamberlin, 1911: 76.

Stanleya elata Jones, squaw cabbage, and *S. pinnata* (Pursh.) were eaten as greens, S–DthV, Coville, 1892. These are among the few plants leached to remove bitter.

Stipa speciosa Trin. & Rupr., porcupine grass. Seeds eaten in Owens Valley, Steward, 1933: 243; called huki. Probably NP–FLk huki is same.

Strombocàrpa odorata (Torr. & Frem.), screwbean (pl. 2, *b*). Plains and valleys, Covillea belt. None north of Ash Meads, Death Valley region.

Trifolium tridentatum Lindl., tomcat clover, and *T. involucratum* Ort., seeds and greens eaten in Owens Valley, Steward, 1933: 243–244.

Triglochin maritimum L., arrowgrass. Seeds eaten by Gosiute, Chamberlin, 1911: 77.

Trisetum subspicatum Beam. Seeds eaten by Gosiute, Chamberlin, 1911: 77.

Troximon aurantiacum Hook. Leaves eaten by Gosiute, Chamberlin, 1911: 77.

Typha, cattail (or *Juncus*, ruoh). Grows in water. Called doi, S DiaV, S–Ely, S–Hmlt, S–Elko, S–RubV (RVJ); toi, NP–MC; to'i, S–Lemhi. Brown seed head burned to procure seeds; roots dried, ground, and stored, S–Lemhi. Another plant, tahonats', NP–MC, was described as similar to toi but smaller. *Typha latifolia* L., eaten by Gosiute, Chamberlin, 1911: 77.

Vaccinium, blueberry. Remy & Brenchley (p. 1929) state that Nevada Shoshoni ate a *vaccinium* berry.

Valeriana edulis Nutt., tobacco root or bitterroot. Roots eaten by Gosiute, Chamberlin, 1911: 78. Frémont says this was abundant along the Bear River (1856, p. 237), in the country north of Great Salt Lake (1856, p. 256), and in Utah County, Utah (1856, p. 464); he called it "kooyah." Remy and Brenchley called this by the Shoshoni name, "kuia" (p. 135). This is probably the important root called kuiyü', NP–Ban; kuiyu, S–Lemhi; goiyu, S–Ely, S–Mor, S–DiaV; koiya, kuia, S–SprV; kuiyu, S–Elko, S–RubV (RVJ), S–Lemhi; küyu, NP–MC; goiyu' u, S–RsRi; goyu' u, S–GSmV. S–Lemhi, dried and stored. According to early travelers, this was poisonous unless roasted. Fremont (1887, vol. 1, p. 206) says 2 days' roasting is necessary.

Weyethia amplexicaulis Nutt. Seeds eaten by Gosiute, Chamberlin, 1911: 78. *W. ovata* T. & G., eaten in Owens Valley, Steward, 1933: 242.

UNIDENTIFIED FOOD PLANTS

Bavo, S–RubV (RVJ); bavogo, S–Elko; bavogo' S–Ely, S–Hmlt, S–SprV; bahmü, S–Lemhi. A plant with a white flower, resembling wild parsnip. Eaten as greens.

Dui, S–RubV (RVJ), S–DiaV; du:, S–Sly, S–Hmlt; duhu, S–SprV; tui, S–SnRv; du'u, S–GSmV, S–RsRi. A root resembling a small sweetpotato. Unknown S–Lemhi. Another plant, resembling *Chenopodium*, the seed of which was eaten, was called dui, S–RsRi; dü:i, S–GSmV, S–Eureka. Possibly neither of these is the plant called tui by Gosiute, a species of *Urtica*, nettle, Chamberlin, 1911: 77.

Dagu, S–Ely; dagü, S–Elko, S–Lemhi, tagü, S–Hmlt. Edible root. This could not be preserved, S–Lemhi.

Duna, S–SprV, S–Elko; tuna, S–Hmlt. Edible root.

Do'gohi, S–GSmV, a large edible root.

Dubwi', S–Ely, S–Hmlt; tübuwi, S–Elko, S–RubV. Greens. It is not certain whether these localities used this word for a certain species or for greens generally.

Ha:pi, S–Elko, ha:pü, S–Lemhi; hape, S–SuRv. An edible root up to 12 inches long, procured by Idaho Shoshoni at Camas Prairie. Roots preserved.

Hugi, S–Ely, S–Lida, S–Hmlt, S–DiaV, S–SprV, S–RubV; hu:gi, S–GSmV; edible seed (?); unknown, S–Lemhi. See *Agropyron*, above.

Huhwi, S–LtLk, unidentified seed of "bunch grass," which grows in mountains, ripens in July.

Hukumbi, S–SprV, S–DiaV, unknown S–Ely, S–RubV;, S–Lemhi; edible berry (?). Hukümbi, S–RsRi, seed; plant has "small white flowers in a bunch on the top."

Hunib, S–DiaV,; hunib:, S–Elko, S–RsRi; hu:nib:, S–RubV, S–Lemhi; huniv*, S–Ely; punib:, S–SprV; hunibui, NP–MC; a low-growing plant, with a long, edible root, growing in the hills.

Hüü, S–DiaV, S–Hmlt. Edible seed (?); unknown, S–RubV, S–Ely, S–Lemhi. Hⁱⁱ ü, S–RsRi, plant with a white flower and edible bulb.

Kan*, S–Lemhi, unidentified root. Gosiute, kana is *Lewisia rediviva*, bitterroot, Chamberlin, 1911: 82.

Kanikc, NP–MC. An edible root, possibly camas, *Quamasia quamash.*

Komuta, S–Ely, S–Hmlt, S–RubV; unknown, S–Lemhi.

Köya, NP–FLk. Seed plant.

Kutzu, NP–MC. Plant with red seeds, growing along the Humboldt River.

Mahavit:, S–Hmlt, S–SprV, S–RubV; rare at S–Elko; absent, S–Ely, S–DiaV. S–RsRi, described as like grass, with many small roots, each little larger than a pea. Possibly *Brodiaea* or *Eleocharis*. Roots eaten.

Mutcki', S–Ely, S–Hmlt; mutcuki, S–Elko, S–RubV. Any plant greens, eaten somewhat like lettuce. Gosiute called any greens mutcigip, Chamberlin, 1911: 85.

Nevingu'nu, S–DthV. Seed plant.

Nəp:, S–DiaV, S–RsRi, S–Ely, S–Hmlt, S–Elko, S–RubV, S–Lemhi. A root; dried and stored.

Pasi, S–Lemhi. Edible nuts of a "spruce."

Pasigo, S–Lemhi. Root, possibly same as sigo. Gosiute called *Osmorhiza nuda*, sweet cicely and possibly *Glycosma occidentalis* both pasigo or pasigwïp but used neither for food, Chamberlin, 1911: 89.

Pä'wa, S–Lemhi. Edible root, possibly of *Rumex* or *Juncus*. Pawaʳ*, NP–FLk, seed, possibly of *Rumex*.

Payai, NP–FLk. Seed plant.

Payump, S–Lemhi. Edible root similar to yamp, *Carum gairdneri*, but grows along streams.

Pit: sogo, S–Lemhi. A root dug at Camas Prairie.

Soiga, S–Lemhi; sowik (?), S–NthFk, S–SnRv. Root.

Takü, NP–MC. Root.

Tonopuda, S–LtLk, a seed plant of considerable importance growing in the mountains.

Töpoi, R–RsRi. Plant with yellow flower and edible root.

To: tǝmb:, S–Ely, S–Hmlt. Unknown or differently named, S–Elko, S–RubV. A large shrub with a berry like a raspberry.

Tsogodzidzina, S–Lemhi (tsogo, earth+dzidzina, any root). Like small potatoes; not suitable for storage.

Tsowiga, S–DiaV, S–Hmlt, S–RubV, S–Elko, S–Lemhi; tsuga, NP–MC. Root.

Wada, S—Lemhi. Seed. Gosiute wada, however, is *Suaeda depressa* Watson, seablite, Chamberlin, 1911: 97.

Wǎ: gova, S–Lemhi, a plant resembling cactus with yellow flowers, growing in mountains. Probably same as wo: gavi, *Opuntia*. Did not occur on Salmon River. Procured by S–Lemhi near Snake River. Root eaten.

Winünu, S–Lida. "Wild cabbage." Tall flower stalk with spike of yellow flowers. Greens eaten.

Yutavo'°, S–Lemhi. Root procured at Camas Prairie.

Yuvikui, S–Kawich. Seed eaten. May be same as yuvikua, S–Tonopah, which is *Chylismia* and was not eaten.

In the Great Basin and Plateau subsistence problems were essentially uniform, though local fertility was somewhat variable. Seeds and roots were the most important foods. Seeds were gathered and prepared largely with twined baskets which were well adapted to the tasks and fairly similar among all groups. Some seeds were knocked into conical carrying baskets with basketry seed beaters, then winnowed and perhaps parched in a basketry tray and ground on metates, or among Shoshoni and a few Paiute boiled in pots. The heads of other seeds were cut with a knife, the seeds threshed, then winnowed. Berries were picked into conical baskets and some dried and stored. Roots were dug with a simple digging stick, and some were dried and stored. Stored seeds and berries were always cached in pits in the earth, located as near as possible to the winter village. For long treks into arid regions, water was carried in basketry ollas.

Whether this highly specialized basketry-gathering complex was widespread because it was ancient (much of it was possessed by Basket Makers) or spread rapidly because of great utility cannot be known at present. But a great functional efficiency of the complex is evident.

There are only three exceptions to the general pattern of wild-seed gathering. First, Owens Valley Northern Paiute sometimes irrigated certain wild-seed patches. Irrigation was communal, but gathering was by individual families. Second, horticulture was practiced by Southern Paiute and, in early post-Caucasian times, by

Death Valley, Lida, Spring Valley, and Ely Shoshoni. It was always a family affair. Third, certain groups in east central Nevada sowed broadcast certain wild seeds, especially *Chenopodium* and *Mentzelia*. It was usually a village activity, though women gathered for their own families. Localities practicing this were: S–SmCr, S–RsRi, S–Mor, S–Hmlt, S–Ely, S–SprV, GS–DpCr, S–Egan. Its southern limit is not known. It was lacking among S–RubV, GS–SklV, and Shoshoni of the Humboldt River, Idaho and northern Utah.

ANIMAL FOODS

Game was less important than plant foods in Shoshonean subsistence. The general aridity of the region restricted the numbers of all species of large game and the limited grasslands largely precluded species which occur in great herds. The infrequency of taking large game is attested by the great premium upon skins. Persons fully clad in shirts and leggings or dresses were rare. Because of the secondary importance of game, the annual migration for foods was directed with reference to plant rather than animal species. Deer and mountain sheep, occurring alone or in small bands, were taken through the wiles and perseverance of single hunters or small groups of men whenever they happened to be in a locality favorable for hunting. Only bison, limited to the northeast, and antelope, occurring throughout the area, were the objects of important hunts. Antelope, forming small herds, lent themselves to communal hunts, but such slaughter so reduced their number that years might be required to restore the herd. Bison never were numerous west of the Rocky Mountains and were evidently not hunted on a large scale until post-horse days when bands traveled east.

Small game was of relatively great importance. Reptiles, rodents, fish, and insects all supplied foods. Rodents and other small mammals had several advantages over large game. They remained in restricted localities and did not require a long chase. Some species, forming large colonies, could be taken in considerable numbers, even warranting construction of ditches for flooding them from their burrows. All of them reproduced rapidly, so that destruction did not diminish their numbers for long periods. Many made large stores of seeds that could be robbed. On the other hand, most of them hibernated during the winter and so were not available when food shortage was most serious.

The country is so generally devoid of water that fish were important only in the Salmon, Snake, Humboldt, Owens, and Bear Rivers and in Utah Lake and its tributaries and in some of the tributaries of Great Salt Lake. In Idaho the seasonal salmon runs had an important effect upon the entire subsistence routine. Elsewhere fish were somewhat less important than in Idaho, but had the advantage of supplying some food throughout the winter and thus providing a motive for the location of winter villages near streams and rivers.

Even insects were sometimes of great importance. In some years grasshoppers and "Mormon crickets" were extremely abundant and could be taken in quantities that would last for months.

The several species of carnivorous animals were not greatly valued in Shoshonean economy. Wolves, coyotes, mountain lions, and wildcats were taken with great difficulty and were rarely eaten. Their furs, excepting that of the wildcat, which was valued for quivers, had no important uses.

Most of the observations on the following species are from Seton (1929) and Barnes (1927). For native names of most of these species, see Appendix B.

Antilocapra americana Ord., pronghorn antelope. Occurrence: Throughout the area, except southern Nevada, in open country, i. e., valleys and hills, migration limited. Herds of perhaps 100, though a herd of 300 was reported in 1911 in Juab County, Utah. Living in the open and being the fleetest American mammal prevented effective chases on foot. But the herding tendency coupled with excessive curiosity made them easy to take by wiles, such as disguises, and to drive into corrals. Their poor jumping ability made moderately high corral fences adequate to impound them. Their tendency to run in a circle facilitated driving by horse relays in the north, where large drives were not undertaken. Weight, about 100 pounds.

Communal antelope drives were among the few economic activities not restricted to family groups. As the animals are wary and fleet of foot, they were taken with considerable difficulty by lone hunters. Large groups of Indians on foot, however, could manage to drive them into a corral. Throughout most of the Shoshoni area these drives were managed by a shaman who had received special supernatural power in a vision to charm antelope. During one to several nights of singing and shamanizing prior to the drive this man was believed to capture the antelopes' souls, rendering them docile and stupid. The next day a large number of men spread out over miles of country and slowly drove the animals toward the corral. A good account of the activity involved has been set down by Egan (pp. 238–241) for the Deep Creek Gosiute, but omits a description of the shamanism:

"For a few days before I came the squaws and bucks were busy repairing and extending the flanking arms of the old corral, or trap pen, which was located near the north end of Antelope Valley and about 20 miles northwest of Deep Creek. It was pretty cold weather, but no snow on the ground. The Indians thought it a good time and expected a good catch.

"After they had all come in from their work a great deal of talking and planning was on and each knew just what part and place he or she was to take. By daylight all were ready for the start, and, in fact, a number of the young men had left early in the evening before to go to the extreme south end of the ground to be covered and about 20 miles from the pen. They were to spread apart across the valley, travel in open order back to the north, being careful that not one of the antelope jumped would run, except in a northerly direction . . .

"An antelope, when started up, will always run directly for one of these [knolls], that lay opposite from where he gets his scare from, and they run from hill to hill. They see no one ahead of them but the party behind being constantly increased, and if they undertake to pass around the drivers a buck or squaw is sure to raise to his feet, and that sends them off to the center again.

"Thus it goes till they come to the line between the outer ends of the arms, which, there, are about 4 miles apart, but gradually closing in as they get nearer the pen. The arms or leads are started at the extreme ends by simply prying or pulling up a large sagebrush and standing it roots up on the top of another brush, thus making a tall, black object visible for miles. The standing of these brush were at first some 10 to 20 feet apart, but were placed more and more near together the nearer towards the pen, and when the two lines came to about 100 yards apart, they were built so the butts of the brush were as close as the tops would allow them to be joined and by this time both wings had swung to the east side of the valley, where there were many ravines to cross and plenty of cedar and pine to use for fencing.

"There were many turns to the lane thus formed, but [it] was getting narrower and stronger till finally, around a sharp turn through a large, thick bunch of cedars, the game were in the corral, which was about 200 feet in diameter and built strong enough and high enough to withstand a herd of buffalo. The pine and cedar trees had not been removed from the inside of the pen and not many from the runway, for a mile back . . .

"The drivers . . . were all on a fast run, yelling like a pack of coyotes. The drive came to an end with a rush and everyone working desperately closing up the entrance . . .

Then began the killing of as many as were wanted that day, the killing was done with arrow and seldom missed piercing the heart. The catch was about 25, mostly all bucks or does . . . There were five or six bucks killed that day . . . to give the squaws time to cut up in thin strips the flesh and dry it on a rack built over a small fire, thus curing it so it would keep for a long time if kept dry . . .

"Three or four young men [had been left] to guard the place." By the next morning the antelope had run themselves down and were huddled in the center of the enclosure . . . The Indians picked out five or six of the largest, which were killed. . .

"The Indians told me that the last drive, before this one at this place, was nearly 12 years ago and the old men never expected to see another at this place, for it would take many years for the animals to increase in sufficient numbers to make it pay to drive. These drives are mostly in the desert valleys, where the poor horseless natives live."

Other antelope drives mentioned throughout this paper are similar to this, though less trouble was taken in many localities in corral construction. It was frequently believed that the shaman's charm would prevent their escape even though the corral were not a continuous fence.

Another method of hunting antelopes was used by Indians possessing horses. It was a true surround. Egan has also described this kind (pp. 240–241):

Near the locality of the hunt previously described, he saw "10 [men] on horses and 5 or 6 foot men. When they arrived at the edge of the hunting ground, they divided into parties, one going to the right and the other to the left and occasionally leaving a man, and so spacing them apart that when the two ends of the line swung around they formed a very large circle.

"We could see where the antelope were running and the plan was to keep them in the circle and on the run all the time and not allow them to rest. When any of them attempted to pass out they were headed off and turned back or around the circle. We could not see an antelope half way across the circle, but could see the dust they raised and the direction they were traveling.

"When, after they had been kept running back and forth till they were very tired, a man would chase one on a fast run and as he neared another man would stop to rest his horse and watch for another run. The second man could run his horse alongside the antelope easily, which I did . . . [and] shot him at a distance of about 8 or 10 feet. There were only three killed and Jack was in high glee."

A lone hunter usually stalked antelope when wearing an antelope head and skin disguise.

Odocoileus hemionus (Rafinesque), mule or blacktail deer. This is the most important species of deer throughout the area, although *O. virginianus* (Rafinesque), the Virginia or whitetail deer, occurs in the northern and eastern portions. Weight, 200 pounds or more. Occurrence: "lower hills or broken ground that is partly wooded" (Seton, 1929, vol. 3, pp. 325–365), ordinarily avoiding open country, dense woods, and high mountains. Occurring thus in the lower altitudes of mountains and limited to small bands, deer were taken by lone hunters or small groups of men. As the country is less heavily covered with brush than the west coast, snares and ambushes on deer trails were of minor importance. Most hunting was by individual men who stalked and pursued the animals, shooting them with poisoned arrows.

Cooperative hunting was much less important for deer than for antelope and rarely warranted special trips for that purpose. Such hunting was most feasible in the fall when deer descended from the mountains by fairly well marked trails into a warmer region or in the spring when they returned to the mountains. At such times people in the northern part of the area sometimes constructed V-wings between which was a hurdle with a pit beyond. The deer's propensity to jump carried him over the hurdle into the concealed pit. In a few localities a shaman charmed deer for these drives. At other times small groups of men who happened to be in the same locality attempted to surround deer in the mountains or, if they could find a deer trail, to drive the animals along it past concealed hunters.

Ovis canadensis Shaw, mountain sheep. Weight, up to 300 pounds. Occurrence: throughout the area, formerly in "grassy foothills and bluffs not far from the crags," but in more recent times in less accessible, high mountains. Though formerly fairly abundant, sheep were taken with great difficulty. Pursued by hunters, often using dogs, they fled to precipices if possible, where the hazard of climbing was often prohibitive. In December, however, when rams were dueling during the mating period, concealed hunters attracted them by thumping logs.

Oreamnos americanus (Blainville), mountain goat. This occurred only in the Bitterroot Mountains and was of minor importance.

Bison bison (Linnaeus), bison or buffalo. The comparative value of this species is indicated by its weight, about 1,800 pounds, which is 18 times that of the antelope, 9 times that of the deer, and 6 times that of the mountain sheep. In addition, its large and heavy hide served many purposes, including house covers, and was a primary object of trade with both Indians and white men.

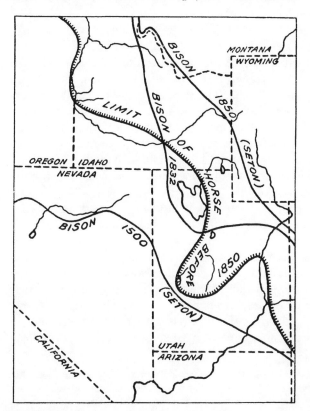

FIGURE 5.—Map of the distribution of the horse and bison.

The former range of the bison, according to Seton, extended in about 1500 through northern Nevada and southern Oregon to northeastern California and through a large portion of Utah (fig. 5). Certain anthropological data corroborate a a somewhat similar pre-Caucasian distribution. Petroglyphs in Nine Mile Canyon, south of the Uintah Basin, and in the Paria River district in southern Utah are unquestionably bison. Caves on the northern shore of

Great Salt Lake contain extraordinarily abundant bison remains associated with a pre-Caucasian culture (Steward, 1937 b). Shoshoni informants said that several generations ago bison were known in northwestern Utah, along the Humboldt River in Nevada, and in the region of Steptoe Valley, eastern Nevada.

Most of this territory west of the Rocky Mountains, however, lacks grasslands and is not the optimum bison environment. A narrowing of the bison's range appears to have begun in pre-Caucasian times. By 1832 it was extinct in northern Utah and by 1840 in Idaho. The final extinction was probably brought about by more efficient hunting made possible by the horse and the arrival of great numbers of trappers.

Cervus canadensis Erxleben, elk or wapiti. This occurred only in Idaho and extreme northeastern Utah. It seems to have played only a minor role in Shoshonean subsistence.

Lepus californicus Gray, blacktail jack rabbit. Weight, 5½ pounds. This species was very important throughout its range, which included the entire area except parts of Idaho and northeastern Utah. The whitetail jack rabbit, *L. townsendii* Bachman, had a more restricted range within the area. The jack rabbit now occurs in enormous herds, having increased both in numbers and range in recent years. Natively, however, it seems to have been sufficiently numerous to have been of major importance. It not only afforded considerable meat when taken in communal hunts, but provided skins which were utilized for the all-important Shoshonean garment, the rabbit-skin blanket or robe.

Its habitat was open, sage-covered valleys. Its speed and ability to hide made it difficult to hunt with the bow and arrow, but the large and rapidly multiplying herds rewarded communal hunts. Drives were held throughout most of the area and were the most important communal activity. The usual plan was to place a number of long, low nets end to end in a vast semicircle many hundred yards in diameter. A large crowd, often including women and children, then beat the brush, driving the animals into the nets where they were dispatched. Egan's account of a Gosiute drive (1917, pp. 235–237) is exceptionally good:

In the vicinity of Deep Creek, the chief took Egan to the site of the drive, 3 or 4 miles from the village. They used "grass native cord nets about 2½ feet high and 2 inches and even smaller mesh. A sharp pointed stick a few inches longer than the width of the net was fastened across 6 or 8 feet apart, to act as fence posts, when the sharp end was pressed into the earth. One buck could easily carry a roll of 150 to 200 yards of the small twisted grass twine nets. Each large family usually have such a roll and at times, when living apart from other families, can use them either as traps or to drive; but then, these are only small catches.

"The drive I witnessed was when there was six or eight of these nets together. When they had decided just where to run the nets, two of the Indians put the end sticks of their nets together and commenced to unroll their nets, going in opposite directions, sticking each cross stick firmly in the ground as they unrolled, making a rabbit-proof fence. When the first two had placed their nets, two more of the Indians commenced where they ended and continued the line in the desired direction.

"I noticed that when they were through stringing their nets in a kind of semicircle form there was part of a roll of nets not unrolled at each end. These ends, when they were ready to drive, were strung out, but not in a circle, but flaring straight out from the opening, making a long U-shaped mouth to the field. When the Indians swung across this mouth they began coming in slowly. But every rabbit that was started went into the pen and kept running back and forth to find a place to get through . . . When the men had reached the opening of the circle the two ends of the net was brought in and strung across the opening, this making a complete enclosure . . . All the Indians were inside with sticks, or bows and arrows, picking up the game . . .

"It took the Indians half a day to get as many as they wanted."

Although rabbit surrounds with fire were not often used because desert shrubs are usually too widely spaced for a fire to spread, Egan also observed this method:

Hunters with torches spread out in a circle about a mile in diameter. "Working all around the circle and towards the center was a continuous ring of fire and smoke, which was gradually closing in, and the rabbits were being crowded together thicker and thicker. Each Indian, squaw, and papoose had a stick about four feet long, the only weapon they carried . . . [They made] as much noise as possible. The rabbits got so dazed by the fire, smoke, and tumult that they simply could not run . . . I saw dozens of them stop within reach of the sticks, and many of them were picked up that had not been hit. When a rabbit was seen to pass out of the human ring, someone would follow him in the smoke and put his body in one of the piles of rabbits they had made as they proceeded towards the center . . . When the drive was over, the field was a black, fire-swept, but still smoking, patch of ground . . .

"The Indians do not like to use fire for a drive, as it takes years for the brush to grow up again."

Lepus americanus Erxleben, snowshoe rabbit. This species probably occurs throughout the area in high altitudes, but it was comparatively scarce and inaccessible.

Sylvilagus floridanus (Allen), cottontail rabbit; two varieties, *nuttallii* in the north and *audubonii* in the south (Seton, 1929, vol. 4, pp. 781–815). Weight, 2 to 2½ pounds. Cottontails are smaller and more limited in numbers than jack rabbits. Occurring in brushy country, especially in the hills, however, they could more readily be taken with snares and with the bow and arrow. Consequently, though never the object of drives, they frequently served to supplement the food supply of families at their winter villages or when traveling in the foothills.

Marmota flaviventris (Audubon and Bachman), rock-chuck or yellow marmot. This species occurs only in a portion of the area, where, however, it was important. Weighing 10 to 15 pounds, its flesh was valued for food and its fur for robes. Living in burrows or rock crannies, it was easily killed, the favorite time being in the fall when it became fat previous to hibernating.

Taxidea taxus (Schreber), badger. This powerful burrowing animal occurs throughout the area. It was used for food only during times of scarcity but its tough hide was valued for moccasins.

Several kinds of small burrowing rodents occur in considerable colonies in valley flats, especially in comparatively fertile localities where they could feed on roots. Considerable effort was made to take these as other animal foods were often not to be had. They were either dug with a digging stick, pulled from their burrows by means of a rodent skewer, smoked out, flooded out, or killed with deadfall traps. If encountered away from their burrows, they could be run down and killed with sticks and stones. Usually weighing but a fraction of a pound, however, large numbers had to be taken.

Among these rodents were various species of the family *Geomyidae*, pocket gophers, the genus *Citellus*, ground squirrels, and *Cynomys*, prairie dogs, in the eastern part of the area.

Other rodents, living among the rocks in the hills and mountains, though taken when possible, were too small to have contributed greatly to the food supply. Among these were chipmunks (*Callospermophilus* and *Eutamias*) and packrats (*Neotoma cinerea* (Ord)). Those living in the water, the beaver, *Castor canadensis* Kuhl, and the muskrat, *Ondatra zibethica* (Linnaeus), were too restricted in occurrence and number to have had great importance.

Reptiles were eaten when they were large enough to warrant the trouble of catching and preparing them. The chuckwalla, *Sauromalus obesus* (Baird), weighing several pounds, was eagerly sought throughout its range in the southern part of the area. Other lizards and horned toads were too small. Most snakes, with the occasional exception of the rattlesnake, were also eaten.

The role of fish in native economy varied with the locality and the species. Owens River, the Humboldt River, and the rivers of the Bonneville Basin had several species in some abundance. The Snake and Salmon Rivers were not only favored with large runs of salmon but had many other species.

Owens River had two important native species. *Catostomus arenarius* Snyder, sand-bar sucker, was up to 7 inches long and occurred in schools (Snyder, 1919). This was probably what the Paiute called huwa, ădăpü̆ᵘ, or atava. *Siphateles obesus* (Girard), lake chub, was up to 5 inches long (Snyder, 1919). This may have been the Paiute potcigi or puitcigi. In addition, there were two minnows, *Agosia robusta* Rutter, black minnow, and *Cyprinodon macularius* Baird and Girard, spotted pursy minnow, both of which were probably called tsoni'ta. Fish were taken by means of diverting streams and stranding, stupefying, shooting, spears, hooks, baskets, and nets (Steward, 1933, pp. 251–252).

Humboldt River.—Of many species occurring throughout the Lahontan Basin of western Nevada, eight were found in the Humboldt River and in some of its tributaries. These were (Snyder, 1917, pp. 42–83) : *Catostomus tahoensis* Gill and Jordan, red sucker, up to 24 inches long; *Catostomus arenarius* Snyder, sand-bar sucker, up to 20 inches long; *Pantosteus lahontan* Rutter, Lahontan sucker, up to 6 inches long, which migrated up the river in July; *Siphateles obesus* (Girard), lake chub, up to 14 inches long and very abundant; *Richardsonius egregius* (Girard), red-striped shiner, up to 5½ inches long; *Agosia robusta* Rutter, black minnow; *Cottus beldingi* Eigenmann, desert rifflefish; and *Salmo henshawi* Gill and Jordan, tahoe trout. The suckers and chubs were important in native economy, but it was probably the tahoe trout which was called agai and was preferred. In addition to devices used in Owens Valley, Humboldt River Shoshoni employed such northern fishing methods as harpoons and complicated dams and weirs.

Although Humboldt River fish were very important because they could be taken in winter, they were, like game and vegetable foods, affected in some measure by dry years. Burche (1864, p. 148) wrote of the Nevada Indians:

Fish, which, with them, is a large item in the sustainment of life, and which they caught in copious quantities in the lakes and rivers of the country, will also almost entirely fail them this season, owing to the extremely low stage of water in all rivers and lakes, caused by the unusually small amount of snow that fell the past winter. The watercourses and lakes being thus reduced in volume, and the alkali properties greatly predominating in the water, great quantities of the fish have died and drifted on the margin of the streams, thereby almost entirely cutting off this, one of their chief articles of supply . . .

In recent years irrigation has almost dried up the Humboldt River.

Several important species of fish occurred in Utah and Bear Lakes and in the streams tributary to these lakes and to Great Salt Lake and Sevier Lake—the Bonneville Basin. Great Salt Lake and Sevier Lake were too salty for fish. The species were: *Salmo utah* Suckley, Utah Lake trout, weighing about 1½ pounds, in Utah Lake and Bear Lake and Bear River; an important species, perhaps the Shoshoni tsapănkwi (good fish). *Pantosteus platyrhynchus* (Cope), mountain sucker, in Utah Lake, in rivers flowing into Utah Lake, and in the Sevier River. *Catostomus fecundus* Cope and Yarrow, Utah Lake sucker, in Bear River, rivers of Utah Lake, Sevier River, and Snake River; perhaps the Shoshoni auwok. *Siboma atraria* Girard, Utah Lake chub, in the streams of the Bonneville Basin. *Leucichthys gemmifer* Snyder, whitefish or "peaknose" in Bear Lake and Bear

River. *Phosopium williamsoni* (Girard), a whitefish in the streams flowing into Salt Lake, Utah Lake, and Sevier Lake. *Prosopium spilonotus* (Snyder), Bonneville whitefish, and *Prosopium abyssicola* (Snyder), Bear Lake whitefish, in Bear Lake. The former occurs 6 to 8 inches long, the latter 12 to 14 inches long. *Cottus semiscaber* (Cope), Rocky Mountain bullhead, in Bear, Utah, Fish, and Panguitch Lakes and their streams. *Rhinichthys dulcis* (Girard), dace, in streams of Great Salt Lake and Snake River. *Richardsonius hydrophlox* (Cope), silverside minnow, and *Richardsonius copei* (Jordan and Gilbert), leather-side minnow, in streams of Utah and Great Salt Lakes. *Apocope carringtonii* (Cope), a very small fish occurring in the streams of Great Salt Lake and in widely scattered springs of the Bonneville deserts. *Apocope abode* (Jordan and Evermann), Sevier system only. (These identifications are from Tanner, 1936.)

It is unfortunate that more information is not available concerning the native names of these species and methods of taking each. It is known only that in the Bear River they were an important and constant supplement to other foods and that Utah Lake was the center of fishing operations of Ute from neighboring territories. In lesser degree they were taken in all streams and even the tiny species of *Apocope* in desert springs were sought when other foods failed.

Fish were more important in the Snake and Salmon Rivers than in other parts of the area. Salmon were taken in such quantities as to warrant preserving and storing. But salmon and several other species were blocked by the falls of the Snake River in southwestern Idaho. Evermann (1896, p. 257) states that Shoshone Falls, height 210 feet, is the absolute upstream limit of salmon, while Auger Falls and Upper and Lower Salmon Falls, below Shoshone Falls, seriously impeded their migration. Some species entered the Payette River but did not pass far beyond in the Snake River. (See map, fig. 4.)

Idaho Shoshoni distinguished several runs of fish, all of which were called agai, salmon. Some of these, however, were not true salmon, for only the Chinook salmon reaches this region in important quantities.

The first run, tahma agai (spring salmon), coming in March or April, was probably *Salmo gairdneri* Richardson, the steelhead trout or salmon trout (Evermann, 1896, p. 282–284; 1897, p. 199), weighing about 15 pounds. Locke (1929, p. 186) says these reach "Idaho waters from the sea from December to early spring, spawning in the headwaters from late winter to spring."

Oncorhynchus tschawytscha (Walbaum), the Chinook salmon, was probably the taza agai (summer salmon) of the Snake River and the agai of the Lemhi and Salmon Rivers. Locke (1929, pp. 181–

182) states that it ascends from the ocean to spawn in the headwaters in July, August, and September. Losing weight in their ascent, in Idaho they weigh from 8 to 20 pounds and rarely reach 50 pounds. Spawning activities leave them emaciated and covered with sores. By September most of them are dead or gone. In the small streams these are probably the wo:vi (board or log) agai. In the upper Salmon River these seldom passed Alturas Creek (Evermann, 1897, pp. 180–186). Locally these are called "dog salmon." The true dog salmon is *Oncorhynchus keta*, a species not ascending these rivers.

Probably a few *Oncorhynchus nerka*, sockeye or red salmon or redfish, probably the Lemhi a ga agai (aŋga, red), reached Payette and Redfish Lakes (Evermann, 1897, pp. 187–198; Locke, 1929, pp. 182–183).

Entosphenus tridentatus (Gairdner), 3-tooth lamprey, occurred in the Salmon River and in the Snake River, probably only below the falls. It was called pado oa (pa, water+toga, snake).

Acipenser transmontanus (Gairdner), Columbia River sturgeon, could be taken below the falls of the Snake River in the spring when the water was muddy. These reached 8 to 9 feet in length (Evermann, 1897, pp. 171–172).

The cut-throat or black-spotted trout, *Salmo mykiss* (Walbaum), and perhaps other species, is the main native trout throughout these rivers. It is probably the Shoshoni tsǎ: pank[w1] (Evermann, 1897, pp. 198–199; Locke, 1929, p. 187).

Coregonus williamsoni Girard, Rocky Mountain whitefish or "mountain herring," is probably the Shoshoni mu:dziwihü' (muvi, nose+dziwihü', pointed), occurring throughout the rivers and streams.

Other native species were *Pantosteus jordani* Evermann, black sucker or blue sucker, occurring throughout the Snake River; *Catostomus macrocheilus* Girard, Columbia River or yellow sucker; *Acrocheilus alutaceus* Agassiz and Pickering, chisel-mouth, square-mouth, or hard-mouth, occurring throughout the Snake River; *Mylocheilus caurinus* Richardson, Columbia chub, occurring in large schools in the Snake River; *Ptychocheilus oregonensis* Richardson, squawfish, occurring below the falls of the Snake River (Evermann, 1897, pp. 171–175). Several small species were *Leuciscus balteatus* (Richardson), shiner, below Shoshone Falls, and *L. hydrophlox* above the falls. *Rhinichthys cataractae dulcis* (Girard) occurred throughout the Snake River. A species, *Uranidea bendirei* (Bean), was limited to Goose Creek and *Cottus leiopomus* Gilbert and Evermann, blob, to Little Wood River. The native names of none of these species is known.

Methods of taking the more important fishes are described below in appropriate sections.

THE ECONOMIC PATTERN

The Western Shoshoni economic system was organized on simple lines. The basic division of labor was sexual, so that each family was, in all but a few activities, a self-sufficient economic unit. As this pattern varied but little throughout the entire area a few illustrations will suffice. Fish Lake Valley North Paiute women did virtually all seed gathering, though men helped somewhat in collecting pine nuts. They prepared foods, did all the cooking and housekeeping, and manufactured pottery, basketry, and most clothing. Men did all large-game hunting, manufactured chipped flint implements, digging sticks and rabbit-skin blankets, built houses, and assisted women in such tasks as hunting rodents, carrying wood and water, transporting seeds, and even gathering some materials for making pots, baskets, and metates. In Owens Valley the division of labor was essentially the same. But men also had the task of irrigating, while women helped make rabbit-skin blankets. Both sexes fished. California and Nevada Shoshoni differed from the Paiute only in that Shoshoni men helped prepare skins and did some sewing, especially of moccasins.

This sexual division of labor covered all essential pursuits. There was no important specialization. For all but a small portion of the year each family was self-sufficient economically and manufactured its own implements. Each sex made implements used by it. Both sexes usually made things used by both—houses, rabbit-skin blankets, and clothing. In a few instances certain men may have been skilled flint chippers and bow makers or women skilled potters who traded their wares, but such specialization was not sufficient for self-support. Trade, as a vital factor of any economy, requires that some members of the society be able to acquire such a surplus of essential goods that they can support other individuals who devote a large proportion of their time if not all their time to certain activities which, alone, would not support them. In this area, surpluses of any kind were infrequent and fortuitous. Commerce of any note was carried on only in the western and northern peripheries.

In Owens Valley and vicinity, where foods were sufficiently abundant to support an unusually dense population and stable enough to leave some margin against starvation, people seem occasionally to have had sufficient surplus of time or goods to indulge in a little commerce. Owens Valley trade has been previously described. It involved direct barter and exchange for bead money. It was principally trans-Sierran, with Western Mono.

Some trade by Death Valley people is indicated, but Shoshoni in Nevada practiced little or none. Probably some salt, procured near Surveyor's Well, was traded, though BD denied that when he was young his family even went as far as Owens Lake. The Death Valley measure of bead money was around the hand as in Owens Valley. At Sigai, BD said, they sold 6 measures for 50 cents; at Lida, 12 for 50 cents, which suggests that beads introduced by the white man may have inflated the currency. He vaguely estimated the following prices: 5 gallons of pine nuts, 10 strings; a sinew-backed bow, about 24 strings; moccasins, 10 to 40 strings; a wife, 100 strings. At the annual mourning ceremony 200 strings might be burned along with other goods for someone who died during the past year. Money was also used here, at Beatty, and by neighboring groups to pay "exhibition dancers." Its main use, however, was probably as ornaments.

TSt described some trade between Beatty Shoshoni and Owens Valley Paiute. Traveling a trail via Death Valley and Saline Valley, Beatty men carried rabbit-skin blankets to exchange for buckskins which were almost impossible to procure locally. No doubt Beatty trade also involved some bead money, for strings of glass beads seem to have reached this district in pre-Caucasian times, from Indians to the south. Beads were red, white, and blue. Four strings, each the length of the circumference of the hand, were worth 25 cents. Small shell beads were somewhat more valuable.

Lida had some shell- and glass-bead money. To the north, money had not been introduced east of Reese River or Great Smoky Valley, where there was probably a little shell-bead money. In the latter valley, ropes of twisted rabbit skins were standards of value, being sold in lengths of twice around the hand. Twenty such lengths were worth $5 and were used to purchase buckskins, etc.

Snake River traded deer hides or roots. Thus three hides purchased a horse from Nez Perce. About one-half bushel of yams or camass purchased a colt.

Ritual was everywhere exceedingly limited and practically none attached to economic activities. There were no group ceremonials, except as the round dance was thought incidentally to bring rain, crop fertility, or general well-being. The main ritual was at birth, girl's puberty (boys had no puberty rites), and death. These were entirely individual affairs involving only the family, except where the annual mourning ceremony was introduced to the Death Valley and Owens Valley regions and the Sun Dance to the Northern Shoshoni. The rites were most like those of California, except that many elements were extremely variable.

Dances were performed only at festivals which were held annually or at most two or three times a year when a large crowd foregathered for a brief period. These were arranged when and where food supplies were sufficient to support an abnormally large number of persons for a week or so. The purpose was dancing (natively, the round dance was probably the only one known in most of the area; certain others spread rapidly within the historic period), gambling, and visiting. These were also occasions for philandering, courting, and for many persons to acquire spouses.

It is important to an understanding of the entire Shoshonean culture that it was stamped with a remarkable practicality. So far as its basic orientation is definable, it was "gastric." Starvation was so common that all activities had to be organized toward the food quest, which was carried on mostly by independent families. Whether other fundamental drives could have been implanted is not known. They had not been except among the eastern groups, Shoshoni and Ute, who attached some importance to warfare. Others carried on activities which were largely devoid of ritual, and of prestige value.

In certain practices the Northern Shoshoni departed radically from their western kin. There is some evidence that at one time they were much like the Western Shoshoni, but the horse wrought fundamental changes in certain, though not all, activities. Economically, they were not primarily seed gatherers, but hunters, and when the bison became extinct in Idaho they ranged on horseback across the Rocky Mountains to hunt in the Plains. The basketry complex had largely given place to skin articles, made on Plains and northern lines—parfleches, skin bags, and the like. Through contact with the Plains they had adopted other traits made possible by the horse—the skin tipi, travois, horse packing, warfare with shields, lances, honors, and some ritual dances, including the Sun Dance. In other respects, however, they resembled their western neighbors except in those traits that were variable among all Shoshoneans—games, dances, and details of crisis rites.

POPULATION DENSITY

Population estimates are derived from three sources of information: Informants' censuses, informants' estimates (which are usually guesses of varying worth), and estimates of early writers, including several rough censuses by the Indian Office. The first is probably most accurate, but is for about 1870 to 1880, a time when the population had been reduced by war and disease and, in some areas, seriously dislocated from its former habitat. Any revision of the estimates derived from this source should be upward. The second is less reliable and sometimes clearly tends to gross exaggeration. The estimates given by early writers are, as the tabulation below shows, extremely variable. Many are mere guesses and, in most instances, the group estimated is neither properly identified nor adequately bounded. The Gosiute estimates, for example, appear often to include Shoshoni of Steptoe Valley, Egan Canyon, and other localities in addition to the people herein called Gosiute.

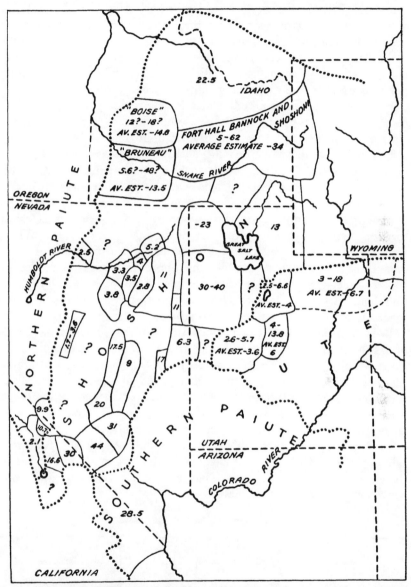

FIGURE 6.—Map of population density. Numerals indicate number of square miles per person for the period of about 1870–1880 within areas bounded by light lines. Heavy dotted lines are linguistic boundaries.

Figure 6 and the following tabulation summarize population esti-mates. Because territories exploited by different groups interlock, boundaries were chosen somewhat arbitrarily in each case to include the territory most often traversed by a group of villages and to exclude that habitually traversed by the next group. This permits a reasonably accurate statement of the relative density of the different localities in the western portion of the area. In the east this difficulty is more serious because territories overlapped to a much greater degree and bands even traveled on horseback into country utilized by other tribes. Several hundred square miles of territory is involved and it is extremely difficult arbitrarily to allot certain portions of it to the different groups in order to determine population density. An additional difficulty in this region is that population figures are generally from early writers who rarely gave precise statements of what peoples were included in their estimates.

The average density for the entire area was probably near Kroeber's estimate of one person to 15.6 square miles (1934, p. 3). There was, however, a striking local variation which correlated with the fertility of the natural environment. Extremely arid regions with large deserts had the lowest density, for example, Gosiute territory which was one person to 30 or 40 square miles. Where high elevation produced increased rainfall or the presence of large mountains made rivers possible, the population was much denser, for example, Owens Valley with one person to 2.1 square miles, the Humboldt River with one to 3.3 to 5.2 square miles, and the Wasatch piedmont with one to 4 to 6 square miles.

It is significant that the density in the area of mounted bands of Bannock and Shoshoni in Idaho and Utah was not exceptionally great—one person to 13 square miles in Utah, one to 34 square miles in eastern Idaho. These bands, as pointed out below, were made possible, not by great density, but by mobility provided by the horse. The impression of a large population is created merely because large numbers of Indians were seen together in early times.

In figure 6 the areas which are bounded and in the following tabulation the areas given in square miles are not always bands, districts, or subsistence areas. They are merely regions which were convenient for making estimates.

SUMMARY OF POPULATION ESTIMATES

Location	Population	Area, square miles	Square miles per person	Approximate date	Reference
All of Nevada	7,000	110,700	15.8	1861	Rept. Com. Ind. Affairs, 1861.
Do	8,500	110,700	13	1865	Rept. Com. Ind. Affairs, 1865.
Owens Valley	1,000	2,125	2.1	1860	Below, pp. 50-57.
Deep Springs Valley	23	250	10.7	1870	Informant census.
Fish Lake Valley	100	990	9.9	1870	Do.
Saline Valley	65	1,080	16.6	1870	Informant estimate.
Death Valley	42	1,260	30	1870	Informant census.
Beatty	29	1,300	44	1875	Do.
Belted Mountains	42	1,300	31	1875	Do.

SUMMARY OF POPULATION ESTIMATES—Continued

Location	Population	Area, square miles	Square miles per person	Approximate date	Reference
Las Vegas and vicinity_____	332	9,450	28.5	1872	Powell and Ingalls, 1874, pp. 10-11.
Reese River Valley_____	530	900	1.7	1872	Powell and Ingalls, 1874, p. 12.
Do_____	250	900	3.6	1875	Informant estimate.
Do_____	1,000	900	.9	1875	Do.
Kawich Mountains_____	90-120	2,025	17-22.5	1875	Informant census.
Little Smoky Valley_____	96	1,700	17.5	1875	Informant estimate.
Do_____	86	(?)	(?)	1872	Powell and Ingalls, 1874, p. 12.
Railroad Valley_____	250	2,250	9	1875	Informant estimate.
Antelope Valley_____	78	900	11	1885	Do.
Spring and Snake Valleys_____	378	2,410	6.3	1885	Do.
Gosiute_____	800	10,000	12.5	1865	Irish, 1865, p. 144.
Do_____	1,000	10,000	10	1866	Head, 1866, pp. 122-123.
Do_____	800	10,000	12.5	1869	Tourtellotte, 1869, p. 231.
Do_____	256	10,000	39	1872	Powell and Ingalls, 1874, pp. 2, 11, 17-18.
Do_____	200-300	10,000	33-50	1859	Simpson, 1876, pp. 35-36.
Do_____	400	10,000	25	1875	Wheeler, 1875, p. 36.
Diamond Valley_____	400	1,550	3.8	1870	Informant estimate.
Ruby Valley_____	420	1,200	2.8	1875	Do.
Huntington Valley_____	246	900	3.5	1875	Do.
Several valleys east of Ruby Valley.	180	2,000	11	1875	Do.
Humboldt River:					
Palisade, Carlin, and Elko__	228	770	3.3	1872	Powell and Ingalls. 1874, p. 12.
Halleck_____	100?	400	4	1875	Informant estimate.
Halleck to Wells_____	264	1,375	5.2	1875	Do.
Battle Mountain to Iron Point.	500	1,280	2.5	1875	Do.
Snake and Salmon Rivers_____	36,000	150,000	4	1855	Ross, 1855, vol. 1, p. 251.
"Bruneau"_____	125	4,800?	30	1866	Hough, 1866, p. 189.
Do_____	400	4,800?	12	1866	Ballard, 1866, p. 190.
Do_____	300	4,800?	16	1868	Powell, 1868, p. 201.
Do_____	850	4,800?	5.6	1869	Powell, 1869, p. 286.
Do_____	100	4,800?	48	1869	Danilson, 1870, pp. 287-288.
"Bruneau" average_____	355	4,800?	13.5	_____	Average of above estimates.
'Boise"_____	200	3,600?	18	1866	Ballard, 1866, p. 190.
Do_____	283	3,600?	13	1868	Powell, 1868, p. 201.
Do_____	300	3,600?	12	1869	Powell, 1869, p. 286.
Do_____	200	3,600?	18	1869	Danilson, 1870, pp. 287-288.
"Boise" average_____	245	3,600?	14.6	_____	Average estimate of above.
Grouse Creek_____	†200	4,700	−23	1875	Informant estimate.
Lemhi and central Idaho_____	1,200	27,000	22.5	1865	Informant estimate and below, pp. 187-189.
Fort Hall:					
Shoshoni_____	1,500	25,000	16.6	1827	Ogden, vol. 11, p. 364.
Bannock_____	650	25,000	38	1832	Irving, 1898, vol. 1, pp. 177-178
Do_____	600	25,000	42	1845	Simpson, 1876, p. 478.
Bannock (2,000)_____ Shoshoni (3,000)_____	5,000	25,000	5	1848	Meek, 1848, p. 10.
Bannock_____	400-500	25,000	50-62	1858	Forney, 1858, p. 213.
Do_____	500	25,000	50	1862	Burton, 1862, pp. 473-474.
Bannock (400-500)_____ Shoshoni (1,100)_____	1,500- 1,600	25,000	15-16	1866	Hall, 1866, p. 200.
Bannock_____	400	25,000	62	1866	Mann, 1866, p. 126.
Do_____	600?	25,000	42	1867	Mann, 1867, p. 189.
Bannock (1,000)_____ Shoshoni (1,500)_____	2,600	25,000	9.5	1867	Head, 1867, p. 188.
Bannock_____	800	25,000	31.2	1868	Head, 1868, p. 157.
Do_____	600	25,000	42	1869	Danilson, 1869, pp. 287-288.
Do_____	800	25,000	31.2	1870	Mann, 1870, p. 274.
Fort Hall average_____	1,200	25,000	34	_____	Average of above estimates.
Bands east of Great Salt Lake___	1,000	13,000	13	1859	Forney, 1859, p. 363, and Burton, 1862, p. 474.
Utah Lake Ute_____	300-800	2,000	2.5-6.6	_____	Below, pp. 224.
Sevier Lake Ute_____	700-1,500	4,000	2.6-5.7	_____	Below, pp. 224.
Sampits Ute_____	144-500	2,000	4-13.8	_____	Below, pp. 224.
Uintah Ute_____	500-3,000	9,000?	3-18	_____	Below, pp. 225.

SOCIOPOLITICAL GROUPS OF DIFFERENT AREAS

WESTERN LOCALIZED NORTHERN PAIUTE BANDS: OWENS VALLEY

The Northern Paiute of Owens Valley were subdivided into true composite land-owning bands. Those in the northern part of the valley have been previously described (Steward, 1933). In the southern part, bands were essentially the same, though many were smaller.

Although the general ecology of this area resembles that of the Shoshoni area, certain local environmental peculiarities affected the subsistence activities of the inhabitants. The valley is a deep trough, more than 100 miles long and not over 20 miles wide. Its floor lies at about 4,000 feet. On the west it is sharply bounded by the lofty Sierra Nevada range (pl. 1, a) and on the east by the Inyo and White Mountains. The crest of the former is nowhere under 10,000 feet altitude, with many peaks surpassing 14,000 feet. Heavy rain and snowfall in these summits is preserved in lakes, springs, snow fields, and even glaciers, from which streams flow out into the otherwise arid valley at intervals of 2 to 15 miles and finally seep out into swamps in the lowlands where they are drained off by Owens River. Deer and mountain sheep could be had in the high mountains; various seeds in the foothills; seeds, roots, antelope, and rabbits in the valley. The arid Inyo and White Mountains on the east give rise to no streams, but support extensive pine-nut groves and formerly had many mountain sheep and deer.

This extraordinarily varied environment afforded all essential food resources within 20 miles of the villages, which were situated on the various streams. Although people sometimes remained away from home several days, it was usually possible to return within a day or two. By way of contrast, the Shoshoni area, which was less fertile, often required travel of many days from the winter villages.

The band territories of Owens Valley were related primarily to the streams emanating from the Sierra Nevada. Where streams are clustered, as in the northern part of the valley, groups of neighboring villages comprised single bands, e. g., those at Bishop (Pitanapatü), Hot Springs (Ütü'ütüwitü), Big Pine (Tovowohamatü) and Fish Springs (Panatü). South of the last, streams are more widely spaced, some having only a single independent village.

Each village or cluster of villages was a band whose unity and independence was expressed in the habitual cooperation of all members in its own communal antelope, rabbit, and deer drives, in local festivals and mourning ceremonies, in the ownership of more or less exactly defined seed territories (and from Big Pine to Bishop, at least, of hunting territories), including irrigated areas, and in the possession of a chief, a common name, and a community sweat house. Occasional cooperation of several independent villages or bands in hunts, dances, or mourning ceremonies united these independent groups only temporarily.

The functional basis of band organization, then, was the habitual cooperation of its members in joint enterprises and its objective expression was the common name, chieftainship, and ownership of territory.

Villages and bands.—Villages and bands in northern Owens Valley have been previously mapped. In the southern part of the valley a village was situated on each stream near the lower edge of the alluvial fan which spread out from the mouth of each canyon, some 2 to 4 miles from Owens River. Such sites afforded an abundance of excellent water and a central location with reference to food areas. Archeological evidence shows some villages to have been located along Owens River, though much of this portion of the valley was swampy.

The following list gives the principal villages on the main streams. It is probably incomplete and omits sites on the river. Exact information to indicate chieftainship and participation in various activities is not available for all. Most of the villages were independent, that is, constituted land-owning, political units. Some, however, especially those which lay in close proximity to one another, were apparently sufficiently allied to constitute larger bands like those at Big Pine and Bishop.

The villages as numbered on the map (fig. 6) were as follows:

1. Goodale Creek, Padohahu: pa (creek?) or padahuhu: matü, a large, independent village with its own chief.

2. Division Creek, Axagüwa (edge of black rocks) matü (place).

3. Sawmill Creek, Tuinü'hu (door?) witü (place).

4. Thibaut Creek, Totsitupi (a whitish rock, perhaps marble or limestone) witü. Perhaps 25 people here. Chiefs of the last three are uncertain. It is possible that they were somewhat allied.

5. Fort Independence, Tsak:'ca (oak—there are many acorns on this creek, now called Oak Creek) witü. Possibly 200 people. Pine-nut lands lay near Paiute Monument and Waucoba Mountain in the Inyo Mountains. Irrigation was practiced with Oak Creek.

6. Independence, Natakâ: (a plant locally abundant) matü. Perhaps 200 people. Irrigation with Independence Creek.

7. Symmes Creek, To''owiawatü (to'owiawü ridge+watü place). (This name resembles that of the native village at Big Pine, Tobowahamatü.)

8. Shepherd Creek, Tsagapu (willow) witü. This village may have been allied through communal activities and chieftainship with George's Creek.

9. George's Creek, Tüpüzi (dübüsi, probably *Brodiaea capitata*) witü. This and the last probably included some 200 people. Band-owned pine-nut lands

were south of Paiute Monument and north of the Cerro Gordo Mine in the Inyo Mountains.

10. Hogback Creek, Mögahu' pina (möga, granite+hu, hills ?pinaɲ. behind). A village, previously recorded (Steward, 1933, p. 325), scattered along Hogback, Lone Pine, Tuttle, and Diez Creeks, west of the Alabama Hills.

11. Lone Pine Creek, Waucova (yellow pine) witü. The village probably east of the Alabama Hills. 200 inhabitants.

12. Tuttle Creek, Pahago watü.

13. Richter Creek, Mogohopinaɲ (high ?) watü.

14. Carrol Creek, Suhu'budu mutü (suhuvi, willow+?).

15. Cottonwood Creek, Hudu (running water ?) matu.

16. Olancha, Pakwazi'(pa, water+kwazi, end) natü.

17. For Fish Springs Creek, i. e., the creeks flowing by Fish Springs, GR gave Suhubadopa. Archeological remains show that an extensive village site existed here.

Subsistence activities.—Food getting was carried on within the band's own territory, except when people were invited to participate in hunts elsewhere. Each territory was roughly a long, narrow rectangle, extending across Owens Valley from the summit of the Sierra Nevada Mountains to the summit of the White and Inyo Mountains. It embraced the various life zones, thus providing all possible local varieties of essential foods.

Seeds were the most important foods. Location, ownership, and methods of gathering seeds in the northern part of the valley have been previously described. Throughout the valley seed areas were band-owned. Testimony conflicted, however, as to whether those in the valley were always subdivided into family plots. Discrepancies may represent local differences or informant error. This is a point for further study.

Pine-nut areas were principally in the Inyo Mountains and White Mountains. Everywhere they were subdivided into family plots, each bounded by natural landmarks known in detail to all band members. At George's Creek in the south, plots were owned by women and inherited matrilineally. Fish Springs and Big Pine plots were owned by men and inherited patrilineally, women picking on their husbands' plots. Trespass on pine-nut areas by other families, and especially by members of other bands, led to fights but not bloodshed. Fear of evil magic seems to have been a potent deterrent to trespass. Owners, however, often invited persons even of other bands, especially their relatives, to pick on their plots.

The trip for pine nuts was made in the fall by the entire band. The chief, having noted the ripening of the nuts, announced the trip a few days in advance. Upon arriving in the mountains each family went to its own plot. When the harvest was complete some nuts were carried back to the permanent village in the valley; others were cached and brought down subsequently when needed. If the harvest were abnormally abundant people might remain in the mountains for a part of the winter.

Most other seeds and roots grew in or near the valley and were accessible from the permanent village. Some, especially the roots of *Brodiaea*, *Eleocharis*, and others, various greens, and the seeds of *Helianthus*, *Chenopodium*, and *Juncus* grew in the swampy lowlands or on irrigated land. In the northern part of the valley the irrigator was elected. Each family harvested where it liked on irrigated land. In the south the village chief was in charge of irrigation, either performing the task himself or requesting young men to do so. Each woman owned a subdivision of the area.

Although this irrigation was previously considered to be aboriginal (Steward, 1933, pp. 247–250) there is some possibility that it was introduced by Americans, who penetrated the valley after 1850, or by Spaniards who had settled at least the southern portion of it much earlier. Wasson (1862, p. 226) said:

"These Indians have dug ditches and irrigated nearly all the arable land in that section of the country, and live by its products. They have been repeatedly told by the officers of the Government that they should have the exclusive possession of these lands, and they are now fighting to maintain that possession."

More arid valley and foothill areas, also within convenient distance of the villages, afforded seeds of *Oryzopsis*, *Salvia*, *Sophia*, *Artemisia*, *Mentzelia*, *Stipa*, and *Agropyron*, various species of cactus, and berries of *Lycium*.

Several species of animals were hunted collectively by each band, participants usually being limited to band members. Jack rabbits were taken principally along the flat portion of the valley near Owens River. Large crowds beat the brush, driving the rabbits into long nets placed end to end to form a large semicircular fence. There were one to three nets, each supervised by its owner. In the north, either the band chief or some older, experienced rabbit hunter, who was perhaps appointed by the band chief, was in charge. In the south, the band chief was director. The kill was equally divided among participants. The largest drives were in connection with the 6-day fall festival. These entailed considerable visiting. For example, Fort Independence people visited George's Creek and vice versa, some people even coming from Big Pine or Lone Pine.

Antelope were hunted communally, especially in the valley flat east of Owens River. A corral but no shaman was used in this area.

Deer were sometimes hunted communally in the mountains on both sides of the valley. Hunts were under the direction of the village chief in the south. Older men hid by game trails to shoot deer driven by young men. Meat was shared by all. In fact, large

game killed by lone hunters at any time was necessarily shared with
all village members. Some deer hunts involved the joint efforts of
several bands. TS's grandfather described a hunt in the Sierra
Nevada Mountains west of Owens Lake in which several hundred
men from throughout the valley participated.

Mountain sheep were also sometimes hunted communally, especially in the Sierra Nevada Mountains, dogs being used to drive
them on to cliffs.

Hunting territory was not band-owned in the south. Men were
permitted to hunt anywhere but naturally tended to restrict hunting
to the mountains near their own villages. In the Fish Springs
portion of the valley, individuals were permitted to hunt anywhere,
but communal hunting groups remained within their own band territory unless adjoining bands cooperated. Thus, band ownership of
hunting territory seems to fade out gradually from northern to
southern Owens Valley. It disappears entirely among neighboring
Shoshoni.

Fishing places were embraced within hunting territories in the
north, but were accessible to anyone in the south. Fish were relatively unimportant, however, and required little communal effort.

Festivals.—Six-day festivals, involving dances, gambling, and rabbit drives, were held by each band in the fall after the pine-nut
harvest. These were planned, organized, and managed by the band
chief. Invitations were sent to neighboring villages. Large villages,
for example those at Lone Pine, George's Creek, Fort Independence,
and Big Pine, attracted people from distant places. Thus, Fort
Independence drew visitors from Lone Pine, Olancha, and Big Pine.
To avoid having festivals at the same time, large villages sometimes
alternated each year, for example, George's Creek and Lone Pine.
Sometimes villages held festivals at different times in the fall so
that people from elsewhere could attend after completing their own
festival. The chief of the host village or band was always in charge.

In post-Caucasian times, with a decreased but more concentrated
population and improved transportation, fewer villages gave festivals. The last was at Fort Independence about 20 years ago.
Visitors brought some of their own food but the hosts slaughtered
beef and presented some to each family. Visitors camped in or
around the large brush dance corral, but were placed in no special
arrangement.

Sweat house.—Band unity was somewhat expressed in and height-
ened by use of a communal sweat house (mu:sa). Throughout the
valley it was like that previously described for the north (Steward,
1933, pp. 265–266). The chief directed its construction and it was
owned and used by the band or village. Men, especially old men,

sweated without steam, meanwhile praying, then plunged into a pool of water always located nearby. All men used it as a clubhouse, gambling place, and dormitory, and spent many hours lounging in it.

The sweat house is particularly significant in indicating that the population was sufficiently stable and clustered to be able to utilize a house centrally located. Nevada Shoshoni were too scattered and the families too unsettled during much of the year to make a community sweat house profitable. Instead, individuals built small houses for sweating only.

Until recently there were sweat houses at Fort Independence, George's Creek, Lone Pine, Big Pine, and possibly Manzanar. They have now fallen into disuse.

Warfare.—Except for temporary conflict with the white man, warfare was an uninportant factor in amalgamating the native population. AG thought all Indians had formerly been at peace with one another. GR had heard only of wars with Indians west of the Sierra and thought the battles had been fought by Paiute who crossed the mountains. TS recounted only a single minor local engagement with a small party of invaders from the south. Paiute bands did not fight with one another or with Shoshoni. Conflicts over pine-nut areas were brief and never involved weapons more dangerous than the sling, which did little damage.

Mourning ceremony.—The annual mourning ceremony contributed somewhat to cohesion of band members. It was usually held in the fall and served primarily to terminate the year of mourning during which relatives of a deceased person were required to abstain from meat and grease, to refrain from washing, and to avoid any festivities. Mourners' grief was symbolically washed away and all the dead of the past year were commemorated by burning certain articles which had been saved from the funerals, together with perhaps $50 worth of articles purchased for the occasion. Each ceremony was led by the band chief. Visitors from neighboring bands and villages frequently attended.

Chieftainship.—As the members of each well-defined sociopolitical group or band of Owens Valley carried on a number of cooperative activities, the position of chief was of some importance. Each band had a chief, pogina'vi (cf. S–LtLk, pakw'navi), whose duties were to direct: irrigation, either doing it himself or appointing a special man (who was at liberty to refuse, however); rabbit, antelope, and deer drives; fall festivals and mourning ceremonies; erection of the sweat house. He also kept informed about the ripening of pine nuts and instructed people to move into the mountains to harvest them; approved or vetoed witch killing; invited other villages to cooperate in some enterprises and, as host, took charge of these activities. (See also Steward, 1933, pp. 304–305.)

The chief was succeeded by his son, provided he were intelligent, good, and persuasive. Otherwise, a brother or some other member of his family, or even an unrelated person who was assured of popular support, succeeded him.

Chiefs had no assistants or speakers but called upon various people as they were needed.

Chiefs had no concern with homicide (except of witches), property disputes, or other difficulties involving band members. These were settled by disputants.

During the wars against the white man, formerly independent bands united. The Big Pine chief took charge of those in the northern part of the valley, the George's Creek chief of those in the south.

Marriage and the family.—Though the bilateral family was the irreducible unit of Owens Valley society, its relative importance was less than among Shoshoni. The Shoshoni family was nearly independent politically and spent much of the year practically in isolation. The Paiute family not only yielded to higher political control for many activities, but, because of the larger, more permanent, and closely spaced villages, was thrown into association with a greater number of related and unrelated families. In marriage, this provided a greater number of potential spouses. In kinship affairs, it threw relatives into more frequent daily contact and gave greater point to observances.

Throughout Owens Valley, marriage between any relatives was forbidden, a fact borne out by genealogies covering several generations (Steward, 1933). A few recent cases of cousin marriage have been strongly disapproved.

The levirate and sororate were so strong that a payment was required to avoid them. Widowed spouses observed mourning taboos and refrained from amorous adventures for a year, fearing witchcraft by their parents-in-law. Even a recent case of "running" with another woman soon after the death of his wife brought a man much censure. In AG's family at Lone Pine his two older brothers married sisters. At the death of the younger brother, AG married the widowed sister-in-law after she had observed the year's mourning. Later, his oldest brother died, then AG's wife died. At the end of a year, after AG had paid $50 to his parents-in-law to purchase articles for burning in the annual mourning ceremony and they had washed him to terminate his mourning period, they tried to force him to marry his brother's widow. AG refused, considering her too old for him, and has not married since.

Though intensification of the levirate and sororate had, among certain Shoshoni, led to fraternal polyandry as well as sororal polygyny, sometimes with concomitant changes in kinship terminology reflecting both practices, Owens Valley Paiute practiced sororal polygyny but not polyandry.

The desire to ally families through marriage was shown in some tendency to infant betrothal and there were special terms designating the relationship to come between prospective parents-in-law, all of whom called one another mukuci'[1] at Fish Springs and Fish Lake Valley, and daiyump, child's mother-in-law, and mukuci, child's father-in-law, at George's Creek.

The mother-in-law taboo, which was lacking among Shoshoni, was strong in northern Owens Valley. At George's Creek it involved a speech taboo and restrained behavior for about a year. At Lone Pine it was lacking.

Although marriage was necessarily with an unrelated person, each village usually had several unrelated families, so that local exogamy was ordinarily unnecessary. In the south, however, there was a strong preference for matrilocal residence, perhaps connected with female ownership of valley seed plots. This tended to convert small villages into female lineages, which approximated but failed actually to be exogamous matrilineal bands. Loss of food lands since the coming of the white man has produced extremely variable residence and much moving.

WESTERN INDEPENDENT NORTHERN PAIUTE VILLAGES

DEEP SPRINGS VALLEY

This valley (pl. 3, b) was occupied by a small group of Northern Paiute which was partially independent. It shared with Owens Valley Paiute those features producing group solidarity—local rabbit drives, sweat house, death ceremonies, and perhaps festivals. The valley is, moreover, such an isolated topographical unit that its small number of inhabitants inevitably cooperated with one another more often than with outsiders. Nevertheless, its unity was incomplete, being reduced by intermarriage with Owens Valley and Fish Lake Valley, by frequent visits to each of these areas for dances and rabbit drives, by lack of local band ownership of hunting and seed areas, and by a chieftainship which interlocked somewhat with that of Fish Lake Valley.

The people called their valley Pato'sabaya (probably patsiat:[a], lake+paya'[a], water), the name of the village on the eastern side of the lake. They called themselves Pato'sabaya nünemua (people). Owens Valley Paiute called the valley Ozaŋ witü (ozaŋ, salt+witü, place), but MH, NP–FLk, called the lower part Ozaŋ witü, the upper part Suhuvawazinatü (suhuvi, willow+wazi, end+witü), after the village at the mouth of Wyman Canyon. TSt, S–Lida, called the entire valley Osamba (alkaline, i. e., the lake).

Villages.—JA remembered only five families in the entire valley, which is undoubtedly somewhat less than the native population. Much interrelated, these families lived together and often traveled together. Archeological remains indicate that the largest and most frequented winter village was on the eastern side of Deep Springs Lake, where a number of excellent springs provide abundant water (village 18 on map, fig. 7). Habitations were generally in the open, though a cave or rock shelter in the vicinity was also used. Sometimes these families wintered near a cave at the mouth of Wyman Canyon at the northern end of the valley, site 19. For several miles south of Wyman Canyon, on the western side of the valley and near Wyman Creek, there are many rock shelters formed by huge boulders where fragments of pottery and basketry and flints indicate encampments, site 20. When pine nuts were plentiful people wintered in the lower portion of the juniper belt near the cached nuts, a favorite place being in the hills near Roberts Ranch in Wyman Canyon, site 21. House remains have been found in the White Mountains near and above timber line (about 10,000 feet) but it is not known whether these were winter or summer dwellings. It is scarcely conceivable that people could have withstood the intense cold or traveled through the deep snow that prevailed in winter at this altitude.

The population given by JA, probably as of about 50 years or more ago, shows 5 families or camps, totaling 23 persons, as follows:

Joe Bowers, the chief, his wife, their daughter, and her husband, all native to Deep Springs Valley. Four persons. The several grandchildren all died before maturity. Joe's brother, Sam Bowers, married a Big Pine woman and moved to Big Pine.

Charlie, who was Joe Bowers' son-in-law's brother, his wife and daughter. Three persons. The daughter married and moved to Fish Lake Valley.

Joe Bowers' brother, Sport, his wife from Big Pine, whom he had met at a Deep Springs fall festival, their two sons, one being Peter Sport, and a daughter. Five persons. The children all married after the family moved to Big Pine and have visited Deep Springs only occasionally since.

Big Mouth Tom, who was chief of Fish Lake Valley and said to reside at Ozaŋwin:' or Tünăva (Pigeon Springs) but whom JA claimed to be the second chief of Deep Springs and to reside there; his wife who was a half Shoshoni and Captain Harry's sister from Tünăva in Fish Lake Valley; and their two sons and two daughters. Seven persons. One of these sons was JA who married a woman from Păŭ'uva (McNett range village) in Fish Lake Valley. Big Mouth was the cousin of Joe and Sam Bowers and Sport, perhaps the paternal grandmothers of each being sisters. It is not certain whether the spouses of JA's brothers and sisters should be counted in this.

Joe Bowers' sister, her husband, their son, Deep Springs Jim. Joe Bowers' second sister possibly should be counted in one of these camps. 3 or 4 persons.

FIGURE 7.—Villages and subsistence areas of the Death Valley and Owens Valley regions.

Deep Springs Jim later married a Big Pine girl and moved to her home. Their daughter, Elsie, married George Collins of Fish Springs and had two daughters.

Of the 9 comparatively old marriages recorded here, there was valley endogamy in 2, exogamy in 4, the others being uncertain. 4 marriages were patrilocal, 2 matrilocal, 1 by parties from the same locality, and 1 uncertain.

Since 4 of these families were those of brothers and sisters, the only marriage choice for the next generation, had the group continued in the valley, would have been into the Big Mouth branch, which was probably no closer than second cousin and therefore marriageable. Lizzie Babock, JA's daughter, thought first cousin marriage, as now sometimes practiced in Owens Valley, shocking, but admitted that second or third cousins might be proper.

The population, however, was not settled and undoubtedly many persons moved to adjoining valleys and vice versa. Hence, with lack of a consistent residence rule there would undoubtedly have been many persons eligible to marry each other in Deep Springs Valley in another generation.

Subsistence activities.—Deep Springs Valley, lying at 5,000 feet, and the surrounding mountains, especially the White Mountains on the west which culminate in a peak over 14,000 feet high, afforded foods in considerable quantities and variety. The valley floor is arid except for a stream which flows down from Wyman Canyon at its northern end and for springs which feed a large salt lake at its southern end. The area usually exploited was about 250 square miles.

Seed gathering was carried on like that previously described in Owens Valley but wild seeds were not irrigated. Pine nuts were gathered in the White Mountains, especially above Dead Horse Meadow on Crooked Creek, above the western side of the valley, and to some extent near Black Mountain and Marble Spring Canyon on Cedar Flat. Grass and other seeds were scattered through the valley and on the foothills. Sometimes, however, trips were made into Eureka Valley to the east for wai (*Oryzopsis*) when it was abundant. Eureka Valley is almost devoid of water and seems to have had few if any permanent inhabitants, but abundant seeds attracted Paiute and Shoshoni from neighoring valleys. Deep Springs people sometimes traveled to Fish Lake Valley when certain seeds were plentiful there.

A woman gathered seeds only for her immediate family. If an older woman, for example an aunt or grandmother, were attached to a family, she gathered for herself if she were able. Relatives and visitors, however, were freely fed and even presented small quantities of seeds. Possibly pine nuts were more freely distributed than other seeds.

Deer were hunted mainly in the White Mountains, antelope in the southern end of the valley, either near Antelope Springs or east of Deep Springs Lake, and mountain sheep near the springs or in the mountains east of the lake. Antelope and deer were tracked by individual hunters or taken by groups of 4 or 5 or more men who, aided by fire and perhaps dogs, drove them past hidden archers. Sheep were either stalked in the mountains or shot from stone blinds near the springs. Ducks were shot in the sloughs east of the lake.

Rabbits were driven into nets during community hunts at the time of the fall festival. Hunters, led by Big Mouth, went out for each of 6 days, to drive them near Deep Springs Ranch and probably in other parts of the valley.

Large game was divided equally among all residents in the village; the hunter kept only one hind quarter for himself. Rabbits killed in drives were kept by the persons who killed them, though hunters who had none were given one or two.

Migrations during the year depended upon local abundance of seeds. Sometimes all families traveled together. sometimes each traveled alone. The whole valley seems to have been exploited. The foothills at the upper end of the valley yielded *Mentzelia*, bunch grass, *Stipa*, and other seeds, which could easily be reached from camps along Wyman Creek. A favorite camp seems to have been in a kind of small valley southeast of Deep Springs Ranch. Another camp was at "Deer Creek" (probably "Beer Creek" on the U. S. G. S. map), used especially for deer hunting. Antelope Springs was base camp for antelope hunts.

Property.—Ownership of chattels and houses was like that in Owens Valley. There was, however, no ownership of food areas. In fact, JA regarded such ownership in Owens Valley as strange and selfish. When local pine nuts failed, Deep Springs people went into Fish Lake Valley or anywhere in the White Mountains, except where Owens Valley pine-nut groves lay. Fish Lake Valley and Owens Valley people were privileged to gather pine nuts and seeds in and around Deep Springs Valley without seeking permission. No quarrels resulted from competition for seeds.

Sweat house.—One sweat house stood at the village at the mouth of Wyman Canyon, another at the village at Deep Springs Lake. Both were communally owned, like those in Owens Valley, and served as club houses, dormitories, and general headquarters.

Festivals.—These were held annually, usually in the fall, and lasted 6 days, the people driving rabbits or gambling each day and feasting and dancing each night. The dance site was either the mouth of Wyman Canyon or Deep Springs Lake. Visitors from Fish Lake Valley and Owens Valley often attended. The local festival leader was Big Mouth Tom. (See, however, Fish Lake Valley festivals, where Big Mouth Tom was the main director.) It is probable, however, that Deep Springs people more often attended the festivals in Fish Lake Valley at Oasis, where Big Mouth and Captain Harry were directors. And sometimes they went instead to Owens Valley.

Chieftainship.—Chieftainship is complicated by a partial interlocking of group activities with Fish Lake Valley. As political control concerned only a few enterprises in which otherwise independent villages rather than a true band cooperated, its extent was not clearly defined. Joe Bowers was the main Deep Springs chief, but as he was away dealing with white men most of the time, especially during the Indian wars, Big Mouth Tom (JA's father) served in his place, organizing festivals and directing rabbit drives. But Big Mouth lived in Fish Lake Valley much of the time, where he was also the chief. Other Deep Springs people, moreover, spent considerable time visiting friends and relatives in Fish Lake Valley. To what extent this linkage with Fish Lake Valley resulted from the reduction of the native population after the arrival of the white man is impossible to say.

Some place names:

Crooked Creek, Suhugo'º (suhuva, willow+go'º, or ko'º, hollow). Cf. Saline Valley, ko'º.

Birch Creek, Hubijava (birch), possibly a recent name.

Antelope Springs, Pazo'º (meadow).

Cedar Flat, Pawahoguma (pawa, juniper+hoguma, flat), possibly also a recent name.

Buckhorn Spring, Si'yabaya (si'ya, pile of rocks+paya'ᴬ, water).

Camp site with tules on northern side of Deep Springs Lake, Tanagwinuᵐ.

The high mountains bordering Deep Springs Lake, Osanakam: (sitting on top).

FISH LAKE VALLEY [5]

The culture of the Fish Lake Valley Paiute differed only in minor details from that of Owens Valley. The environment, however, is much less fertile. The White Mountains which separate it from Owens Valley on the west are large and massive and rise above 10,000 feet, White Mountain Peak surpassing 14,000 feet. This great altitude produced considerable rain (though much less than at similar altitudes in the Sierra Nevada Mountains) and some abundance of plant growth. But this range is so precipitous on the Fish Lake Valley side that habitations were almost impossible and seed gathering was extremely difficult. Other sides of the valley are bounded by low, arid ranges except in the vicinity of Lida, where they are

---

[5] A somewhat dynamic picture of a Fish Lake Valley family is provided by the informant's thumbnail biography, Appendix F.

covered for miles with junipers and pinyons, and part of the Silver Peak Range, which rises into the juniper belt. The valley floor is about 5,000 feet, generally arid, for only a few streams enter it, and supports largely xerophytic plants which are worthless for food.

Although Fish Lake Valley is a fairly well-defined topographic unit, it is so large that the people scattered through it seem to have been able to cooperate only with difficulty. A certain amount of unity, however, was induced by the necessity for each family to forage nearly the entire area of about 990 square miles for foods and by the custom of assembling annually for hunts and dances. It was not a true band, for chieftainship was tenuous and people in certain villages seem to have cooperated with Lida or Deep Springs Valley people about as often as with Fish Lake Valley neighbors. They had, moreover, no band name, no communal sweat house (the only sweat house was at Oasis), and no ownership of food territories. Mourning observances were merely village affairs. MH explicitly observed that an individual's sense of allegiance was with the village rather than the valley as a whole. And even this allegiance was not always permanent.

Villages.—The population known to MH at about 1870[6] comprised 100 individuals, distributed among 8 villages, each having 1 to 4 camps or families. There was a total of 16 such camps, averaging 6.2 persons each. Six of the villages were located on streams, not far from where they issued from the White Mountains. Two were at springs in the mountains at the eastern end of the valley. The villages were more or less permanent, being occupied throughout the year, except when, during summer and fall, trips were made for seeds and pine nuts.

The census of the villages, representing but a single point in time, conceals the actual fluidity of the population. Like Nevada Shoshoni and in contrast to Owens Valley Paiute, attachment even to a village was impermanent. Families changed residence so often and traveled so widely that relatives were scattered over several valleys while even small villages might embrace unrelated families. For example, MH's paternal grandfather had lived at Hot Creek, Paŋwihumadü (fish creek place) in Long Valley, northwest of Owens Valley, and her paternal grandmother somewhere north of the White Mountains. They had moved to North Bishop, Kuhavahi'natü, when her father was born. Her maternal grandparents had lived at West Bishop, Paoka'matü (rock ridge place) where her mother was born. Her parents moved to a village in Hamil Valley, Tepo'siinatü, where MH was born not long after white men began to enter the country. But

[6] Ranches were probably started in the Fish Lake Valley region about 1865, borax works in 1875. Mining began at Gold Mountain to the east in 1864 and near Columbus to the north in 1865. (Bancroft, vol. 25, p. 260.)

after her maternal grandfather's death they moved to Tu:na′va in Fish Lake Valley. After her marriage to Captain Harry, MH lived at Sohodühatü.

Names of individuals are generally omitted from the census because they have been dead and not mentioned for so many years that MH had forgotten many of them. For our purpose the only loss is the knowledge which might have been obtained of the relationship between members of different villages. This, however, is probably unimportant, for it is clear that a good deal of relationship existed between members of all villages. Villages, moreover, did not necessarily comprise only relatives, for lack of a rule of post-marital residence split families in all ways. Village numbers correspond with those on figure 7.

22. Suhuyoi, at the Patterson ranch, 5,000 feet. One camp: a man and his wife; his sister and her husband; his daughter and her husband, who was probably born in the same village. Five persons.

23. Yo:gamatü, several miles from the mountains at the present Chiatovich ranch, 4,900 feet. Ten persons in two camps or families, as follows: in one, MH's mother's father's brother, his wife from Watühad:ᵃ, and their two sons and daughters; in the other, MH's great uncle's male cousin, his wife from an unknown locality, their daughter and two sons.

24. Tu:näva, the present Geroux ranch, marked McFee on the U. S. G. S. map, 4,825 feet. Fourteen persons in two camps, as follows: in one, MH's father's father, his wife, and their son, all from the North Bishop village; MH's step-mother from Watühad:ᵃ, MH, her brother who died at the age of 7 or 8, and her two half-sisters; MH's mother had died; in the other, three male cousins. One married a woman from Big Pine and later moved to Big Pine. The other two married women from Yo:gamatü, whose relationship to each other was unknown. Six persons.

25. Watühad:ᵃ, Moline ranch on "Moline Creek" (probably Leidy Creek on the U. S. G. S. map). One camp of four brothers, one of whom married a woman from Suhuyoi, the other a woman from Yo:gomatü. The other two were unmarried. Six persons.

26. Tü′näva, at Pigeon Spring, several springs at 6,200 to 6,500 feet in the mountains at the eastern end of Fish Lake Valley. This was advantageously located in the midst of pine-nut country. Thirty-one persons in four camps. In one, the chief, his wife from Palmetto, a son and a daughter, both of whom died before they were married, and a daughter whose husband came from Paŋwihumadü, Hot Creek, in Long Valley to Tü′näva. In the second, the chief's sister, her husband from Tü:näva, their daughter, her husband from Paŋwihumadü (Hot creek in Long Valley) or Benton, and their three children, who have subsequently married. The third, the chief's older brother, his wife from Sohodühatü (Oasis), their daughter, their son, and his Shoshoni wife from Lida Valley or Tule Canyon. The fourth, the chief's younger brother, his Shoshoni wife from Lida Valley, their oldest daughter and her Shoshoni husband from Grapevine Springs Canyon, and their three children. A second daughter, her Shoshoni husband from Lida Valley, and their two children. And a third, unmarried daughter with her child.

27. Sohodühatü (sohodü, cottonwood? tree under + hatü, place), at the present Oasis ranch, 5,031 feet. Twenty-four people, four camps. In one: Sohodüviji; his wife probably from Big Pine; a daughter, her husband from

Bishop, and their two daughters, Minnie Piper and Kate; a son and his wife from Yo: gamatü; a younger daughter, her husband probably from Tü: năva; and their son. Kate, now dead, first married an Oasis man named Greyhaired Johnny and had a boy, Omi, now dead; later she married a white man and had another boy, Lewis. Sohodüviji's son died childless soon after his marriage. His youngest daughter's son Bill has since married and separated. Of these persons 11, who were living at Sohodühatü at the time of the observation, are counted. The second camp, a man related to Sohodüviji; his wife also from Sohodühatü; two daughters who died unmarried; an older son who brought his wife to Sohodühatü from Big Pine, but whose children all died; and a son who died unmarried. The third camp, a man related to the other two in some way; his wife, a Sohodühatü woman; two daughters who died unmarried. The fourth camp, a man, related to MH's family and also to the other three local household heads; his wife, most of whose relatives were in Bishop; a daughter and son who died unmarried.

The great number of deaths in this village MH thought due to gonorrhea.

28. Ozaŋ'win:[1] (oza, ozap, alkaline+?), probably at various springs at about 7,000 feet on the eastern or southern slope of the Sylvania Mountains and near Tü: năva. This name, however, may be confused with Ozaŋ'win:[1] in Deep Springs Valley. Five persons in one camp: A Shoshoni from Tule Canyon or Lida Valley, nearby; his local Paiute wife; their son, Captain Harry, who moved to Oasis after marrying MH; their daughter; her local husband who was a cousin of the main chief at Tü: năva and who served as a lesser chief.

29. Păü'üva, a village in the vicinity of McNett ranch, 5,600 feet. One camp of six persons, as follows: JA who was Captain Harry's sister's son and came from Ozaŋ'win:[1]; his wife from Păü'üva; her mother's brother (her parents had both died) and his wife from Watühad:[2]; the latter's son and daughter, both of whom died unmarried.

Subsistence activities.—Food resources seem seldom to have been sufficient to permit laying up reserve stores against the future. Seeds might last through the winter, but rarely longer. Meat, especially that from lesser animals such as fish, lizards, rodents, and caterpillars, was usually consumed at once, so that techniques for preserving and storing it were unimportant. While there was probably little starvation, life entailed constant food seeking. Men seem to have hunted throughout the year, including the months when their wives gathered. Men's share in gathering was relatively slight, except in pine nutting, when they gave women some assistance.

Seed gathering required extensive wandering through the area, especially within the valley. MH described the seasonal activities of her family as follows: Their usual winter home was at Tu: na'va on a creek on the western side of the valley. In early spring they procured Joshua tree buds from the low hills of the Silver Peak Range (pl. 2, *a*) and sand grass and *Mentzelia* seeds from the vicinity of Păü'üva, 10 miles to the north. Then they went 5 miles northeast to Yo': gamatu, taking the seeds with them. The principal crop at Yo': gamatu was nahavita roots (*Eleocharis* ?) which grew on ground irrigated by her maternal grandmother's brother. He was the only person in the valley who practiced irrigation. Although he seems to have owned the irrigated plot, he freely assigned portions of it to families from the vicinity, even though they were not related to him. He received no compensation for his trouble. In moist places near Yo': gamatu they also dug tupusi (*Brodiaea*?) roots which were not, however, deliberately irrigated.

In late June they traveled some 8 miles to Sühüyoi at the foot of the White Mountains to gather posida (chia) and mono. Here and other nearby places where the crops were good they gathered *Helianthus*, *Sophia*, *Aster* (?), payai, *Salvia*, *Stipa*, and *Erogrostis*. These and dried berries of *Ribes* and *Lycium* they carried back to Tu:na'va to store for winter use.

In the fall they ordinarily went for pine nuts to the Silver Peak Range to a place called Tohoyavi, some 10 miles directly east of Tu:na'va, and south of Piper Peak. Several unrelated families in Tu:na'va had a kind of claim to this area. Visitors whose local crops had not been good could not be denied access to the pine nuts, but they were assigned places to pick. Even where true ownership of plots does not exist it is customary throughout the Shoshonean area for families to agree before harvesting begins to confine their picking to certain delimited tracts. Sometimes even Shoshoni from the east came to this region for pine nuts. On the other hand, when the Silver Peak crop was poor, MH's people went into the White Mountains or even to the Palmetto Mountains, some 25 miles distant, which were customarily frequented by Oasis and Pigeon Springs people. Trips were usually made by all the members of a village. Harvested nuts, however, were family property. Most families carried as many nuts as possible down to the winter village and cached the remainder in brush-lined pits in the mountains. These were brought down when needed, usually in the spring. Families occasionally remained in the mountains near their pine nuts. MH's family did so only once when a heavy snow fell while they were gathering. They built a winter house. Sometimes in the spring when cached seeds ran short people suffered hunger, but MH denied that they ever starved.

Before returning to the winter village after the pine-nut harvest people usually assembled for the fall festival. If the pine-nut harvest were good it was held at Tünǎva or Ozaŋ'win:'. If poor, it was perhaps held at Sohodühatü (Oasis Ranch) in connection with the rabbit drive.

After she had married Captain Harry and moved to Oasis MH usually crossed the low pass into the northern end of Deep Springs Valley, 10 miles away, each year to gather chia, *Stipa*, and pasida seeds from the sunny slopes of the hills and *Mentzelia* and sand bunch grass seeds and hupuhya ("buckberry" *Lycium ?*) from the valley. They also ranged through Fish Lake Valley gathering seeds. Sometimes they gathered paŋwibuhya berries on the eastern side of the White Mountains. For pine nuts they generally went to the Sylvania Mountains near Oza 'win:¹, where Harry's family gathered, or else to the Silver Peak Range where MH gathered nuts on the tract that had been frequented by her maternal grandmother before her death. This place was generally used by MH's brother, but he shared it with her. Sometimes they gathered nuts on the rugged slopes of the White Mountains. Other Oasis families usually went to the Palmetto Mountains and made their base camp at Indian Garden Spring, A:bünüwi.

Animal foods were of secondary importance. Deer were usually procured in the White Mountains, antelope in the plains at the western base of the Silver Peak Range, mountain sheep in the mountains east and south of Deep Springs Valley, and rabbits within a few miles of the various streams in Fish Lake Valley. There was no ownership of hunting areas.

Deer hunting was both individual and communal. Game procured by individual hunters was divided among the members of the village, the hunter keeping only the hind quarter for himself and family. When hunts were communal, some men beat the brush, while others, usually older men, hid by game trails. The kill was shared equally by all hunters. As a matter of convenience, men usually hunted deer in the White Mountains near the headwaters of the streams on which their villages lay.

Antelope and mountain sheep were also sometimes hunted by groups of men. All communal hunts were informal, with no special director.

In the fall people from throughout the valley assembled for rabbit drives. Shoshoni from the east and Paiute from Sodaville, Montgomery Pass, and other places to the north (known collectively as Kwinawatü, north place), and from Deep Springs Valley might participate. Drives were directed by the lesser valley chief, living at Ozaŋ'win:¹ or by some experienced hunter. Net owners remained by their nets; others beat the brush. Drives usually started from Oasis, especially when the fall festival was to be held there, and might last for several days, the hunters moving through the valley in the vicinity of various villages.

Chieftainship.—Need for centralized authority in this valley was slight compared with that in Owens Valley. The rabbit drive and fall festival, nüga süwüduwa'dü (dance gathering), which were usually held at the same time, were the main activities requiring supervision. Palmetto Dick had been director of these. He was

succeeded by Big Mouth Tom, JA's father, who lived at Oasis and
Geroux's ranch in Fish Lake Valley as well as in Deep Springs
Valley. Big Mouth's qualifications were ability to manage these
activities, popularity, and oratorical ability. He would have been
succeeded by his son or other male relative if any of them had been
suitable. Instead he was succeeded by Captain Harry, who was part
Shoshoni and bore no relationship to him. Captain Harry died
in 1919.

There was no formal office of chief's messenger, but when the chief
had planned a dance he sent a man to the different villages to announce it. The same person served each year if he were available.

Marriage.—Marriage was regulated only by blood relationship,
first cousins, at least, being prohibited from marriage. There were
no social or local exogamous groups.

The census as MH remembered it in her girlhood, about 1870, has
32 marriages. Although the birthplace of all older persons was not
known, 19 of these seem to have followed valley endogamy, 13 valley
exogamy. Of the first, 15 were exogamous by village, 4 endogamous.
This degree of village exogamy is not remarkable as villages aver-
aged but 2 families, or 13.5 persons, each. Marriages outside the
valley were with Northern Paiute of Owens Valley, Round Valley,
and Benton, and with neighboring Shoshoni to the east. Five of
these marriages were with Shoshoni, of which four were contracted
by inhabitants of Pigeon Spring and one by an Ozan'win :[1] person.
Both villages are but a few miles from the Shoshoni villages of Lida
Valley. In three cases the women were Shoshoni, in two cases men.
Thus 5 persons in a total of 36 at these two villages were full-blood
Shoshoni. No doubt an equal number of Paiute had gone to live
with Shoshoni, though persons who had married and moved away
would be less readily remembered by MH.

These figures suggest that proximity was an important factor in
choice of mates. With a taboo on marriage between blood relatives,
however, some small villages were necessarily exogamous. Frequent
change of residence, even to other valleys, and wide acquaintance
engendered through visiting at festivals and communal hunts brought
marriages with interrelated neighboring valleys to a high degree.

MH asserted that residence after marriage was matrilocal until
the birth of a child, when the couple set up an independent household.
The census provides no reliable data on this, but it is not difficult
to see that the type of house built in Fish Lake Valley would not
readily accommodate more than the average household of 6.3 persons
per family. In spite of the theory of residence with respect to
village, actually 10 of the instances of village exogamy were patrilocal, 5 matrilocal. To these should be added the 13 cases of valley

exogamy, of which 6 were patrilocal, 7 matrilocal. A total of 16 patrilocal, 12 matrilocal. In addition, four marriages were between members of the same village. In one or two cases the married couple moved to a new locality.

Whether or not matrilocal residence was theoretically preferred, it is certain that practical considerations predominated and that such considerations favored residence at the home of either spouse about equally. Thus, couples might move to a more sparsely settled area. In the camp at Sühüyoi a brother and sister married a sister and brother and lived together as a single household. In one camp at Tu:na'va there were three male cousins with their wives, while at Watohad:ᵃ were four brothers, two of whom had brought wives. The presence of the chief at Tü'năva may have influenced his sister and two brothers to remain there after marrying.

WINNEMUCCA

Northern Paiute occupied Nevada west of the Sonoma and Hot Springs Mountains. Scraps of information indicate that, like the Shoshoni, they lived aboriginally in independent villages, but that the wars with the white man had caused a rapid consolidation into temporary bands.

CTh's family, living at Mill City, south of Winnemucca, seems to have foraged the local region, but claimed no ownership of food territory. They had local festivals under Boinəbi, dancing at Mill City or nearby at pine-nut camps. Lovelock, to the south, also had festivals. Communal shamanistic deer and antelope hunts were held under CTh's grandfather, who charmed both species.

CTh denied pseudo parallel-cousin marriage, polyandry, and marriage by abduction. His reliability, however, is not unquestioned.

WESTERN INDEPENDENT SHOSHONI VILLAGES

LIDA AND VICINITY

Separate treatment of the Lida region is somewhat arbitrary. Its population, though predominantly Shoshoni, was linked with Fish Lake Valley Paiute and the Gold Mountain, Stonewall Valley, and Clayton Valley Shoshoni through extensive intermarriage and co-operation in various activities. In short, it was not a distinct socio-political group and did not occupy a natural geographical area. It was but a link in the network of interrelated villages that extend throughout the entire Nevada Shoshoni area.

The present town of Lida lies at the eastern end of the Silver Peak Range at 6,037 feet at the base of Palmetto and Magruder Mountains, the latter called Ko:wa (cut with a knive), and is less than 10 miles from the Northern Paiute village at Pigeon Springs. In the vicinity of Lida the country is fertile and the mountains are clad with pinyon and juniper trees, but broad, arid valleys broken by a few low ranges which seldom reached the pinyon belt stretch away to the north, east, and west. These deserts have little water and in native times supported but a few small encampments at favored spots. The population was so sparse that there are few informants today who know anything about it.

Villages.—Data on these are incomplete. The numbers correspond with those in figure 7:

29. Lida, Pauwahã'ᵃ, five families, predominantly Shoshoni, but some speaking Northern Paiute.

30. Tule Canyon, Saiyogadü (tule place), 6,500 feet. At least one family formerly: Old Paty and his sister. Palmetto Fred was born here, but the relation of his family to the last is unknown.

31. Stonewall Mountain, camp called Tumbasai'uwi (tumbi, rock+pa, water+sai'uwi, fall down) probably at Stonewall Spring, 5,900 feet, on the northern side of Stonewall Mountain. Palmetto Fred's family, totaling seven persons, had lived here. These people gathered seeds mostly in the vicinity of Corral Spring.

Clayton Valley, 4,300 feet, perhaps had a few residents, though it was visited only temporarily for seeds and *Lycium* berries by people in neighboring regions. Cow Camp: called Tsaiyiyugwi (tsaiyi or tsaip: ?, tule+yugwi, sitting).

22. Old Camp, a former village on the north side (?) of Gold Mountain (Tumbákai), at 7,500 feet (?). One family: Tciwanuitcugaᵖᵘᵗˢⁱ (tciwanui, a stick vertical in the ground+old man), his wife, two sons, two daughters; total, six. The sons went to Beatty and there married sisters (see "Beatty Shoshoni," below). The daughters married two brothers from the Belted Range and remained here part of the time. One brother was Gold Mountain Jack, Tundukwiᵛᵃ (brownish black); the other, Deaf Charlie, Niavi. These four marriages were all matrilocal. Niavi's daughter, Paiwuŋguʷᵃ (sandy wash), married BD and moved to Death Valley.

33. Montezuma. One family, that of LJB's maternal grandfather, lived at two springs near here, Kweva (kwe or kwina, north+pa, water) and Yudugiva (yudugi, sleet). The family consisted of his grandfather, grandmother, their two sons and four daughters; total, eight. One son went to Big Pine and married a Northern Paiute. One daughter went to the Kawich Mountains and married LJB's father's cousin. Another married LJB's father.

34. There were probably also a few people at three springs several miles east of Goldfield at about 5,800 feet, called Kamuva (Kamu, jack rabbit), Hugapa (hugapi, cane) or Wildhorse, and Wi꞉pa (wi꞉, knife) (LJB). It is possibly these springs that were called Matsum, where Matsum Sam lived (JS).

Subsistence activities.—These were carried on by Lida people within a short distance of their village. Pine nuts were gathered in company with Fish Lake Valley Paiute in the vicinity of Pigeon Spring or wherever there was abundance in the local mountains.

Several families usually camped together but gathered independently. If the local crop failed people went westward in the Silver Peak Range or some 40 miles south to the Grapevine, or even farther to the Kawich Mountains. These long journeys were facilitated by the introduction of horses. There was no ownership of pine-nut groves.

Within a few miles of Lida, on Magruder Mountain, brush was burned in the fall so that plants would grow better. These plants were principally üyüp: (*Chenopodium*?), waiyabi (probably *Elymus*, wheat grass), waciüp: (unidentified), and a root, tüi (unidentified). A few miles farther south, in Tule Canyon, they got *Mentzelia* and pasida (*Salvia*) seeds. Sand-bunch-grass seeds occurred in Stonewall Valley about 25 miles to the east. *Lycium* berries grew in great quantities in Clayton Valley and near Gold Point. Near Lida could be had seeds of hu:gi (probably wheat grass), *Sophia*, *Salvia*, and *Artemisia tridentata*. Greens called wiwünu, and roots, sego (*Brodiaea* ?), also grew locally.

Except for pine nuts, Lida people did not go into the vicinity of Pigeon Springs or vice versa, because each had ample seeds locally.

Deer, sheep, antelope, and small game could be hunted within no great distance of Lida. There were few antelope, however, and no antelope shamans. Of communal hunts, little information was obtainable. JS knew of communal rabbit hunts only in comparatively recent times, held near Oasis in Fish Lake Valley.

Festivals.—Lida and neighboring camps seemed to have joined Fish Lake Valley people at Tünăva (Pigeon Springs) where Palmetto Dick and later Big Mouth Tom were directors. Gold Mountain, Stonewall Mountain, Palmetto, and Pigeon Springs people also participated in these. Sometimes, however, festivals were held at Oasis instead. That these were strictly native festival groupings, however, is not certain.

Political organization.—The villages in this area are unusually small and widely spaced. For all practical purposes, each family was the political unit, villages as such carrying on no important activities. If a family joined a festival it usually went to Pigeon Springs and submitted to the direction of Palmetto Dick and, later, Big Mouth and Captain Harry.

Kinship and marriage.—Information on these was scant. Marriage was, like that among Paiute, probably only with unrelated persons. The partial census shows the usual preference for multiple marriages between two families.

EASTERN CALIFORNIA

The Shoshoni of eastern California were slightly marginal with respect to those of Nevada, showing slight influence of adjoining tribes. These Shoshoni occupied the northern halves of Death Valley and Panamint Valley, all of Saline Valley, the southern end of Eureka Valley, the southern shore of Owens Lake, the Koso Mountain region, the northern edge of the Mojave Desert, and the eastern slope of the Sierra Nevada Mountains. Owens Valley Paiute called them Sivinaŋwatü (sivi, east+ ?+ watü, place), AG, or Tavaduhütcᵘ, GR. Fish Lake Valley Northern Paiute similarly called Shoshoni Sivina'watü (eastern place), Tavai'nüwᵘ (sun people), or Tavai'-duhatü (sun place). Southern Paiute called them Koets.

Southern Paiute lived east of Death Valley, being mixed with Shoshoni at Ash Meadows. These Paiute called themselves Nu. Those at Ash Meadows were called Sivindü by Shoshoni (GG, TSp). Shoshoni at Ash Meadows were called Koyohutsᵘ (GG) or Kwoiaxo'tza (GH) by Shoshoni. Railroad Valley Shoshoni called Southern Paiute Tavinai (tavi, sun, i. e., east+nai, dwellers).

The inhabitants of the southern end of Panamint Valley, the Argus Mountains, probably the region around Trona, and the territory to the south and west to an undetermined extent were called Mugunüwü (GG, TSp, TS, SS, TSt). They were mixed with Shoshoni in at least the central part of Panamint Valley and, perhaps, in the vicinity of Trona. The latter region was called Üwā'gatü and its inhabitants Owa'dzi. The Mugunüwü were unquestionably Kawaiisü, as the vocabulary,[7] (pp. 274–275) corresponds with Kroeber's Kawaiisü vocabulary from the region of Tejon and Tehachapi, though it shows slight affiliation also with his Chemehuevi (1907, pp. 68, 71–89). Kroeber's Shikaviyam, Sikauyam or Kosho vocabulary from Koso Mountains, southeast of Owens Lake, is clearly Shoshoni and is very similar to the present vocabularies from Little Lake, Panamint Valley, and Lida Shoshoni (pp. 280–281).

The probable derivation of Mugunüwü is mugu, point+müwü, people. This seems to have been taken either from Telescope Peak in the Panamint Mountains, which was called Mugudoya (mugu+doyavi, mountain) or Kaiguta, or from the Argus Mountains, called Mugu or Tinda'vu. AH and MHo, Southern Paiute at Ash Meadows, however, called these people Panümünt and BD, Death Valley Shoshoni, called them Panamint, but were not able to translate these words.

Probably Tübatulabal adjoined the Shoshoni on the south, occupying part of the Mojave Desert west of the Kawaiisü and extending across the Sierra Nevada Mountains. The division of this region between Tübatulabal and Kawaiisü, however, is not certain. Little Lake Shoshoni called the Tübatulabal Nawavitc or Wavitc, trans-

---

[7] Given by TSp, who is one-half white, one-quarter Shoshoni, one-quarter Mugunüwü and resides in Grapevine Canyon in the Sierra Nevada Mountains. There is said to be only one other surviving Mugunüwü, Long Jim, living in Pahrump Valley, Nevada.

lated "tough" or "mean." Owens Valley Paiute called the people on the western slope of the southern Sierra Nevada Mountains, who were probably Tübatulabal, Wawa'" or Túbadüka (pine-nut eaters).

The geographical variation of the Shoshoni habitat in eastern California probably exceeds that of any other area of equal size in North America. Its life zones range from lower Sonoran in the valley bottoms, including Death Valley, part of which lies below sea level (pl. 1, c), to the Boreal zone in the Panamint and Sierra Nevada Mountains. So large a proportion of it consists of arid and infertile valleys, however, that the simple Shoshoni hunting and gathering economy supported only a very sparse population.

The main foods were vegetable. GR rated pine nuts as most important because in years of good harvest enough were gathered to last through most of the winter, whereas other seeds were ordinarily consumed within a few weeks or, at most, 2 months. Next to pine nuts, he rated *Mentzelia, tonopuda* (unidentified species), and *Salvia* in the order named. These occurred in the mountains. Also of importance were *Oryzopsis* (sand bunch grass) seeds, occurring in mountains and somewhat in valleys, acorns near the foot of the Sierra Nevada Mountains west of Olancha, *Lycium* berries in the valley flats, especially near the Koso Mountains, and several unidentified species, mostly in the mountains. Mesquite (*Prosopis glandulosa* Torr.) grew in limited areas in low portions of Saline, Panamint, and Death Valley, where it was of some importance. In addition, foods listed by Coville for Death and Panamint Valleys include: Seeds of devil's pin cushion (*Echinocactus*), reed (*Phragmites*), buds of Joshua trees growing especially in the Mojave Desert, seeds of evening primrose, and greens of large crucifers. Soon after the arrival of the white man a small amount of horticulture was introduced to Death Valley and Panamint Valley.

Subsistence activities.—Economic life rested upon a particularism of the family, though several families might travel together, especially when gathering pine nuts. Communal rabbit hunts and occasionally antelope hunts were the only activities involving extensive joint effort; these usually involved several cooperating villages.

For the greater part of the year each family pursued subsistence activities independently. It usually wintered in the same village, though various circumstances might take it elsewhere. In the course of a normal year it ranged over a certain minimum food area, the limits of which depended upon occurrence of essential foods, their abundance that year, and the distance that it was possible to travel on foot with one's entire family. Inhabitants of neighboring villages naturally tended to forage the same general terrain, though each exploited most extensively the country nearest it. The limited supplies of food and poor transportation facilities prevented all inhabitants of a given area from living together in a single large village. Often villagers from different valleys foraged near one another in the same mountain seed area, though each family gathered seeds independently. For rabbit drives, however, some of these families went elsewhere and might cooperate with people from the opposite side of their own valley. For pine nuts they might go many miles away if the crop were promising.

Apparently family ownership of pine-nut plots existed only among Saline Valley Shoshoni, adjoining Owens Valley Paiute, from whom it may have been borrowed.

After harvesting pine nuts, some nuts were carried down to the winter villages, which were located on streams in the low, warm valleys; the remaining nuts were cached in the mountains.[8] Robbery of cached nuts, even by brothers or sisters of the owners, led to fights with sticks and stones but no killing. Permission to open caches, however, was sometimes extended to relatives.

When stored seeds were exhausted in March or April, and hunger became acute, families left the winter villages. They procured greens, which were the first food plants to be available, and hunted antelope and rabbits. In May some people went to Owens Lake for larvae. During the summer different seeds ripened in various places, mostly in the mountains. This required considerable travel from place to place, as observation or information from other families informed them of the whereabouts of good crops. Journeys into the mountains were a welcome escape from the excessive heat of the lower valleys. Finally, in the fall, families which happened to be in certain areas assembled for communal rabbit drives, went for pine nuts, held a festival-mourning ceremony, then returned to the winter village.

Property.—The linguistic boundary between the Owens Valley Paiute and Shoshoni tended to divide areas of property concepts. The Paiute family and band ownership of food areas were largely unknown to Shoshoni.

GG, BD, GH, and TSt all denied any form of family, village, or band ownership of seed lands. Although people from certain localities habitually exploited the same areas, anyone was privileged to utilize territory ordinarily visited by other people. There is some evidence that Saline Valley families, like those in Owens Valley, owned pine-nut lands and resented trespass. Other Shoshoni emphatically denied such property rights.

---

[8] See descriptions of pine-nut gathering in this region by Dutcher, 1893, and Coville, 1892.

JN said his grandfather had described fights in Death Valley because of trespass on mesquite lands, the fights involving merely shouting and stone throwing. This probably applied only to Furnace Creek, for the Southern Paiute of Ash Meadows and Pahrump Valley had definite concepts of family ownership of certain seed lands and may have introduced them to Death Valley.

Hunting areas also were claimed by no one, even though men habitually visited mountains near their villages.

An explanation of the Shoshoni lack of ownership of food areas will be offered in a concluding section on property.

All other natural resources, including water, were also entirely free to anyone. No doubt the extensive seasonal travels of families and the constant shifting of residence, even from one valley to another, prevented habitual utilization and hence ownership of village sites.

Gathered seeds were private property. Women shared them only with their husbands, children, and sometimes parents whom they supported. Brothers, sisters, and, upon occasion, other relatives were presented gifts of food.

Large game, on the other hand, was shared communally with all village members, whether they were related or not. The hunter was privileged to keep only the skin and some special portion of the animal.

Houses were built by men, but in case of divorce usually kept by the one who remained. At death, houses were burned or abandoned. Other goods belonged to their makers or users.

There was no question of inheritance, for the meager number of material objects were burned at the owner's death, so that potential heirs received nothing whatever.

Festivals.—The fall festival, which included the circle dance, gambling, and annual mourning observances, was the only noneconomic motive for large numbers of persons to assemble. There were no other group ceremonies. Small groups of people who happened to be in the same vicinity might hold a minor circle dance during the summer, dancing one to several nights. The fall festivals, however, were annual events, enlisting people from a considerable territory. The temporarily increased food supply following the communal rabbit hunt and pine-nut harvest supported these large aggregates for a brief time.

The location of fall festivals depended partly upon the whereabouts of large villages, which acted as hosts, partly upon the annual occurrence of good seed crops, especially pine nuts. There seems to have been considerable reciprocity between certain villages which acted as hosts in alternate years. It had somewhat crystallized in the institution of the exhibition dance, performed by visitors who were paid by their hosts.

The main gatherings recorded were at Koso Hot Springs, Olancha which drew many Northern Paiute as well as Shoshoni, Saline Valley or Sigai (below), and northern Death Valley. People participated in these with great enthusiasm as they afforded an opportunity to visit and revel with families seen only rarely or not at all in the course of the year. As new factors introduced by the white man made it possible to travel farther there were fewer but larger festivals. They were abandoned a few years ago.

Direction of festivals was the most important task of the "chiefs."

Political organization and chiefs.—Family particularism prevailed throughout so great a part of the year and an individual's behavior was governed to so large an extent by kinship that political controls were not extensive.

Beyond the family, allegiance was primarily to the other inhabitants of the winter village. One most frequently cooperated with them in games, dances, and hunting. He was designated by the name of his village. But he did not share with them exclusive rights to any food areas. And his residence was always liable to change for various reasons. Information was not obtainable on village headmen, but there is little doubt that, like the headmen in Nevada Shoshoni villages, their functions did not extend beyond keeping informed on the few matters of village interest, such as the ripening of pine nuts.

Intervillage alliances were too temporary and shifting to permit them to form politically stable aggregates or bands. In spite of the fact that the valleys were definitely delimited by high mountain ranges so as to give an apparent topographic predisposition to band formation, villages did not always associate with their neighbors in cooperative enterprises. Local crop failures or abundance of pine nuts elsewhere took families away from their customary haunts, so that they drove rabbits or participated in festivals with very different people from year to year.

The occasions for cooperation, moreover, were limited to rabbit drives, some antelope hunts, and fall festivals, which gave but brief unity to participants. And even festivals were impossible when a poor year afforded insufficient food to maintain them.

In spite of disruptive factors, however, certain villages naturally associated more often with one another than with others. The areas embracing such villages are called districts. The unity within some of these approached true band organization and the people were even known by a collective name, for example, Sigai or Ko'önzi (see below).[9]

Chiefs controlled intervillage activities, but it is clear that the scope of their powers varied and even overlapped in some ways. A chief was called pakwi'navi (GG), pokwi'navi (BD), usually translated as "big talker," though BD also gave naŋgawin (talker). There seems to have been at least two in each district, either working jointly or perhaps specializing, one in hunting, the other in festivals.

Saline Valley had two, Caesar and Tom Hunter, both of whom died many years ago. Tom Hunter probably succeeded his father. Together, they directed rabbit drives and fall festivals. When these were held in Saline Valley people from Sigai and from near Eureka Valley participated. When held in Sigai, Death Valley as well as Saline Valley people often attended.

Little information was obtainable about chiefs in the Koso Mountain region, though there seems to have been one for communal rabbit and antelope hunts and another for festivals.

In upper Death Valley, BD's grandfather and later BD's father, Dock, living at Grapevine Canyon, directed rabbit drives. He was assisted by Pete Sam's father, who lived at Surveyor's Well. The latter directed festivals, assisted by Dock. When Beatty or Sigai people joined Death Valley people in these activities they were under Dock and Pete Sam's father.

Upper Panamint Valley seems to have held its own cooperative hunts and dances or to have joined Saline Valley or Death Valley people when convenient. No data are available on lower Panamint Valley, occupied by Kawaiisü.

Similarly, Death Valley south of Furnace Creek was occupied by mixed groups, especially Kawaiisü, and its political affiliations are undetermined. Furnace Creek was, from all accounts, independent of the villages in the upper part of the valley, though it no doubt associated with them at times.

Though the chief's power was limited, chieftainship was regarded as a real office to be inherited patrilineally. Lacking an acceptable son, the chief was succeeded by a brother or other male relative.

SALINE VALLEY.—This district had an extraordinary range of life zones.

The deep valley floor, 1,100 feet, is in the Lower Sonoran zone. It is mild in winter and almost unbearably hot in summer. It supports a little mesquite but has few edible seed annuals, the majority of its

---

[9] For the people of Koso Mountains, Panamint Valley, and Death Valley, Kroeber, 1925: 589, gives Koso, Kosho, Panamint, Shikaviyam, Sikaium, Shikaich, Kaich, Kwüts, Sosoni, and Shoshone. None of these except Shoshoni was known to informants in the area. They called themselves nuwu, people. Shoshoni they could not explain. Koso is Northern Paiute for fire.

sparse flora being extremely xerophytic and unfit for human consumption. The bordering mountains, especially to the north and south, are in the Upper Sonoran and Transitional zones, where cooler temperatures make summer living possible and where greater precipitation supports many flowering annuals, which supply the greater part of plant foods. Pine nuts are also abundant in these mountains.

The high and massive Inyo Range which bounds Saline Valley on the west is too precipitous to be readily inhabitable but affords the greatest range of life zones. Better watered than ranges to the east, it supports many square miles of pine-nut trees. Its crest, however, extends above 10,000 feet into the Canadian and even Hudsonian zones, thus capturing greater precipitation, supporting a variety of flora, and feeding the one stream that reaches the valley floor. The vast area of the range and the greater vegetation maintained in turn many deer, which are largely lacking in the ranges to the east, and large numbers of mountain sheep.

This remarkable variety of habitat zones and of species of both plants and animals within a comparatively small area enabled the Saline Valley people to maintain existence securely if not abundantly without having to exploit an inconveniently large area.

This district embraced about 1,080 square miles and, according to the census, had about 65 persons, or 1 per 16.6 square miles. The aboriginal population may have been denser.

There were four main winter villages in three subdivisions of the district. The subdivisions were: A, Saline Valley; B, the mountains between Saline Valley and Eureka Valley; and, C, the mountains between Saline, Panamint, and Death Valleys. The inhabitants of each tended to forage within their own subdivision, though they sometimes ranged more widely. People from the entire district, however, assembled for rabbit drives and for fall festivals, and associated with one another at least more often than with people from elsewhere. Two men, Caesar and Tom Hunter, who acted jointly, were chiefs for these communal undertakings. There was, however, no common name for the entire district.

The villages as numbered on map, figure 7, were:

A. 35, the main village and division of the district was Saline Valley, Ko'° (deep place, descriptive of Saline Valley, which is very deep), elevation 1,200 feet. The people were called Ko'önzi. The village lay in the midst of a barren, infertile expanse of valley at the mouth of Hunter's Canyon, where the stream maintains some mesquite and a few other edible plants.

Its inhabitants exploited the surrounding mountains, especially the Inyo Range to the west, where deer and pine nuts could be had. SS claimed that pine-nut tracts lay on the Saline Valley side of the Inyo Mountains and in the vicinity of Waucoba Mountain and that, like those of the Owens Valley Paiute, they were family owned. Trespass led to argument but not to serious fights. Caesar was said to extend permission to outsiders to gather on them without consulting their owners. The last point is doubtful. GG thought that there was no ownership of pine-nut areas. It seems clear that, however former ownership was conceived, families went to the same fairly well-defined tracts each year and that, as SS asserted, the entire family "inherited" them. In years of good crops, however, any tract afforded far more nuts than the owners could possibly gather in the brief period between the time when the nuts ripened and when they fell from the trees and winter cold and snow drove people down to the winter village. It is entirely understandable that, in such years, outsiders should be allowed freely to utilize the tracts. For this reason the Saline Valley people frequently gathered in the Pauwüji or Eureka Valley area to the north and in Sigai to the south. Nelson observed people from Hunter's Canyon in 1891 gathering at the latter place. Occasionally they gathered in the Koso Mountain district. SS thought permission of the Koso chief was necessary; GG said people went there as they pleased, without asking anyone.

The Ko'o villagers obtained mesquite from the vicinity of their winter village. Other wild seeds, such as sand grass, grew in certain parts of the valley, but most seeds occurred in the surrounding mountains. Often they went into the Sigai country and other parts of the mountains separating Saline and Death Valleys.

Game, distinctly of secondary importance in Shoshoni economy but requiring considerable time of hunters, occurred largely to the north and west. Deer were procured in the Inyo Mountains and antelope in the lower ranges north of Saline Valley. There is no evidence of ownership of hunting territory, although certain accessible regions were naturally utilized most often.

Other foods were procured in various places but did not as a rule require extensive travel. Rats, mice, chuckwallas, rabbits, and birds could be hunted in all parts of the territory. Occasionally, however, trips were made, probably by single families, to Owens Lake for larvae or for duck hunting.

Saline Valley yields great quantities of salt which was traded for goods or shell money to Owens Valley Paiute, who in turn often traded it across the Sierra Nevada Mountains.

Rabbit drives were held in connection with fall festivals. Usually people from throughout the district assembled for them. Sometimes, however, individuals took part in drives in the Koso Mountain or Death Valley districts.

BD said the Ko'o village as he remembered it about 50 or 60 years ago comprised five families or camps whose heads were as follows: (1) Caesar, the chief, (2) Caesar's father, who had been chief before him, (3) Wakin, (4) Tom Hunter, the other chief, (5) Patu'ku. If, as in Fish Lake Valley, the average family consisted of 6 persons, the total population was not over 30 individuals. BB thought this village had had a communal sweat house, like those in Owens Valley.

Some place names in Saline Valley territory are:

Upper Warm Spring, Pabu'inü (water reservoir ?).
Lower Warm Spring, Puigĕt:ü (green rock).
Dodd's Spring, Bast:ª (?).
Willow Spring, Honovĕgwa'si (a yellowish gravel), little frequented except as temporary camp on route to Waucoba Mountain for pine nuts.
Paiute Canyon Spring (?), Yadadüp (kind of rock), a camping place on pine-nut trips.
Cerro Gordo Springs, Wiva'ª (?), a pine-nut camp.
Burro Spring, Yĕtum'ba (?), a pine-nut camp.
Unnamed spring east of Burro Spring, Pakwü'tsi (?), a pine-nut camp.
Quartz Spring, Pambu'iva (?), little frequented.
Jackass Spring, Ica,ªwumba (icaʼª coyote+pa, water), a pine-nut and seed camp.
Inyo Mountains, Nününop:ü (high), mythologically the only land remaining above the waters of the flood.
Ubehebe Peak, Tinguhu (tinguta, play+?) or toyavipiap:u (mountain—big) has little of value.
Dry Mountain, Sü:ndugai (?).
Tin Mountain, Sia (gravel).
Vicinity of Keeler on Owens Lake, Tono'musa (tonovi, greasewood+musa, sweat house ?) or Tonomádü, a spring, visited during trips for larvae and ducks in the lake.
Waucoba Mountain (waucova, pine tree, Paiute word), Wuŋgo (juniper) doyavi (mountain).

B. The second subdivision, Pauwü'ji (BD) or Pauwü'jiji (GG), lay between Saline and Eureka Valleys, where low mountains were suitable for winter dwellings. The principal and perhaps sole village was probably at Waucoba Spring, Icam'ba ("coyote water") (36), on the eastern slope of Waucoba Mountain at about 5,600 feet. There may have been another camp at Lead Canyon Spring, Pau'-onzi, from which the area was named. GG called the people Pau'on-jüjü. These people procured most foods locally. They gathered pine nuts and hunted deer in the Inyo Mountains immediately to the west. They procured seeds, antelope, and rabbits in the low hills around them and got some seeds also in Eureka Valley to the north and in Saline Valley.

As Eureka Valley is practically waterless, it could support no permanent residents, but it had important quantities of sand-grass seed and págampi (unidentified). Water was obtained from a well near the sand dunes in the southern end of the valley. It is doubtful, however, whether temporary visits by small parties could account for the vast archeological site which stretches for several miles along the northern foot of the dunes on the edge of the playa. The site has untold quantities of flint and obsidian chips but relatively few artifacts, except some spherical stone mortars of the type commonly used by Shoshoni for grinding mesquite. But there is now no mesquite in the valley. An extended search produced no pottery, which is usually present at Shoshoni and Paiute sites in this region. The mortars, however, are more distinctive of Shoshoni than of Paiute.

C. Sigai (flat, on the mountain top) or Sigai watü, the mountains separating Saline, Death, and Panamint Valleys. People called Sigaitsi. Two villages. One at Goldbelt Spring, Tuhu (black ?) (37), at about 5,000 feet, the people called Tuhutsi; the other at the springs in Cottonwood Canyon, which runs westward from Death Valley, called Navadü (big canyon) (38), at about 3,700 feet, the people called Navadünzi.

Sigai people procured pine nuts, various seeds, rabbits, and mountain sheep in their own territory. When local seeds were unusually abundant visitors came from Saline Valley and sometimes from Surveyor's Well to gather them near Navadü. SS thought rabbit drives were held independent of Saline Valley; BD, that Saline Valley people always came to Sigai for rabbit drives.

For festivals Sigai people either went to Saline Valley or Saline Valley people came to Sigai, but both places never held them simultaneously. Caesar and Tom Hunter (and GG said George Button's wife's father's father whose identity is otherwise undetermined) directed festivals at both places. Chiefs' powers were definitely extended and groups more closely associated in post-Caucasian days.

The village census given by BD for perhaps 1890 showed:

Navadü, 2 families totaling 14 persons, as follows: One camp, Pete Sam's father (who later went to Surveyor's Well, Ohyu, in Death Valley and became director of the fall festival and mourning ceremony); his wife from Ohyu; their sons, Pete and Johnny, each of whom married a Saline Valley woman in the levirate (the only levirate recorded in this district) and lived at her home; a daughter, May, who later married. The other camp: Jackass Sam (Pete Sam's mother's brother from Ohyu); his wife, two sons, two daughters, his wife's two sisters; the husband of one of the sisters from Saline Valley. This makes the unusual total of nine persons in one house.

Tuhu, one family as follows: Tuhudzugo (tuhu+tsugoputsi, old man; Caesar's paternal grandfather); his wife, probably from Sigai, four daughters and one son.

These data accord more or less with Nelson's observations in 1891 when he found two or three families on Cottonwood Creek.

These few Sigai marriages were probably all exogamous by village and show a preference for matrilocal residence.

LITTLE LAKE AND KOSO MOUNTAINS.—This district, known as Kuhwiji, is a relatively large subsistence area, embracing about 1,000 square miles and centering in the Koso Mountains, where the greater precipitation in the Upper Sonoran and Transitional zones supported most of the important food plants, but including also the surrounding plains and the eastern escarpment of the Sierra Nevada. The inhabitants, who lived in three winter villages, exploited the entire territory, but lacked sufficient intervillage cohesion to constitute a true band.

Villages.—The four main villages as numbered in figure 7 were:

39. Pagunda (lake), Little Lake, at 2,948 feet; one of the largest, GG thought with 50 to 60 persons in 1870. People called Pagundünzi.

40. Müa'ta (boiling), Coso Hot Springs, at 3,635 feet; formerly 100 or more people. Visited by Northern Paiute and Shoshone for medicinal water, which was used for bathing and drinking.

41. Üyuwum'ba (a black rock ?), springs about 5 miles south of Darwin, probably Cold Spring at about 6,200 feet.

16. Pakwa'si (probably pa, water +kwasi, end) at Alancha, at 3,700 feet; people called Pakwasitc'. Paiute and Shoshoni intermarried here.

Some place names:

Sierra Nevada Mountains, Manovü putoyavi[tu] (long mountain).
Owens Lake, Patsiata (any large lake); called by Paiute, Panowi.
Upper Centennial Spring, Tcia'navadü (rose bush place).
Lower Centennial Spring, Tcia'bugwai (tciabip:, many rose bushes).
Black Spring, Tuwa'dambahwatü (tuwada, a bush+pa, water+watü, place).
Crystal Spring, Tcivügund:[ü] (?).
Springs near Millspaugh, Pa'[a] (water).
Cold Springs, south of Darwin, Ogwedü, Ogwaidü (creek), a place visited frequently in summer, but no winter village.
Springs by Maturango Peak:
    Paga'wagandü (paid:[u], watering place for animals).
    Tuhupa (from hupai'hya, shade ?, of the mountain+pa, water).
    Pag[w]o'i (?).
    Tuŋwuvi (?).
Spring in the canyon running into Panamint Valley, east of Darwin, Ogwedü (creek).
Haiwee Springs, Hugwata (?).
Springs near last, Icamba (coyote water).
Rose Spring, Tunahada (?).

Subsistence activities.—The following sketch of seasonal activities is largely from the point of view of the inhabitants of the Koso Hot Springs village. In winter they dwelt in pit houses, eating stored seeds and hunting rabbits. In April some families moved to Haiwee Springs, Hugwata, about 12 miles away, where they spent 1 or 2 months, finishing up any stored seeds and gathering greens. In June they usually went to Cold Spring, where a few people sometimes wintered and hunted rabbits. This hunting was done by individual men using spring-pole traps. Meanwhile, a few families sometimes joined together for a communal antelope hunt.

Antelope were most numerous in Indian Wells Valley, near Brown, about 10 miles south of Little Lake. There were also some just south of Owens Lake and at the northern end of Saline Valley. Drives near Brown involved mostly Little Lake Shoshoni and some Nawavitc (probably Tübatulabal), their neighbors to the south. A few Saline Valley Shoshoni might participate, but the trip of nearly 75 miles was generally too long.

The antelope hunt director announced the hunt several days in advance. Antelope were driven by 8 or 10 men, perhaps aided by fire, into a corral built of posts spaced about 20 feet apart and covered with brush. The corral had a wide opening but no wings. As the animals milled around inside, archers stationed between the posts shot them. There was no shaman.

In midsummer some families might go into Saline Valley and occasionally into Death Valley to gather mesquite. They removed the seeds and ground the bean pulp into flour which could be readily transported. But if they had gotten any considerable surplus it was cached to be procured on subsequent trips.

Between July and September most families wandered in the Koso Mountains, which, lying in the zone of greatest plant growth, afforded many different seeds. They remained as near their winter villages as possible in order that trips during winter to seed caches should not be too long. But if certain species were sufficiently abundant elsewhere, they went several days' travel from the winter village to get them.

During September or October, if they were not already in the Koso Mountains, families ordinarily went there for pine nuts. Large crowds preferred to travel together on these trips, under the direction of the village chief. Sometimes the Koso Springs villagers joined the people from Üyuwumba, the Cold Spring village, and if the crop in that vicinity were unusually heavy they might even winter there. If the Koso Mountain yield were small, some families might go into the Panamint Mountains, where perhaps they kept company with Death Valley Shoshoni who had come for the same reason.

In the fall some families also went to Owens Lake to hunt ducks. Although a few minor rabbit drives were held during the summer, this was the season for large drives.

For large rabbit drives, families who happened to be in the vicinity of places with numerous rabbits cooperated. The main drives were at Rose Valley, Darwin Wash, the vicinity of Cold Spring, Little Lake, and Olancha. Visitors came from a convenient distance to join these. For example, people from Keeler came 25 miles and people from Saline Valley came perhaps 50 miles to Olancha, but Panamint Valley was too far away. Panamint people either had local drives or joined one closer to home.

In the drives they used one or two nets, each about 2 feet high and 100 or more feet long, propped at intervals with sticks. Eight or ten men beat the brush, driving the rabbits into the nets, while the owners remained behind their nets to dispatch the ensnared animals with clubs. There is some question about directors of these drives. BD thought district chiefs were in charge; GG that net owners were directors and divided the kill.

The annual round of food quest, which was scarcely sufficiently fixed to be a routine, varied in different ways. Mountain sheep might be hunted by individuals in the Koso Mountains or the Sierra Nevada and deer in the Sierra Nevada. Fish were taken in Rose Valley and, with poison, in Little Lake. Larvae were procured in Owens Lake. Caterpillars (piüga) could be had on the ground around Koso Springs, Little Lake, and elsewhere. Other animals eaten were bear, badger, chuckwalla, gopher, mice, rats, doves, eagles, hawks, crows, snakes, mountain lions, wildcats, but not coyotes, wolves, frogs, magpies, or grasshoppers. To vary the vegetable diet, acorns might be procured from the eastern foot of the Sierra Nevada.

Relative scarcity of animals made meat a minor food. Dried rabbits would not keep over 2 weeks. Large game meat, cut into thin slices and dried in trees, would keep longer but was usually consumed quickly. Hunting was of relatively greater importance during seed shortage, but considerable reliance was placed on rodents. Even in good years stored seeds rarely lasted more than a year. GG's grandmother recalled a period of several months when a complete lack of seeds, rabbits, or other important foods caused several deaths.

Warfare.—Although Kuhwiji adjoined several other tribal groups, GG thought they had warred with none. He recalled but one fight, when some people from far south invaded the country. The fight occurred at Coso Hot Springs. The invaders were all killed.

Mourning ceremony.—There was no large mourning ceremony to unite different villages. GG thought that each year property, saved from funerals, was burned simultaneously for several dead, but that only close neighbors participated.

Sweat houses.—The sweat house probably served as a village meeting house, but information about it is lacking.

Marriage.—An extensive genealogy, covering several generations, bears out informant testimony that any relationship was a bar to marriage. Village endogamy was permissible if persons were unrelated. Of 21 recorded marriages, including some in neighboring districts, 10 were exogamous by district, 8 endogamous by district. Of the last, at least three were exogamous by village. People shifted residence so often that villages usually consisted of unrelated families.

Parents arranged their children's marriages, the man's parents paying shell money to the girl's parents, the latter reciprocating with buckskins and food.

Post-marital residence was theoretically matrilocal until the birth of the first child. After that, is was independent, though preferably patrilocal, because a man preferred his home territory for hunting. There was no strict rule about this, however, and many factors entered into the choice. Of recorded marriages, 3 were patrilocal, 10 matrilocal, 3 in a new locality, 4 in the same locality where both had lived.

Intertribal marriages were: Two with Mugunüwü (Kawaiisü), one with Wavitc (Tübatulabal), one with Owens Valley Paiute, four with white men.

The levirate and sororate were both practiced. In fact, to avoid following them upon the death of a spouse, a payment to the parents-in-law was required. But only one case of the levirate is shown in the genealogies.

Though kinship terms accord with marriage of a brother and sister to sister and brother and of several brothers to several sisters, no instance of these was shown in the genealogies.

PANAMINT VALLEY.—Little information is available from this locality. The valley proper was so low (1,000 to 1,500 feet) and so arid that the native population was extremely sparse. There is virtually no water within the valley where winter villages could have been located. The Panamint and Argus Ranges which bound it on the east and west respectively have many springs which were frequented between spring and fall by people from neighboring valleys but had few winter residents.

North of Ballarat, Panamint Valley was predominantly Shoshoni with some admixture of Kawaiisü.[10] South of Ballarat it was largely Kawaiisü. The principal and probably only village within the northern part of the valley was at Warm Springs, 1,100 feet, called Ha:uta (village 42 in fig. 7). This entire portion of the valley was also called Ha:uta. The people were called Ha:utans[i].

Wildrose Springs, Su'ᵘnavadu (su:vi, willow+navadu, flat), at about 4,500 feet in the Panamint Mountains about 8 miles north of Ha:uta (43), also had a few winter residents, called Su'ᵘnavadunzi.

Subsistence activities.—Subsistence activities could be carried on by these people largely within a short distance of their villages. Though the valley was devoid of important foods of any kind, except some mesquite which grew at Ha:uta and at Indian Ranch (the latter had no running water until a well was recently dug), the Panamint Range surpasses 11,000 feet and provided many seeds, pine nuts, and mountain sheep. People went sometimes, however, near Maturango Peak in the Argus Mountains for chia or to the Koso Moun-

[10] Nelson in 1891 observed about 100 Indians in upper Panamint Valley whose language was the same as that in Saline Valley, which is Shoshoni.

tains for sand bunch grass seed. Dutcher saw families from Panamint Valley in 1893 gathering pine nuts in the mountains between Saline and Panamint Valleys, that is, in Sigai.

Political organization.—It is improbable that any important communal activities were held within Panamint Valley. Saline and Death Valleys were within convenient distance for festivals. Panamint Tom, however, seems, at least in post-Caucasian times, to have gained some prominence in connection with hostilities against the white man. Whether he was a Kawaiisü is uncertain. TSt thought that he had been chief of the Death Valley Kawaiisü.

Marriage.—Parents of young men and women seem to have taken less hand here than among groups to the west in arranging marriages. A man desiring to marry a girl gave her perhaps 20 to 30 dollars, which she gave to her mother, who reciprocated with food to the man's mother.

Marriage was matrilocal until the first child was born, then independent.

To avoid the sororate a man paid money to his wife's parents, and they in turn gave him seeds and food. If he failed to do so, his deceased wife's mother told his new wife he had not paid. A woman similarly paid the mother of her deceased husband to avoid the levirate.

There was little polygyny, no mother-in-law avoidance.

Some place names:

Emigrant Springs, Tiŋgah'ni (cave), probably a temporary seed-gathering camp of Ha: utans[1].

Springs near Modoc mine, Hunupa (hunupi, canyon+pa), seldom visited.

Springs by Snow Canyon, Tahahunü (tahavi, snow+canyon ?), seldom visited.

Springs by Wood Canyon, Pipum'ba or Pibump': (a plant), seldom visited.

Spring in Revenue Canyon, Tusi'gaba or Tusi'gava (a canyon that narrows sharply), the most important camp on the rare trips made by Ha:utans[1] to the Argus Mountains for seeds.

Springs in Upper Shepherd Canyon, Nia'va (?), visited occasionally for *Mentzelia*, chia, and sand-grass seeds.

Springs in Lower Shepherd Canyon, Taka'goba (taka'go, valley quail), a camping place on trips.

The five springs in upper Tuber Canyon were pine-nut camps.

NORTHERN DEATH VALLEY.—Death Valley, stretching more than 100 miles north and south, lying partly below sea level, and bounded partly on the west by the lofty Panamint Range, has an extraordinarily varied natural landscape.

The valley floor, much of which is more than 250 feet below sea level, is incredibly arid (pl. 1, *c*) and has summer temperatures ranging commonly up to 130°, with a record of close to 140°. It and the bounding foothills fall into the Lower Sonoran life zone, among whose limited plant population Jepson (p. 12) includes: *Phyllogonum luteolum, Boerhaavia annulata, Oxystylis lutea, Astragalus atratus* var. *panamintensis, Brickellia knappiana, Amphiachyris fremontii, Viguiera reticulata,* and *Enceliopsis argophylla* var. *grandiflora,* most of which are endemic and none of use for food. Probably the only important food species on the valley floor is mesquite, which grows in limited quantities at springs.

Most of the bounding mountain ranges rise into the Upper Sonoran zone and provided a few species of edible seeds. But vast areas, especially of the Funeral and Black Ranges, which scarcely exceed 5,000 feet, were practically worthless for gathering and were devoid of large game. The neighboring ranges extend upward into the tree zone at only three places. One of these was the Sigai region in the Panamint Range north of Darwin. It was more accessible to and was therefore utilized more habitually by the Sigai and Saline Valley people. The Grapevine Mountains, reaching to nearly 9,000 feet, form a massive block of pinyon-covered hills and were utilized by all the villages north of Furnace Creek. These and the comparatively treeless Tin and Dry Mountains to the west sheltered a small number of mountain sheep but no deer. The third high mountain area is the Panamint Range which bounds lower Death Valley on the west and culminates in Telescope Peak, 11,045 feet, which rises abruptly from below sea level to about timber line in the Boreal life zone. Except during the short winter when the residents of Furnace Creek and Lower Death Valley remained at water holes in the valley, they were driven by heat and virtual absence of foods in the valley floor into the cool Panamint or Grapevine Mountains. Here the various species of seeds and a limited amount of sheep hunting maintained them until pine nuts were ripe.

The distribution of population within Death Valley was also determined by water supply. Water is not only extremely scarce, but many springs are poisonous or undrinkably saline. At each usable source of water there were, therefore, winter residents, the number depending upon the amount of water and quantity of accessible foods.

North of Furnace Creek the three main villages were at Mesquite Springs, Grapevine Canyon, and Surveyor's Well. Their total population was 42, or 1 person to about 30 square miles. Though the census may be low, it is probably not much too low. These villages had no collective name for themselves, but TSt of Beatty called them Yo:gombi (flat, i. e., the valley floor). They were independent in most activities; in fact, their component families were independent throughout most of the year. Communal rabbit drives and fall festivals, however, united villages temporarily with one another and in some measure with Beatty on the east and Sigai on the west.

Villages.—The following numbers correspond with those on figure 7:

44. Mahunu (from hunupi, canyon), springs in Grapevine Canyon and probably Grapevine Springs, about 2,500 to 3,000 feet. The people called Mahunutsi. BD gave the following census as remembered from his boyhood, about 75 years ago: 4 camps or families, totaling some 27 people, as follows:

BD's grandfather, born at Mahunu, and his wife from Cottonwood Canyon in Sigai.

BD's father, Dock, a shaman; BD's mother from Surveyor's Well; his mother's brother; BD; BD's brother and sister; also, BD's father's second or polygynous wife (BD's mother's sister), and her 2 children, both of whom died young.

BD's father's mother's sister (her husband from Lida had died); her daughter and daughter's husband from some other village; her three sons, Bob, Longhair John, and Jack; Bob's wife from Lida and his son; Longhair John's wife from Lida (but not related to Bob's wife).

Cold Mountain Jack and his family, which he moved back and forth between Grapevine Spring and Mesquite Spring, as he owned cultivated land at each place. His family consisted of his two polygynous wives who were sisters, Susy and Maggie from Grapevine Spring, and seven children. Susy had four children: a son and a daughter who died when young; Tule George who moved to Lida where he lived with his wife Tudi until she died, childless, then married Lizzie from Surveyor's Well and lived with her at Tule Canyon, also childless; Kittie, who married a Beatty man and lived at Tule Canyon and had two children (one died; the other, a daughter, married an Italian and had seven children). Maggie had two sons and a daughter, all of whom died young. This camp also included Susie's mother. The 10 individuals in this family occupied a single house.

45. Ohyu (mesquite), at Surveyor's Well, 60 feet below sea level. The people called Ohyutsi. BD's census gave 2 camps totaling 14 or 15 persons, as follows:

Ike Shaw's father, from Grapevine Canyon where Ike had been born; his father's second wife born at Ohyu; three daughters, all of whom died before marrying.

Tule George's father-in-law from near Telescope Peak in the Panamint Mountains; his mother-in-law born at Ohyu; their four daughters and three sons. Total, nine persons. This family is of interest because of its exceptional fertility. The oldest daughter, Anne, married an Ohyu (?) man and had two sons, one of whom died young. The next daughter married BD's half-brother, Shoshoni John, from Grapevine Canyon, and had 13 children, of whom 10 died. The third daughter was unmarried, but had a child who died. Lizzie, mentioned above, married Tule George at Tule Canyon. The oldest son, Cottonwood Frank, married Tule George's sister, Kittie, whose husband had died. This is the only reported case of a brother and sister marrying a sister and brother. Cottonwood Frank's daughter, Minnie, was unmarried, but, probably by several white men, she had seven children, of whom four died. The next son, Joe Button, married Maggie (?) from Sigai and moved to Saline Valley when the borax works opened, then to Furnace Creek, spending the summers at Wildrose Canyon. He had three daughters and two sons who died young and 6 daughters and one son who survived. When Joe died his younger brother married Maggie and they moved to Beatty. They had no more children.

Thus, at least 28 grandchildren were born to the seven children of Tule George's parents-in-law.

46. Mesquite Springs, Panuga (no meaning ?), at 1,730 feet. This village was only semipermanent. Cold Mountain Jack and Dock each had ranches here after the introduction of horticulture in early post-Caucasian times. These and other families, however, often visited it for ducks, seeds, grapes, and mesquite, and sometimes wintered here. Even Saline Valley people visited Mesquite Springs, though they seldom remained long. Its most frequent visitors appear to have been Cold Mountain Jack's large family which lived there about half the time.

Sand Springs, Yogomba (yogömi or yogombi, a flat+pa, water), in the northern end of the valley; no winter residents.

Salt Creek, Tugu'mü[m1] (tuguwü, sand+wutü, place), below sea level. The water was too saline to permit extended residence.

Various small springs on the eastern slope of the Grapevine Mountains served as temporary seed camps but seldom as winter residences.

Subsistence activities.—The subsistence area for these villages lay largely within the confines of the mountains enclosing Death Valley. Except for the short period of residence at the winter village, families moved independently. Thus, Dock, chief of the district and resident at Grapevine Canyon, traveled with his family without reference to the movements of Cold Mountain Jack of the same village. All the people assembled only for communal rabbit drives and fall festivals, under the leadership of Dock and Tule George's father.

Dock's family ordinarily wintered at Grapevine Canyon. In the spring, when food shortage brought hunger—BD remembered crying for food in the spring during his childhood—residents of Grapevine Canyon usually went to near Mexican Spring and Mud Spring on the western side of the Grapevine Mountains to spend about a month picking *Mentzelia* and *Oryzopsis* seeds. They then went to Surveyor's Well to pick mesquite which ripened in June or July and which was free to anyone. Or, in early spring, perhaps April, they went to Cottonwood Canyon in the Sigai district to gather chia, *Oryzopsis* seeds, *Lycium* berries, and pine sugar, wapihavi (wapi+havi, sugar). Sometimes they visited Mesquite Spring in the spring or fall to hunt ducks and to gather wild grapes and mesquite. After the white man came, Dock started a ranch there. At Grapevine Canyon they got grapes and various seeds.

In the fall, people from Grapevine Canyon, Surveyor's Well, and Mesquite Springs went into the Grapevine Mountains to gather pine nuts, Dock having announced when they were ripe. Families habitually gathered from the same tracts, but did not actually own them, for other persons were privileged to gather from them if they wished. Dock and his two wives carried as many nuts as they could down to Grapevine Canyon and stored the remainder in the mountains. This naturally limited the distance from the winter village that it was feasible to go for pine nuts. But after Dock got horses, pine-nut gathering was greatly facilitated.

Cold Mountain Jack's family, meanwhile, wintered at Grapevine Canyon, Mesquite Springs, or Mahunu, and foraged for food either with Dock's family or alone, as they pleased.

No wild seeds were planted or irrigated in northern Death Valley, but horticulture was introduced in early post-Caucasian times. The plants and pattern of cultivation seems to have been borrowed almost completely from neighboring Southern Paiute. Few Death Valley people had farms. When BD was a small boy, perhaps in 1870, his father, uncle, and grandfather owned about 50 acres in Grapevine Canyon which, apparently, they subdivided, each cultivating his portion. Cold Mountain Jack also had a "ranch" about a mile below the village and one other family had a plot.

Before shovels were introduced, plain digging sticks were used for planting. Each species or variety was planted in a separate row. Work, including irrigation, was performed by both sexes. Because of the short winters, crops were planted in February and harvested in July.

Plots were family owned. This conformed to the principle of use ownership and conflicted with no native patterns. Inheritance was a simple matter. Plants, even those ready for harvest, were usually destroyed at the owner's death, as among Ash Meadows Southern Paiute, and the field lay fallow for a year or two, when any relative resumed cultivation.

Cultivation had not acquired an important place in native economy, though it was becoming important by 1890 (Nelson, 1891; Coville, 1892). Crops were usually consumed by the end of summer and helped little to relieve the want of food during the following winter. The increasing importance of the white man's economy, moreover, drew people into new activities and into regions outside their native districts. Thus, during the Rhyolite mining boom in 1906 they left their farms to haul wood for the mines. Some farming is still carried on, but odd jobs offered by the white man relegate it to a secondary place.

BD thought that soon after its introduction horticulture had spread also to Lida, Beatty, and Tupipah Springs east of Beatty.

So far as seed gathering was concerned, Death Valley people were split into families. That they habitually exploited approximately the same territory was a question of convenience, not of social or political coercion. And even seed gathering sometimes brought people from neighboring districts into the same area.

The annual rabbit drive, however, more or less consistently united all the inhabitants of the northern part of the valley under a single chief and outsiders were recognized as mere visitors. The chief was Dock. Normal participants were residents of Grapevine Springs, Surveyor's Well, and Mesquite Springs. Beatty people often attended. In October, before pine-nut trips, all the families went to the vicinity of Mexican Spring at the lower end of Sarcobatus Flat. Dock addressed them each morning, announcing the location of the drive and of the feast at the end of the day. Only men took part in the hunt. The kill was divided equally among all participants, the flesh being roasted for the evening feast and the skins preserved for rabbit-skin blankets. Drives lasted about a month.

Large game was of secondary importance. Antelope occurred in small numbers in Sarcobatus Flat and perhaps at White Rock, but were never hunted communally and were rarely sought by individuals. There were virtually no deer nearer than Lida, an inconvenient distance away. Mountain sheep could be had on Tin Mountain, Dry Mountain near Sigai, and probably in the Grapevine Mountains. BD's father hunted little. Cold Mountain Jack hunted often, especially for mountain sheep.

Lesser game, especially rodents and chuckwallas, were of some importance. Birds were also taken when possible.

A little trade was carried on. This has been described on page 45.

Festivals.—The fall festival, held after the pine-nut trip, was combined with the annual mourning ceremony. When given at Surveyor's Well, families from Grapevine Canyon, Mesquite Spring, Sigai, and a few sometimes from Beatty, Panamint Valley, Darwin, and perhaps even Saline Valley, but not Ash Meadows, attended. In some years it was held at Sigai or in Saline Valley instead of Surveyor's Well, especially if pine nuts had been abundant in those regions. It may be that people in this wide area were able to forgather only when horses, introduced after the white man arrived, facilitated transportation.

When held at Surveyor's Well, Dock was director. Panugatsugo (or Patuko) probably had this task before Dock. At Sigai and Saline Valley, Caesar and Tom Hunt were jointly directors.

The festivals started with the exhibition dance, mugwa nukana. At Surveyor's Well this was performed by Saline Valley men, and at Saline Valley by Surveyor's Well men. The dancers were paid in goods and shell money by the host village. This dance was followed by burning goods for the year's dead, then by the circle dance.

Sweat house.—The large community sweat house was not used. Instead, the sweat house was small, conical, with a center pole, earth-covered, and not more than 10 feet in diameter. Anyone desiring to do so built his own. BD's father, who greatly enjoyed sweat baths, had built one in Grapevine Canyon, one in the Grapevine

Mountains, one at Surveyor's Well, one at Furnace Creek, and one at Navadu. Anyone was privileged to use these, but they did not serve as club house and dormitory, and therefore had no connection with group unity. BD knew of no sweat house having been built at Sigai.

Warfare.—Warfare was unimportant. BD recalled but one episode. Sigai women picking sunflower seeds in upper Panamint Valley saw strangers. The next morning Sigai men pursued them into a dry cave and killed them. The identity of the invaders and the final disposal of them was unknown.

Marriage.—Marriage with any relatives was forbidden and it is probable, though not certain, that marriage with a pseudo cross-cousin, i. e., mother's brother or father's sister's stepdaughter, as practiced among Shoshoni of northern Nevada, was prohibited. Though kinship terms were not collected from Death Valley, Shoshoneans on all sides of them used the same system as that given for Little Lake, which has no features indicating either pseudo cross-cousin marriage or polyandry.

Choice of mates was not delimited by locality as such, but the inhabitants of these small villages and even the entire valleys were naturally much interrelated. Of 15 marriages recorded, 8 were with persons outside the valley, 5 within the valley but exogamous by village, 2 endogamous by village.

In arranging a marriage a man or his parents asked the girl's parents for the match, then paid them perhaps $20. They gave seeds and other presents in return.

Marriage was supposed to be matrilocal for about a year, then independent. Of the eight cases of valley exogamy, two were matrilocal, three patrilocal, in three the couple moved to a new locality. The last, especially, were determined largely by factors introduced by the white man, the couple seeking work at a ranch or mine. Of the five cases of valley endogamy and village exogamy, one was patrilocal, two matrilocal, one in a new locality, one uncertain.

The levirate and sororate were both stressed, the census showing two cases of the former. Polygyny, especially sororal polygyny, was practiced, two cases being revealed in the census. Cold Mountain Jack's second wife, a sister of the first, was given him because of his outstanding ability as a hunter. There is one case of the marriage of a brother and sister to a sister and brother.

CENTRAL AND SOUTHERN DEATH VALLEY.—No detailed information is available for the central and southern parts of Death Valley. Furnace Creek (village 47 in fig. 7) was apparently the point of contact and intermixture of three linguistic groups: Shoshoni from the north, Southern Paiute who were also mixed with Shoshoni at Ash Meadows 25 miles to the east, and Kawaiisü (also called Mugunüwü and Panümünt) who occupied the southern portions of Death Valley and Panamint Valley. JH, from Saline Valley, called Death Valley people Tsagwadüka (chuckwalla eaters), the only instance of naming by foods eaten recorded south of Benton, California.

There seems to have been a small winter village at the several springs at Furnace Creek, Tümbica (tumbi, rock), which is at about sea level. TSt remembered an old man, Pa: sanats (bat), whom he thought was chief, his two or three daughters, and several men. These people spoke Shoshoni, Southern Paiute, and Kawaiisü. BD, however, knew of no residents until the borax works were founded by the white man, when Bill Bullen and his son and five daughters moved there from Sigai. Subsequently, Furnace Creek has been headquarters for Shoshoni from a considerable distance. They live in a colony adjoining the modern winter resort, but move to Beatty, Saline Valley, and elsewhere during the summer.

The native subsistence area for the Furnace Creek people was predominantly in the Panamint Mountains, a few miles across the valley to their southwest. The Black and Funeral Ranges to the east were almost totally devoid of foods. The main summer camps were at Wildrose Spring, Blackwater Spring called Bast: (GG), and a spring near the head of Death Valley Canyon called Ko' (Kawaiisü for tobacco). Considerable mesquite, however, grows at Furnace Creek.

South of Furnace Creek the Death Valley population was predominantly Kawaiisü. Kelly (1934, p. 555) describes the boundary of the Las Vegas "band" of Southern Paiute as passing between the "Funeral mountains and Black range, thence south along the western slope of the latter, bringing the Vegas people to the very borders of Death Valley. More than likely Black range was held jointly by the Death Valley Panamint [Kawaiisü] and the Las Vegas; at best it was useful only as a source of mountain sheep and certain edible seeds." It is impossible to trace a boundary with any precision in an area like this. Ash Meadows was a mixture of Southern Paiute and Shoshoni, while southern Death Valley undoubtedly had an appreciable Shoshoni and Southern Paiute element in its population. Moreover, Ash Meadows and Pahrump Valley inhabitants went primarily for foods to the vicinity of Mount Shader and the Spring Mountains to their east and southeast rather than cross 20 miles of waterless, infertile desert to the barren Black Range, which has few peaks which rise even to 5,000 feet elevation in the Artemisia zone. Death Valley people sought foods in the Panamint Range. Thus a considerable territory between Ash Meadows and Death Valley was unoccupied and very little utilized.

TSt remembered three families which lived some 15 miles south of Furnace Creek. They probably spent some time during winter

in the vicinity of the Borax Works and Bennetts Well, which are
about 250 feet below sea level, though there is some question as to
the adequacy of water here in native times. Their main headquarters were Hungry Bill's ranch (village 48 in fig. 7), at 5,000 feet,
well up in the Panamint Mountains east of Sentinel Peak. This was
called Pūaituŋgani (pūai, mouse + tuŋgani, cave). Foods were procured in the Panamint Range.

There were 17 persons: Panamint Tom, the "chief," his wife, 2 sons and 4
daughters; Tom's brother, Hungry John, his wife, 2 sons and 2 daughters;
Tom's sister, her husband, and son, Nūaidu (windy). They spoke both Shoshoni and Kawaiisü.

Some Shoshoni place names in this vicinity:

Hanaupah Canyon, Wici (from wicivi, milkweed). Panamint Range, Kaigota
(J. H), Kaiguta (GH).

Telescope Peak, Siümbutsi or Mu:gu (pointed).

Spring at head of Wildrose Canyon, Wabüts¹; sometimes a summer camp for
seed gathering.

BEATTY AND BELTED MOUNTAINS

Shoshoni occupied southern Nevada from the Amagrosa Desert
eastward to the Pintwater Range and possibly beyond, including
Desert Valley. Southern Paiute dwelt to the east, though it is probable that the population along the area of tribal contact was a mixture
of Paiute and Shoshoni, like that at Ash Meadows.

This region is even less fertile than the Death Valley region, for the
valleys are low, extremely large, hot, and generally arid. Few of
the low mountain ranges penetrate even the pinyon zone. The great
Amagrosa Desert, lying east of Death Valley, is some 40 miles long,
12 and more miles wide, only 2,500 to 3,000 feet above sea level, and
almost devoid of water and edible plants. Valleys and flats to the
north become gradually higher and hence somewhat more favorable
to subsistence: Sarcobatus Flat, 4,000 feet; Pahute Mesa, 5,500 to
6,000; Gold Flat, 5,000; Kawich Valley, 5,500; Cactus Flat, 5,500.
But the mountain ranges were too low to contribute streams to these
valleys and, indeed, had few springs. The highest points of the
Yucca and Bullfrog Ranges and of Bare Mountain near Beatty
barely surpass 6,000 feet. The Shoshone, Cactus, and Timber Mountains reach only 7,500 feet, Pahute Mesa 7,000 feet, and the Belted
Range 8,500 feet.

Some detailed information is available concerning two population
centers, the vicinity of Beatty and the Belted Range, where, because
there was an unusual number of springs, winter villages were clustered. Each of these centers is, in a sense, a district, for the residents naturally found it most convenient to associate with their nearest neighbors. But the two were somewhat interlinked through considerable intermarriage and some cooperation. But Beatty also asso-

ciated occasionally with Death Valley and the Belted Range residents with Kawich Mountain people. Indeed, TSt said the language differed slightly in the two districts, and JK linked the Belted Range linguistically with Desert Valley to the east.

Camps.—TSt's census for about 1875 or 1880 gave some six camps in the vicinity of Beatty. There were 29 persons in 4 of these. The others were alternate camp sites. As the camps were scattered because of limited water and scarcity of foods, it is hardly proper to call them villages. These were at springs and along the Amagrosa River which flows for a few miles in Oasis Valley but fails to reach the Amagrosa Desert. Other springs in the general region, for example, those in the Bullfrog Hills to the west, were merely temporary seed-gathering camps. People of the Beatty region were called Ogwe'pi (creek), GH, BD, TSt. The winter camp sites are numbered to correspond to figure 7. They were:

49. Indian Camp, at the head of Oasis Valley, about 4,000 feet. Permanent inhabitants, if any, unknown.

50. Howell Ranch, near Springdale. This was sometimes occupied by the family of Takanüasugu from 54, below.

51. Hu: nusü (hu: nupi, canyon+suüvi, willow), at Burn's Ranch (probably Goss Springs on the U. S. G. S. map). One family: a man, his wife (a cousin of TSt's father), and daughter.

52. Ta: kanawa (takapi, obsidian+nawa, between or close to), at Hick's Hot Springs, 3,600 feet. One family: Tu: na k (tuhu, black+nank, ear) from some other locality, his wife (TSt's father's cousin), and son.

53. Sakainága (willow ?), at the mouth of Beatty Wash on the Amagrosa River. Three camps scattered in this vicinity. The first: TSt's father, who was born there; his wife from Wuniakuda in the Belted Range; two sons and a daughter. It also included two brothers (TSt's father's cousins). One of them, named Kadupuaganda, had a wife from Furnace Creek and a son. Total, eight persons.

The second and third camps were headed by two brothers from Gold Mountain, each of whom had married one of TSt's father's sisters. One brother, Tuwunsugu (tuwu, black+tsugupütsi, old man) had three daughters; the other, Na: sonimuju (na: sonip, grass+muju, head ?), had four sons.

54. Pa: navadu (pa, water+navadu, flat), somewhere near the last. Two families. One: two local brothers, Jack and Ego^bsugu (ego, tongue), and their wives who were sisters from Tupipah in the Belted Range. The other: Takanüasugu (takanua, crooked foot) from Hu: nusü, his wife (a cousin of Jack and Ego^bsugu), and their daughter. This family alternately wintered at Pa: navadü and Howell Ranch.

The chief of these encampments was TSt's father, who directed rabbit drives and festivals until his death. He had no successor because these activities were discontinued.

The other group had about 42 people in winter encampments along the southern end of the Belted Range (Tunga'tunu). They were collectively called Éso (little hill). They were:

55. Wuniakuda, a place 2 or 3 miles east of the Ammonia Tanks (Tuna^xkuwa, low hill) at about 6,000 feet, where TSt's mother's sister's family

wintered in a rock shelter called Tavondo'wâyo (standing rock). The history
of this family illustrates the lack of permanent connection with a locality and
the possible far-flung marital connections. It had formerly consisted of TSt's
maternal grandparents and their three sons and three daughters; total, eight.
After the parents died, there remained at Wu lakuda only one daughter, her
husband from some other region and her three daughters and a son; total, six.
Of TSt's other maternal aunts and uncles, one aunt went somewhere to Southern
Paiute territory to the east to live with her husband. The oldest uncle married
a Southern Paiute woman at Pahrump, where he lived, because hunting was
better. The second married a Paiute woman at Indian Spring, where he
moved. The third, Panamint Joe, married a Paiute woman in the Charleston
Mountains and lived with her but seems later to have returned to Beatty where
he was "chief" of the Shoshoni at the time of the Rhyolite mining boom,
about 1906. TSt's mother moved to the vicinity of Beatty to her husband's
home.

During the summer Wuŋlakuda was visited for seeds by Tu:naŋki and
his family from Ta:kanawa, near Beatty.

56. Mütsi (thistle ?), in the vicinity of the water holes marked merely
"Tanks" on the U. S. G. S. map; elevation, probably more than 7,500 feet.
One family: Mütsitsugutsi or Mütsitsuguputsi, his wife, from Sivahwa (below),
one son; total, three.

57. Sivahwa, at "Small Tank," a few miles north of the last; about 7,000
feet. One family: Mütsitsugutsi's son, his wife, two daughters; total, four.

58. Tünä'va, at Whiterock Springs, to the east of the last; 5,400 feet. One
family: Wandaᵍwana (?+daᵍwana, chief), chief of this general region; his
wife, Tsuŋga huvijiji (?+huvijiji, old woman), from Mütsi; four or five children; his wife's sister; total, seven or eight.

59. Wi:va (a plant), Oaksprings, a few miles to the north; 6,000 feet. An
old woman and one or two children. Also, an old man of unknown relationship
to the woman. Total, three or four.

60. Kuikun:', Captain Jack Spring; 6,000 feet. One-eye Captain Jack and
his wife.

61. Tupipa (tupi, rock+pa, water), Tippipah Springs, about 8 miles to the
south on the northern side of Shoshone Mountain, 5,400 feet. Kapitasugupiitsi,
his wife (Mütsitsuguputsi's sister), two sons, one daughter, and his unmarried
brother; total, six.

62. Topopah Spring, Pokopa (poko, ?+water), at 6,700 feet on the southern
side of Shoshone Mountain, probably had occasional winter residents.

63. Cane Spring, Pagaˣmbuhan (Southern Paiute, Pagaˣm, cane+buhan, much)
or Hugwap: (Shoshoni, cane). This site is to the east of the preceding, at the
end of Skull Mountain at 4,300 feet. It probably affiliated with Ash Meadows
Southern Piaute as much as with Shoshoni and had a mixed population. One
family: Wiˣna, born at Tupipa; his wife, Pagaˣmbuhan huvijiji; probably born
locally; two sons and one daughter; total, five.

Subsistence activities: seed gathering.—Scarcity of game in this
general region forced the population to subsist to an unusual degree
upon vegetable foods. The annual round of food seeking of the
families near Beatty during TSt's childhood required travel over an
extensive area of about 1,300 square miles.

In early spring, when stored seeds were exhausted and hunger usually caused much suffering, greens (tuhwada) and Joshua-tree buds

could be had in the vicinity of Sakainãga, so that it was not necessary to move camp. The greens were boiled, squeezed, then eaten.

In May and June, women, perhaps accompanied by a few men, went to gather sand bunch grass (*Oryzopsis*) seeds. If they were fortunate, these could be had about 10 miles to the north, near Indian camp, where another, unidentified species of seed, yubihuva, also grew. Otherwise, they went either 25 miles north to the southern side of Black Mountain or an equal distance south or east to the vicinity of Big Dune, Iron Tank, or the southern side of the Calico Hills in the Amagrosa Desert. They remained a week or two, then transported their seeds back to Sakainãga.

Meanwhile, a group of men spent perhaps a month mountain-sheep hunting in the Grapevine Mountains. As these mountains are about 25 miles away the hunters dried the meat to facilitate transporting it home.

After the women returned to Sakainãga they gathered *Mentzelia* in Beatty Wash, within a few miles of the village, *Salvia* on Bare and Yucca Mountains 5 to 10 miles to the east, and *Lycium* berries in the Bullfrog Hills a few miles to the west. During this time men usually hunted rabbits.

In July it was necessary to move camp from the southern portion of the Belted Range to the vicinity of the villages near Ammonia Tank and Mütsi, where they spent several weeks. First, they gather hu:gwi, a large grass seed resembling wheat, and later rye grass (*Elymus*) seeds.

On rare occasions, instead of going to the Belted Range they went to Surveyor's Well in Death Valley for mesquite.

By August the seeds of the most important food plants had ripened and fallen to the ground, so that people had to subsist until pine-nut time on stored seeds and such miscellaneous items as rabbits, chuckwallas, rats and other rodents, and insects.

In late September or early October pine nuts ripened. Beatty people gathered these in the Belted Range, some 40 miles distant. Though each family customarily picked from the same place, it did not own it; trespass was not resented and permission was not asked if someone else desired to pick there. Where pinyon trees grow, they generally cover thousands of acres and if the crop is abundant in the region there are many good picking places. The only practical consideration was that different families should agree not to utilize the same few acres.

If the Belted Range pine-nut crop were poor, Beatty people went to the Grapevine Mountains, where northern Death Valley people habitually picked. It is not clear why they did not always go here, as these mountains are about 15 miles nearer Beatty than the Belted

Range. A possible explanation is a sociological one. They were more intermarried with the Belted Range people and may have taken this occasion to visit relatives, with whom they would remain for the fall rabbit hunt and perhaps festival. On the other hand, this intermarriage may have resulted from association at pine-nut time and at hunts.

If neither the Belted Range nor Grapevine Mountains had a pine-nut crop, they went to the Kawich Mountains, 50 miles to the north, or to the vicinity of Lida, equally far to the northwest. TSt remembers a trip made on foot to the latter during his youth. Such long journeys, however, were made only when there was acute danger of food shortage. Ordinarily, the distance was excessive and illustrates the limitations which facilities for travel and transportation imposed on the size of the Shoshoni food areas.

Domesticated corn, melons, pumpkins, sunflowers, beans, and perhaps other plants were procured about 1860 but were cultivated on such a small scale that they seem to have contributed little to economic security.

Subsistence activities: hunting.—Animal foods were of secondary importance. Deer were virtually unknown within the distance that hunters could conveniently travel. Mountain sheep could be had in the Grapevine Mountains, where individual hunters or small groups of men often went while women were gathering seeds elsewhere. Antelope were either lacking or unimportant in this area. Sometimes, however, Belted Range people went into the Kawich Mountain district, to the north, to participate in large communal drives directed by an antelope shaman. Thus the Belted Range residents, though linked with Beatty in many ways, were also linked with their northern neighbors.

The fall rabbit drive was the only truly communal economic activity. These were usually held in the flats south of Whiterock Springs, under the direction of Wangaᵍwana, the local chief. Local residents and Beatty people who had come for pine nuts drove together. There were also sometimes visitors from the Kawich Mountains, Ash Meadows, Lida, and even Death Valley. Visitors were most likely to be present when their own pine-nut crop had been poor and that in the Belted Range abnormally good. Sometimes, however, when the Beatty people had not come to the Belted Range for pine nuts, they drove rabbits with Death Valley people in Sarcobatus Flat, 10 to 20 miles north of their villages. TSt's grandfather directed these drives.

At Whiterock rabbit drives lasted about a month, men driving each day while women gathered pine nuts, if any remained. Each morning Wangaᵍwana informed hunters about the plans for the day, say-

ing, "We will build fires to show you where to go." If the Kawich
Mountain people were participating, Kawich, their chief, also talked.
Young men drove the rabbits, shooting them meanwhile with bows
and arrows, into 10 or 12 nets, each of which was owned by an old
man. Each man kept his quarry but unsuccessful hunters were given
a few. The main motive of the hunt was to provide skins for twined
robes and blankets. The meat was consumed at once.

The fall festival.—The fall festival was held either at Wuṇiakuda
where Wangaᵍwana was director, or at Beatty where TSt's paternal
grandfather was director. It was probably rare that each place
had a festival the same year; instead, the two districts seem to have
alternated each year, playing host to each other. The Wuṇiakuda
festival was held during pine-nut time, and before the rabbit drive,
probably in October. At Beatty it was held in conjunction with the
rabbit drive. Occasionally Beatty people attended a festival at
Willow Spring on the eastern side of the Grapevine Mountains, given
by Death Valley people during pine-nut time under the direction of
Dock.

The festival lasted 5 days. Wangaᵍwana and an old man from
Oak Springs or other chiefs, depending on where the festival was
held, talked from time to time. The first night there was an exhibition dance, performed by visitors who were paid by their hosts.
The second to fifth nights were given over to the round dance,
wegi (round) nük:ǝp (dance), after which people dispersed. There
was no associated mourning ceremony.

Sweat house.—The sweat house was unimportant in integrating
the residents of a large territory, though it served as a meeting place
for people of neighboring camps. A sweat house was located
wherever there were enough people to make it worth while, for
example, at Sakainãga and Indian Camp for Beatty people, and at
White Rock and Oak Spring for Belted Range people. These were
used by men and women for smoking, gambling, sweating, and as
a dormitory (?), thus being somewhat more important as community
centers than those in Death Valley.

Warfare.—Warfare was unknown in these districts. TSt had
heard only of the fight in upper Panamint Valley, previously described. JS had heard of some fighting with Southern Paiute
who had objected to Shoshoni fishing in the stream flowing into the
Pahranagat Lakes.

Political organization.—Because of the distribution of water holes
the population was clustered in two centers, that at Beatty almost
constituting a group of relatives. To the extent that each was independent, having its own chief, gathering seeds in its own locality,
and holding its own rabbit hunts and festivals, it approximated a

band. The two were linked with each other, however, in that Beatty
people gathered pine nuts and drove rabbits sometimes in the Belted
Range and the two districts reciprocated with alternating festivals.
But Beatty was sometimes linked with Death Valley by gathering
pine nuts in the Grapevine Range and participating in rabbit drives
and even festivals in that region, while Belted Range people sometimes associated with Kawich Mountain people for antelope drives,
pine-nut gathering, and festivals.

In spite of these varying outside associations, however, members
of each district usually cooperated with one another in the few
communal affairs and had a local chief to direct them. The chief
was called taghwani (talker) or pokwinavi; his wife was called
taghwani huvitc: [1] (huvitc: [1] old woman).

Marriage.—The only bar to marriage was blood relationship. So
far as is known, no marriages between even second cousins were
recorded. There was no rule of local exogamy nor of postmarital residence. Actually, however, the probability that these small clusters
of camps would consist of related nonmarriagable persons was
great. Five of the 7 families (29 persons) in the Beatty district
were related through one spouse or the other to TSt's father's
family; the other 2 were related to each other and possibly to
TSt's family. Of nine marriages, seven and possibly eight were
exogamous by district, three and possibly four being matrilocal,
four being patrilocal. One was possibly endogamous by district,
exogamous by camp site, and matrilocal. There were two instances
or four marriages between two brothers and two sisters. One of
these formed a single camp.

The extent of relationship between inhabitants of the Belted
Range district is unknown, though some is evident. Greater endogamy, however, is manifest in that three marriages were exogamous
only by village; these were patrilocal. Four marriages were exogamous by district. Three of these were previously mentioned, the
spouses going to the Beatty district. In the fourth, the woman
remained, matrilocally. Of four intertribal marriages, all by TSt's
mother's siblings and all with Southern Paiute, three were matrilocal, one patrilocal, the Shoshoni in all cases moving away.

Marriage was arranged by the boy's father, who gave 10 to 20
strings of bead money (nauwaku) and a basket to the girl's father.
The girl's mother reciprocated with seeds. Marriage simply entailed
the couple's living together.

The sororate and levirate, both junior and senior, were compulsory.
To avoid it when remarrying, either party had to pay. Sometimes a
sororal marriage also required a slight additional payment to the
girl's family.

IONE VALLEY, REESE RIVER, AND SMITH CREEK VALLEY

Ione and Reese River Valleys were more densely populated than the region of Tonopah, but the study of this and of practically all of the remainder of northern Nevada was greatly handicapped by the total lack of suitable maps for location of sites, sources of water, and food resources. Only the extreme southern parts of Ione and Reese River Valleys are covered by the U. S. G. S. "Tonopah" quadrangle.

The Paradise Range which bounds Ione Valley and the Desatoya Mountains which bound Smith Creek Valley on the west are roughly the boundary between Shoshoni and Northern Paiute. (See Wasson, 1862, p. 218.) But a good many Paiute lived in Ione Valley where they had intermarried and some Shoshoni had settled with Edwards Creek Valley Paiute. In 1860, Burton (1862, p. 487) observed that Smith Creek was in Paiute territory.

The culture of these Shoshoni is fundamentally the same as that of neighboring Shoshoni, though slight influences from the Paiute are evident. Borrowed, either from the Paiute or from Shoshoni to the north was the custom of naming people of a general though not definitely bounded region after some prominent food. Thus:

Kuivadüka (Kuiya, the root of *Valeriana edulis*+düka, eat), people of Smith Creek Valley.

Waidüka (wai, *Oryzopsis hymenoides*), people in the vicinity of Cloverdale, to the south.

Wiyumbitükanü (wiyumbi, buffalo berry, *Lepargyrea*+düka, eat+nü, people), people in Great Smoky Valley, which was called Wiyumbahunovi (buffalo berry+pa, water+hunovi, valley).

Shoshoni of Reese River called themselves Nü (people) or Mahagüadüka (mahagüa, *Mentzelia* seeds+düka) and their valley, Mahaküa bahunovi.

Paiute were called Paviotso (TH), Paviyodzo'° (JK). Neither could be translated.

It is probable that in native times Ione, Reese River, and Smith Creek Valleys were separate though not completely independent districts. As the information given by informants comes largely from late post-Caucasian days, it shows a single, persuasive chief, Tu:tuwa (called Totoi by the white man), extending his influence over these and neighboring valleys, as far north as the Humboldt River. This almost certainly does not represent the scope of political unity in native times.

JF thought the dialect was a little different north of Eureka, east in Great Smoky Valley, south near Cloverdale and Tonopah, and west in Ione Valley. WJ denied the last.

Reese River Valley, lying between two high ranges, is unusually fertile and is one of the few valleys favored with sufficient water to maintain a perennial stream. The Toyabe Range on the east

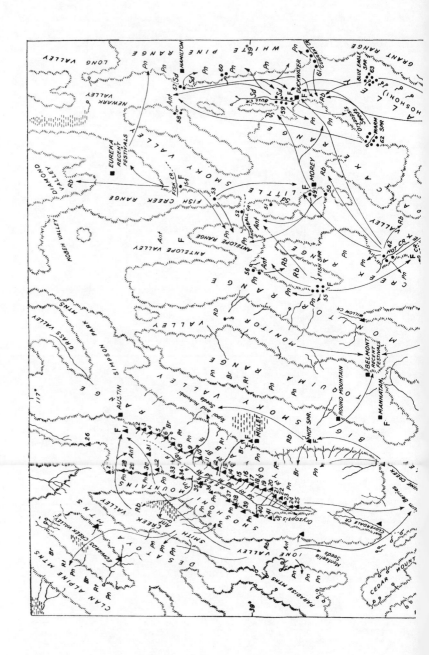

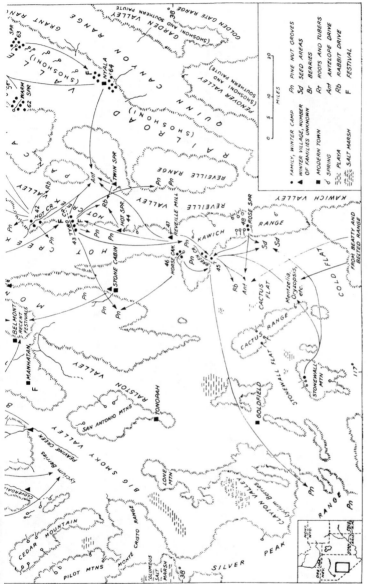

FIGURE 8.—Villages and subsistence areas of central Nevada.

extends upward beyond the pinyon zone, having several peaks which surpass 11,000 feet. Though precipitous, this range had many plant foods and gave rise to numerous springs. The Shoshoni Mountains on the west are lower, the highest peak being just over 9,000 feet, but they contained some springs and important food resources.

Although the local population was undoubtedly denser than in most parts of the Shoshoni area, there is no reliable estimate of it. If each of the 41 camps in Reese River Valley listed by JF had but 1 family of 6 persons, the total population would be 250 persons in 900 square miles, or 1 per 3.6 square miles. This seems too much and JF's guess that there were 1,000 to 2,000 persons is certainly excessive. In 1872 Powell and Ingalls (1874, p. 12) estimated it to be 530 persons.

Village or camp sites.—The following is the approximate location of camp sites in the Reese River Valley south of Austin, the numbers corresponding with those on the map (fig. 8). Although JF thought each was a winter encampment of several families, it is more likely that some were mere temporary seed camps, or even place names. Those which were camp sites, however, were conveniently located, for the mountains behind them afforded pine nuts, roots, and seeds, while the low and partly marshy valley floor provided seeds and roots, most of which grew within 4 or 5 miles of each camp. In fact the only long trips that were necessary were for pine nuts when the local crop failed and for communal antelope and rabbit drives and festivals. These might require travel up to 40 or 50 miles, depending on the location of the village.

Reese River Valley slopes gradually upward from probably about 6,000 feet or slightly less in the vicinity of Austin to 7,400 feet at the head of the Reese River at Indian Valley.

Starting at Austin and proceeding south, down the western slope of the Toyabe Range (hunupi in these names means canyon), the camps were:

1. Wiyunutuahunupi (wiyümbi, buffalo berry+nutua, close, i. e., the thick buck brush closes the canyon), the first creek south of Austin, about 2 miles from Austin. Fall festivals held here.

2. Äŋgasikigada (äŋga, red+siki, sideways+gada, sitting), 1 mile from last; a canyon here; the name is from a peak in the vicinity.

3. Tutumbihunupi (tu, black+tumbi, rock), 1½ miles from last.

4. Ohaogwaihunupi (óha, yellow+ogwai, ground), 1 mile from last.

5. Bambicpahunupi (bambic, stinking+pa, water), about 2 miles from last.

6. Soŋgwatumbihun (soŋ'gwa, lava+tumbi, rock), about 1½ miles from last.

7. Gunuvijǝp (gunuvip, elderberry bush+jǝp, here, i. e., occurs here), about 1½ miles from last.

8. Biahunupi (bia, big), Big Creek, west of Kingston.

9. Mǝzagüahunupi (mǝza, the round cactus+kiia, peak), 2 miles from last.

10. Oapihunupi (oapi, a yellow stone used for paint), 2 miles from last.

11. Tüdüpihunupi (tudupi, turquoise) ; 1½ miles from last; turquoise mined here aboriginally for beads.

12. Yudigivo'ihunupi (yudigip:, thin slabs of rock+vo'i, on top; so-called because the trail to Eureka crossed over these rocks) ; 2 miles from last.

13. Aihyu'hunupi (aihyu', the pole used to pull down pine nuts), about 2 miles from last.

14. Navahodava (navahoda, dug out+pa, water; named from the fact that wells were dug here to procure water) ; 3 miles from last.

15. Gu:vadaküahunupi (gu:vada, long+küa, peak), 2 miles from last or about halfway between Austin and Bell's ranch.

16. Baiămbasa'hunupi (baiya'ᵃ, yellow jacket+basa', dried up), about 1 mile from last.

17. Kwinahunupi (kwina, gwina, hawk or eagle), 2 miles from last.

18. Tosaküahunupi (tosa, white+küa, peak), 3 miles from last. This is probably near Clear Creek, at about 7,000 feet.

19. A:suŋguahunupi (ă:suŋ, yellowish+küa, peak), 1 mile from last.

20. Wakaihunupi (wakai, pinyon tree), 1 mile from last.

21. Böyü'wihunupi (böyü', trail+wia, pass), 3 miles from last. A trail to Great Smoky Valley passed over here.

22. Yümbahunupi (yümba, yomba, root of *Carum gairdneri*), 3 miles from last.

23. O:nihunupi (o:ni, winding or crooked ?), about 2½ miles from last.

24. A:dumbihunupi (a:, white+dumbi, rock), about 2½ miles from last.

25. Bukwiyo'°hunupi (warm water in a pool or small spring), about 4 miles from last and a little south of Bell's ranch.

Winter sites similarly were located at sources of water along the eastern slope of the Shoshoni Mountains, near pine nuts, which were gathered in this range. These were:

26. Sünuŋgoi (sünu'ᵘ, seeds of *Lappula*+koi, peak), about 10 miles northwest of Austin and slightly north of Mount Airy. It is possible that this fell into the territory of the district to the north.

27. Sova, sofa (so, much+pa water), a spring near the summit of Mount Airy; Tu'tuwa, the chief, lived here.

28. Tüosava (tüosa, boulder+pa, water), 2 or 3 miles south of last.

29. Yü'tomba (yü'tom, badger hole+pa, water, i. e., water in badger holes), 1 mile from last.

30. Evimba (evi, white chalk+pa, water), 3 or 4 miles from last.

31. Dumboi (dumbi, rock+boi, cave), at foot of hill near river, with some camps nearby. No one occupied the cave. Two or three miles from last.

32. Hukumba (hukumbi, "pine needles" or seeds ?, which cover up the spring+pa), about 2 miles from last.

33. Kosiva (kosi, dust+pa, water, i. e., muddy water), 3 miles from last.

34. Wü:payagahunupi (wü:payaga, spreading or expanding, i. e., at the canyon mouth), 3 miles from last.

35. Dawiciwühunupi (dawiciwəp, rabbit brush), 2 miles from last.

36. Kü:nuvidumbihunupi (kunuvi, elderberry+dumbi, rock), about 1½ miles from last. A source of elderberries.

37. Pazuyuhoi' (pa, water+zuyuhoi', dripping, i. e., down the rocks), 4 miles from last.

38. Waŋgodüsikihunupi (waŋgovi, "white pine"+dusiki, a peak which rises gradually on one side and precipitously on the other), 2 miles from last.

39. Ava (a, white+pa, water; named from the white ground in the vicinity), 2½ miles from last.

40. Bohoba (bohovi, *Artemisia tridentata*+pa, water), a spring, 3 miles from last.

41 Dongwicava (dongwicəp, wild cherry+pa, water), slightly south of Ione, west of the Bell ranch.

Another camp, which properly fell into the Ione Valley district, was south-west of Berlin Peak at a spring called Wánzi awa'ᵃ (wanzi, antelope+awa'ᵃ, chest; significance unknown).

No village sites were obtained for Ione Valley. The population was predominantly Shoshoni with some Northern Paiute intermixed. Two Paiute villages in Edwards Creek Valley given by TH were:

Wanahunupi (wana, net or string), on a creek on the eastern side of the valley.

Acamüdzi'¹, near a little mountain southeast of Alpine.

Place names. Shoshoni Mountain, Hotoya' (ho, wood+toyavi, mountain). The following places are in this range.

Berlin Peak, Duvanoha' (duva, pine nut+noha', ?)

Ongua (on, rocky+kau, peak), a low, rocky peak on the pass between Peterson's and Welch's ranches.

Nagaho: ngua (naga, smallest+ho:n, rocky+küa, peak), about 2 miles south of last.

Wedodo' (?), a small peak standing out in the flat of the valley near the hills about 3 miles south of the last. Used as a point of reference in giving direction.

Dügungüa (dügu, "wild potatoes"+küa, peak), about 1 mile from the camp at Evimba. A place for gathering "wild potatoes."

Boinawiya (boina, *Sophia* seeds+wiya, pass), about 1 mile south of last, where a trail crosses the mountains and where boina was abundant.

À:güa (à:, white+küa, peak), a peak about 1 mile west of the camp at Dumboi.

Tungwigadü (tumbi, rock+gwip:i, smoke+gadü, sitting, i. e., the bluish, smoky looking rock ledges on the hill somewhat below the summit on the eastern side of the range). About 4 miles south of the camp at Wü:payaga hunupi.

Toyabe Mountains, Biatoyavi (bia, big+toyavi, mountain). The following are in this range:

Tumüza:pi (tumbi, rock+za:pi, point), a peak about 2 miles south of the camp at yudigivo'i.

Welch's ranch in Reese River, Wandonawüuun: (wando, pole+nawünun:, standing up). This name seems to have been taken from the fact that the white soldiers erected some kind of signal poles.

Near Edwards Creek Valley:

Yundumba (yun, ?+tumbi, rock+pa, water), springs in the Clan Alpine Mountains southwest of Alpine, which served as a pine-nut camp.

Sonaduhaga (?, a Paiute word), springs south of the last, also a pine-nut camp.

Nadapika'ᵃ (nadapi, their rock+ka'ᵃ, peak), a peak in the Mount Airy Range.

Düt:sofe'ᵃ (Paiute word), Eastgate.

Subsistence activities.—Economy differed here in minor ways from that farther south. First, there are more roots and berries in proportion to seeds, though the pine nut continues to be of outstanding importance. Second, certain characteristic southern plants disappear, among them *Salvia*, tonopuda (unidentified), Joshua tree, and mesquite. Third, the practice of sowing wild seeds was first encountered here. The brush in "basins" in the hills near the winter villages was burned and *Mentzelia* and *Chenopodium* seeds were broadcast. There is no question that this practice was native, for it was described in all parts of north central Nevada. Planting was done by all village members and the plot protected against trespass. Reese River, Ione, and Smith Creek Valleys all planted in the same way. It was, however, probably a minor factor in subsistence.

Plant foods were nearly all gathered within convenient distance of the encampments, thus permitting the population to be somewhat more stable and sedentary than most Nevada Shoshoni.

Seeds procured in the valleys were: Sand bunch grass (*Oryzopsis*), second in importance only to pine nuts and sometimes gathered in sufficient quantity to last all winter; June, July. *Sophia;* June, July. *Mentzelia;* June, July. Dui, unidentified; July, August. Hukümbi (unidentified), especially in Great Smoky Valley; September. Tule, in marshy places; August, September. *Lappula. Artemisia tridentata*, some eaten. Most of these required trips of only three or four days, people carrying water into the arid desert in basketry ollas.

Seeds from the canyons and mountains were: Pine nuts, the most important. *Chenopodium;* August. Sihū, red top grass; August. *Elymus*, wild rye; August, occurs also in valleys. Sunflower; August.

Practically all seeds were stored in some quantity for winter use.

Roots, mostly from the mountain, were: hü'ü (unidentified), yomba (*Carum gairdneri*), onions, and hunib: (unidentified) in June, July. Töpoi (unidentified), July; Reese River Valley, where Ione Valley people secured permission to gather; also Big Smoky Valley. Du'u, "wild potato," valleys, canyons; July. Goiyu'u (*Valeriana edulis* ?), valley near Ione; July. Mahavit (*Eleocharis* or *Brodiaea* ?), wet parts of valleys; June, July; people from all parts of the valley usually dug it between Welch Ranch and Ledlie, near Austin. Nəp: (unidentified), swamps in valley; ripe in July but could be dug throughout winter. All but hü'ü and du'u were dried and stored.

Berries, practically all growing in canyons and mountain sides, were: Buffalo berries (*Sheperdia*); crop only in certain years; August. Service berry (*Amelanchier*); July. Wild cherry (*Prunus*); August. Elder (*Sambucus*); September. Gooseberries (*Grossularia*); July, August. Wild currant (*Ribes*); July. The first four were dried and stored. *Lycium*, none in Ione and Reese

Valleys, but procured with permission or by invitation of local residents around Peavine and Cloverdale Creeks, to the south; dried, stored.

Communal antelope and rabbit hunts were the main collective economic activities.

Antelope hunts depended upon the whereabouts of antelope and of an antelope shaman. There seems to have been only one shaman, Wanzigwəp tsugu' (wanzi, antelope+gwəp, fence, i. e., antelope corral+tsugu', old man), for Reese River, Ione, Smith Creek, and Edwards Creek. (There was another shaman in Great Smoky Valley.) Drives were held in March (gwámua; gwəp, corral+mua, month) in Reese River Valley, usually just below Austin, or in neighboring valleys to the west.[11]

Rabbit drives were held after pine-nut trips, in connection with the fall festival, which lasted 5 days. The location seems to have varied from year to year, but it is uncertain whether each valley performed independently. In Reese River, Waŋgodo'° was director. Ione Valley people usually went to Reese River, but may have had their own hunts, under a local director. Sometimes they went to Smith Valley, where Wagon Jack was probably director. Hunts involved several nets and large crowds of drivers.

Deer were unimportant in this region. They were hunted either by individuals or small groups, probably involving little more than village members.

Ownership of seed areas.—In both Ione and Reese River Valleys, choice pine-nut tracts were owned and protected against trespass by villages, whether or not village members were related. Villages, however, probably were often but single families or related families. Each tract embraced some 100 to 200 acres and was bounded by natural landmarks known to everyone. Tracts were in the mountains behind the villages. Thus, camps on the eastern side of Reese River Valley owned tracts in the Toyabe Mountains, those on the western side in the Shoshone Mountains. The same was true of Ione Valley. MJ's people in Ione Valley owned a tract on the western slope of the Shoshone Mountains a few miles southeast of Mount Berlin, near their winter village, and another in the Paradise Mountains, on the western side of the valley, perhaps 12 miles away. If the crop failed at these, her family was usually invited by her mother's step-father to pick on his tract in the "Alpine" (Desatoya or Clan Alpine ?) Mountains.

Plots which were burned and sowed with wild seeds were also village-owned. There is some doubt whether plots of other wild seeds were similarly owned. GJ and JF held that all seed areas were di-

---

[11] A detailed account of the procedure of the antelope shaman during a hunt has been given elsewhere.

vided into village-owned tracts, the owners inviting others to gather if the crop were abundant. That trips to near Cloverdale to gather *Lycium* berries and to Great Smoky Valley to gather topoi roots and hukumbi were made only with permission of the local residents substantiates this. Gus Thomas, however, thought people were at liberty to gather where they pleased, except on pine-nut and sowed-seed land.

Trespassers were driven off with words, if possible, but there was no fighting or killing. Tutuwa's brother, a weather shaman, once produced a heavy downpour of rain and hail to drive trespassers from his seed lands.

Inheritance is confused by the claim of village ownership. It seems to have been patrilineal, however, when a single family was involved, women gathering on their husband's tracts.

Ownership of seed territory is contrary to Shoshoni custom. Two explanations are possible for its occurrence here. First, the idea may have been borrowed from neighboring Paiute, who, according to all Shoshoni, had property rights in seed areas. (This, however, was denied for Paiute in the vicinity of Winnemucca, to the north.) In this case the situation would perhaps resemble that of the Saline Valley Shoshoni, who also adjoined Paiute with such concepts and were also exceptional in claiming property rights in pine-nut tracts. Second, it may have developed from the fact that the population here was denser, more stable, and able to get all essential foods within a small radius of the village, so that habitual use led to ownership. In this case the ownership would presumably have developed somewhat like the Owens Valley Paiute ownership of seed lands.

Smith Valley people, immediately north of Ione Valley, did not, however, have ownership of any tracts except those of sowed seeds. Trespassers on these were shot. (TH.)

Ownership of sowed plots accords with the Shoshoni principle that there are property rights only in things on which work has been done.

Festivals.—The fall festival was held in conjunction with the rabbit drive. This was usually at Wandonawunum: and sometimes at Wiyunutuahunupi in Reese River Valley, but might be in other valleys if, for any reason, rabbits were hunted in them. JF said that they followed, FS that they preceded, pine-nut trips.

The aboriginal area participating in festivals is open to question. In post-Caucasian times Austin became the site of large festivals which drew people from not only throughout Reese River Valley north to Battle Mountain, and from Ione, Smith Creek, and Edwards Creek valleys, but even Paiute from Walker River and Walker Lake, 100 miles away. Tutuwa was director.

For 5 days the men drove rabbits daily and everyone danced at night. Dances were the round dance, the horn dance, which is a variation of the round dance, and the recently borrowed back-and-forth dance. Though danced primarily for pleasure, there was and still is some belief that the round dance brings rain.

FS's account of the Austin festivals introduces a few elements which may have been native but are suspiciously like practices of Northern Shoshoni whom he observed at Owyhee. When visitors arrived, FS said, Tutuwa assigned each family a place in the camp circle which surrounded the dance ground in place of a dance corral. It had an opening on the eastern side, directly opposite which Tutuwa camped, and a pine-nut tree or post in the center. People merely erected temporary windbreaks for shelter. During the dance Tutuwa talked from time to time, telling the boys not to steal or make trouble and urging people to bring out food for feasts. Captain Charlie also talked.

In addition to the main fall festivals, lesser gatherings were held in spring and summer for the round dance. These were generally also directed by Tutuwa.

Warfare.—Several casual fights with Paiute from the west were recorded, but these contributed little to social solidarity, and were conducted with a lack of specific war procedure. Two or three times, before the arrival of the white man, marauding bands of Paiute men bent on sheer mischief, according to Shoshoni accounts, killed women and children in the festival camp in Ione Valley, while men were away hunting rabbits. The Shoshoni men, without a special leader, followed the Paiute and killed them. In one instance the Shoshoni killed all the Paiute except one man. They cut off his ears and sent him home as a challenge. Eventually an old Paiute man came over to give shell money (GJ and JF thought shell money had not been used) to the Shoshoni, asking that they be friends and trade rabbit-skin blankets and other goods with the Paiute (PH).

Political organization.—Natively, the land-owning village seems to have been a fairly stable political unit, though I have no information on village chiefs. Cooperation between villages, as elsewhere in Nevada, seems to have been variable. Probably the people of Reese River Valley south of Austin habitually assembled for the combined festival and rabbit drive. Ione Valley and sometimes Smith Valley people joined them, though it is not clear whether they came merely as guests. The whereabouts of an antelope shaman determined which people cooperated in antelope hunts. There were no other native activities to weld the inhabitants of the different areas into true bands.

In recent times, however, people of Reese River Valley and Ione Valley seem to have held a common festival and looked to the same chief to represent them, so that they were thought of by informants as being something of a band. Austin, settled in 1860, has long been a center of Shoshoni population from a large area.

The main task of the chief, dagwani, in native times was to direct
the festival. The earliest known Reese River Valley chief was
Tutuwa (Totoi). In 1862, Wasson (p. 219) estimated his followers
to number 300 to 400. He was succeeded by his brother, Tom Totoi.
Tom was succeeded by his sister's son, Captain Joe Gilbert. Joe was
succeeded temporarily by his brother-in-law, Jim Butcherman, who
was too old but became temporary chief at the request of the white
people until someone else could be found. Eventually, Joe Gilbert's
son, Aleck Gilbert, took the position, but today it means little and
Aleck has moved to Duckwater. Succession thus seems not to have
been primarily governed either by inheritance or public choice, but
by appointment by one's predecessor.

Powell and Ingalls (1874, p. 12) list four chiefs for the Reese
River Valley in 1872: To-to'-a, Koo-soo-be-ta-gwi, Behr-ha-naugh,
and Uhr-wa-pits; and three for the vicinity of Austin: Weg-a'-whan,
Wedg-a'-gan, and Kush-sho-way; To-to'-a was the chief of the "alliance" or entire group, called Na-hae-go.

Antelope shamans received their powers in dreams.

Though Tutuwa was said to have been festival chief for all valleys,
Reese River, Ione, and Alpine Valleys probably had their own rabbit-
drive directors. TH, Smith Valley, thought that Tutuwa appointed
the rabbit-drive director.

Marriage.—The relationship of marriage to communities was not
distinctive. Districts and probably many of the larger villages were
made up of unrelated families which could intermarry, so that there
was no rule of local exogamy. Blood relationship was the only bar
to marriage and recent cases of second-cousin marriage are strongly
disapproved.

In this region, however, we first encounter certain new types of
marriage which are practiced by most Shoshoni to the north. The
most interesting of these is a kind of cross-cousin marriage. A number of localities to the northeast and east, described below, had true
cross-cousin marriage. Others, like Reese River and Ione Valley,
prohibited marriage of true cross-cousins but preferred marriage of
what may be called pseudo cross-cousins. That is, marriage was preferably with the mother's brother's or father's sister's stepchild, but
was prohibited with the pseudo parallel-cousin, the mother's sister's
or father's brother's stepchild. The relationship of these forms of
marriage to social structure is discussed in a concluding section, as
none is wholly intelligible unless set in the perspective of a comparison of a number of areas.

Marriage was arranged largely by a man's parents, who gave gener-
ous presents of goods to the parents of the prospective bride. Although the latter gave some reciprocal presents, these gifts seem to

have constituted a semibride purchase. There are no census data, but informants declared that there was temporary matrilocal residence, during which the boy hunted for his parents-in-law in a kind of bride service. Permanent residence was usually patrilocal, but was determined by individual circumstances rather than by any rule.

The levirate and sororate were both extremely strong, informants believing that a person had no choice but to follow them. Lack of children made no difference. The reason for these customs was said to be the strong affection which existed between brothers-in-law and sisters-in-law. No additional payment was required when the levirate and sororate were followed. Disregard of them led to the assassination of the offender. (The last seems improbable.)

Two other methods of obtaining a wife, which were common to the north and east, were abduction and personal combat. In the first, a man, aided by several friends, went to a girl's house and, beating down opposition should it be offered, carried her off without regard to her or her family's desires. In the second, a man, coveting the wife of another man, went with his friends to her home. He and the husband fought with their fists and the winner took the woman. Neither involved use of the bow and arrow or intentional bloodshed. Both practices have more point where the population was sparser and potential spouses scarcer.

It is not known whether fraternal polyandry was practiced. It has been reported among Paiute to the west and northwest and occurred among Shoshoni to the north and east (Stewart, O. C., 1937; Park, 1937), but not to the south. Throughout the area including Shoshoni to the south, however, the levirate and sororate were very strong and polygyny was preferably sororal.

GREAT (BIG) SMOKY VALLEY AND MONITOR VALLEY

Geographically, these valleys resemble Reese River Valley, though they are somewhat less fertile. Virtually no information is available, however, for the region of Ralston Valley and the extreme southern portion of Great Smoky Valley, north of Tonopah. The area is comparatively arid and probably had a sparse, scattered population.

Great Smoky Valley is enclosed by the Toyabe Range on the west and the Toquima Range on the east. The former is comparatively arid on the Great Smoky Valley side in the north but the southern portion, which culminates in Arc Dome (11,775 feet), gives rise to many small creeks at intervals of a mile or two. There were probably camps on each of these but the largest villages were at Millett's Ranch on the South Twin River (6,002 feet), at Darrough's Hot Springs (5,609 feet) called Üdü'ba (hot water), and at Peavine Creek. There may also have been other villages but it was not possible to procure a list of them.

Even less information is available about Monitor Valley. It, too, was between high ranges, both the Toquima Range on the west and the Monitor Range on the east having a number of summits above 10,000 feet and a general elevation which produced considerable moisture but no important rivers in the valley.

Fragments of information suggest that Great Smoky Valley Shoshoni were like other Nevada Shoshoni in all important features.

Subsistence activities resembled those of Reese River, except that there was no ownership of seed areas. Thus, Hot Springs people gathered seeds in their own valley and in the Toquima and Toyabe Ranges where they pleased. There was probably no danger of their trespassing on Reese River pine-nut groves in the Toyabe Range, for they ordinarily gathered on their own side of the summit.

The Great Smoky Valley 5-day fall festival was held, after pine nuts were harvested, at Hot Creek, Millett's Ranch, Manhattan, or elsewhere. They were directed by Captain John. After the dance, Captain John would announce the 10-day rabbit hunt, held at various places in the valley. Visitors from Reese River, Austin, and elsewhere attended these and it is possible that, in post-Caucasian times, at least, Monitor and Ralston Valley people had customarily joined forces with the Great Smoky Valley people under Captain John. (JK.)

Belmont, a mining town settled in 1865 in the southern end of the Toquima Range, however, became the center of a fairly large white and Indian population at an early time and seems to have had local festivals and rabbit drives under a special director, Old Joe (JK). JS, who had lived in Belmont during his childhood, circa 1875 or 1880, said the early, post-Caucasian director was Timpanovo'tsugupu'ʦⁱ (timb:, rock+pa, water+novo', tank, i. e., water in a rocky basin after a rain+tsugupu'ʦⁱ, old man). After he retired, Bill Kawich, who had come from the Kawich Mountains, became director. He is probably Powell and Ingalls' Kai'-wits, who was chief of 116 persons at Belmont and vicinity. These authors name "Brigham" as chief of 25 Indians in Big Smoky Valley (1874, p. 12).

Festivals at this time drew Indians, traveling now with horses, from most neighboring valleys. PH, however, named Bogombits dagwani (bogombits, wild currant+dagwani, chief) as director of joint festivals held by people of Belmont and Stone Cabin. At what period he was director is not known.

KAWICH MOUNTAINS

The Kawich Range, north of the Belted Range, gives rise to a few springs where a small number of winter camps were clustered.

These, together with the camps at Tybo Creek and Hot Creek, to the north, are shown on the map, figure 8. There is no information about camps in the Reveille Mountains or extreme southern Railroad Valley. The northern part of Railroad Valley is described with Little Smoky Valley, below.

Some idea of the aridity which restricted population in this area may be had from the fact that all the sources of water in the Kawich Range and the territory to the south and west are entered on the map, figure 8, from the very detailed U. S. G. S. "Kawich" quadrangle. The valleys are all in excess of 5,000 feet, however, and the mountains, though not high, extended into the pinyon zone in several localities, so that foods, while not abundant, sufficed for this sparse population.

Encampments.—In the area for which encampments are given, JS thought there had been a total of 20 families, LJB estimated 15. This would be about 90 to 120 persons. As these families ordinarily ranged over some 2,025 square miles, the population would be 1 person to 17 or 22.5 square miles.

Winter encampments frequently shifted, especially with respect to good pine-nut crops. They were usually at springs at 6,500 to 7,000 feet but might, if pine nuts were plentiful, be higher in the mountains where snow was used for water.

42. Hot Creek, about 10 miles north of Tybo, had two families, one headed by Hot Creek John, Kawüsi, the other by Brigham. Total, about 10 persons (AC). For festivals, they went to Duckwater, in Railroad Valley, or Biabahuna, in Little Smoky Valley, and later went with people from Stone Cabin to Belmont; for antelope hunts they probably occasionally joined Tybo and Kawich; for rabbit drives they joined Little Smoky Valley people, under Morey Jack.

43. Tybo Creek (from taivo, white man); native name, Kunugiba (kunugip, elderberry+pa). Three or four families under a chief named Kunugipajugo. These people got pine nuts near Rocky Peak, to the west, in the southern part of the Hot Creek Range, in the Kawich Range, and sometimes in the Reveille Range, but never as far away as the Quinn Canyon Mountains to the east. The maximum length of these trips was about 25 miles. They usually joined Kawich Mountain people for antelope and rabbit drives, some of which were held in southern Hot Creek Valley, others near the Kawich Mountains. They either had local festivals with Kawich Mountain people participating or went to the Kawich Mountains.

44. Hot Springs, to the south, had several winter encampments.

The Kawich Mountains, called Piadoya (big mountain), had several scattered camps at the various springs. These totaled nine or more, and included that of the chief of this region. These were:

45. Breen Creek, 6,800 feet, 3 families, totaling 15 persons known to JS. These were: Kawatc (Kawich), the chief, whose first wife was unknown, and one son; second wife from Tybo, one daughter; third wife a Southern Paiute, two sons, two daughters; total, eight. Second, Kawatc's sister, her husband from Tybo or vicinity, two daughters. Third, Kawatc's second sister, her husband, a Shoshoni from somewhere east, and one daughter. (JS.)

46. Longstreet Canyon or Horse Canyon, 7,000 feet, Hugwapagwa (hugwa, cane+pagwa, mouth of canyon). Three families; total 23 persons. Family heads were three brothers. One, the oldest and so-called chief, his wife from a local camp, four sons, one daughter. The next brother, wife from Hugwapagwa, seven sons, one daughter. The third brother, LJB's father, his wife from the Montezuma Mountains, two sons, two daughters. (JS.)

47. Reveille Mill probably had several persons. (JS.)

48. Rose Spring, Tüava (probably tuambi, service berry+pa, water). Two families. (LJB.)

Of 6 marriages recorded here, 5 were with persons from regions other than the Kawich Mountains. Three of these were patrilocal, 2 matrilocal. The sixth marriage followed only village exogamy and was patrilocal.

Subsistence activities.—Pine nuts were gathered by Kawich Mountain people in the local mountains. When they were scarce, the chief directed each family where to gather; when abundant, each family gathered where it liked. When there was no local crop they went to the Monitor Range east of Belmont, 25 to 50 miles distant, and even to the Silver Peak Mountains near Lida, 75 miles distant. (LJB.)

Other seeds were gathered in the vicinity of winter villages in the Kawich Mountains. Also, Antelope Spring in the Cactus Mountains was base camp for gathering seeds of bunch grass, *Mentzelia*, yuvikui (*Chylismia* ?), and tiüga (unidentified) during May and June. Belted Range and even Lida people sometimes went to the Cactus Mountains. No one wintered there because there were no pine nuts.

In November, after pine-nut harvests, all Kawich Mountain people assembled, usually in Cactus Flat, to drive rabbits for several days or even a month. Each morning the director, LJB's father's oldest brother who was the chief's, Kawatc's, cousin, announced plans for the day's hunt and told people where to go. Sometimes Kawich Mountain people visited Whiterock Spring in the Belted Range to drive rabbits under the direction of the local chief. (LJB.)

Communal antelope drives directed by a shaman were held in the spring. Participants are not known, though some Belted Range people took part.

Festivals.—These were held during pine-nut harvest and therefore wherever the crop was good, for example at different villages in the Kawich Mountains. Sometimes they were held at Tybo. Recently, at least, people joined forces with Indians at Belmont, Tom being director of these enlarged festivals and Kawatc also rising to prominence. Kawich people did not participate in Belted Range festivals. (LJB.)

Political organization.—For the greater part of the year, the nine or more individual families of the Kawich Mountains were independent. Had they cooperated exclusively with one another in communal hunts and festivals they would have formed something of a band. Actually, though they usually assembled for these activities, some families were likely to join peoples to the north or south. Also outside people frequently came to the Kawich Mountains.

There seems to have been a kind of village chief where the cluster of camps was large enough to warrant giving the leader of the several generally related families this title. The chief of the general area, at least in post-Caucasian times, was Kawatc. He directed festivals, pine-nut trips when nuts were scarce and when all the families traveled together, and possibly rabbit drives. A shaman directed antelope hunts. Kawatc's influence was later extended, when, after the mining boom in 1865, Belmont acquired a large community of Shoshoni who held festivals of some magnitude.

LITTLE SMOKY VALLEY AND VICINITY

Information about this valley is mostly from BH; a little is from his brother, PH. They formerly lived near Morey, an old stage station on the road between Warm Springs and Eureka. As the activities of the residents of Little Smoky Valley were extremely interlinked with those of neighboring valleys, it is necessary to include the latter in some matters.

The dialect spoken in Little Smoky Valley seems to have been shared by people with whom its occupants were in most frequent contact. BH said it was the same in Hot Creek Valley, around Tybo, in Willow Creek, Fish Creek, and Little Smoky Valleys. It was slightly different at Belmont, Duckwater, Antelope Valley, Eureka, and in the Kawich Mountains. This would suggest that people of Hot Creek and the Kawich Mountains were not in as close contact as information from informants to the south had indicated. But as the language changed in a gradual, progressive manner and not through distinct, well-bounded dialets, present data from language sheds little light on alinement of social groups.

This valley had no local name for itself but was called by Railroad Valley people Yuwinai (yuwin, south+nai, dwellers).

Its geography is essentially like that of the regions to the south and west, just described.

Villages and camps.—The following were recalled by BH from his boyhood, about 1880. Locations were necessarily approximate because of want of a suitable base map. The total population for the 9 villages and camps of Little Smoky Valley and Fish Creek Valley was about 14 families, or 96 persons. The subsistence area was about 1,700 square miles. This gives about 1 person to 17.5 square miles.

Numbers of camps correspond with those on map, figure 8.

49. Moore Station, Dzicava (dzica, dried juniper+pa, water), 4 miles north of Morey. One family: BH's paternal grandfather, his 3 wives, 3 children by one, 4 by the second, 3 by the third; total, 14.

50. Tutoya (tu, black+toya, mountain), a spring 4 or 5 miles south of Morey on the western side of the valley. Possibly 2 families. Morey Jack's father, mother, 4 brothers, 1 sister; total, 8. Possibly also BH's father-in-law's family.

51. Hick's Station, Sap:ava (sap:a, scum+ba, water), 12 miles north of Morey. One family: BH's father's sister's relatives, about 7 persons.

52. Snowball, 8 miles farther north, Kwadumba (kwadu, antelope+ba, water, i. e., antelope come for water), 4 or 5 persons.

53. Indian Creek, 6 or 7 miles north of last, Ba gumbuc (?). One family.

54. Fish Creek. One family: Kwatsugu, (i. e., Fish Creek Charley's father), the antelope shaman, his wife, three sons, including Fish Creek Charley; total, five.

Sigi Canyon, near Eureka, Basōba'; about 8 or 10 miles north of Fish Creek. One family of 8 or 10 persons.

North of this lies Eureka with a different dialect. BH gave the following census for Fish Springs Valley, west of Little Smoky Valley.

55. Woŋgodoya (woŋgovi, white pine+toyabi, mountain), a spring in the hills west of Fish Springs, where there is now a sheep ranch. Probably several families, totaling some 30 persons.

42. Hot Creek, Üdüifa (üdüind, hot+pa, water), two or three families.

56. Butler's place, about 20 miles north of Woŋgodoya in the same valley where there are 2 or 3 springs. Perhaps 10 people.

Some people lived at Twin Springs, to the south, affiliated with Tybo for festivals and spoke like Kawich Mountain people.

Powell and Ingalls' incomplete census in 1873 gave 24 Indians under To-po-go-om'-bi in the vicinity of Morey and 62 under Wau-go-vwi in the vicinity of Fish Lake (1874, p. 12).

Subsistence activities.—For pine nuts, Little Smoky Valley families went into the Antelope Range to the west and northwest of Sap:ava, usually to the same place each year. If the crop were poor and if people from other valleys had come here, they arranged with the local residents that each family should harvest in some specified place. If a number of families were camped together at a favored locality the chief announced each morning where each was to pick. People from the vicinity of Eureka sometimes came to these mountains or went to the White Pine Range east of Railroad Valley. The Pancake Range was too low and arid to have many pinyon trees, though Little Smoky Valley people sometimes went there where they met Duckwater families.

Fish Springs Valley residents gathered pine nuts in the Monitor Range, Suŋgadoya (suŋgavi, cottonwood+toyabi, mountain), which was too far for Little Smoky Valley families. Hot Creek people went to Six Mile, probably in the Hot Creek Range.

Little Smoky Valley families procured most other seeds at various places in their own valley. When they had a surplus of *Mentzelia* and *Chenopodium* seeds they sometimes sowed them near their villages.

Groupings for communal rabbit and antelope drives alined the Little Smoky Valley and Fish Springs populations in various ways.

For rabbit drives the villagers of the northern part of Little Smoky Valley joined Fish Springs, perhaps driving in the latter valley. The villages near Fish Creek, however, sometimes went to Diamond Valley, north of Eureka. Villages near Morey and in southern Little Smoky Valley went south to Hot Creek Valley, joining forces with local people to drive under the Morey chief, Morey Jack. Meanwhile, residents near Tybo, not far to the southwest, drove with families from Twin Springs to the southeast, from Willow Creek to the northwest, and sometimes even from the Kawich Mountains to the south.

All Little Smoky Valley people assembled near Snowball under Kwatsugu' (kwəp, corral+tsugu', old man), the shaman, to build a corral and drive antelope and sometimes deer. As Kwatsugu' seems to have been the only antelope and deer shaman in a large area Fish Springs people participated in these Little Smoky Valley hunts, though they sometimes held their own nonshamanistic deer hunts in the Antelope Mountains under a local director. Pine Creek Valley and Diamond Valley, both north of Eureka, had also to call upon Kwatsugu' for antelope drives (see p. 142). That he should have served so large an area is doubtless due to the fortuitous fact that no one to the north had received a vision for antelope charming. Dukwatsugu' (not to be confused with Kwatsugu'), living at Potts. shamanized for communal antelope and deer drives in Monitor and Antelope Valleys to the west and northwest. Tybo people probably also had local antelope drives under their own shaman. Eureka people often went to Railroad Valley.

Some communal and probably shamanistic deer drives, with fences, hurdle, and a concealed pit, were held by Fish Creek people in the Monitor Range.

Big game hunting was carried on by individual hunters in accessible mountains. Meat was distributed freely to one's neighbors, though it was not obligatory.

Festivals.—Little Smoky Valley festivals were held at pine-nut time and sometimes in spring and midsummer.

Festivals brought population alinements somewhat different than those for other activities. Little Smoky Valley people assembled under Morey Jack's brother, who lived at Tutoya, and Dosamasidu' (dosavitü, white+masidu', fingernail), BH's paternal grandfather who lived at Dzicava near Morey. The Fish Creek village, however, held festivals at home or went north to Eureka, where one of their own chiefs, Fish Creek Charlie, was a talker. For Eureka two local festival directors were named: Buffalo Jim and Bitjüt, the latter also managing pine-nut trips.

Antelope Valley, to the northwest, had its own festival under Bai- yana. Fish Springs either danced locally or went south to Tybo, though Tybo people sometimes went to the Kawich Mountains. Hot Springs undoubtedly also participated in Tybo festivals, though the people often went to near Morey and even to Duckwater. Later, peo- ple from this general southern region went either to Belmont or Hot Creek, where post-Caucasian conditions had made large festivals possible.

There were other independent festivals in Railroad and White Pine Valleys and at Ely.

Warfare.—BH recalled only one fight. Ute, armed with guns, came to Little Smoky Valley and captured women and children. The Sho- shoni seized their guns and drove the invaders out. There was no organization, regalia, or method for warfare.

Marriage.—Marriage was forbidden between all blood relatives, in- cluding cross-cousins, and between pseudo parallel-cousins, i. e., with the stepchild of the mother's sister or father's brother. The preferred mate was the pseudo cross-cousin, i. e., the stepchild of the mother's brother or father's sister. There was no rule of local exogamy, though some people got spouses from a considerable distance. For example, BH's paternal grandfather was from near Morey, his paternal grand- mother from the Kawich Mountains; his father also from Morey, his mother from Willow Creek.

In normal marriages the parents of the couple concerned first agreed upon the union. Then the boy's parents gave presents of food and the boy gave perhaps half a deer to the girl's parents. The boy's parents then took him to the girl's house, where, after about 2 weeks, he slept with her and was thus married. For a month or two he remained, hunting for her family, then took her to an independent residence. There was a strong preference that permanent residence should be patrilocal, as evidence whereof BH cited Black Eye's son, who married a girl from Sharp but returned to live with his father in Duckwater. Occasional visits were made, however, to the wife's family.

Polygyny was probably not uncommon and was preferably sororal. BH's grandfather had three wives.

Polyandrous relations were an intensification of the levirate with an extension of sex privileges to the brother rather than true polyandrous marriage. One brother actually married the woman and was considered father of her children. The other brother lived in the same house and the woman cooked for both. But the second had sex privileges only when the first was away and with consent of the wife. He anticipated marriage to another woman at some future time. In a case observed by BH in Little Smoky Valley, the husband was the older brother.

When two brothers each had wives they did not grant each other sex privileges. There was no wife lending to visitors.

The levirate and sororate, junior and senior, were so strong as to be mandatory. In following them, a man did not have to make further presents to the woman's family.

When a girl's family would not consent to marriage a man might recruit his friends and try to abduct her. BH thought the fights sometimes involved shooting and killing. Similarly, a man sometimes attempted, with the aid of his friends, to abduct a married woman. PH boasted that his grandfather traveled widely, seducing men's wives and, if necessary, killing the men.

RAILROAD VALLEY

This valley is more than 100 miles long, extending from the region of Hamilton (S–Hmlt) in the north to the latitude of the Kawich Mountains in the south. It is bounded on the east by the high White Pine, Grant, and Quinn Canyon Ranges, which afforded seeds, pine nuts, and many sources of water for village sites. Parts of these ranges even extend upward to the white-pine belt, with summits above the timberline. The Pancake Range on the west, which is topographically a mesa rather than mountain formation, is lower and has few pine nuts. The valley floor is broad, level, sage-covered, and favored only a few seeds. It had, however, some antelope and jack rabbits.

Villages.[12]—The population of the northern part of the valley, excluding Curran Creek, was, using JW's and AC's estimate of Duckwater, 70 persons, or 1 per 13.5 square miles. Using BH's estimate of Duckwater, it was 89 persons, or 1 per 9 square miles. The entire valley from Hamilton to a little south of Nyala was approximately 2,250 square miles. Assuming that each family at Curran Creek, Warm Springs, Blue Eagle, and Nyala had an average of 6 persons, and adding the population of these villages to those in the north, the valley total was 250 persons, or approximately 1 per 9 square miles.

---

[12] Powell and Ingalls (1874, p. 12) state that there were 101 persons in the vicinity of Hamilton under Chief Que-ta'-pat-so.

Camps in the northern end of the valley listed by JW are numbered to correspond with map, figure 8.

57. Bambasa (ba, water+basedaiəp, dry, i. e., it dries up in summer), on the west side of Mount Hamilton, Kaidandaya (kaidan, peak+toyavi, mountain). Two families. One, JW's father, her mother who was abducted from the Kawich Mountains, two sisters, five brothers, and JW. JW's father had been born here and raised by his grandmother. The other, JW's father's brother, his wife, two sons, and probably one daughter. Total, 15.

58. Akamba (akü, sunflower+ba) or, probably also, Watoya (wa:vi, wild rye seed+toyavi, mountain), a spring west of Mount Hamilton, probably on the eastern slope of the Pancake Range. Two families. One, A: taŋgisugo (a: taŋgi, grasshopper+tsugupu', old man) and his wife. The other, Nokosugo (noko, roast), two wives, two daughters, one son. Total, eight. These people remained here throughout most of the year.

59. Duckwater, Sühuva (sühuvi, red top grass), BH; Wandabamuts (wanda, hooked willow pine-nut pole+bamuts, a pool, creek, or pond), JW; Payagombi (paya, water?+gombi, flat). People called Tsaidüka (tsaip, tule+düka, eat), BH. JW and AC remembered 4 families, perhaps 24 persons. BH thought 50 persons. Powell and Ingalls (1874, p 12) give 60 persons under Chief Mo-tso'-gaunt. A locality with many seeds and a center for rabbit drives and festivals.

60. Woŋgodupijugo (probably, woŋgovi, "white pine"+tupi, flint+?), a place southeast of Green Spring frequented by two families.

Some villages in the central and southern part of the Railroad Valley were given by AC. Though the total number of families may be nearly correct, it is probable that they were more scattered at the various springs than her information indicated.

61. Currant Creek, Bawãzivi (ba, water+wãzi, end+vi, long), AC; Icagooəp: festival chiefs, Kwitavui (kwita, stink bug+bui, eye) and Ba:kəp (ice) lived here.

62. Warm Spring, Baüdüiŋ (üdüiŋ hot). Seven families. Village chief, who managed pine-nut trips, was Dughoviadzugu.

63. Biadoyava (biəp, big+toyavi+pa), at Blue Eagle Springs. Seven families. Village chief was a shaman. These people participated in western antelope hunts.

64. Nyala, native name unknown (a spring near Nyala was called Hugapə, from hugap:, cane). Ten families. Village chief, Hunatsi (huna, badger+tsi, diminutive or personal ending). These people picked pine nuts in the Quinn Canyon mountains, Biadoya.

Subsistence activities: seed gathering.—JW's relatives, two families, wintered together at Bambasa near Hamilton, but, if pine nuts had been plentiful, they remained in the mountains, using snow for water. In the spring they set out for seeds, traveling at night in warm weather and carrying water in basketry ollas. Though local hills supplied most seeds, they sometimes went as far as Duckwater, especially if they wished to attend the 5-day festival held in May. About the same time there might be an antelope hunt nearer home. These families remained alone, near home most of the summer, caching seeds for the next winter, though occasionally they went to Duckwater for a midsummer festival.

In the fall they usually went to Duckwater for the festival and rabbit drive. After this they set out alone to gather pine nuts, going usually to the White Pine Mountains near Bambasa or to the northeast of Curran Creek, possibly near White Pine Peak, Tumbaiwia (tumbi, rock + wia, summit), some 25 or 30 miles from home. If crops in the White Pine Mountains were poor longer trips were made.

Families of other villages procured pine nuts from the nearest mountains, traveling together under their village chief.

In the fall men burned brush and in the spring sowed üəp: (*Chenopodium*) and perhaps wu꞉sia and other seeds. There was probably no native horticulture in this area.

Areas of wild seeds were not owned, though it is almost certain that sowed plots were protected against trespass. Outsiders, however, might be given permission to gather seeds on these plots. In fact, they might be given seeds if they were in need. But gathered seeds were strictly family property. Each of the two families of Bambasa gathered for itself, though they traveled together. They shared their seeds, however, when necessary.

Duckwater was a fertile locality, the stream flowing some 8 or 10 miles and today supporting a dozen or more ranches. In native times people came from other villages to gather seeds in June. Seeds included: sunflowers, redtop grass, nəp꞉, wüsia, and pamambi. JW thought that even before getting horses they came afoot from Morey, Tybo, and Belmont when the crop was good. Residents of Duckwater had little need to travel far from home except for pine nuts and rabbit drives. BH said they sometimes went to Stoney, about 10 miles from Locke, for sand bunch grass seeds, or to a little south of Duckwater or to "Sand Spring Valley," 7 or 8 miles west, for other seeds—all short trips.

All the villagers traveled to the Pancake Mountains for pine nuts. The village chief directed the travel and talked each morning, telling people where to gather.

Subsistence activities: communal hunts.—These were principally antelope and rabbit hunts.

Duckwater people drove rabbits about 15 miles south of Duckwater in the valley flat near Biadoya. The director (known as wuhwutoi or wàmuwutci dăgwani) was Biadewatsi (biand꞉, big + dewatsi, talk), an old man living at Duckwater, who announced hunt plans each morning. Twenty or thirty men had nets; the remaining men drove the rabbits to them. Hunts might last 6 weeks, though they did not drive every day. They were called kamu dükaya (kamu, jack rabbit + dükaya, eat).

Villages participating with Duckwater were Curran Creek, Warm Springs, Hamilton, and the other villages in the northern part of the valley near Duckwater, and perhaps sometimes even Nyala and Hot Creek. But Hot Creek, according to BH, had local drives under Morey Jack, and Eureka sometimes drove with near neighbors under Captain John.

Antelope hunts were held in the spring in a low pass in the northern end of Railroad Valley between Akamba and Mount Hamilton. The shaman in charge was Duŋgwajugu'ᵘ (BH) or TꞮ ŋgwainjugo (tuŋ, fat+gwai, summit+jugo, old man; tuŋgwai, a mountain southwest of Hamilton in the Pancake Range) or Tuŋgwaibuagənt (buagənt, shaman) (JW, HJ), who was also a deer charmer, medicine man, and talker at festivals. He died about 1900 at Wells, Nevada. AC named Ombatsuga at Hamilton as antelope shaman. It is not certain what relation he bore to Tuŋgwainjugo. People built a corral, kwadunzkəp (kwadunzi, antelope+kəp, fence). Tuŋgwainjugo shamanized five nights, charming the antelope which were driven into the corral by two or three men. Bowmen around the corral shot the animals, which were then skinned, butchered, and the meat dried. The hearts, which were taboo to young people, were placed in a pile for old people. Meat was divided equally, not even the shaman receiving an extra share.

Villages participating under Tuŋgwainjugo were those of the northern part of the valley, Curran Creek, and Warm Springs. Neither the southern part of Railroad Valley nor Hot Creek seems to have had an antelope shaman, so that they either did not take antelope communally or joined people from Tybo or the Kawich Mountains.

Festivals.—The main festivals were held at Duckwater, under Haidüka (hai, crow+düka, eat; so called because as a little boy he ate crows), living at Duckwater, Tuŋgwainjugo helped talk. Festivals were held in March, April, or May, when plants began to grow, in midsummer when seeds had ripened, and in the fall.

In native or early post-Caucasian days participants included villages north to Hamilton, Curran Creek, Warm Springs, and sometimes Nyala, and even Hot Creek. Nyala, however, sometimes went to a place nearby with Blue Eagle people under Másoniba or to Little Smoky Valley. After the introduction of horses and improved transportation Duckwater festivals drew people from Deep Creek (Gosiute Shoshoni), Belmont, Eureka, and places equally distant. Even Kawich, chief in the Kawich Mountains, sometimes attended and talked. In recent years, when festivals were discontinued in other localities, they were still held at Duckwater. Festivals are no longer held, but the present "chief" is Black-eye.

Political organization.—Unity in Railroad Valley centered in a core of villages—Bambasa, Akamba, Duckwater, Woŋgodupijugo,

Curran Creek, and Warm Springs—which usually participated in hunts and festivals at or near Duckwater, the largest village, under Duckwater chiefs. But circumstances of annual seed occurrence might take people of one or more of these to distant places. Unity diminished in proportion as villages were remote from Duckwater. Thus allegiance of Biadoyava and Nyala was divided. Sometimes they seem to have held a local festival under Màsoniba (mà, hand + soniba, rub), sometimes they joined Duckwater, and sometimes they joined Hot Creek or Little Smoky Valley, each of which was another nucleus of cohesion for neighboring villages.

Marriage.—Little information was obtained on marriage except that it was accomplished in the two ways characteristic of central and northern Nevada: (1) By the orthodox exchange of presents between the families concerned; (2) by the abduction of a married or unmarried girl.

Fraternal polyandry was sometimes practiced; HJ's grandmother at Hamilton had two husbands. Sororal polygyny was also preferred; Black-eye had three wives who were sisters. The levirate and sororate were also strong.

There is no information about cross-cousin or pseudo cross-cousin marriage.

STEPTOE VALLEY

Steptoe Valley was called Bahanai by Railroad Valley people (AC).

This valley is arid, though the Egan Range on the west and the Shell Creek Range on the east were high enough to afford many pine nuts and other seeds and to give rise to numerous springs and two streams, Steptoe Creek and Duck Creek, which flowed some distance into the valley. The valley lies at nearly 6,000 feet near Ely.

A complete list of the villages could not be obtained. There were, however, villages at Ely, on Duck Creek, about 8 miles northwest of McGill, and at Warm Springs, Schellbourne, Egan Canyon, and Cherry Creek. That at Ely was probably largest. These villages were interlinked like those in neighboring valleys.

Information about Steptoe Valley comes largely from Ely. Egan Canyon is discussed separately (pp. 146–147).

Subsistence activities.—Ely people gathered pine nuts at various places in the Egan Mountains, near Ely, and also across the valley in the Shell Creek Range. North of Cherry Creek the mountains are low and the region so arid that few pinyon trees grow.

Pine nuts were gathered by independent families. In good years a sufficient quantity to last 2 years might be obtained. In this case the nuts were roasted so that they would preserve better, then buried, preferably in a cold place in the high mountains. Egan remarked

(p. 242) that Indians gathering pine nuts in the Shell Creek Range cached them "all through the pine-nut grove to save carrying them too far and save time, for the harvest does not last long, for a heavy frost will cause the cones to open and the nuts to drop to the ground, where squirrels and coyotes feast on them."

There was no ownership of pine-nut areas among Shoshoni, though it was known that Southern Paiute owned or at least competed for pine-nut grounds.

Other seeds, especially sand bunch grass, were formerly abundant on the mountains south of Ely, but have been largely destroyed by sheep.

AR's grandfather told her that, just prior to the arrival of the white man, horticulture had been introduced from tribes to the south (undoubtedly Southern Paiute). Plants grown were variegated corn, a large blue pumpkin called padagada, and large white beans. The last were no doubt lima beans, procured from the white man. AR thought that only two families had practiced horticulture.

Steptoe Valley people did not sow wild seeds.

Rabbit drives were held about November, after the pine-nut harvest, and continued during December and January. These were at various places in the valley, each locality having a hunt director (who was probably a different man from the festival director). Probably, as in Spring Valley and Snake Valley, participants were members of only one or a few villages.

Antelope were driven communally under a shaman. Ely people went to Spring Valley near Cleveland for drives. But there were also independent drives under different shamans in southern Steptoe Valley, in northern Steptoe Valley around Cherry Creek, at the village at Indian Spring near Shoshone in southern Spring Valley, and in White River Valley.

The antelope hunt involved a corral called kwaduŋgwəp (kwahadu, antelope+gwəp, fence), antelope disguises, and one night of singing by the shaman.

Deer were also driven communally into a corral with a shamanistic performance like that for antelope, but it was not clear whether the same man or different men charmed both antelope and deer.

Festivals.—Festivals, involving the round dance, back-and-forth dance, "war dance" or paminukəp, and considerable gambling, were held, usually after pine-nut harvest, at various localities, depending partly upon abundance of seeds. People, after dancing at home, often went elsewhere to dance again; there was frequent reciprocation in this manner.

In early post-Caucasian times dances with local leaders might be held on Duck Creek in Steptoe Valley under Duck Creek Charley, at

Ely, at Cherry Creek, at Cleveland, where Gosiute sometimes attended, at Baker, where Indian Sam was director, and in White River Valley. If dances were held at so many places in post-Caucasian times an aboriginal separatism is certainly indicated.

Perhaps 60 years ago, when the population had been reduced through warfare and transportation had been improved, festivals were directed by Duck Creek Charley wherever held and seem to have drawn people from a wider area. It is impossible, however, to define the limits of the people participating under this single director.

Chieftainship.—Few names of chiefs could be obtained, but festivals, rabbit hunts, and antelope hunts apparently had different directors. Probably there was a dance and hunt director for every two or three villages.

Marriage.—At Ely both true and pseudo cross-cousin marriage were encountered.

Marriage of several brothers to several sisters, though not group marriage, and of a brother and sister to a sister and brother, were favored. Polygyny was preferably sororal. The sororate was preferred but not required.

Polyandry was fraternal with two brothers, never three. It was unknown with other than brothers. Paternity of children was not known and seems to have made no difference under polyandry. AR heard also of a case of polyandry among Southern Paiute at Panaca, Nevada, in which two brothers were married to one woman. One brother slept in a wagon, having access to the wife only when the other was away.

In orthodox marriage a man served his prospective bride's parents for 2 or 3 years prior to marriage, during which time they ascertained his hunting ability. The parents were at liberty to reject him if he did not acquit himself well. Postmarital residence varied, being determined by individual choice.

Wives were also acquired by abduction. Aided by his friends, a man attempted to make off with a woman, fighting her husband or family if necessary. Such fights only involved fists.

SPRING, SNAKE, AND ANTELOPE VALLEYS

The population of these valleys was Shoshoni. But in Lake Valley and in the extreme southern portions of Spring and Snake Valleys it was mixed with Southern Paiute. In Snake Valley and in the vicinity of Sevier Lake in Utah it was also somewhat mixed with Ute. Gosiute, who were indistinguishable, culturally and linguistically, from Shoshoni lived in the region bordering the Great Salt Lake Desert. Spring Valley people have sometimes been called Gosiute.

Spring and Snake Valleys are particularly favored environmentally by the presence of lofty ranges. The Shell Creek Range, which separates Steptoe from Spring Valley, rises above the pinyon belt and has numerous springs and streams which permitted many villages on its eastern slope. The Snake Range (pl. 3, *a*) is even higher, Wheeler Peak rising to 13,058 feet, and several other peaks towering above timber line. The greatest run-off of moisture is on the eastern slope, where, in the vicinity of Baker, Nevada, and Garrison, Utah, several villages were concentrated.

Villages.—The following population estimate of the villages is that which JR believed to be native, though he was a young man in 1885. It is probably representative for Spring and Antelope Valleys but incomplete for Snake Valley. Even these data, however, show an unusually dense population which was naturally concentrated near the high mountain masses where precipitation was greatest and streams most numerous. In the total subsistence area of these three valleys, which was about 4,400 square miles, there were about 100 families, or 1 person to 7.3 square miles. Omitting Snake Valley, there were about 456 persons in 3,310 square miles, or 1 person to 7.2 square miles. Antelope Valley, which is much more arid, had about 900 square miles and 78 persons, or 1 per 11 square miles, while the more fertile Spring and Snake Valleys had about 378 persons in 2,410 square miles, or 1 to 6.3 square miles. The density for the last would probably be greater if all the villages for Snake Valley were known. Powell and Ingalls (1874, p. 12) said there were 60 persons in Spring Valley and the Robinson district.

Many of these villages were sufficiently large to give point to the existence of a village chief, though, in some instances, several smaller villages were under the same chief. Families were independent during most of the year. In cooperative enterprises, villages were the maximum stable unit.

The following numbers correspond with those on the map (fig. 9). Some of the locations are only approximate. A bracket on the map indicates villages under the same chief.

Spring Valley:

1. Tupa (black water), about 7 miles north of Anderson's ranch. Two families; about 15 people.
2. Supuva, at Anderson's ranch. Three camps; about 20 people.

The chief of these two villages was Sitümp, living at Tupa. These villagers most often went to Antelope Valley, where they joined local residents and Deep Creek people in antelope drives and occasionally in festivals; sometimes, however, they went south to Cleveland in Spring Valley. Wherever they went, Puyunzugo (puyu, duck+zugu, old man) was the "talker and organizer" who assisted

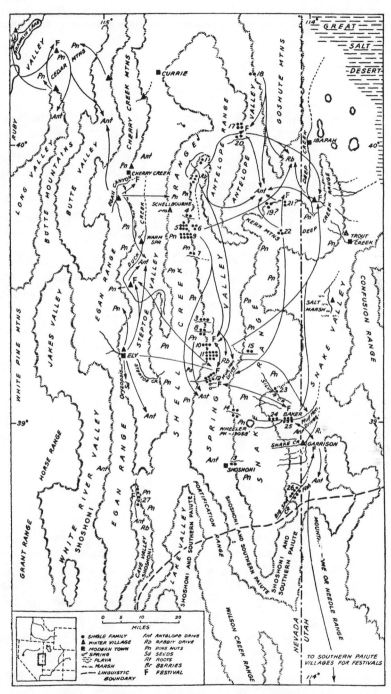

FIGURE 9.—Villages and subsistence areas of eastern Nevada.

the shaman in antelope drives. (Puyunzugo, however, JR later gave as chief of village 10, below.) These two villages usually held their own rabbit drives locally.

3. Woŋgovitwüninogwaṗ: (woŋgovi, "white pine"+wünin, log+ogwaṗ:, creek), on Valley Creek, at Yellen's (?) ranch, about 10 miles north of Cleveland. Probably about three families. Nüaidu (wind), living at (8), below, was chief for this village.

4. Basawinuba, location uncertain; either 3 or 4 miles northwest of Aurun at a spring about 1 mile north of village 5, or near Anderson's ranch. About two families.

5. Aidumba (aidu, murky+pa, water), at a spring west of Aurun. About seven families. Some doubt about chief. He was either Ovitc, Mugin (who directed pine-nut trips), or Kwati who seems later to have gone to Deep Creek). Possibly all three men served at once or at different times.

6. Sogowosugu (sogoṗ:, earth+wosugu, "bridge", i. e., a bridge over some creek), at Aurun. Either 3 or 4 families; about 20 persons. Chief was Bauwi (a plant ?), known as Bob.

The people inhabiting villages 4 to 6 allied themselves either with the Antelope Valley people or with Cleveland people for festivals and antelope hunts. Thus Sogowosugu people went north to Pǎŋwiowǝp or south to near Cleveland for dances.

7. Basawinuba (basawinu, mud), Mud Springs, about 7 miles south of Aurum. About 2 families here.

8. Haiva (hai, crow, so called because crows had nests in the rocks here), about 6 miles north of Cleveland, or two canyons south of village 3. Four families. Village chief called Nüaidu (wind).

Nüaidu announced pine-nut time and directed pine-nut gathering, when all four families went and camped together. Haiva people attended festivals at Cleveland ranch, where Nüaidu was one of the talkers. Sometimes they visited festivals at Baker. For antelope drives and rabbit drives they affiliated with Cleveland people.

9. Basamba (basa, dry, i. e., dry in summer because of small local winter snowfall), slightly up the hill west of village 6, above. About 8 camps here, or some 35 people.

The village chief, who served mainly as pine-nut director, was Sigodagitci (sigo, sego lily+dagitci, ?). Sigodagitci aided in leading antelope drives wherever the Basamba people went, but was not an antelope shaman. They held rabbit drives in brushy country near Suhuva, in Antelope Valley, where Sigodagitci may have been director.

10. Tuhuva (tuhu, black+pa, water), between Yellen's and Cleveland ranches. About three families. Village chief, Puyunzugu (but see villages 1 and 2, above).

11. Biabauwundü (biandu, big+pa, water+wundü, down canyon), at Cleveland ranch; the largest and most important village in the valley. About 11 families. The chiefs in order of importance were: (1) Bohoa, also called One-Eye, (2) Kuviji (short or stocky+man ?), also known as Biabauwundü

Pete, (3) Duuyumbo'° (duuyu, deer+bo'°, ?), (4) Nəpia (white man's money), (5) Tünamp: (mountain mahogany), (6) Takavi (snow).

These men talked and directed such communal activities as pine-nut trips, festivals, and communal hunts, and had authority more or less in the order listed. In addition, there was a special messenger, appointed by the chief, who invited people of other villages to co-operative enterprises. After the deaths of the other chiefs, Kuviji or Biabauwundü Pete continued as chief. He was disliked because he scolded the people every morning, but was tolerated as he was the only remaining chief.

Dances were directed by Bohoa, Kuviji, and Duyumbo'°. Buda (arm) Jim also had a part in these. Dances were held in the spring at Biabauwundü and sometimes at Basonip:, village 12, below.

Antelope hunts were directed by Tünamp:, an antelope shaman, aided by Nəpia and Takavi, who were probably not shamans. Antelope drives were held in March with a corral about 1 mile west of Basonip:, the spring festival often occurring at the same time.

Rabbit drives, held in late fall and winter, were directed by Kajugo (Ka, ?+jugo, old man).

Mud-hen drives, which were held in Spring Valley only near Biabauwundü, as no place else had sufficient water, were directed by Jambazugo. People from other Spring Valley villages were invited to participate. Sometimes Spring Valley people communally hunted a few mud hens at Baker and Garrison in Snake Valley.

12. Basonip: (ba, water+sonip:, grass), a creek with a village site near the present highway, about 7 miles (?) south of Cleveland ranch. About seven families; all were killed by the white soldiers.

The village chief was Yuhudumbi (yuhu, "soapy"+dumbi, rock), also called "White," director of pine-nut trips and festivals when held locally. In lieu of local festivals, Basonip: people sometimes went to Deep Creek or Steptoe Valley to visit (and no doubt also to Biabaunwundü).

Rabbit drives were held locally under Kinumbe, Yuhudumbi's brother.

13. Bauumba (bauu, clear+ba, water). A village near Shoshone. Probably two families. The chief may have been Ziwitci. Festival and hunting affiliations are doubtful.

In spite of the enormous height of the Snake Mountains, the greater part of its drainage runs off the eastern slope into Snake Valley, where it supported several large communities. There was sufficient water to support only three villages on the western or Spring Valley slope (pl. 3, a).

14. Basiamba (named from mountain back of Oceola, Basiandoya), village in vicinity of Oceola, a present-day mining town. About four families. Village chief, Yagatcu'. Many local seeds.

15. Toziüp:, site on the western slope of Mount Moriah, Dadia'. Two families; one that of Muvigund (muvi, nose ?+gund, tall) and his four sons; the other, that of Muvigund's half-brother, Konogund or Charlie. No chief.

16. Taiwudu, somewhere on the western slope of the Snake Mountains.

Pine nuts were habitually gathered by the above villages in localities most accessible to them or where the crop was good. There were no property rights of any kind in pinyon groves. All families of a village traveled together to the mountains and camped together, under the direction of the village chief. In the morning the chief told each family where to gather. A family gathered only for itself and cached the nuts secretly if possible.

JR thought some horticulture had been practiced prior to the arrival of the white man, plants grown being maize, called korn, and wheat. Each family had its own garden. Men dug shallow trenches with a digging stick into which women dropped bunches of seeds at intervals and covered them with earth. JR thought all people in Snake Valley and Spring Valley had irrigated, HJ claiming the same for Ely. Farmed plots were inherited by a man's wife or children.

Hunting was carried on anywhere, there being no ownership of hunting territories. Antelope hunts were communal, under shamans who sang 5 nights. Forty or fifty men and women helped corral the animals. Deer were not shamanized. Collective hunts, in which deer were driven over cliffs, were infrequent. Mountain sheep were hunted by individual men. Buffalo disappeared when JR's grandfather was a young man. Hunting methods used for them were not known.

The occupants of Antelope Valley were called Gosiute by some informants, Shoshoni by others. As they cooperated and intermarried with the neighboring Deep Creek Gosiute, whose language and culture differs in no way from Shoshoni, it makes no difference what they are called.

In "Fish Creek Valley" [Antelope Valley] Beckwith in May 1854 saw 20 mounted Shoshoni who had blankets and buffalo robes and appeared more prosperous than the Gosiute to the east (1855a, p. 25).

Seeds were procured by Antelope Valley people in and around the valley and pine nuts from the Gosiute Range.

Though the villages of this valley generally cooperated with one another in communal enterprises, they were linked with neighboring valleys, especially Deep Creek. Thus Deep Creek contributed the antelope shamans, Go:sitci and Taibc (white man), who directed the communal antelope drives at Äsiŋgwoi in the northern foothills of the Kern Mountains, and Kwatüip, who directed the communal rabbit drives west of Ibapah in Deep Creek Valley. People from Spring and Snake Valleys sometimes attended these. But Bohoba (village 22) often cooperated with Spring and Snake Valley people.

Antelope Valley villages held festivals at Wadoya (village 18) or, more often, went to Păŋwiowəp: at or near Deep Creek. Magunt (moccasin) living at Deep Creek, assisted by Dabanai (chipmunk) and Antelope Jack, living at Toiva (village 17), directed Deep Creek festivals. Antelope Jack had succeeded his father, Kutanzip (kutan, firewood+sip, exploding), in this task.

It is apparent that the Antelope Valley people had frequent association with the Deep Creek Shoshoni or Gosiute, though this may have come about in part after the arrival of the white man and establishment of the Deep Creek Reservation which drew Indians from neighboring valleys.

For all of Antelope Valley, Antelope Jack was the main chief and Dabanai was second chief. They directed such activities as pine-nut trips and dances. Often they officiated at Deep Creek functions.

The villages in Antelope Valley were:

17. Toiva (probably toip, cattail+pa, water), a spring at the northern end of the valley. Three or four families; about 18 to 24 people. Chief, especially director of pine-nut trips, named Winjugo (wi, knife+jugo, old man).

18. Wadoya (named from the Antelope Mountains, wadoya), a spring, 15 miles north of the last, east of Dolly Varden. Two families.

19. Kwadumba (antelope water), a spring about 3 miles south of Tippetts. Three families, the heads of them being brothers.

20. Hugapa (hugapi, cane+pa, water), Chinn Creek. There was abundant water here, much cane, and many rabbits. About two families.

21. Suhuva (suhuvi, willow+pa, water), a spring near (east of ?) Kwadumba. Two unrelated families.

22. Bohoba (bohovi, sagebrush+pa, water), Mike Springs, south of the villages in Antelope Valley. Three families. These people went to Suhuva for festivals, to Kwadumba for antelope drives, where Bo: stici and Taibo were shamans, and to Cleveland, in Spring Valley, for rabbit drives.

Villages in Snake Valley were:

23. Tosakowaip: (tosa, white+kowaip, ground), Silver Creek. Two families; one, that of Tuhuzu' (tuhu, black+zugo, old man), the other, that of Tuhuzu''s brother, Tuwuk:.

24. Tuŋkahniva (tuŋkahni, cave), a cave near Lehman Cave in the canyon west of Baker. Three families, one of each of three brothers. Chief: oldest of the brothers, Tuŋkahnijugo.

Rabbit hunts were held near Garrison in Snake Valley by people of Tuŋkahniva and other neighboring sites and were directed by Tuŋgwip. Antelope drives were held against the foothills between Baker and Garrison and were directed by Wiyunjugo, who lived on the other side of Garrison.

25. **Bauwunoida** (water zigzagging, i. e., probably meandering, in a flat). At present Baker. Six families. The chief for festivals was Tsuguputsi (old man), who was Sam's father.

Festivals were sometimes held locally; sometimes the people went to Spring Valley, Garrison, or Deep Creek. Biaba people attend local festivals. Antelope drives were held at a corral between Garrison and Baker, with Budazugo (buda, arm) of Biaba as shaman and director. Wiyunzugo also performed as shaman. Sometimes they drove antelope at Big Spring (below) or at Indian Spring. Dances were held in conjunction with these drives, which were in the spring. Fish drives, held only here in Snake Valley, were under Bahu.

26. **Biaba** (biaund, big+pa, water), Big Spring. Seven camps. Chiefs were, first, a one-arm man named Budazugo, the antelope shaman, and, second, Á: wihi (yellow), the pine-nut and festival director.

Although these villages were predominantly Shoshoni and seem to have cooperated most often with residents of village 25 in communal activities, some persons spoke or could speak Paiute. Also, Budazugo shamanized for Paiute antelope drives to the south and southwest. Biaba people often joined Paiute for festivals.

Villages south of Biaba were Southern Paiute, the borderline settlements having the usual admixture produced by intermarriage. Relationships between Paiute and Shoshoni were entirely amicable.

Wheeler (1875, p. 11), in 1869 encountered some 200 "Snake Indians" in Snake Valley, "who are in the habit of occupying the valley in planting and harvesting season, raising scanty crops, which they cache for the winter use, and then retire to the mountains." He states their chief to be Blackhawk, but (p. 36) gives Blackhawk as chief of the Pahvants (pp. 224–230).

The Indians between Snake and Meadow Valley, Wheeler (1875, p. 27) states to be mixed "Snakes, or Utes proper, and Pah-Utes." See also reference to Jarvis (p. 132).

Warfare.—In aboriginal times warfare was evidently too infrequent and unimportant to have produced organization and leadership, though war implements, especially the shield, were first encountered in this group. JR knew only of a minor, probably post-Caucasian, fight between Shoshoni and Ute (?), which occurred somewhere west of Deseret in the Sevier Desert, Utah. It was provoked by Ute theft of horses. Konustü, a Shoshoni (Gosiute) living at Salt Marsh, just northeast of Snake Valley, was leader of the Shoshoni.

Marriage.—Preferred marriage was between pseudo cross-cousins, who called each other hainz. True cross-cousins, who called each other niwa, and pseudo parallel-cousins, who called each other "brother" and "sister," could not marry. As elsewhere, there was also strong preference for several brothers and sisters to marry sisters and brothers. The levirate and sororate were strong if not obligatory.

Polygyny was sororal if possible. But Tüimb, a Shoshoni at Deep Creek, had a Ute and a Paiute wife at the same time. "Mother" was not extended to mother's sisters. But a man's plural wives, whether sisters or not, were called doka, mother's sister, by his children. Plural wives called one another's children duep: (boy) or bĕdup: (girl).

Polyandry was usually fraternal, though this was the first locality where it was asserted that plural husbands might be cousins as well as brothers and that there might be as many as three husbands. If so, this was something more than the extension of sex privileges to a brother, which is the essential feature of polyandry elsewhere. All these spouses lived and slept together and the husbands seemed to be of equal status. There was no interest in determining biological paternity. Although "father" was not extended to father's brother unless he was involved in polyandry, all of the mother's husbands were called "father."

Postmarital residence was not ascertained by marriage data, though there is no question that village exogamy was necessary only where all village members happened to be related. In two villages all the families were those of several brothers. Residence was actually determined by the various factors of food supply and individual preference.

CAVE VALLEY [18]

Inhabitants of this small valley, south of Steptoe Valley, occupied one main village near the cave (village 27, fig. 9). Both the village and the people were called Daint. In JR's youth 5 families totaled only 17 persons. This would give 1 person per 17 square miles for the valley, which may well be less than the aboriginal figure.

Some unity and separatism of these people was expressed in local rabbit drives, antelope drives, and festivals. The general headman was Jimku, father of Bigitci. The antelope shaman was Evidadawunu (spotted) or Pinto (because of red and white marks over his body).

Pine nuts were gathered from the Ely Mountains, Nogadu (sits), around Mount Grafton, Pasindoya (pasi, quartz+doyavi, mountain), and as far south as Willow Creek, northwest of Pioche, in Southern Paiute territory. JR thought Cave Valley Shoshoni and Southern Paiute permitted each other access to pine-nut lands. They frequently intermarried and carried on no warfare.

---

[18] Legends are recorded (Wheeler, 1875, p. 60, and Egan) that this cave leads to another world where superior and well-dressed people lived.

GOSIUTE SHOSHONI

There has been much confusion about the identity and location of the Gosiute.

Beckwith (1855a, p. 21), traveling west from the Wasatch Mountains in 1854, entered their territory in Tooele Valley.

Forney (1858, p. 212) said that the "Go-sha-Utes" lived about 40 miles west of Salt Lake City. They were impoverished, living on snakes, lizards, roots, etc. Forney also said (1859, pp. 363–364) that they spoke Shoshoni and were predominantly Shoshoni with a few Ute intermarried.

Jarvis (1859, p. 378) mentioned a band of "Gosha-Utes" 50 miles south of Pleasant Valley, 150 miles west of Fillmore, which is probably near Baker, Nev. They numbered about 100 and had 2 chiefs, Ta-goo-pie and Wan-na-vah.

Simpson (1876, pp. 35–36, 54), quoting his guide, stated that their language is a combination of Shoshoni and Ute, that under Chief Gosip they had split off from the Ute two generations earlier, and that they occupied the country south of Great Salt Lake as far west as Steptoe Valley. Chamberlin (1909, pp. 27–28), however, stated that Gosip was not a Gosiute chief and that the name Gosiute was taken not from Gosip but from ku'tsĭp or gu'tsĭp, ashes or dry earth+Ute.

Hatch (1862, p. 207) said that "Goshee Utes" were under White Horse and lived between Simpson Springs and Egan Canyon, being concentrated at Deep Creek and Shell Creek stations on the stage road. In midwinter they were in a deplorable condition, not one-half having blankets or shirts. There was but one "wickiup" among them, most families using shelters of sagebrush or boughs [probably windbreaks].

Burton (1862, p. 475) said the "Gosh Yuta or Gosha Ute" have the "Shoshonee language" and (p. 467) that Egan Canyon was their western limit.

Doty (1864, p. 175) mentioned 200 "Goships" in the southern portion of the region south of Great Salt Lake, where they were mixed with "Pahvontees" [Pahvant Ute]. They were poor and miserable and lacked guns and horses. He also mentioned (p. 173) "Shoshonee bands" of the "Goship tribe" who were also called "Kumumbar."

Irish (1865, p. 144) said there were 800 "Goships or Gosha Utes," who talked "nearly the Shoshonee language," under "Tabby (the Sun)," and several subchiefs. They were poor and lacked guns and horses.

Head (1866, pp. 122–123) said the "Goships or Gosha-Utes" numbered 1,000.

Tourtellotte (1869, p. 231) said there were 800 "Goships."

Douglas (1870, p. 96) said there were 895 Gosiute in the vicinity of Egan Canyon and that their language was entirely different from Shoshoni.

Powell and Ingalls (1874, pp. 2, 11, 17–18) stated that the Gosiute numbered 460. "They inhabit a district of country west of Utah Lake and Great Salt Lake, on the line between Utah and Nevada, a part being in the Territory and a part in the State." They "speak a language much more nearly allied to the Northwestern Shoshones than the Utes, though the greater number of them affiliate with the Utes, and are intermarried with them." In 1872 they were "scattered in very small bands, cultivating the soil about little springs here and there . . ." They list 5 "tribes": Un'-ka-gar-its in Skull Valley, numbering 149 under Si'-pu-rus; Pi-er'-ru-i-ats in Deep Creek under Tu-gu'-vi; Pa-ga'-yu-ats in Otter Creek under Pi-av'-um-pi-a; Tu-wur-ints in Snake Creek Valley under Tat'-si-nup; the last three groups totaling 107 persons; the To-ro-un-to-go-ats in Egan Canyon under To-go-mun-tso, numbering 204. The whole "alliance" of Gosiute was under Pi-an'nump. The total of these population estimates, omitting Egan Canyon, which I have treated separate from Gosiute Shoshoni, is 256, or about 1 person to 39 square miles.

Egan, observing the Gosiute subsequent to 1850, stated (1917, p. 166) that "Go-Shute" country was "from Salt Lake Valley on the east, to Granite Rock [Granite Mountain ?] on the desert on the west, and from Simpson's Springs on the south to Great Salt Lake on the north."

Wheeler, calling these people "Gosiats," "Goshi-utes," or "Goshoots" (1879, p. 410) stated (1875, p. 36) that "they differ in no material way from the Shoshones, the language being similar, and habits and disposition the same, always having lived at peace with each other." He defined their territory as extending from Sevier Lake Desert west to the mountains bordering Spring, Steptoe, Sierra, and Gosiute Valleys and south to latitude 38°. The last is certainly too far south.

The Handbook of the American Indian (vol. 1, pp. 496–497) indicated the close affinity of the Gosiute with Shoshoni but leaves doubt about their exact identity.

Kroeber (1909, p. 267) suggested their similarity to the Shoshoni. He recorded their name as Kucyut.

Gottfredson (1919, p. 6) described the Gosiute as a band living in Cedar, Tintic, and Skull Valleys under Chief Tintic, a "renegade chief." But Armstrong (1855, p. 206) had stated that Tintick was a Ute chief at Utah Lake.

Nevada Shoshoni, especially those some distance to the west, believed the Gosiute to be a distinct group, but were unable to bound them accurately. BG at Elko thought that, at least since the Indian wars, Gosiute had lived in Steptoe Valley in the vicinity of McGill, at Cherry Creek, and in Duck Valley. BM from Egan Canyon placed them in Gosiute, Independence, Spring, and Snake Valleys. JR of Spring Valley was at a loss whether to call people of his vicinity Gosiute or Shoshoni.

This confusion was dispelled when it became apparent that Gosiute are Shoshoni and that informants' opinions merely reflect attitudes toward the impoverished inhabitants of the Great Salt Lake Desert. Linguistically, as the vocabularies (pp. 278–279) show, the Gosiute are wholly Shoshoni, having dialectic distinctiveness no greater than that which exists in Shoshoni localities throughout Nevada. Culturally, as the element list survey showed, the Gosiute were essentially like their Nevada neighbors. In spite of the comparative isolation of many of their small camps there is no reason to regard them as fundamentally different from other Shoshoni. They intermarried somewhat with Ute to the east, but intertribal marriage is a common phenomenon where two groups are in proximity; it made Gosiute no less Shoshoni.

For these reasons the name Gosiute (gosip:, dust, referring to the dust storms over the salt deserts + Ute) is misleading. How they came by the name Ute is not known. It is similar to the use of

Weber Ute for Shoshoni in the vicinity of the present Salt Lake City.

The Gosiute habitat is one of the least favorable in the entire Shoshoni area. Lying between the fertile piedmont of the Wasatch to the east and the relatively high terrane of central Nevada to the west, it is an area of true desert and semidesert. It is within the drainage basin of Great Salt Lake (4,200 feet) and occupies a great part of the area once covered by Lake Bonneville. The Great Salt Lake Desert consists of a level plain of alkali and pure salt, 20 to 40 miles broad, more than 100 miles long, and perfectly level, which supports no vegetation and has no fresh water. It was uninhabited and could be crossed only with great difficulty. Most neighboring valleys are also low (rarely above 4,500 feet) and arid. Few mountain ranges have sufficient altitude to intercept moisture in important quantities.

The only fertile areas are Deep Creek Valley and Trout Creek, which lie on the western and eastern sides of the lofty Deep Creek Range, and a few localities with small springs and streams in the Oquirrh and Cedar Mountains which bound Tooele and Skull Valleys. The remainder of the area had only a few widely separated sources of water.

The population was probably sparser than in any other part of the Shoshonean area of the same size. Exact population data are not available. Early estimates (Irish, Head, Tourtellotte, et al.) probably included more persons than are herein designated Gosiute. Simpson (1876, pp. 35–36) estimated it to be 200 to 300 persons and Wheeler (1875, p. 36) 400 persons, though the territory included was not stated. It is probable that, including the Great Salt Lake Desert, there was not over one person to 30 or 40 square miles. In the vicinity of the Deep Creek Range, of course, the population was much denser and probably compared favorably with the more fertile localities in Nevada.

Gosiute culture and subsistence was fundamentally like that of other Shoshoni but their environment is so exceptionally unproductive that their poverty was extreme. Contrasted with their more favorably situated and horse-owning Ute neighbors, their condition was deplored by early travelers.

Russell, observing them between 1834 and 1843, described them (p. 122) as "depraved and hostile savages who poisoned their arrows." Simpson (p. 35) said they were "very low and dirty, eating rabbits, rats, lizards, snakes, insects, rushes, grass seeds, roots, etc." Somewhat similar comments, however, were made about other Western Shoshoni. Bryant (p. 168) described Tooele Valley Indians, 1846, as "naked, and the most emaciated and wretched human objects I had ever seen," and probably Skull Valley Indians as "miserable Digger Indians calling themselves Soshonees. They were naked, with the exception of a few filthy ragged skins, fastened about their loins. They brought with them a mixture composed of parched sunflower seeds and grasshoppers." Beckwith (1855a, p. 24) described those near the Goshoot Mountains in 1854 as "extremely filthy and very naked, and emaciated by starvation during the long winter, during which their supply of rats and bugs fail, and they are reduced to the greatest extreme of want. . . ."

When the Mormons arrived in Utah in 1847 the Gosiute seem to have had a few horses, which had probably been acquired from Spanish sources or perhaps from the Ute. A traveler in 1854 noted that Indians between Salt Lake City and the Ruby Mountains had some guns, horses, and clothes (Aveson). But it is improbable that enough families owned horses to have greatly affected the ecology of the whole population.

There are occasional reports in the Great Basin that extreme want impelled families to leave their aged and hopelessly infirm to perish.

Egan (pp. 251–252) recounts the abandonment of an old man at Fish Spring, about 30 miles east of Deep Creek. Totally blind, deaf, and emaciated, he was put in a semicircular sagebrush windbreak near a spring, given a small rabbit skin robe, and left to perish. He had been subsisting miserably on a few small fish that he could seize in the springs. The white man's efforts to provide for him were apparently thwarted by his relatives, for he soon disappeared and probably died.

Though my information about Gosiute society is wanting in many details, there is little doubt that the Gosiute ecology was fundamentally like that of Nevada Shoshoni.

Groups and villages.—There is evidence that there were several somewhat distinct local subdivisions of the Gosiute and that the members of each associated together more frequently than with members of the other subdivisions. These, however, were not based upon any real sense of band solidarity but upon expediency. When they possessed few or no horses the occupants of each small locality where there were foods and water found it easier to associate with immediate neighbors for dances, antelope drives, and other activities, than to cross the great deserts. But even these local communal affairs were insufficient to weld the population into true bands.

Tooele Valley inhabitants are little known. M thought they were mixed Weber Ute (Shoshoni, pp. 219–222) and Gosiute who lived near the present town of Tooele under Weber Tom (probably in post-Caucasian times).

Rush Valley, adjoining Tooele Valley on the south, was probably also Gosiute. Lander (1860, pp. 28–29) speaks of this valley as the headquarters of "Mormon Snakes" under Pay-e-ah, who, now possessing horses, raided immigrant trains. They were also called Southern Snakes or Salt Lake Snakes under Jag-e-ah ("the man who carries arrows") in Lander (1860, pp. 28–29).

Although Utah Lake was held by true Ute, Cedar Valley, lying between Utah Lake and Rush Valley, was, with Tintic Valley, according to Gottfredson (p. 6), occupied by Gosiute. Whether these be called Weber Ute or Gosiute probably matters little, for there was no cultural or linguistic distinction between them. Because of intermarriage and relative independence of native villages nomenclature for inhabitants of these regions is largely arbitrary.

The greater number of Gosiute villages named by M lay in Skull Valley and Sink Valley. Deserts prohibited occupation of the

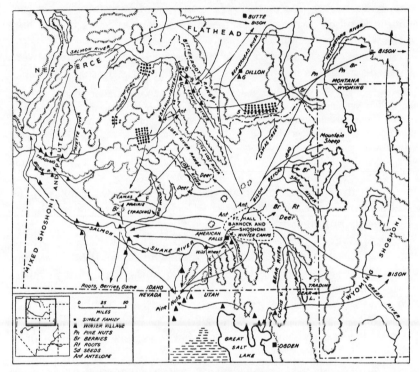

FIGURE 10.—Villages and subsistence areas of Idaho.

country to the west, northwest, and south, and Great Salt Lake lay to the north. The known villages of Skull and Sink Valleys, which are indicated by number on map, figure 12, are:

11. Tutiwunupa, on the western slope of the Cedar Mountains, just east of Clive.

12. Utcipa, somewhere to the south of the last on the western slope of the Cedar Mountains.

13. Tozava, at a spring on the western side of the Lakeside Range.

14. A cave on the northern end of the Skull Valley Mountains, a short distance from the present highway. This and several other caves in Skull Valley were visited by the writer, but they yielded little evidence of occupation and nothing distinctive of Shoshoni except a single muller.

15. Haiyacawiyəp (haiya, pass+?), near the present town called Iosepa.

16. Iowiba, in the mountains just east of the present Skull Valley Reservation.

17. Tiava, on the present reservation where there is a fairly ample creek.

18. Suhudaosa, at the present Orr's Ranch. This was the site of dances for all these villages.

19. Oŋgwove, a few miles south of Orr's Ranch (?).

20. Wanapo'ogwaipi (wana, string?+po'o, pole?+ogwaipi, stream) at Indian Springs, south of the last.

Between this region and the Sevier Desert to the south and between the House Mountains and the Utah-Nevada boundary lie vast deserts with little water. They probably had a sparse population living at isolated springs. M and JPi thought they were Gosiute who had mixed somewhat with the Ute of the Sevier Lake and the Sevier River regions.

The people living around Trout Creek, village 21, on the eastern slope of the Deep Creek Mountains were also called Gosiute. Trout Creek Valley, though small, is relatively fertile. Isolated by the lofty Deep Creek Mountains on the west and by deserts in other directions, the inhabitants apparently had slight unity. The local chief, according to FBo, was Editawump. Egan (p. 252) mentions the vicinity of Fish Springs, just northeast of Trout Creek, as the habitat of a group of Indians. At Pleasant Valley, in this territory, Jarvis held an election by 73 warriors in 1859 and had an old man, "Arra-won-nets," made chief and "Ka Vana" made subchief (p. 377).

Deep Creek Valley, 22, site of the present Deep Creek Indian Reservation, also was a comparatively fertile oasis supporting a number of camps. The chief here, according to FBo, was Unu', who was also hunt chief. JR named a Deep Creek Village Păngwiowəp. In 1859 Forney reported (p. 363) that about 60 Gosiute had settled down to farm in Deep Creek Valley.

There may also have been other Gosiute with some independence and chiefs.

Subsistence activities.—A thorough study of Gosiute ethnobotany has been made by Chamberlin (1911). His list of edible plants is more complete than my own and includes the important species which were also utilized in Nevada. Seeds were gathered by independent families. Though exact location of different species was not ascertained, they were in general limited to moister areas, namely mountains, stream borders, and swamps; valley plants were rarely edible. As water is particularly scant and the deserts unusually wide, this meant that families ranged limited areas in comparative isolation.

Pine nuts, of great importance here, were procured by Skull Valley people from near Murker, south of Tooele, or from near Deep Creek. If the Deep Creek crop were good, families might remain in the mountains during the winter. Deep Creek people, however, had to

go no great distance, getting them from the Deep Creek Mountains
at the southern end of their valley and carrying them home. Any
surplus could be cached, for the distance from the winter villages
was not excessive.

There was no ownership of seed or pine-nut areas, even Ute being
permitted to gather in Gosiute country. When a group of Gosiute
went into the mountains for pine nuts they merely agreed that each
family would pick from a certain area.

Wild seeds of tui (unidentified, possibly *Urtica*) were sowed in
the spring where brush had been burned off in the fall by Deep
Creek but not by Skull Valley Gosiute. There was no native horticulture of domesticated plants.

Minor deer surrounds were held. At Deep Creek they were directed
by Unu', the valley chief.

All Gosiute probably held shamanistic antelope drives. Deep
Creek people held them usually in Antelope Valley, about 20 miles to
the northwest, under two of their own shamans, Bo: sitci and Taibo
(white man). An excellent account of one of these drives related by
Egan has been quoted above (pp. 34–36). The Skull Valley shaman
was Tcub, who usually directed drives somewhere west of the Cedar
Mountains or just south of Delle. Some Gosiute, according to Chamberlin (1911, p. 27), even traveled to Mill Creek Canyon in the
Wasatch Mountains, about 30 miles east of Skull Valley, where they
drove deer and antelope down the narrow canyon.

Rabbit drives were held in the fall. In Skull Valley they were
minor affairs and did little to unite families of different camps.
One net, perhaps 20 feet long, was placed across a trail and three
of four men drove rabbits to it. In Deep Creek Valley drives were
held along the flats at any time during the winter. All people in
the valley participated. Egan's account of these drives has been
quoted (pp. 38–39). Chamberlin (1911, p. 28) has described great
drives involving the whole "tribe" (probably principally Deep
Creek) and even neighboring peoples and employing an unusual
method. Rabbits were driven through V-wings of sagebrush into
an underground passage where they were killed.

The importance of rodents was considerable in this region. Egan
(p. 237) describes taking them with deadfall traps. He met an
Indian whose "plan was to go up one side of the canyon, setting
the traps wherever he saw the sign of rats, and the same down the
other side. The next day, taking the same route, gathering the catch
and resetting the traps. The rats . . . were 6 to 8 inches long . . ."
The extent of operations is indicated by the fact that though this
man had set most of his traps, he had over 100 triggers he had not
used. Egan (pp. 245–246) also saw 8 or 10 women at Creek Hollow

diverting water by means of little ditches into gopher holes. In part of a day some of them acquired up to half a bushel, with several days of work ahead. One woman got 25 to 30 within half an hour. These rodents were skinned, eviscerated, and dried without removing the bones. Beckwith remarked (1855a, p. 22) that a small "ground-rat or gopher and a black beetlelike cricket" furnished a large portion of Gosiute food.

There was no ownership of hunting areas.

Festivals.—Festivals were held independently at Skull Valley, Deep Creek, and perhaps elsewhere under different directors. In Skull Valley the director was Tave (sun); in Deep Creek, probably Unu'. Festivals were held by members of several neighboring villages, principally in the spring. They performed the round dance to make seeds grow. If, however, many people were assembled in some area of abundant seeds during the summer, and especially when gathering pine nuts in the fall, they might also hold dances. The chief of the nearest villages served as director. When such dances were to be held the chief sent out messengers to invite people to attend. The main festivals lasted 5 days.

Chieftainship.—The Great Salt Lake Desert area is too large for unmounted Gosiute to have cooperated with one another to any important extent. Simpson (p. 54) recorded that there was no chief among them until the United States Government demanded it and that even then "they do not know how to respect him."

Present data, however, indicate that people of limited and isolated portions of the desert usually cooperated under a certain chief who directed hunts (except antelope drives, which required shamans) and festivals.

Chiefs recorded were:

Deep Creek, Unu' (FBo). Wheeler (1875, p. 36) gives the Deep Creek chief in 1869 as Big Horse.

Trout Creek, Editawump (FBo).

Skull Valley, Weber Tom, living in the vicinity of Tooele in Tooele Valley (M). OD, probably referring to the period of the wars with the whites, said that Tave (sun), living in Skull Valley, and Siplus, a "Weber Ute," living in Tooele Valley, were chiefs for all the people from Skull Valley to Ruby Valley. This Tave is probably the Taby We-pup who lived in Tooele Valley a few miles from Grantsville, according to Egan (1917, p. 166) and who, in early Mormon pioneer days, contrived numerous cattle thefts.

In 1860 Davies (1861, p. 131) attempted to organize the scattered "bands of Goshu-Utes," which were then under Green Jacket, Teekutup, Jack, Tabby, Wonibijinnu, and others, under Ads-Sin as head chief.

Powell and Ingalls (1874, p. 7) named Pi-an-nump, brother of Kanosh, the Pah-vant Ute chief, as chief of all Gosiute. The extent of his power, if accurately recorded, may be the result of the wars. Other Gosiute chiefs listed by Powell and Ingalls are given above.

Warfare.—Though the Gosiute carried on depredations against the white man, especially along the stage road which passed through their country, they were not aboriginally inclined to war. Probably their only fights in pre-Caucasian days had been with the Pahvant Ute (called Pavandüti, FBo), who raided them from time to time. Such raids were continued in post-Caucasian times, at least one motive for them being acquisition of "slaves." But raids must have been generally unprofitable, because Gosiute were too scattered and could readily escape into the deserts and mountains. When forced to fight, Gosiute did so without organization, special regalia, or ritual.

Simpson (1876, p. 54), describing the Gosiute soon after the arrival of the Mormons, said that they lived some distance from water for fear of capture and that they carried water in ollas.

Marriage.—Some indication of the status of Gosiute women is indicated by M's assertion that Gosiute sold girls and even wives for horses. Most women, however, ran away from their purchasers and returned home.

Marriage was preferably either with a true or a pseudo cross-cousin. Skull Valley preferred that a man marry his father's sister's daughter but prohibited his marrying his mother's brother's daughter. If this information is correct, the reason is not clear, except that here, as elsewhere, the father's relatives seemed somewhat closer to the children. A man's sister would ask his son to marry her daughter. Deep Creek permitted marriage with either cross-cousin. Parallel-cousins, real and pseudo, were prohibited from marriage.

There was no bride price or present exchange.

I have no census data on postmarital residence. In both valleys it was said to be matrilocal for about a year as a kind of bride service, and thereafter depended upon circumstances.

Polygyny was commonly but not necessarily sororal. The sororate was preferred but not required.

Polyandry was permitted at Skull Valley but only one instance was recorded. One of two half-brothers was married to a woman, but all three lived in the same house. They did not sleep in the same bed, but one slept with her when the other was away. Sex privileges were sometimes extended to a brother, though it was not customary. Some men became angry and would not tolerate it.

Men wishing wives sometimes abducted married or unmarried women, their friends assisting them. There were no general fights; instead, pairs of champions from opposing camps kicked each other

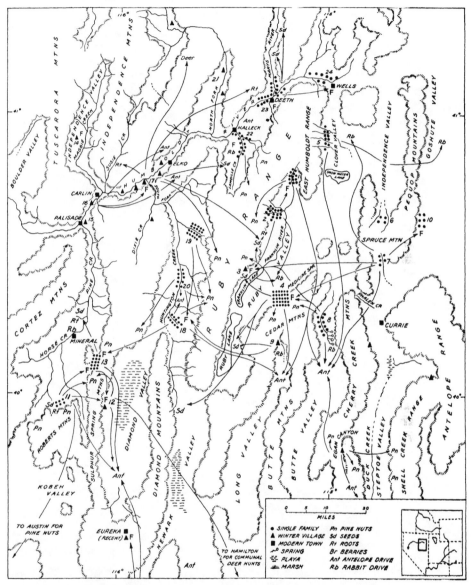

FIGURE 11.—Villages and subsistence areas of the upper Humboldt River region.

(there is a Shoshoni game of kicking) and wrestled. The bouts continued until all the men of one side had been bested.

An account by Egan (pp. 252–253) gives some idea of the ruthlessness involved in wife-getting, though it is more drastic than informants' accounts.

A young Fish Springs man, Indian Bill, sought a girl "who lived in the Shell Creek country with her father, there being no more of the family or relatives left. The father had lost one eye. He was getting old and feeble, so the young girl had a hard time of it gathering enough food for both. There had been many a young buck that wanted her for a wife, but the old man had driven them off . . . Indian Bill made . . . that camp his home and helped out the food supply with game. This went on a month or more. The old man still said no one should take the girl from him. But Bill soon solved the problem . . . " One afternoon he loaded his gun. "The girl was busy shelling nuts, the old man sound asleep on the sunny side of the camp, with his face towards Bill, who aimed his gun at the old man's good eye and fired. The ball passed through the eye and the brain, too, killing the old man instantly.

"The marriage ceremony was completely over. Bill coolly reloaded his gun, turned to the girl and said, 'Come,' and the girl picked up her blanket and followed her lord and master . . . All they owned on earth they had on, or carried in their hands."

There were no parent-in-law avoidances, though a man was required to show respect to his mother-in-law. Brothers-in-law, who were often cousins, were close friends and maintained a relationship in which they aided and joked with each other, especially about sex.

PINE CREEK AND DIAMOND VALLEY

These valleys are in the midst of an area about which I have little information. They are not unusually fertile, except around the Roberts Mountains, which have great altitude.

The total area was about 1,550 square miles. If SF's guess that the native population was 400 persons is correct there was 1 person to about 3.8 square miles. This seems excessive, however.

As usual, villages were somewhat clustered where the mountains were highest and consequently water and foods most abundant.

Villages.—Some of the winter villages, as numbered on figure 11, were:

11. Bauwiyoi, a group of at least six encampments at the foot of the Roberts Mountains where there are four sloughs.

12. Tupagadü, west of the alkali flat in Diamond Valley. The spring and fall festivals were held here with Wovigünt as director.

13. To:dzagadü (to: dzap, a medicinal plant+kadü, sitting), on the western side of the Sulphur Spring Mountains. Fifteen or sixteen families (perhaps 90 individuals), scattered along the mountain side at springs a few miles apart. Chiefs were, in order of importance: (1) Kuwaigunt, festival chief (called nukadägwani, dance chief, or kwinidägwani, mush chief) and rabbit drive director. Kuwaigunt decided upon the time and place of festivals, *sent out*

invitations, directed activities, and talked.   (2) Papadom, also called Buffalo Jim, a talker at dances and communal hunts.   He had been preceded in this by his father.   (3) Kandugəp (wood rat smell, a nickname given because a wood rat once ate his blankets and other property) or Pipotsi (his untranslatable real name), one of SF's polyandrous fathers who announced pine-nut time and talked at festivals and antelope hunts.

Powell and Ingalls list 60 persons at Mineral Hill under Chief Tú-ka-yan-na (1874, p. 12).

Subsistence activities.—These are outlined largely from the point of view of the To:dzagadü people.

Most pine nuts occur mainly on the western sides of ranges, especially on the Sulphur Springs and Roberts Mountains. A few grow on the Cortez Range. SF thought most of the people of these two valleys forgathered on the Sulphur Springs Range, traveling and camping in large groups. Papadom, Kuwaigunt, and other chiefs talked each morning, telling the different families where to gather.

There was no band, village, or family ownership of pine-nut lands. Outsiders were welcome and even encouraged to come when the crop was good. When local crops failed Diamond Valley and Pine Creek people went as far south as Austin to gather pine nuts and to participate in festivals.

When local pine nuts were harvested as many as possible were transported to the winter camps, the remainder being moved on subsequent journeys.

Spring often found people weakened by insufficient stored foods and many died. When the first plants began to ripen two to four families foraged together, going from place to place until fall. In one of the tributaries of Pine Creek, probably to the west or southwest of Mineral, called Pabomba (pabom, clean+pa, water), they took small fish about 4 inches long. Similar fish could be had at Tupagadü. They went north of Mineral to gather yomba, tsowiga, and other roots, then perhaps west to near Cortez or Tinaba (tina, a white rock+pa, water) to gather roots and seeds, or to kill woodchucks, chipmunks, and other smaller mammals. Roots not consumed at once were sun-dried and cached in pits.

Prior to the fall pine-nut trip people assembled in the southern end of Diamond Valley, south of the alkali flat, to drive antelope into a corral (tuzikwəp). As there was no local shaman, Kwatsuga was invited to come up from Little Smoky Valley and probably was paid for his services. The four local chiefs listed below helped direct these hunts. Three preliminary nights of shamanistic singing preceded 1 day of driving.

Deer were sometimes hunted communally but this was done near Hamilton in northern Railroad Valley, when deer were migrating.

Brush wings converged to a hurdle built on a deer trail. Pine Creek and Diamond Valley people did not hunt deer communally.

Each fall, following pine-nut trips, people remained together to hunt rabbits west of To:dzagadü near the present town of Blackburn. Papadom was the director but other talkers assisted him.

Fesivals.—Festivals were usually held before the pine-nut trip. At To:dzagadü, Kuwaigunt, assisted by Papadom, Kandugəp, and Wovigunt, was director. If held at Tupagadü, Wovigunt was in charge.

Chiefs.—The ranking of chiefs among the combined Pine Creek and Diamond Valley people was probably based largely on personal prestige. It was: (1) Kuwaigunt, living at To:dzagadü, main director for festivals and perhaps for rabbit drives; (2) Papadom, also at To:dzagadü, possibly the main rabbit-hunt director, but assistant in antelope hunts and dances; (3) Wobigunt, local chief at Tupadagü but third chief for the entire group; he talked at festivals and announced the ripening of pine nuts and the location of good crops; he also announced to Tupadagü people the ripening of other seeds and prayed to Icavaip (coyote), "father of the people," for good crops; (4) Kandugəp, talker at various communal enterprises.

Chief's succession was not strongly hereditary. The son or cousin of a chief often, though not necessarily, succeeded him. A new chief needed group sanction, which was procured at big meetings where people talked in his favor.

Marriage.—Blood relatives, with the possible exception of real cross-cousins, were ineligible for marriage. Though some features of kinship terms accord with cross-cousin marriage, it is not known whether real or pseudo cross-cousin marriage was practiced. There was no local exogamy or rule of postmarital residence.

In orthodox marriage a man gave presents to his prospective mother-in-law, who reciprocated with presents to his own parents.

Polygyny, which was usually though not necessarily sororal, was contracted by a good hunter who was able to support plural wives or by a man who was desired by women.

Polyandry was always fraternal and was restricted to two brothers. The younger brother did not anticipate future marriage with other women. Ordinarily one brother remained with the wife while the other hunted. When both were home together all occupied the same house and slept in the same bed. They did not quarrel. But SF seemed convinced that both brothers were rarely home at once. Children call both men father, üpü'ü. If one were called father's brother, hai', it would indicate a relationship which would prevent his sleeping with his brother's wife.

SF's mother had two husbands, one being Kandugəp. SF thinks Kandugəp was his biological father, but could not explain why. Perhaps SF likes to believe that his real father was the chief. HJ's grandmother, living at Hamilton, also had two husbands.

Marriage was also accomplished by abducting a girl or a married woman, aided by one's friends, and fighting only with the fists.

RUBY VALLEY AND VICINITY

Compared with the territory of eastern Nevada, Ruby Valley is exceptionally fertile. Long, Butte, Independence, and Goshute Valleys to the east are so barren and arid that they supported only a sparse and scattered population which lived in small encampments at the few springs and streams. Ruby Valley, however, is flanked on the west by the massive and lofty Ruby Range, Takadoya (takavi, snow+mountain) or Biadoya (biap:, big), the great peaks of which extend into the aspen and spruce belt. Though slightly north of the optimum pinyon environment, the western slopes of the range have many pine nuts. The lofty summits sheltered numerous mountain sheep. Many streams running down into Ruby Valley water extensive areas of wild seeds and create two large lakes which attracted water fowl.

Ruby Valley had an exceptionally dense population which served as the focal point for communal affairs of a considerable area. Though the census data are incomplete, the northern two-thirds of the valley for which population estimates are available had about 420 persons in 1,200 square miles, or 1 person to 2.8 square miles. This omits the inhabitants of one village, who were not known but who, if included, would give a denser population. The comparatively fertile Huntington Valley to the west had about 1 person to 3.5 square miles and the Humboldt River to the north about 1 to 5.2 square miles. Simpson (p. 64) estimated that there were 1,500 Indians in Ruby Valley in 1859. If correct, this was certainly a temporary massing of the population from a considerable area during the war, for it would be more than one person per square mile, which is unbelievably dense for native times. Wasson saw 100 persons under Chief Buck, who had succeeded Chief Sho-kab, in 1862 (p. 219) or Sho-kub (Davies, 1861, p. 138). The series of more arid valleys east of Ruby Valley had about 180 persons in 2,000 square miles, or 1 person to 11 square miles.

The people of Ruby Valley were called Wadadüka (wada, rye grass seed+düka, eat). Kroeber (1909, p. 267) recorded this as Warü-dika-nü.

Villages in Ruby Valley.—These were somewhat larger than villages of southern and eastern Nevada.

Instead of being situated in the valley proper, they were located in the lower portion of the juniper belt, where wood for house construction and for fuel could be had during the severe winters. In the spring, however, people moved into the valley and remained there through the summer, gathering seeds.

The list of villages is probably not complete. Some of them, as numbered on the map (fig. 11), were:

1. Suhuwia (suhuvi, willow+wia, pass), on the headwaters of Franklin River, on the Ruby Valley side of Secret Pass. Thirteen families. Village chief, Pokinänk (pokəp:, a species of brush+nänk, ear); also director of festivals which were held here. Suhuwia people got pine nuts in the Ruby Mountains near Waihamuta, a few miles south. They went to Long or Butte Valleys, nearly 60 miles south, for antelope hunts (RVJ).

2. Waihamuta (waiha, make a fire+muta, place ?; because everything here once burned), on the creek against the hills, west of the Neff Ranch. Sixteen families. Village chief, Navinutsa (broken back), directing rabbit drives. People went to Suhawia or south to near Franklin Lake for festivals (RVJ).

3. Baguwa, in the flats near Overland.

4. Medicine Spring, on the western slope of the "Cedar Mountains," east of Franklin Lake. Twenty to forty families. Tümok, who had previously lived in Huntington Valley, became chief. He directed hunting and gathering trips to near Overland in Ruby Valley during the spring, summer, and fall. Medicine Spring was preferred to Ruby Valley because the Cedar Mountains have more pine nuts than the Ruby Mountains.

Villages near Ruby Valley.—People in certain neighboring valleys and villages having some connection with Ruby Valley were:

5. Clover Valley, Toyagadzu (toyavi, mountain+gadzu, sitting), lying east of the Humboldt Range, Taindandoi or Tainyandoya (holes in the top) and extending from near Wells south to Snow Lake. About 10 families under Ängatumbijugo (äŋga, red+tumbi, rock). These went to Butte Valley for antelope hunts, to north of Shafter near some big spring for rabbit drives under a local director, to near Tuwagusaba for pine nuts, and to Ruby Valley for festivals directed by Tümok. They got seeds in and around Clover Valley.

6. Spruce Mountains, Woŋgogadu (woŋgavi, "white pine"+gadu, sitting). On the northern side of the Spruce Mountains there were three or four families, probably scattered on Cole and Latham Creeks, and called Kubadoogwe. No chief.

7. On the southern side of the Spruce Mountains there were four or five families under Hunivutsi. These people went to Ruby Valley or at pine-nut time to Biabaduzəp:, on the eastern side of the Pequop Range, for festivals, to Butte Valley for antelope hunts, and to Clover Valley for rabbit drives which were led by Hunivutsi.

Two localities between the Spruce Mountains and Currie, Bugunobegwic and Biazunt, were temporary camp sites. They lacked sufficient wood for winter habitations (RVJ). BM, however, said a man living on Phalen Creek had directed rabbit drives held in northern Steptoe Valley near Currie.

8. Butte Valley. A village of perhaps 10 families was located in the northern end of Butte Valley in a canyon called Natsumbägwic ("big water coming

down"), near the Taylor Ranch. This was probably a tributary of Butte Creek. There may also have been a family or two at Pony Spring, on the eastern side of the Butte Mountains. BM said there are no inhabitants of this valley alive today. The chief was Hugamuts, an antelope shaman who directed local hunts. These hunts were participated in by people from a wide area, including Ruby Valley, Cloverdale Valley, the Spruce Mountains, and elsewhere. BM also described an old woman who conducted antelope hunts in Butte Valley, the only instance recorded of a woman antelope shaman. These people held local rabbit hunts under a man who lived at Immigrant Spring. They went to Baguwa, near Overland in Ruby Valley, for festivals. They got pine nuts on the "Cedar Mountains" (east of Ruby and Franklin Lakes), called Tubuŋgadu (probably tuba, pine nut+gadu, sitting). These trips were managed by Paŋguma, who lived at Natsumbăgwic.

Beckwith (1855a, pp. 26–27), who observed some of these people in 1854 west of Goshute Lake, probably near Butte Creek, observed that these "Diggers" "live a family or two in a mountain, and know nothing beyond the rat-holes of their own hills, being afraid of their next range neighbors." The camp he saw was but a fire built beside a cedar tree. The family lacked shelter and blankets, had only a couple of deer skins, a few ground-rats, grass seed, and a variety of artemisia seed.

9. Long Valley, Yuogumba (flat) or Sihuba (sihu, redtop grass), is separated from Butte Valley by the Butte Mountains, Tudundoya (tuhu, black+dun, spots, i. e., on the ground+doya of Má'áwǝt (má'á, hand+wǝt, lackiug; BM). It is almost devoid of water except in the extreme northern end, where the "Cedar Mountains" give rise to a number of springs, Ponhiaba (ponhiats, skunk+ water). Several families wintered here and in the mountains where snow was used for water. Icagumbui (ica'ᵃ, coyote+gum, cross+bui, eye), the local antelope shaman, was chief. Long Valley people got seeds in the vicinity of Ruby Lake. They sometimes had joint festivals with Huntington Creek under Basimugwini, of the latter.

10. A village was situated somewhere on the eastern slope of the Pequop Mountains, Blagwǝp (blap., big+gwǝp, fence), south of Shafter. It was called Biabaduzǝp: (big+baduzǝp:, creek ?) and had about six families under Winjuganbaduzǝp:. Like Ruby Valley people, these were called Wadadüka. Tapsudo had been chief here, but traveled too much. His son, Hunib, refused to be chief and lived mostly in Ruby Valley where, though not a shaman, he directed some communal deer hunts.

Egan Canyon. Though located in the Egan Range on the western side of Steptoe Valley, the residents of this canyon were linked with people to the west as much as with their Steptoe Valley neighbors. Their chief was Togoamuts (togoa, rattlesnake) or Egan John. Kükwijugo or Mose (BM's father), a signer of the treaty of 1863, has been called a "chief," but BM and RVJ said he merely "talked" during the Indian wars and previously had had no authority.

BM and his father were both born in Egan Canyon, his mother in Ruby Valley. Most of their subsistence activities were carried on near home, though they went west for some purposes. They preferred to gather pine nuts in the surrounding Egan Range, which Steptoe Valley families also frequented, but sometimes crossed the valley to gather in the Shell Creek Range, Panandoya (pani, yellow-jacket), near Schellbourne. They got other seeds near home and sowed wild seeds, especially *Mentzelia*, in Egan Canyon. For ante-lope hunts they either went west to Butte Valley or south to Steptoe Valley, where corrals had been built at various sites. For rabbit drives they went to the Warm Springs near Magnuson, where they joined local residents and Ely families. Partly because of family ties, partly because mountain sheep were more numerous there, they spent considerable time hunting in Ruby Valley.

Jakes Valley and White Sage Valley. Little information is avail-able about these valleys, which probably had few inhabitants. HJ said that two chiefs, Padugutsa kahudua (mud face ?) and To:nai (corn on his foot) served Jakes and probably White Sage Valley. The former lived at Yunaŋgwa bahunovi (a species of seed which was very abundant in Jakes Valley+valley). Biwonoonzuga was director of festivals in which these people sometimes joined Butte Valley residents at Pony Springs.

Subsistence activities: seed gathering.—People of the various localities listed above gathered most seeds near their winter villages. Those from Suhuwia, Waihamuta, and Medicine Spring usually went to Ruby Valley where the moist canyons and valley bottoms afforded abundant yampa (*Carum gairdneri*), tsowiga (unidentified), and other seeds and roots. They might go as far as Connor's Creek, Sunadaint (sunavi, cottonwood+daint, cluster), 15 miles south.

Pine nuts were procured in the Ruby Mountains or "Cedar Moun-tains." Medicine Spring people preferred the latter. When gather-ing nuts in the Ruby Mountains people from various localities as-sembled under Tümok, who directed operations. Sometimes people remained in the mountains near their caches.

Journeys were made on foot. A few horses were acquired during RVJ's childhood, about 1860, but these were usually eaten.

Subsistence activities: communal hunts.—Apparently lacking a local antelope shaman, Ruby Valley people hunted antelope commun-ally in or near either Butte or Long Valley, each of which had a shaman. People from other neighboring valleys also went to these valleys (RVJ). Corrals were built in the northern end of each valley. There was also one at White House Spring, two on the west-ern side of Spruce Mountain, and one on the western side of the Cedar Mountains.

Ruby Valley people held drives for white (probably snowshoe) rabbits in the Ruby Mountains or for ordinary jack rabbits near Medicine Spring, Baijuk[wa] being director at either place. Butte and northern Steptoe Valleys, however, held their own more or less local rabbit drives. Drives were during the winter. Four to eight nets were used.

Some communal deer surrounds were held in the Ruby Mountains. These were directed by Tümok and were not shamanistic, though the Long Valley antelope shaman charmed deer which were caught, when going south, in a V-fence and pit on the Cedar Mountains. Mountain-sheep surrounds were held without any leader.

BM's father had seen a few buffalo near the Butte Mountains, but these, like the buffalo in northwestern Utah, were probably not hunted communally.

Festivals.—The main festival seems to have been at Medicine Spring, the largest village. It was held either in the spring or fall. Papadop:, BM's maternal grandfather's brother, was director, his leadership extending probably in post-Caucasian times to Egan Canyon. BM also said another festival might be held after summer harvests 2 or 3 miles from the present Ruby Valley post office at a small sand hill. Tukumuts (mountain lion) was director.

Political organization.—Throughout most of the year and for most purposes the family was largely independent, even when living in the winter village. But, as population was relatively dense in the vicinity of Ruby Valley and as food distribution permitted clusters of some size, village control of a minor sort was necessary. Hence each village had a chief whose main duty was to keep people informed of the whereabouts of ripening seeds and especially to lead trips to the pine-nut areas. In some cases the village chief was also antelope shaman, festival director, "talker" at festivals, or rabbit-hunt leader.

For communal activities different villages were the center of operations. As there was more water and more food in the mountains than in the valleys, cooperative enterprises involved villages which were clustered around certain mountains rather than those located in the same valley. The nuclear center for such activities was the "Cedar Mountains," with its villages on the Ruby Valley, Butte Valley, and Long Valley sides. Medicine Springs was the location for the main festivals, people attending from far and wide when harvests had been sufficient to support a large gathering. Long Valley and Butte Valley drew people from neighboring regions for antelope drives because each had an antelope shaman. Rabbit drives were more local affairs, only adjoining villages ordinarily participating. Communal deer, mountain sheep, and water-fowl hunts involved only people who happened to be wintering or gathering seeds in the same locality.

Chieftainship was preferably patrilineal, except, of course, the antelope shaman who acquired his powers supernaturally with only

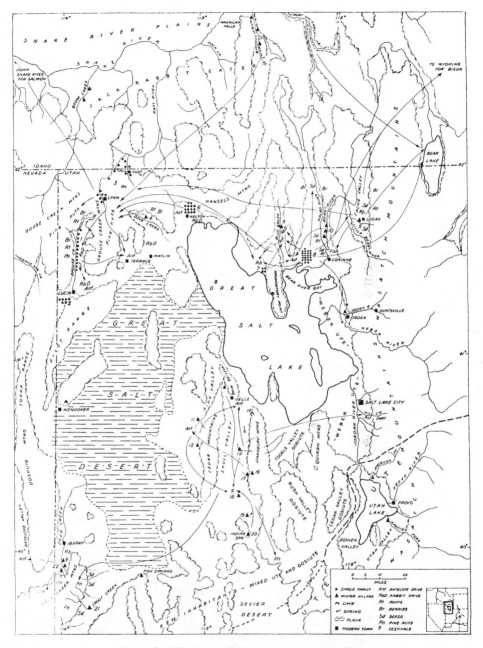

FIGURE 12.—Villages and subsistence areas of northern Utah.

some predisposition to inheritance. Patrilineal succession, however, was not a rigid rule and if the son were disliked, a general meeting decided upon a successor.

Warfare has not been mentioned as a unifying factor because it was unimportant in native times. After the coming of the white man, however, the Indian wars amalgamated people along the Humboldt River, in Ruby Valley, and in neighboring valleys under the leadership of Tümok. The new political alinements produced by the wars are shown by Powell and Ingalls' list of chiefs for Ruby Valley in 1872: Tim-oak, To-sho-win'-tso-go and "Mose" (1874, p. 12). The first and second were from Huntington Valley, the third from Egan Canyon. A thumbnail sketch of Tümok, given by BG, throws light on the nature of this sudden spread of political and military control which occurred in a very similar manner in other parts of the area. This sketch is, of course, one Indian's version, not an objective chronicle.

Life of Tümuko'°.—Tümuko'° or Tümok (rope, because he braided rope) or Tümukunaiwüp was born at Camp Creek, probably a tributary of Susie Creek. (RVJ, however, said he had lived in Huntington Valley, west of Ruby Valley, as a young man.) He had two brothers, Tozawinzugupü' (white knife old man) being the eldest.

As a young man, Tümok traveled with his family and lived at various places on Susie Creek and North Fork up to Jarbridge, where they went to hunt. They wintered ordinarily at the large village at the mouth of South Fork. The group comprised 600 to 700 persons [certainly far too large an estimate] who traveled on foot. Sometimes they went to Ruby Valley for mud hens. At this time Tümuko'° was neither a chief nor a leader of any activity.

One March, about the time when the first white immigrants arrived, while Tümok was trapping sage hens alone in Ruby Valley, he met three white men with long beards, the first he had ever seen. They greeted him with raised hands, but Tümok was frightened. By motions, the men asked directions for the trail and Tümok directed them to Harrison Pass. They rewarded him with a huge plug of chewing tobacco and food, promising to bring him more which they would leave at a certain place in 3 months. Tümok went home and announced his encounter with the "dog face people." Three months later the white men left food and tobacco as promised and Tümok was convinced of their friendship.

At this time Tümok was about 25 or 30 years old but had no authority. He rose to power among his own people purely through personal influence. He was intelligent, jolly, well-liked, and widely known because of his extensive travels in Shoshoni territory. He settled in Ruby Valley and rapidly gained influence.

Meanwhile the number of immigrants increased, the stage line passing south of the Great Salt Lake Desert and through Steptoe Valley was put in operation, and friction developed between the whites and Indians and between certain Indian groups. Trouble with Shoshoni in and near Steptoe Valley and with Gosiute Shoshoni led the whites to construct a fort in Ruby Valley. Shoshoni near Wells committed depredations against immigrants. Northern Paiute, it was claimed, had fought Shoshoni without provocation in pre-Caucasian times and later had clashed with the white man. And Gosiute had stolen Shoshoni children in Steptoe Valley. [The last statement is improbable as Gosiute are Shoshoni and were on friendly terms with their kin. It is possible, however, that a few Gosiute, like the Ute, captured children which the Mormons, out of pity, redeemed from them.]

Tümok's part in these affairs was made possible by his connection with the white men, with whom he seems to have become fast friends. His task was to keep the Shoshoni, who had forgathered in and near Ruby Valley, at peace with the white man and to recruit Shoshoni to aid the soldiers in punitive expeditions against certain Indian groups. Tümok's Shoshoni kept out of the wars with the Northern Paiute [see Hopkins, 1883] but aided in quelling the Wells Shoshoni. [Jr and other Ely Indians recounted massacres of Shoshoni in and near Steptoe Valley by soldiers. It is not known whether Ruby Valley Shoshoni took a hand in this.] To maintain peace between the Shoshoni and whites it was arranged that any offender should be brought to justice only by members of his own race.

Tümok had begun to assist the white men some time between 1854 and 1857. The wars were over in 1862 and the next year a treaty, which included Shoshoni as well as the hostile Indians, was signed. The Shoshoni were promised certain privileges, territory, and rewards for permitting the white man free access to their lands. BG insisted that it was Tümok who actually negotiated this treaty and that the other 11 signers were only "witnesses." Of the others, however, several had been leaders of festivals or other activities in different localities, so that they were assumed to be competent to represent the entire area embraced in the treaty. [This area extended from Jarbridge near the Idaho border south to Ely and from the Great Salt Lake Desert west to Smith Creek and Great Smoky Valley and had, in native times, embraced several hundred independent villages.]

After the treaty was signed, Tümok's task was completed and his authority vanished. Until his death in 1891 he remained in Ruby Valley where the native foods, of which he was fond, were plentiful. He was no longer a "chief" but merely a popular citizen who could tell interesting stories of the wars and of his travels and trading journeys to the east. He had many friends among the white people.

Tümok's political and military career was thus as brief as it was spectacular, lasting probably not more than the seven years between 1854 and 1863. After 1863 he seems to have made no effort to force the white men to fulfill their treaty obligations. It is only in recent years that various self-appointed leaders have assumed this task.

Marriage.—This is one of the few localities in which true as well as pseudo cross-cousin marriage was approved. I have no information as to the frequency of such unions, however, nor, indeed, any genealogy to bear out the informant's assertion about them. Parallel-cousin marriage was taboo.

In orthodox unions, preferably with the cross-cousin, the man asked permission of the girl's father, giving her family buckskins. Some couples went at once to the man's family to live, but most stayed with the wife's family for a year, in a kind of bride service or until the first child was born. Permanent residence, however, seems to have depended largely upon circumstances of food supply and preference. Wherever they resided, they frequently visited the other family.

There was a preference for marriage of a brother and sister to a sister and brother.

Polygyny was not uncommon but there was no feeling that it should be sororal (BM, RVJ). Charlie Tümok had two wives from Steptoe Valley who were not sisters. The sororate was common but not mandatory.

Polyandry was, unlike most other localities, not necessarily fraternal (BM, RVJ). Although it seems, as elsewhere, to have been arranged so that one husband was usually away hunting, neither had prior rights. When both were home the three slept in the same bed. Both husbands were called "father" by the children. BM had heard of cases of polyandry in Ruby Valley, Steptoe Valley, Elko, and Eureka. In the last case the husbands were not related. The wife has since left both of them and is married to another man.

Wives were also acquired by abduction. A man, assisted by his friends, abducted a married or unmarried girl from her home.

It was impossible to procure census data that would show village composition in terms of relationship and intermarrying localities, but a few marriages were recorded which shed some light. Most of these, however, involve chiefs and are not therefore wholly typical, for there is a strong reason in the case of chiefs to practice patrilocal residence.

1. RVJ's mother and father were both born at Kinome, on Huntington Creek.
2. Tümok and his wife both from Kinome.
3. Pokinănk at Suhuwia, Ruby Valley; his wife from Toygadzu Wells.
4. Guwuwutawa at Sahoogap in Huntington Valley; his wife from Halleck.
5. Biadapana at Kinome; his wife from Kinome.
6. Winjugo, at Kinome; his wife from Egan Canyon.
7. Icagumbui, at Long Valley; his wife, a Gosiute Shoshoni.
8. Kusip and his wife both from Halleck.
9. Basimugwini, Hunting Creek; his various wives from various other places.
10. Bokoni and his wife both Clover Valley.
11. Hunivutsi, on the south side of the Spruce Mountains; his wife from Wells.
12. Pisatoya near Carlin; his wife from Kinome.
13. BM's wife's mother from near Egan Canyon; her father from about 4 miles south of Currie.
14. BM's mother from Ruby Valley; his father from Egan Canyon.

Of these 14 marriages, 5 were endogamous by village, 9 exogamous, demonstrating that villages were not lineages, and did not follow a rule of local exogamy. Few of the smaller villages to the south comprised only relatives, and it is less expectable that these larger villages should have.[14]

---

[14] A traveler in Ruby Valley in 1854 visited a camp of an old man and six other persons, including his sons and sons-in-law (Aveson, p. 94).

Place names.—Toana Mountains, Tuana (tuhu, black+ana, top of hill).

HUMBOLDT RIVER

Shoshoni occupied the Humboldt Valley westward approximately to Iron Point between Battle Mountain and Winnemucca, where they were somewhat intermixed with the Northern Paiute or Paviotso, their western neighbors. Wheeler (1875, p. 36) incorrectly places Shoshoni also at Winnemucca, "named after their old chief," where, he states, they had their headquarters. Actually the vicinity of Winnemucca was entirely Paiute and the town was named from one of their headmen. (See, for example, Hopkins, 1883.) Humfreville (pp. 289–293) is wrong in supposing that the Humboldt River Shoshoni were made up of the individual outcasts of Snakes, Ute, Bannocks, and others. East of Iron Point the Humboldt River Valley was entirely Shoshoni.

Although the Humboldt River was the main immigrant thoroughfare, early descriptions of its natives were generally limited to comments on their poverty.

Ogden, traveling somewhere on the upper Humboldt River in November 1827, described the Indians (vol. 10, pp. 384–385) as numerous, wretched, and wild, "with scarcely any covering, the greater part without bows and arrows and without any defense." Walker (Irving, 1898, vol. 2, p. 94) said they were shy, forlorn, and scattered in 1825. Leonard, traveling down the Humboldt River in 1834, said (p. 157) that "the natives . . . still continued to be of the most poor and dejected kind—being entirely naked and very filthy." Near the present town of Wells, Bryant, in August 1846, met six Shoshoni, of whom he said (pp. 194–195), "The bodies of two or three of them were partially covered with the skins of hares sewn together. The others were entirely naked." One had a "miserable gun," two or three had bows and arrows, and several had hareskin pouches. Near the Humboldt River he met 5 naked Indians (p. 198) and probably at or near the present town of Elko they saw 200 or 300 Indians in a group (p. 205). Between Goose Creek, Utah, and the headwaters of the Humboldt River, Delano, in July 1849, saw Indians who were entirely naked except for breechcloths and who carried bows and iron-tipped arrows (p. 159). Farther down the Humboldt River they saw the "palace of a 'merry mountain Digger.' It was simply a cleft in the rocks—a kind of cave, strewn with wild grass, and might have served equally well for the habitation of a Digger king or a grizzly bear" (pp. 170–171). Humfreville (pp. 289–293) stated that they stole horses and mules to eat but not to ride, had no homes, often went entirely naked, ate what they could get, including crickets, frogs, toads, snakes, insects, grasshoppers, and clay, had no war, sometimes sold their children to get food, had small, dirty houses, were too lazy to fight, forage, or stir, and only sometimes lived in families which broke up readily. Simpson in 1859 (p. 37) wrote that the Humboldt River Indians "were of Sho-sho-nee origin, but had no chief. They lived scatteredly, and, like the Go-shoot, are of a low type and live and dress in the same way."

Leonard makes the surprising observations that in 1834 in the valleys west of Great Salt Lake he met Indians en route to the buffalo country (his own party had killed one buffalo west of the lake) to "lay in their winter's supply of meat." Shortly after this he met "a few straggling natives, who were in a manner naked, on the trail of the main body to the buffalo country" (pp. 149–150). It is possible that a few Humboldt River Shoshoni had acquired horses by 1834 and traveled into southern Idaho, where some buffalo remained. But too much credence cannot be given this statement, as Leonard's journal was frequently confused as to time and place. Horses were extremely rare for many years in this region. In 1854 Beckwith met a party of Indians, probably near Deeth, who had but one pack horse among them (1855a, p. 31).

Holeman in 1853 supposed there were 500 Humboldt River Shoshoni under Ne-me-te-kah (man eater), subdivided into a group of 200 or under at the first crossing of the river, near the present town of Wells, under Paut-wa-a-raute (the drowned man), and 450 at Stony Point under Oh-hah-quak (yellow skin). In summer these Indians were scattered in hunting parties (1853, pp. 444–445).

Forney in 1859 (p. 363) said there were seven bands along the Humboldt River.

Compared with other portions of the Western Shoshoni area, the Humboldt Valley was a fertile region. Lying at a considerable altitude (5,000 to 6,000 feet) and traversed by many mountain ranges of great height, it had exceptional rainfall (up to 10 or 15 inches in the valleys and more in the mountains) and a large number of perennial streams. Fish could be had in the Humboldt River and its tributaries, game, especially antelope, in the valleys, and seeds and tubers in important quantities in the valleys and mountains. Although pine nuts occur well north of the Humboldt River in this region according to Sudworth (1917), the only locality where they are sufficiently abundant to warrant gathering is the Grouse Creek region northwest of Great Salt Lake. There are a few near Wells, but north of Wells and along the Humboldt River west of Wells they are unimportant. Even the vicinity of La Moille in South Creek Valley has but few. The greatest native supply was gathered in the Ruby Mountains. In recent times Humboldt River people have gone 100 miles south to the White Pine Mountains for them.

Districts and villages.—Owing to the unusual fertility of the area and diversity of landscape along the Humboldt River, the areas foraged for food were somewhat smaller and the villages somewhat larger than among most western Shoshoni.[15] But the foods were somewhat erratic in their occurrence, so that subsistence activities had not become a fixed routine and families often found themselves in different places associating with different people from year to year. Communal hunts and dances which tend to amalgamate large groups of people consequently did not always unite the same people.[16] In short, there was no band organization whatever.

---

[15] Leonard observed (pp. 159–160) that the natives became more numerous as he proceeded downstream.

[16] There is not the slightest evidence for Humfreville's 2 "tribes," one of about 500 persons on the upper Humboldt River, another of about 600 persons on the lower river, unless by "tribes" he meant the Shoshoni and Northern Paiute.

The districts listed below are more or less arbitrarily bounded. Each included several semipermanent camps, which certain families considered home and returned to when they could. These camps were often clustered in fairly large villages.[17] District members assembled with one another more often than with outsiders for festivals, communal hunts, and some fishing. But, although they ordinarily gathered food within the district, they frequently ranged into adjoining districts or even beyond, where they might participate in local hunts and dances. There was consequently incomplete attachment to a locality. There was no idea of inalienable membership in the local group, nor group ownership of food rights, no resentment of trespass by outsiders or even dialectic distinctiveness. In fact, dialectic areas given by BG were far larger than districts, which is expectable in view of the frequent and wide wandering of the people. BG said the Elko dialect was spoken at Battle Mountain, Wells, and Ruby Valley, while Eureka, Austin, and Owyhee spoke a slightly different dialect.

It is significant that districts adjoining the river are smaller than those at some distance from it. The inhabitants of the former depended to a relatively greater degree upon fish and found within a small territory sufficient vegetable foods (excepting the pine nut). Those away from the river had to range over a larger territory to gather foods in sufficient quantity and variety and probably had a much smaller per mile population.

None of these districts was named, except as prominent villages had place names. A few names have gained some prominence in literature but are not band designations. Thus, Tosawi (tosa, white + wi, knife) has been thought to designate a band occupying different parts or all of the Humboldt Valley. Actually it was usually applied only to a small group at Iron Point, near Battle Mountain, where good white flint occurred, though there was no consistency in its application.[18] More often people of general regions were designated by foods. Thus, Snake River Shoshoni called the Elko region people Tsogwi (a root) yuyugi (shakes, like jelly) and those in the vicinity of Deeth, Tu:koi (tu:, black + koi, peak). BG called Deeth people Kuiyu (*Valeriana edulis* root) düka, Pine Valley people Pasia (redtop grass) düka, the Jarbridge region Woŋgogadu toyavi (woŋgovi, pine + gadu, sitting + toyavi, mountain), and Northern Paiute, paviodzo (meaning unknown). Northern Paiute called Shoshoni Tovomb (meaning ?). Some place names were North Fork Mountain, Sütoya (sü, cold + toyavi, mountain); mountains 4 or 5

---

[17] Ogden (1827) stopped at a village of 50 "tents," which was possibly on the Humboldt. Here he was visited by 150 Indians.

[18] Tümok's brother was named from this Tosawinugo (tosawi + jugo, old man) though he did not live in the Tosawi region.

miles west of Austin, Sunundoya (sunu'ᵘ, a seed ?) ; a district south
of Ely, Bohonovi (bohovi, sage+novi, house ?). White man, Tosaic
(tosa, white+ic, wolf ?), though usually Taivo.

Some of the Humboldt region districts, as numbered on the map
(fig. 11), were:

14. Independence Valley. People lived in the valley of what is called Magpie
or Maggie Creek. These people seldom reached the river. They held their
own local festivals.

15. Palisade. Elevation, 4,846 feet. People lived along the Humboldt River
in this vicinity. BG included them with the Pine Creek people, but SF thought
they were separate, perhaps associating with some other Humboldt River
people. For 1872, Powell and Ingalls list 56 persons here under Chief Pit-si-nain
(1874, p. 12).

16. Carlin. The main village was about 3 miles below Carlin, called Badukoi (pa, water+dubihand, middle+koi, peak), because of a rock in the middle
of the river. Certain families usually wintered here but joined the Susie Creek
and Elko residents for festivals. Badukoi head man was Badukoin. Powell
and Ingalls list 82 persons here under Chief Pit-si-nain (1874, p. 12).

17. Elko. Elevation, 5,066 feet. People lived along the Humboldt River from
Susie Creek to South Fork and somewhat on both tributaries, and near Hot
Springs. Although camps were scattered, perhaps 1 or 2 miles apart, the preferred site was a village at the mouth of South Fork, Puŋodudumoin, where
perhaps 1,000 people gathered (probably after the horse was introduced). This
general region was called Puŋodüŋgahnivain (place where the house is) (BG).
Powell and Ingalls list 90 persons here under "Capt. Sam" (1874, p. 12), but
see below (pp. 163–164).

The general region of the Palisade, Carlin, and Elko groups had
about 770 square miles and, according to Powell and Ingalls' figures,
about 228 persons, or one per 3.3 square miles.

In a valley a little south of Elko (?) Beckwith met about 50 Indian men.
They had been shooting gophers with blunt arrows, digging them by hand,
or catching them in figure-4 traps, each man getting 40 to 50. These men had
hidden their "treasures, one bringing out a piece of an old buckskin, a couple
of feet square, smoked, greasy, and torn; another a half dozen rabbit skins
in an equally filthy condition, sewed together, which he would swing over his
shoulders by a string—his only blanket or clothing; while a third brought out
a blue string, which he girded about him and walked away in full dress—one
of the lords of the soil." (1855a, pp. 32–33.)

Dixie Valley. Probably a small, somewhat distinct group here.

Huntington Valley. There were several camps and villages along
Huntington Creek above Puŋodudumoin. This locality was some-
what favored by having access to the Humboldt River with its fish
and by proximity to pine nuts on the western slope of the Ruby
Mountains. These nuts are the best in the general area and were
sought by other groups from along the Humboldt River (BG).
This area of about 900 square miles had 246 persons, according to
RVJ's estimate, or 1 per 3.5 square miles.

RVJ gave three villages:

18. Kinome, 5 miles north of Huntington. Eleven families. Village chief, Biadapana, who had succeeded his father. At his death, Biadapana was succeeded by a younger brother, Tümok (who later moved to Ruby Valley and rose to fame during the Indian wars), who was in turn succeeded by another younger brother, Winjugo (RVJ), Tosawinjugo (tosa, white+wi, flint knife) or "Charlie Temoak." (BG, BM.)

19. Sahoogəp (water runs down ?), at Lee. About 20 families. Village chief, Guwewutawa ("tied up head"). (RVJ.)

These two villages gathered pine nuts at Wakwe, on the western slope of the Ruby Mountains, near Jiggs.

20. There was another village of perhaps 10 families somewhere on upper Huntington Creek, under Basimugwini (basip:, grass+mu, ?+gwini, mush). People remained here throughout the year except when traveling to near "Cold Creek" (?), southeast of Huntington to pick pine nuts in the Ruby Mountains or to Long Valley to hunt antelope under a Long Valley shaman. (RVJ.)

Huntington Valley people had local festivals under Basimugwini or went to South Fork or to Pine Creek. Often, people from South Fork, Diamond, Newark, and other valleys wintered in the vicinity of Huntington Springs when pine nuts had been abundant.

21. North Fork. People occupied most of the drainage of the North Fork of the Humboldt River with the exception of the vicinity of its mouth. People from Susie Creek and Elko often ranged over this country to hunt antelope and small game, and, in winter, to gather cactus. They crossed it en route to the vicinity of Jarbridge to hunt deer. The chief, though not festival director, was Ziaŋkasü (ziavi, rose bush+kasü, end of a finger). People lived in scattered camps, each having 4 to 5 families and some perhaps 10 families. BG thought there were 500 to 600 persons, but this would give 1 per 2 square miles, which is undoubtedly excessive.

22. Halleck. Elevation, 5,229 feet. The people called Kuiyudüka (BG, RVJ); the village, Banadia (RVJ). A village of about 100 persons, scattered along both sides of Lamoille Creek. These people ranged a fairly small territory of about 400 square miles. The country along Lamoille Creek between the Humboldt River, where fish could be taken all winter, and the Ruby Mountains provided foods in considerable variety and quantity. They got pine nuts and squirrels in the Ruby Mountains near Lamoille, called Wapeguc (many pine trees), or in Ruby Valley, where they sometimes remained during the winter. The village chief was Pooŋgwatsa or Poaŋutsa (poa, skin+gwatsa, gravy), probably a signer of the treaty of 1863 (BG), or Kusip: (ash), RVJ. He directed pine-nut trips, local rabbit drives, and local festivals.

A Halleck man named Sokəp (sometimes written Cho-kup) joined the white soldiers and thereby acquired himself the title of "chief." Powell and Ingalls list "Capt. Sam" as chief of 36 persons here as well as of Elko people (1874, p. 12).

23. Deeth. People also called Kuiyudüka. The village, called Tukwampandai (tuhu, black+kwam, hill+pa, water+nadai, under; from 2 small, black hills on the south side of the river); 16 to 20 families, scattered in the vicinity of Mary's Creek and the Humboldt River. These people ranged all of Mary's Creek for seeds and took fish in both streams. They held local festivals under

Pihazugo or Bill Antelope (BG); or went to Wells where Poangwatsa (see Halleck, however), was director (RVJ).

24. Wells. Elevation, 5,630 feet. Also Kuiyudüka. The village, called Toyagadzu (toyavi, mountain+gadzu, sitting), comprised 6 to 8 camps, scattered from Bishops Creek to near Wells. Festivals were held here under Poangwatsa (RVJ).

The last 3 centers of population, Halleck to Wells, had about 264 persons utilizing 1,375 square miles, or 1 person per 5.2 square miles.

Another group of camps was scattered on the headwaters of the Salmon Falls Creek, near Contact. There were probably others near Montello, in northeastern Nevada near the Grouse Creek Shoshoni of northwestern Utah (pp. 173–175). This territory was sparsely populated, however, and little information is available concerning it.

Thousand Springs Valley, northeast of Wells, was occupied by 600 persons under Too-ke-mah (rabbit) in 1853, according to Holeman (1853, pp. 443–444). Most of these people went to Fort Hall "where there is more game, and where they intend to winter" (p. 446). Hurt (1856, p. 227), however, gives Setoke as chief in Thousand Springs Valley. Holeman's population estimate is undoubtedly excessive and probably was of a transient population, perhaps from Fort Hall.

Subsistence activities.—Information on economic life is from BG of Elko, but probably is representative of most Humboldt River peoples.

Pine nuts could not be had near Elko. BG's grandmother had to go south into Huntington Valley, a distance of 20 or 30 miles, to gather from the western slope of the Ruby Mountains. A number of families made this trip together, but gathered individually, having no chief. Each gathered where it pleased. If the harvest were large, they wintered there. Usually, however, they returned to their village at the mouth of South Fork. They transported the pine nuts by carrying as many as they could in a day's trip and making subsequent trips until all the nuts were at that place. Then they made several trips to carry them to another point, and so on until they were home. A good crop might last through the winter until March, but never longer.

Other seeds were gathered at various places by family groups. For sand bunch grass they went sometimes to Ruby Valley, as there was little near Elko. Uəp: (*Chenopodium*) was abundant along the Humboldt River and especially near Lamoille. Quiyu (*Valeriana edulis*), also along the river, ripened in August. Dagü, abundant around Austin and on Susie Creek. Yumb: (yamp), ripening in spring, abundant on hills just south of Elko. Boina (*Sophia*), foothills south of the river. Bogombi: along the river. Nəp: (a root) from Hot Springs near Carlin. Sowigo on Camp Creek, i. e., on Susie Creek. Mahavita known but too rare to be important. Wiyumbi did not grow on the Humboldt River near Elko but was abundant in Star Valley near Deeth, 35 miles away. Although 35 miles seems a considerable distance to carry food, the dried berries were so light that they could easily be transported. BG's family frequently carried them on foot back from Star Valley even before horses were introduced. Large groups made trips to Star Valley together for "company and for fun."

When stored seeds were insufficient to last the winter people might go to the low ridges north of the Humboldt River near the mouth of North Fork Creek, to gather cactus, wogavi. This cannot be gathered and dried in summer, like roots, but may be picked at any time during the winter.

Thus, for vegetable foods Elko people foraged an area some 20 to 30 miles in diameter. They preferred to winter at the mouth of South Fork, where they cached seeds and dried roots. When special circumstances arose, such as an unusual abundance of pine nuts in some locality or a general dearth of food, families governed themselves by the circumstances and wintered where most practicable.

Hunting was carried on along the Humboldt River but game was none too plentiful. A man was lucky to kill enough large game to make a complete outfit of skin clothing. Early accounts indicate that such small game as ground hogs, gophers, and rats were perhaps economically more important than such large game as deer, antelope, and sheep. But there were no communal rabbit hunts in which nets were used.

Buffalo, though occurring in Utah until 1832, were unknown here.

Antelope hunts probably involved larger groups of people than any other economic activity, though the same people did not always participate. Antelope must have been fairly common along the river. During 1 day's travel below Wells, Bryant observed 300 or 400. There was one antelope shaman in the region of Elko and another in Ruby Valley. Hunts occurred whenever people needed food, corrals at different places being used. There was a corral on the hills north of Elko and another on the mountain south of Elko, both of which were used by people from the vicinity of Elko and Carlin. There was also a corral in Ruby Valley, one on the mountain west of Jiggs in Huntington Valley, and probably another near Halleck.

Small groups of people without any director sometimes hunted mud hens in Ruby Valley. They drove the birds out of the water and killed them with clubs as they ran through the marsh grasses. This was done any time of the year.

Mountain sheep were hunted in the Ruby Mountains, Swails Mountain, "North Fork Mountain" (probably the Independence

BASIN-PLATEAU ABORIGINAL GROUPS

Range), or the Jarbridge Mountains. Individual hunters either trailed them or attracted them by pounding logs together to make a noise like rams fighting, then shot them with a bow.

There were many fish in the Humboldt River and some in South Fork, Mary's River, and Lamoille Creek, but none in North Fork.

The main species was a trout (?), said now to be extinct, called agai (the Snake River name of salmon; the Shoshoni name for fish is usually paŋgwi), probably the Tahoe trout. There were also several suckers, chubs, and minnows.

Individuals took fish in summer and winter with nets and hooks. Communal fishing involved stone dams or willow weirs equipped with baskets. A stone dam was photographed in the Humboldt River 13 miles west of Elko. This site had been chosen partly because the talus of the canyon wall provided ample rock for the dam, partly because it was near the village at the mouth of South Fork. Donai-gunt (donai, bunion) was in charge of this dam.

The maker of a trap or dam was director of fishing operations. He called for assistance to drag out the baskets full of fish every 2 to 4 days, as each weighed up to 200 pounds. The fish were then distributed among the various families.

There was also a dam on Susie Creek not far from its junction with the Humboldt River. Another was on South Fork about 12 miles from the Humboldt River, where Sowaiji was in charge. BG's grandmother, living sometimes near Elko, sometimes at the mouth of South Fork, helped catch fish at both places.

Ownership or even habitual utilization of fishing places was not strongly if at all developed. BG denied any family, village, or district rights to fishing places among Shoshoni, though he had heard of such rights among Walker River Paiute.

Festivals.—The two important Humboldt River festival sites were South Fork and Halleck. At South Fork the chief was Wubaba (BG's grandfather), who had dreamed the power to direct dances and who was also a shaman. These festivals drew people from as far west as Carlin and sometimes even from Beowawe. At Halleck, Bihazuga or Bill Antelope (BG's father-in-law) was director. His father had preceded him as director. Other festivals were held in Ruby Valley and at localities mentioned elsewhere.

Festivals were usually held but once a year, in the fall before pine-nut time. Sometimes there was a spring dance. For 5 nights the round dance was performed. About 35 years ago the bear dance was adopted. Formerly dances served not only as an occasion for much festivity but also for courtship. More recently they had become somewhat disorderly and philandering broke up many marriages. The effect of dances in disrupting marriages, however, was probably not entirely recent.

Warfare.—Shoshoni never fought one another, but BG depicted Shoshoni as the inoffensive victims of raids by Gosiute from the east and by Winnemucca Northern Paiute from the west. Ute had stolen children from Steptoe Valley Shoshoni but did not reach the Humboldt River. BG believed that an ancient enmity existed between Shoshoni and Paiute who continue to dislike one another.

This corroborates the testimony of other informants that native warfare was not an important factor in integrating social or political groups. Events following the arrival of the white man, however, stimulated strife and gave temporary cohesion to many formerly independent Humboldt River and neighboring groups under Tümok.

Chiefs.—BG claimed that prior to the arrival of the white man there had been no village chiefs. There were no rabbit drives. Pine-nut trips and fishing activities required no important management. Antelope and deer shamans acquired powers supernaturally. This leaves only festivals requiring chiefs. The South Fork director acquired his power in a vision; the Halleck director inherited his power from his father.

Tümok's rise to power as a "chief" has been described.

Marriage.—There was no local exogamy. Cross-cousin and pseudo cross-cousin marriages were preferred, not required. Parallel-cousin marriage was prohibited.

Polygyny was common, being sometimes but not necessarily sororal. One man had 4 wives, by whom he had respectively, 4, 6, 2, and 3 children, a total of 15 children in a family of 20. Children of one woman called the other wives biatsi (little mother).

Polyandry was denied, BG believing that multiple husbands would fight. He professed incredulity at its practice to the south, though he knew one of SF's polyandrous fathers, Kandukup.

In normal marriage there was bride service for a year or so prior to marriage to permit the bride's parents to ascertain the boy's hunting skill. He lived with the girl's parents during this time but did not have access to the girl. After such a marriage the couple determined the whereabouts of their future residence but frequently visited their parents. There was no bride price.

Marriage was also accomplished by abducting a girl, e. g., one with whose parents the boy had not found favor or a married woman. The abductor was aided by his friends. If a fight ensued, it was with fists only. The girl was held aloft on the hands of her abductors, presumably to protect her from being trampled, while a man watched to see that she was held out of danger. Ruby Valley Johnson's father abducted BG's mother; she did not like him and walked back from Ruby Valley to Elko. Once, during such a fight, the woman was dropped onto greasewood (tonovi) and hurt, whereupon the fight stopped. When a woman so abducted did not like her new spouse she ran away to return home.

The family which occupied a single house was apparently restricted to the mother, father, and children, unless grandparents had to be cared for. In this case the grandparents helped raise the children. The aunts and uncles were present only when visiting. Economically they were independent of the mother and father.

BATTLE MOUNTAIN AND VICINITY

The Humboldt River cuts through a series of mountain gorges below Elko and emerges into a comparatively broad and fertile valley plain in the vicinity of Battle Mountain [19] (elevation, 4,511 feet). Shoshoni occupied the region to and including Iron Point, beyond which lived Northern Paiute or Paviotso. Although these Shoshoni are essentially like their upstream kin, their slight geographical isolation from the latter makes it convenient to treat them separately.

Shoshoni relationships with Paiute in this region were somewhat ambivalent. They intermarried with them and sometimes cooperated with them in antelope hunts and perhaps other activities. At the same time there seems to have been some feeling of antagonism and occasional bloodshed because of woman stealing.

Shoshoni villages and camps.—The population was comparatively dense and undoubtedly exceeded Powell and Ingalls' figure of 194 in 1872. It was somewhat clustered in nuclei in several districts where families tended to concentrate. None was named after prominent local foods, however, like the areas farther up the Humboldt River.

One area of concentration was along the fertile lowlands of the Humboldt River between Battle Mountain and Iron Point. The population was fairly dense (one estimate is 500 persons in 1,280 square miles) but the winter encampments were somewhat smaller and less permanent than those of most Shoshoni and lacked headmen. There were few large winter villages. Instead, related families associated in groups of three to five. They generally foraged together during the year and chose a winter camp site where seeds and fish were plentiful. These sites varied from year to year. To some extent, of course, different camps were often made in the vicinity of one another, but this was because local food abundance drew them to the same general region.

Why they did not deliberately concentrate in larger winter villages, which local economy would certainly have permitted, is not clear. Apparently they had no great urge, innate or learned, to associate with large numbers of people.

---

[19] Battle Mountain was named from a fight between a party of immigrants and Northern Paiute in 1857. White men first settled here in 1867. (Bancroft, vol. 25, pp. 206, 268.)

JP's family ranged the river between Ellison and Iron Point, usually wintering at Pagowe, a place about 2 miles upstream from Herrin, where nəp: (unidentified root) was abundant. Captain Sam's family, unrelated to JP's, sometimes stayed there also. The camp usually had 15 to 20 persons. JP's family sometimes went to Bohowia (bohovi, *Artemisia tridentata*+wia, pass) near Iron Point, where perhaps 10 families wintered.

There was probably another concentration of camps in the vicinity of Battle Mountain called Tonomudza (tonovi, greasewood+mudza, point). People from part of the northern Reese River Valley, which was very arid, wintered here also. These people rarely went west of Battle Mountain for foods.

As pine nuts did not occur in sufficient quantities locally, people along this section of the river sometimes went 80 miles south toward Austin to gather them. They did not winter there, but carried the nuts home. Sometimes they went an equal distance to the headwaters of the Owyhee River and other tributaries of the Snake River to get salmon (tahma agai and wovi agai) and perhaps to visit the Snake River Shoshoni. They usually consumed the salmon before reaching home, however, unless there were extra men to carry them.

People who wintered on the Humboldt River above Battle Mountain were called Tosawi (tosa, white+wi, knife) because they procured a high quality of white flint for knives in the mountains to the north. This name, unfortunately, became prominent and led to the fiction that all the Shoshoni in a large area around Battle Mountain had comprised a band by this name. Because, like other Shoshoni group names, Tosawi did not designate a definitely bounded linguistic, political, cultural, or even geographical division, no two writers have agreed in its use.

Holeman (1852, p. 152) applied "White Knives" to people of the Humboldt River and Goose Creek Mountains. Hurt (1856, pp. 228–229) restricted Tosow-witches or White Knives to about 250 people living near Stony Point. Burton (1862, p. 481) extended the terms to include even the Shoshoni in the vicinity of Diamond Valley. Powell and Ingalls (1874, p. 12) used it for people in the vicinity of Battle Mountain and Simpson (1876, pp. 34–35) considered the To-sa-witches to be a separate division of "Sho-sho-nee" who ranged along the Humboldt River in small parties between the Un-gowe-ah and Cooper's Ranges.

The hunting and gathering area of the people most often called Tosawi was in the mountains around Rock Creek. Many of them often wintered on the Humboldt River below Battle Mountain.

There were other winter encampments on the Humboldt River in the vicinity of Beowawe. Residents here gathered seeds in Crescent Valley, but preferred not to remain there as winters were too cold.

Sometimes they wintered near Cortez or Grass Valley to the south instead of returning to the Humboldt River. Grass Valley was a good place to hunt rabbits in winter.

Communal hunts.—Rabbit drives were held in the fall and winter when furs were good. Drives were organized wherever there were enough people. One center for drives was Rock House, Pagawi, where the rabbit-drive chief (called kahmudagwani, from kahmu, jack rabbit) sent out two announcers (dagwowəp) to visit different camps along the river plain and tell people where to assemble. JP could not, however, remember any hunts that involved more than about 7 families or 40 persons.

There were probably other drives at Battle Mountain under a local director. Beowawe did not have enough people and it is doubtful whether Golconda to the west, where Paiute and Shoshoni adjoined, could muster enough people for drives.

Sometimes several different localities joined for an extraordinarily large drive.

The task of rabbit-drive director was not inherited. Any good hunter and talker assumed the responsibility.

Lacking a local antelope shaman, these people went to Pü:wünük: (plain against the hills) near Iron Point to drive antelope under Musuwitsiüm, a Paiute shaman from the west. JP knew of no shaman among the Shoshoni. Large crowds of people, formerly on foot but more recently on horseback, drove antelope into a corral. The kill was shared equally by all; even the shaman received no more than the others. This was usually done during the winter.

There were also minor cooperative nonshamanistic deer hunts.

Festivals.—Probably festivals were held in native times at Iron Point and at Battle Mountain. The latter location subsequently became more important and drew people from Iron Point and Beowawe. Captain Bob was director (kwinidagwani; kwini, mush + dagwani, chief). The Tosawi and Beowawe groups, however, sometimes went to South Fork, near Elko, which was the next locality east to hold festivals.

In more recent times people often went south to near Austin, especially when pine nuts were plentiful there, to dance under Tutuwa (see "Ione Valley—Reese River").

Chieftainship.—Though several names figure prominently in literature, there is no information about native village headmen or directors of communal activities. The so-called chiefs appear to be men who were elevated to rank during the Indian wars. Powell and Ingalls list six for the vicinity of Battle Mountain (1874, p. 12): Pie-a-ra-poo'-na, Se-no-wets-o, No-wits-ie, Pie'-a-nang-gau, "Sam," and Tim-pits'. "Sam" is perhaps the Captain Sam who, with Captain Charlie, CTh named as "chiefs" in the Owyhee region, probably in post-reservation times. Other Battle Mountain Shoshoni who acquired titles were Captain George Dick, Captain George, and his son-in-law, Captain George Washington. Captain Sam or Picedai had also been named as "chief" of the Tosawi, but his functions were not known.

Marriage.—Marriage with any blood relative including a true cross-cousin and with a pseudo parallel-cousin was forbidden. The preferred mate was a pseudo cross-cousin. A man's father's sister, who was usually considered his closest relative, urged him to marry her stepdaughter. If the paternal aunt had no stepdaughter a man married any girl whose mother approved of him.

Polygyny was usually sororal, a man marrying the oldest sister first, then taking the others in order of age, one at a time, up to three or four. Likewise, the sororate was usually followed but was not obligatory.

Polyandry was always fraternal and temporary. A woman married the oldest brother first, then, if she liked a younger brother, took him into the household and allowed him sex privileges. Although both brothers were regarded as fathers of any children born during this time, the younger brother looked forward to acquiring a wife of his own. He preferred a sister of his polyandrous wife, but if she had none, he took an unrelated woman. Marriages of two brothers to two sisters were not group marriage. The couples maintained separate households and did not permit each other sex privileges.

The levirate and sororate were preferred but were not compulsory.

Acquisition of a wife by abduction was less common than among other Nevada Shoshoni. It was a last resort to get a wife, an unmarried woman from some distant village being stolen. The fighting was without weapons. Battle Mountain Shoshoni did not abduct married women, although JP had heard that people to the south and southeast had done so.

Kinship terms were little used for address. A man addressed his wife as hu:viji (old woman); a woman called her husband tsugu (old man). A son was called dui or duivitc (boy). Any person called to from a distance was addressed üü (you) instead of using the kinship term for a relative or the personal name for anyone else. If there were several persons, the one desired was designated by his position in the crowd.

Brothers-in-law were the closest friends, playing jokes on each other, privileged to say anything to each other, and helping each other. They could not, however, as to the north, appropriate one another's property.

SNAKE RIVER

The Shoshoni of western Idaho differed from those at Fort Hall in two important respects. Inhabiting streams where salmon could be taken, fishing was their principal subsistence. Having few horses, they lacked any important degree of band organization. But the population was not homogeneous. Some were impoverished and pursued a restricted annual subsistence routine on foot, while others, possessing a few horses, ranged over a wider territory which afforded more varied resources.

The density and prosperity of the native population depended in large measure upon the environment. Below Fort Hall, the Snake River, Biahunuvi (bia, big+hunuvi, creek) flows through a gorge cut deep in the lava. Between Shoshone Falls, which is the upper limit of salmon, and American Falls above, the country is exceptionally infertile and there were few if any winter residents. People preferred to remain downstream near their stores of salmon and in proximity to one another so as to have some protection against raids by an unidentified tribe from Oregon called Saiduk: a.[20]

Below Twin Falls, Shoshoni villages were scattered along both sides of the Snake River. The people here called themselves **Agai-düka** (agai, salmon) or Yahandüka (yaha, ground hog), CT. They were also called Yamb: düka by Bannock and Tutwanait (tuwa, below+nait, people or inhabitants of ?) by Fort Hall Shoshoni, who included, also, northern Nevada Shoshoni in this term. Either these or the Shoshoni farther west were also called "Cat foot" by Nez Percés because they sometimes stole into Nez Percé dances undetected. They called the Nez Percés Dzoigadüka (dzoiga, a root).

The southern Idaho Shoshoni called Kuembedüka or Squirrel eaters (Lowie, 1909, pp. 206–208) were unknown to TP. JP named Güəmbedüka as a Lemhi camp site, 7 miles north of the town of Salmon.

Encampments.—Winter encampments occurred below Twin Falls. Although families sometimes remained many miles from the Snake River, they preferred to transport any foods collected to the vicinity of the river so as to be near cached salmon. Encampments were scattered, however, some being as much as 6 miles from the river, because the country would not support them if densely clustered. Moreover, they were small, each having only about three families.

CT named three villages between Hagerman and Bruneau:

Saihunupi (saip, tule+hunupi, canyon), about 4 miles below Hagerman.

---

[20] These may be Powell's Shoshonean-speaking Saidyuka on the Klamath Reservation (1891, p. 110).

Pazin:tumb:ᵃ (pazin:, thistle+tumb:ᵃ, rock or rocky pass), about 8 miles below Hagerman.

Ötotumb:ᵃ (öto, silty soil), near Bliss.

Between these, individual families made scattered camps. There were also some on the tributaries of the Snake River.

Many of these Agaidüka were without horses, having nothing to trade the Nez Percés for them. Others, however, especially those on the northern side of the Snake River, had acquired a few through trade and theft. A factor preventing maintenance of horses was the very small amount of good pasturage along the lower Snake River.

Observations by early travelers do not always distinguish the local residents of this region from Shoshoni and Bannock who visited it on horseback and Shoshoni from Camas Prairie and northern Nevada who came here on foot. They are, however, of considerable interest.

On the Snake River, probably in the section between Shoshone Falls and Salmon Falls, the Astoria party saw a number of dwellings which, in October 1811, "were very comfortable; each had its pile of wormwood at the door for fuel, and within was abundance of salmon, some fresh, but the greater part cured . . . About their dwellings were immense quantities of the heads and skins of salmon, the best part of which had been cured, and hidden in the ground." Along this part of the river, the shores were "lined with dead salmon." "There were signs of buffalo having been there, but a long time before." Along the northern side of the Snake River in the vicinity of Salmon Falls they saw evidence of a great many horses, though the Indians "were never willing to part with their horses, having none to spare." Indians on the opposite side of the river were more impoverished (Irving, 1897, vol. 2, pp. 38–40). On August 25 they saw about 100 lodges of Shoshoni fishing at Salmon Falls. On the northern side of the river below Salmon Falls they "passed several camps of Shoshonies, from some of whom they procured salmon, but in general they were too wrechtedly poor to furnish anything" (op. cit., pp. 169–171).

In 1832 Bonneville said that the Indians near Salmon Falls were on foot, timid, impoverished, and had houses in groups of three or four or even more to form a small "hamlet" (Irving, 1898, vol. 1, pp. 329–330).

In 1843 Farnham (p. 312), about 20 miles above Shoshoni Falls on the western bank of the river, found a family of "Root Digger Indians, the man half clad, children naked, all filthy."

In 1842 Frémont mentioned no camps above Salmon Falls, but saw several at the falls and below it. "We now very frequently saw Indians, who were strung along the river at every little rapid where fish are to be caught." He described the Shoshoni at Salmon Falls as "poor" and "but slightly provided with winter clothing; there is but little game to furnish skins for the purpose; and of a little animal which seemed to be most numerous, it required twenty skins to make a covering to the knees . . . [the Indians] grow fat and become poor with the salmon . . ." and lived in "semicircular huts made of willow, thatched over with straw and open to the sunny south." These were "unusually gay savages, fond of loud laughter" (1887, vol. 1, pp. 249–252).

In August 1845 Palmer saw 18 or 20 Indian huts at Salmon Falls (p. 93).

Wyeth (Schoolcraft, 1851, p. 216) says "these Indians nearly starve to death annually, and in winter and spring are emaciated to the last degree; the trappers used to think they all eventually died from starvation as they became old and feeble. In salmon time they get fat."

Subsistence activities.—Each village was completely independent economically as there were virtually no subsistence activities requiring communal effort.

Hunting of large animals was rarely undertaken and involved no communal effort. Neither mountain sheep nor elk could be had within convenient distance. Deer were generally procured about 20 miles south of the Snake River where hunters ambushed them on game trails. There were no communal drives or corrals.

The main economic life centered around fishing and seed and root gathering, both essentially family affairs. Vegetable foods were gathered by individual families and fishing was carried on either by individual families or by small groups of related families. Seasonal activities of all were similar, varying only as one family or another wandered to a place of abundant roots, seeds, or fish, and remained there instead of returning to the Snake River for the winter.

Having generally wintered near the Snake River, living on dried salmon, insects, and roots, and frequently starving, spring found most families awaiting the first run of salmon.

The first "salmon," probably the salmon trout, *Salmo gairdneri*, came about March or April and were called tahma agai (tahma, spring+agai, salmon). These were caught both by people who had wintered on the river and by others who had stayed at Camas Prairie near their caches of dried roots but returned to the river in spring for fishing. The best fishing was near Hagerman, that is, at Upper and Lower Salmon Falls, at the bottom of which the fish were taken in nets. They were also caught with hooks, and especially with dams and weirs.

About this time people procured some yamp :, tui, boina, and other seeds and roots along the Snake River.

A second run of salmon came in May or June, called taza agai (taza, summer). This is probably *Oncorhynchus+schawytscha* (Walbaum), Chinook salmon. These were speared in pools under falls.

In July people who had fished in the Snake River usually traveled to Camas Prairie to gather yamp, camass, and other roots, and remained there until the fall salmon run. Individual families traveled and camped independently. Camass was gathered in great quantities and preserved for winter either by boiling in clay pots, grinding on a metate, spreading in the sun to dry and winnowing to remove the skins, or by merely drying without cooking. It was put in bark bags and buried. As much as possible was transported to the Snake River and stored in rocks in the canyon walls. While at Camas Prairie, gray ground squirrels, paizĭp, afforded the main meat.

Families gathered and camped where they pleased, all informants agreeing that there was neither ownership of food areas nor disputes arising from competition for food.

Before leaving Camas Prairie there was usually a large gathering for a dance.

Upon reaching the tributaries of the Snake River the tahma agai were called wo: vi agai (wo: vi, board, plank, or log, referring either to their large scales or to the fact that in the small streams they go under logs). Nets were better adapted to these small shallow streams than to the Snake River. People sometimes went up small streams, e. g., the Owyhee River, for the purpose of procuring roots and berries as well as of taking these salmon. Also, mugadu, described as a sucker, and ondiawox, a boney fish with a wide mouth and yellow stomach, were sometimes taken in the Owyhee River. Families might remain on these streams until fall, procuring some yamp:, hape (especially south of Jack Creek), sowik (the last two unidentified roots), chokecherries and service berries. Sometimes, if the salmon catch were good, people from both the Snake River and the Humboldt River wintered on the South Fork of the Owyhee River, called Sohohunub: (soho, cottonwood + hunub, creek), for although it was cold there was much timber. Fish could be taken through the ice.

About September some families went to the hills south of Camas Prairie to gather chokecherries. These were picked by hand, mashed on a metate, and dried in cakes to be mixed with other foods subsequently. Here also people got different kinds of sunflowers, which were gathered with a seed beater, the flowers perhaps being rubbed on a metate to remove the seeds. These seeds were parched before storing to prevent their sprouting if the ground became damp.

Even though families had to store surplus foods near where they gathered them, they preferred to return to the Snake River, where it was warm, for the winter. Here they could catch "trout," yuhubank[w1] (winter? + fish) and a small, shad-like fish with a small mouth, called natzika'[a].

In the fall there was another run of salmon or, perhaps, salmon trout, called kua agai (from kuəp, fence, referring to the fish weir) or yu: va agai (yu: va, fall). These could also be taken with hooks.

At Salmon Falls in August 25, 1812, the Astoria party "saw Shoshonies busily engaged killing and drying fish. The salmon begin to leap shortly after sunrise. At this time the Indians swim to the center of the falls, where some station themselves on rocks, and others stand to their waists in the water, all armed with spears [harpoons], with which they assail the salmon as they attempt to leap, or fall back exhausted . . . Mr. Miller, in the course of his wanderings, had been at these falls, and had seen several thousand salmon taken in the course of one afternoon" (Irving, 1897, vol. 2, pp. 169–171).

At the same falls, Frémont, 1842, observed that in the spring the salmon are so abundant "that they merely throw in their spears at random, certain of bringing out a fish." The Indians were paddling about in "boats made of rushes" (1887, vol. 1, pp. 249–250).

Ordinarily there was no ownership of fishing places. In fact people were encouraged to visit good places. When a dam or weir was built, however, four or five families cooperated in its construction under the direction of a person with the necessary knowledge. The director was called kuwədagwani. He was considered to be the owner of the dam. He took the responsibility of visiting the dam to remove the fish from the basket traps and of distributing them among the people who had assisted him. For his trouble he kept the greater share of the catch. Dams and weirs were rebuilt each year. If the director died any other competent person took charge. A single stream often had several dams along it.

It was probably infrequent that Snake River Shoshoni went south for pine nuts, because the trip was too long to make on foot. Pine nuts could be had no nearer than Grouse Creek, Utah, or Beowawe, Nevada. CT thought that people perhaps went for pine nuts if salmon failed, but does not remember any famine or any cannibalism which was common elsewhere. Pine-nut excursions were probably not undertaken until reservation days, when they possessed horses and traveled south from Owyhee.

Sometimes the residents of the vicinity of Salmon Falls made brief trips to Fort Hall. And Fort Hall people (pp. 202–207) and Shoshoni from the south frequently visited this section of Snake River for salmon. The latter came mostly from the high territory near the Nevada border, called Woŋgogadu (woŋgavi, "white pine"+gadu, sitting), where, CT said, starvation and cannibalism were frequent.

Political groups.—From the foregoing it is apparent that the true political unit was the village, a small and probably unstable group. Virtually the only factor besides intervillage marriage that allied several villages was dancing. Dances, however, were so infrequent and the participants so variable that they produced no real unity in any group.

TP said the leader of the dances was the te'gwani, an office inherited patrilineally. This man was chief at other times over a small group of villages, his main function being "to talk." Besides leading the dance, TP could not say what he directed or what he talked about. But he thought there were several such chiefs along the Snake River.

Dances were held at different places and at different seasons, depending largely upon whether there were sufficient persons within convenient distance and sufficient food to support them. Therefore the same people did not always participate. Paiute from the west frequently joined them. Dances lasted 5 days, the people playing the hand game, football, and woman's hockey during the day and dancing the round dance at night.

The director of the dance encampment was called the kwinidagwani (kwini, mush+dagwani, chief or talker). When the people arrived for the dance he assigned each family its place in the camp circle. He then planned the "feasts," telling the women to prepare the food. Sufficient food to support these gatherings for any considerable time was always a major problem.

The te'gwani, who probably directed the actual dancing, had a "talker" or interpreter, degwowəp. There were no messengers, the news merely being "spread."

TP added comments on chieftainship, his information coming partly from his grandfather on the North Fork of the Humboldt River, partly from recent activities at Owyhee, Western Shoshone Reservation, where the status of the chief was undoubtedly exalted. He said that the duties of the chief were to plan and direct dances, announce pine-nut crops, and, in recent years, to deal with white men, especially preventing warlike acts on the part of his people. This office was hereditary patrilineally. The incumbent chose the best of his sons who became chief upon his father's death. If he had no son any well known and highly esteemed man succeeded him.

The tegwowəp: (tegwü, to talk; tegwəp:, word+w p:, doing) was the chief's talker. He was chosen by the chief for his speaking ability and served only while the chief lived. When encamped for a dance he rode around in front of the camp circle announcing what was to be done and telling the young men to fish or hunt and the women to dig roots.

The kwinidagwani or boina (the seed of *Sophia*, often used for food) was sometimes also the chief's speaker, sometimes not. He chose a different dance ground each year and planned the camp circle around it with the opening east, placing a willow where each family was to erect its house. The chief's house was always on the western side, opposite the opening. The kwinidagwani also planned a large feast, to which one day during the middle of the dance was devoted.

At Owyhee, in reservation times, the general dance place was called Posiadung [api] (posia, louse+dung[api], dance place), located near Meadows, east of Owyhee. Although Shoshoni and Paiute from various regions participated in these dances, the leaders were Snake River Shoshoni or Agaidüka. The main chief was a famous Owyhee dance leader named Waimozo (waip:, dying of old age, i. e., becoming white+mozo, mustache). His tegwowəp was named Wahni (fox). He arranged for the young men to get meat for the feast and did the talking. The main singer was named Biahuvia (bia, big+huvia, sing).

TP also said there were hunt chiefs at Owyhee, tugu (hunt) tegwani, who directed communal antelope and deer hunts and fishing. These men had received dream powers, unsought, during their youth, which gave them hunting methods. Such men were unknown on the Snake River where there were no communal hunts. Even North Fork Shoshoni hunts were not shamanistic as farther south in Nevada.

Warfare.—There was no warfare, though Ballard (1866, p. 190) remarked that Shoshoni were afraid of the hostile "Pi-Ute" of southwestern Idaho and Oregon.

Marriage.—Blood relationship was a bar to marriage. Local exogamy was not barred per se, but it frequently happened that the two or three families comprising a village were related so that village exogamy was necessary.

The preferred spouse was a pseudo cross-cousin, the father's sister's (baha's) stepdaughter. The baha usually requested the young man to marry the girl. There was no bride service and no obligatory matrilocal residence. The young man, however, was obligated to "keep his baha's mouth plugged with fat," i. e., keep her supplied with game. This naturally militated against moving too far away from her. CT knew of no outstanding factors which determined whether marriage was matrilocal or patrilocal, saying that it was determined by the couple.

A man might also marry ("inherit") his mother's brother's wife (though she was also called baha), at his uncle's death if she were "pretty", but was not obliged to take her. He could not, however, marry the wife of his father's brother (called biatsi, little mother) if this uncle died. The implication of this is that the father's brother's wife might become his stepmother, through the levirate or sororate.

CT knew of no Snake River instance of brothers marrying sisters or a brother and sister marrying a sister and brother, but knew of a case at Fort Hall wherein three brothers married three sisters.

As many as three wives might be married polygynously. They were not necessarily sisters, though sororal polygyny or the sororate was desired under certain circumstances. When a man's wife died he became her sister's "cry house" (yage kah[nt]), meaning that they were now related through sorrow. If the sister-in-law had children needing a father or if the bereft husband had children he often married her.

CT knew of no instance of polyandry among the Agaidüka but said it would not have been disapproved. He described a case among Bannock, in which two unrelated men were married to one woman and slept on each side of her. He did not know whether they married her simultaneously. Both eventually left her, each marrying a different woman. A Fort Hall Shoshoni woman had married two unrelated men but the marriage did not endure.

In addition to orthodox marriage, men sometimes abducted married or unmarried women. This seems not to have differed from its practice elsewhere and need not be described in detail.

BOISE RIVER AND VICINITY

Shoshoni seem to have extended westward about to the Snake River which forms the boundary between Idaho and Oregon. They also occupied the Boise River Valley and probably to some extent the valleys of the Payette and Weiser Rivers. They probably never penetrated Oregon beyond the Blue Mountains.

The valleys of the several rivers in western Idaho were favorable for occupation. The rivers afforded salmon, the meadows had roots, especially camass, and pasturage for horses, and the low altitude produced mild winters.

This population was neither well defined politically nor territorially. It was scattered in small, independent villages of varying prosperity and tribal composition. Along the lower Snake, Boise, and Payette Rivers Shoshoni were intermixed with Northern Paiute who extended westward through the greater portion of southern and eastern Oregon. Slightly to the north they were probably mixed somewhat with their Nez Percé neighbors. Ballard (1866, p. 190) said they were much intermarried with "Bruneau Shoshonee."

The general name for people of this area was Yahandüka, Groundhog Eaters, though they imperceptibly merged with the Agaidüka of the Snake River and the Tukadüka of the mountains to the north. WH called them Yahandüka only so long as they remained in this region. He said families sometimes went south into Nevada for pine nuts, and were then called Tubadüka. He called this region Su:woki (suhuvi, willow + woki, striped; referring to the striping of the general landscape by willows along the streams).

As this territory was frequented by Fort Hall and Lemhi Shoshoni and by Nez Percés as well as by local residents, descriptions by early travelers may be somewhat misleading. The general impression is that it was a rendezvous of trading and fishing parties who mingled temporarily with the local residents.

Hunt, in 1812, observed that people near the Boise River were better clad and had more horses than Indians up the Snake River, though somewhere on the Snake River below the Boise River he met starving Shoshoni (Irving, 1897, vol. 2, pp. 42, 45). He said that the vicinity of the mouth of the Payette was a famed Snake salmon fishery (p. 160).

In 1839 Farnham saw a camp of "Snake" fishermen on the Boisais (Boise) River, who were "laying in their winter supply of salmon. Many horses were feeding on the plain" (1843, p. 316).

In the vicinity of the Boise and Snake Rivers, Townsend saw several groups of about 20 "Shoshoné" fishing (pp. 253–254).

Palmer saw 30 to 40 Indians on the southern side of Snake River, a little above the Boise River. Some were mounted and some had guns (pp. 244–245).

Frémont called the Boise River Indians "Shoshonee or Snake" in 1842. He observed that there were several encampments strung along the river. The Indians visited him on horseback, bringing dried and fresh fish to trade. "While the summer weather and salmon lasted, they lived contentedly and happily, scattered along the different streams where the fish were to be found; and as soon as the winter snows began to fall, little smokes would be seen rising among the mountains, where they would be found in miserable groups, starving out the winter; and sometimes, according to the general belief, reduced to the horror of cannibalism—the strong, of course, preying on the weak. Certain it is they are driven to any extremity for food, and eat every insect, and every creeping thing, however loathsome and repulsive. Snails, lizards, ants—all are devoured with the readiness and greediness of mere animals" (1887, vol. 1, pp. 255–257).

In 1833 Townsend saw 40 lodges of Shoshoni (?) in a single encampment (p. 247).

Lander (1860, p. 137) includes with "Western Shoshoni," people ranging on Camas Prairie; their "chief, Am-a-ro-ko; in English, 'Buffalo Meat under the shoulder.' Lodges, 75; subsistence, buffalo meat and wild vegetables; horses, large number." He also mentions "Bannacks of Fort Boise . . . Chief, Po-e-ma-che-ah; in English, 'Hairy man.' Lodges, 100; subsistence, salmon fish, wild vegetables, and roots; range, in the neighborhood of Fort Boisé; horses, large number."

That the latter observation does not wholly agree with those previously cited may be explained by Lander's misnaming this population, emphasizing its Paiute content, or mistaking Fort Hall Bannock visitors, who sometimes wintered here, for local residents. In fact, Ross (vol. 2, pp. 91–92) observed Shoshoni from Wyoming on what is probably the Boise River. However, Lander (1860, pp. 28–29) speaks of "Kamass Prairie" and "Fort Boisé Pannachs."

GROUSE CREEK

These people occupied a comparatively isolated territory centering on Grouse Creek northwest of Great Salt Lake. They were separated from Shoshoni to the west by broad deserts. GCJ stated that the next real village to the west was near Wells, Nevada, but there were probably at least a few scattered families in the intervening region. Bryant, for example, saw three huts built of "cedars" and grass on the western edge of the Great Salt Desert, probably near the Pilot Range (p. 184). The Great Salt Desert and Great Salt Lake separate the Grouse Creek district from that of the Gosiute Shoshoni and the "Weber Ute" (Shoshoni). The nearest neighbors were the Kamudüka of Bannock and Goose Creeks, the Promontory Shoshoni, and the Snake River Shoshoni.

The population was more than 200, the area exploited about 4,700 square miles, and the density therefore something less than 1 person per 23 square miles.

Grouse Creek Shoshoni were called Tubadüka (pine-nut eaters) by Shoshoni to the north because they are the northernmost Shoshoni in the pine-nut area. They were, however, also included among those people designated by Fort Hall Shoshoni as Tutwanait (beyond or below people).

Villages.—There were four main areas of settlement, as follows:

1. Grouse Creek called Tu: said (black tule) or Aŋgapuni (red eye), where about 12 families lived. No chief.

2. A little southwest of Lucin, called O'° (a shaly rock) or Podoŋgo'e (podo, stick+go'e, top). About 6 or 7 families.

3. On Raft River, probably near Lynn and Yost, called Kuiya (*Valeriana edulis*). About 15 families. Pocatello was formerly chief here, but later left to live among the Kamudüka, and finally went to Fort Hall, where he was considered "chief."

4. Dove (?) Creek, called Paduyavavadizop:ᵃ (spring+seeds of some species?).

Apparently the first three groups tended generally to live along Grouse Creek during the winter. The fourth wintered independently.

A partial census of these villages is as follows, the numbers referring to village numbers on the map and above; M, man; W, woman; m, married.

Residents of 1, Grouse Creek:

Yuhuduso m. W, both born at 1; 2 sons. 1 son m. a Kamudüka W, lived at 1, but killed her and went to Wells, never returning. The other son m. W at Wells, stayed there, killed her, and was killed.

Sogoyuwatsi m. local W ⫲ 1 daughter. She married a boy from 2, Tugitci'n son, see below.

Residents of 2, near Lucin:

Tugitici (born 2) m. W (born 2); 2 sons, 2 daughters. 1 son married two sisters polygynously, daughters of Icavaip (below, from 3, near Yost), whose son m. daughter of Sogoyuwatsi, above, but died soon afterwards. The first came to his father's house, patrilocally. He was unrelated to the girls. Second son m. daughter of Sogoyuwatsi, above, but died soon afterwards. The first daughter married a boy of unknown parentage, died; the second daughter married him and soon died.

Muwiŋjanəp m. W (born 2); 3 daughters, 1 son. 2 of the daughters m. polygynously a son of Bianunəp: (at 4) and went to 4 to live. A son m. a daughter of Bianunəp: (at 4) and brought her home to live. The third daughter m. a Skull Valley Gosiute and went there to live.

Residents of 3, Raft River, near Yost:

Icavaip (coyote; born 3) m. W (born 3); 3 daughters. The first m. a local man; lived locally. The other two polygynously m. a son of Tugitci and went to his father's house to live.

Tamawats (born 3) m. W (born 3) ; 1 son, who m. daughter of Kakwipuint (4) and went there to live.

Residents of 4, Rosebud Creek:

Bianunəp: (bia, big+nunəp:, chest) m. W (4) ; 2 sons, 2 daughters. 1 son polygynously m. 2 daughters of Muwiŋjanəp and brought them home. The other son went to Fort Washakie, Wyoming, and did not return. 1 daughter m. a son of Muwiŋjanəp and went to his home to live. The other m. a Shoshoni man at Wells, Nevada, and lived there; then later married a Fort Washakie Shoshoni and went there.

Tusuwatsi (tusu, muller+watsi, lost) m. W (born 1) ; 1 daughter, 3 sons. The 3 boys died before marrying. The girl married a man from 1, and her parents accompanied her there to live.

Suhidazigi (shining hair?) m. W (born 4) ; 2 sons, 1 daughter, all of whom married into the same family at the Kamudüka village of Biagamugəp:, near Kelton. Tsoaputsi (tsoap:, ghost+putsi, dimunitive ending) m. 1 daughter; Hugunəp: (bow and arrow) married the other. When Tsoaputsi died, Hugunəp: married her. They lived at Biagamugəb:. The daughter married Tsoaputsi's and Hugunəp:'s wife's brother.

Hugunəp: (above) had 2 daughters who lived long enough to marry. 1 married an orphan at Biagamugəp: and they moved to 1 where they lived next to the husband's sister and her husband from Washakie. The other daughter married Kutsvata's (the headman's) son's son at Biagamugəp: and moved to Washakie where the husband's mother's mother lived.

Kakwipunt m. W (born 1) ; 2 sons, 1 daughter. 1 son died before marriage. The other son went to Washakie, married a woman there. The daughter m. the son of Tamawats (above at 3) but lived at 4.

In addition to these, there was Hukuwət, a Hukundüka at Biagamugəp: who married a woman of the same village, their son and 2 daughters marrying Suhidazigi's children, mentioned above.

Subsistence activities.—Seasonal movements were not unlike those of people to the west. Pine nuts and various seeds and roots could be had in the local mountains, and salmon could be procured from the Snake River, though the necessity of going below Twin Falls for them somewhat restricted the feasibility of procuring them. Sometimes various families wintered among the Kamudüka to the east, especially at the village of Biagamugəp:, whose residents they often married. Trips for foods elsewhere, however, often led to marriage and a permanent change of residence to another district. Thus, GCJ's father was a Yahandüka Shoshoni from western Idaho, near Boise, who came to Dove Creek, then married at Grouse Creek where he remained.

Communal antelope hunts were held near Terrace and in Grouse Creek Valley, near Lucin. A new antelope corral was built each year. Hunts were held when antelope went south in the fall and in early spring; in the summer antelope were too scattered to hunt. There were at least 3 shamans. They were at O'°, at Kuiya, and at one other village.

Rabbit drives were held after snow had fallen in Grouse Creek Valley, near Lucin, and at a place north of Matlin. Several nets were used, the old man who owned each taking charge of it.

The few "trout" in Grouse Creek were a minor factor in the economy.

For communal hunts, Kumbidagwani (kumbi, a small, brown ground squirrel + dagwani, chief), the general hunt chief, living at Grouse Creek, was leader.

Warfare.—These people were sufficiently isolated in the deserts to have escaped the warfare to the east. They had no regalia and no interest in war. And when hostile war parties happened to enter their country they simply ran away to the mountains. Having few or no horses, however, they were not the objects of deliberate raids.

Political organization.—There was evidently sufficient joint activity involving all these people in hunting and dancing to give them some slight though unstable unity.

JP said the general chief was Tumozo, living at Dove Creek.

Marriage.—Marriage was prohibited between any blood relatives. Pseudo cross-cousin marriage, but not pseudo parallel-cousin marriage, was preferred. There was no bride price or bride service.

Polygyny was not necessarily sororal. Though the sororate was practiced it was not obligatory. Polyandry was necessarily fraternal and, though it was contracted with a view to permanency, one brother frequently got a wife for himself alone later. The levirate was practiced but was not required.

GCJ said marriage should be matrilocal for about a year, when the couple visited the husband's family. They then returned to the wife's family, where they lived until two or three children were born. Then they made a separate home near the wife's family.

Although the marriages recorded above probably do not represent wholly native custom, they occurred during GCJ's youth when any native pattern should have retained some strength. They do not, however, indicate temporary residence. Summarizing the data of the marriage of children (their parents are omitted because there is question whether GCJ actually knew the groups from which they came) and assuming for the moment that this static picture was a permanent one, there were nine cases of village exogamy, three of village endogamy, five of district exogamy (when the person married as far away as Wells (Nevada), Washakie (Utah), or Skull Valley). Because, however, the various villages listed tended to form a single winter encampment much of the time, the number of marriages endogamous by group would be increased considerably if 1, Tu:sai; 2, O'ᵒ and 3, Kuiya were merged. In post-marital residence, four cases were matrilocal (two where the marriage was with a distant group), six patrilocal (of which three were in a distant group), three where the spouses moved to a new locality, one where they remained in the same place. Again, however, if villages 1, 2, and 3 were merged, the bulk of residence would be neither patrilocal nor matrilocal with respect to locality.

These figures, of course, do not give anything like precision to the picture and may not be a wholly fair sampling. They do show, however, a lack of a consistent rule. The main controlling factor was convenience and relationship. GCJ said any blood relationship prevented marriage, but pseudo parallel-cousins as well as pseudo cross-cousins could marry.

Because people moved about, visited, and changed residence because of considerations of food, whereabouts of relatives, and other factors, no rigid rule of exogamy or post-marital residence could have developed.

The preference for alliances which bind families is illustrated in the occurrence of two cases of sororal polygyny, two of the sororate, two of marriage of a brother and sister to a sister and brother, and one of several brothers marrying several sisters, one of the levirate.

It was probably the Grouse Creek Shoshoni who, according to Remy and Brenchley (pp. 85–86), did not permit their women to be prostitutes for immigrants, but who sold their wives for horses. GCJ thought infidelity was taken lightly and little done about it.

In case of separation, which might occur because of infidelity or incompatibility, the woman took the children.

There were no avoidances of relatives.

PROMONTORY POINT (HUKUNDÜKA)

Four Shoshoni villages comprising a loose band lay in a district on the northern shore of Great Salt Lake. This territory extended from Promontory Point on the west to and including the lower portion of Bear River Valley on the east. Deserts separated it from the territory of the Kamudüka (Pocatello's band) to the west. It adjoined that of the Cache Valley band, Paŋwidüka, on the east. It is not known whether there were any villages to the immediate north.

This population as well as that on Bannock Creek (see also Hoebel, 1935) was formerly called Hukundüka (huki *Stipa*, seeds+duka, eaters). But as Bannock Creek people were also called Kamudüka (rabbit eaters) and as both Kamudüka and Hukundüka were variously used by different individuals, it seems preferable to reserve the former for Bannock Creek and the latter for Promontory Point, though to do so is somewhat arbitrary. A small remnant of Promontory Shoshoni now lives under the care of the Mormon Church at Washakie, Utah (not to be confused with Fort Washakie, Wyoming), in company with a few converts to the church drawn from Washakie's band of Wyoming Shoshoni. Because of their church membership, they are now called Mömun ündudua (Mormon children) by Fort Hall Shoshoni. Bannock call them Navagiu'.

Information about this group is inadequate. It comes from OD who was born on Promontory Point.[21]

The four villages listed, as numbered on the map, figure 12, were:

7. Toŋgicavo (toŋgica, chokeberry tree+pa, water), on the western side of Promontory Point near Mount Tarpey. Population: Four families, including that of Segwitc (father of Yegai Timbimbu, an old man now living at Washakie), who was village headman and band chief.

8. Nanavadzi (nana, our+badzi, sisters; so-called because several sisters had lived here), near Little Mountain, east of Promontory Point. Population, 23 families. Headman, Kwüdawüatsi, who was a secondary leader of the entire band. Segwitc sometimes wintered here.

9. Nagwitüwəp (smoking ?, i. e., smoke from a fire in a cave), on Blue Creek, north of the old railroad. OD saw little of these people; headman unknown.

10. Südotsa (sühuvi, willow+dotsa, round place), an encampment scattered along the low, flat valley of the Bear River from near Bear River City to Deweyville. Headman, Poibonoip.

Of these, OD regarded Nanavadzi as the main village. Probably a few horses provided some mobility which facilitated band cooperation. In fact, the people sometimes traveled to Bear Lake on horseback to assemble with Cache Valley and Kamudüka people.

Subsistence activities.—Little information is available about the territory in which vegetable foods were gathered. It was said that people traveled sometimes as far as Brigham City, Ogden, Huntsville east of Ogden, and Cache Valley. They sometimes went to Grouse Creek country for pine nuts, when families without horses made four or five trips if necessary to carry the nuts home.

Near the mouth of the "Roseaux" (Malad) River, Utah, in August 1842, Frémont met an encampment of two families gathering seeds and kooyah (*Valeriana edulis*) and thistle roots. They had 12 to 15 horses. Some miles upstream was another camp of several families gathering seeds, roots, and service berries (1887, vol. 1, pp. 238–239).

Promontory Cave shows evidence that considerable bison had once existed in the area (Steward, 1937). These had been fairly abundant along the lower Bear River but had not, to OD's knowledge,

[21] OD was born in a cave a little north of the large cave excavated by the writer in 1930–31, Ancient Caves of the Great Salt Lake Region, 1937. Although there is little doubt that the numerous caves in this region were frequently occupied by Shoshoni, the distinctive culture abundantly represented in this cave does not at all correspond to that of the Shoshoni. OD said that once his people retreated to the large cave where Gosiute Shoshoni attempted to smoke them out. It is doubtful that Gosiute ever traveled this far from home and more doubtful that they fought their kinsmen. A similar story is related of different caves in Nevada.

ranged farther west. After acquiring sufficient horses, people sometimes joined Chief Washakie and his Wyoming Shoshoni for bison
hunts.

Communal antelope hunts, both with and without corrals, involved
all the villages under Nagwowǝp, the antelope shaman. These were
held along the Bear River flats, near Sudotsa and south of Lampo
along Blue Creek.

Communal rabbit drives were relatively unimportant in pre-Caucasian days, as all informants agreed that there had been few jack
rabbits at that time. Promontory Point is near the northern limit
of the black-tail jack rabbit. Instead of using nets, they surrounded
and killed the rabbits with clubs or drove them into series of loops
suspended from horizontal cords, arranged somewhat like nets.
Drives were held in the fall, after the first snow, under the direction
of Taiwatsi, who lived at Toŋgicava. All the villages forgathered
and hunted along Blue Creek near Nagwitümǝp or on the western
side of Promontory Point near Toŋgicava. Sometimes they joined
forces with people from Biagamugǝp, to the west.

Communal duck drives were held under the direction of Segwitc
in the marshes around Bear River Bay which abounded in water-
fowl.

Deer were sometimes driven over cliffs by groups of hunters. The
leader was Hubiünoki, who was in charge of all hunting.

Fish, taken in the Bear River, especially near Corinne, were auwok
(suckers), widjavănkw (?), and tsapănkw (trout). Use of weirs
involved some communal effort, but how much is not known. Near
the mouth of the Bear River in August 1842 Frémont came upon
"several families of Root Diggers, who were encamped among the
rushes on the shore, and appeared very busy about several weirs
or nets which had been rudely made of canes and rushes for the
purposes of catching fish . . . They had . . . matted hair, and were
almost entirely naked; looking very poor and miserable . . ." Their
language seemed to be "Snake" (1887, vol. 1, p. 223).

In 1855 Hunt (p. 198) found Shoshoni from Wyoming fishing at
the mouth of the Bear River.

Warfare.—These people were sufficiently exposed to raiding parties
from the east and sufficiently in contact with warring Shoshoni and
Ute to have acquired some interest in warfare. They were not
numerous enough to undertake major campaigns, though they doubtless sometimes joined forces with other Shoshoni. They did, however, have war regalia. Small parties undertook horse-stealing
expeditions.

Political organization.—For activities concerning the entire band—
trips to Wyoming for bison, antelope hunts, and festivals—Segwitc,

assisted somewhat by Kwüdawüatsi, was chief, dagwani. Another man, Tuandumi, was chief of some importance, though his special rank and duties are not clear. Though chieftainship tended to be patrilineal, there was no strict rule, any good man being chosen at the death of a chief. The chief chose two or three announcers, dagwaniwǝp, who met and smoked with him while receiving important information. The announcers then went among the camps, "spreading the news."

In addition to these general chiefs, a man named Tonihünt was the special dance director.

Marriage.—All blood relatives and even pseudo cross-cousins were prohibited from marriage. Thus marriages were entirely outside the family. Villages included unrelated persons, so that there was no rule of local exogamy.

Marriages were arranged with the consent of parents. The man's parents gave the girl's parents presents of buckskins and other goods, but received nothing in return.

Polygyny was usually sororal, but rarely more than two wives were kept in the same house. The sororate was common, but not required.

There was no true polyandry, but sexual privileges might be granted a brother. The levirate was common, but was not required.

Post-marital residence was variable.

There was no abduction of women, married or unmarried.

Some respect but no avoidance was required between a man and his mother-in-law and between a woman and her father-in-law.

WESTERN INDEPENDENT SOUTHERN PAIUTE VILLAGES

Much of the territory occupied by Southern Paiute is, like that of the Nevada Shoshoni, a succession of arid mountain ranges and aggraded, sage-covered desert valleys. In extreme southern Nevada and adjoining California, however, it is more arid and lies within the area of the Mojave Desert basins and ranges. Southern Paiute territory in southern Utah and northern Arizona was only slightly less arid, embracing a portion of the Great Basin and a portion of the Colorado Plateau.

Though certain plant species in this territory differed from those in western Shoshoni territory, the basic ecology of both linguistic groups was very similar. Some horticulture was probably practiced by all Southern Paiute, but it seems to have been a minor supplement to hunting and gathering and contributed little to their prosperity. Frémont (1887, vol. 1, pp. 378–379) described the Paiute of the Muddy and Moapa Rivers as barefoot and nearly naked predatory Diggers. Horticulture did not permit large or stable populations which greatly affected sociopolitical groups.

Kelly (1934) divided the Southern Paiute, including the Chemehuevi, into 15 "subgroups, bands, or tribes," which are "dialectic units with political concomitants." It is questionable whether all of these groups fulfilled the requirements of "bands" according to the present definition. Dialectic distinctiveness is an insufficient criterion of a band. Band members must habitually have cooperated in a sufficient number of economic and social activities under a central control to have acquired a sense of community of interest. It is difficult to understand how people who were scattered over such vast territories and often separated by wide, waterless deserts could, when traveling on foot, habitually have joined forces in any important communal undertaking. Yet the Southern Paiute, in contrast to the Western Ute, apparently lacked horses until very recently. Möllhausen (1860, vol. 2, p. 296) testified to the Paiute's lack of horses in the Searles Lake region near the Mojave Desert, and Sale (1865, p. 155), Head (1867, pp. 174–176; 1868, pp. 148–149), and Fenton (1869, p. 203) said Southern Paiute in general had no horses. Though Southern Paiute frequently raided travelers between Utah and southern California, horses which came into their possession were more often eaten than ridden. Frémont, for example, observed in 1843 that Indians in the vicinity of the Mohave River and Agua Tomaso "make no other use of horses than to eat them" (1887, vol. 1, p. 373).

It is probable that the aboriginal number of politically independent groups was nearer to Powell and Ingalls' list of 31 (1874) than to Kelly's 15. Indeed, if the whole area were organized on a village basis, 31 is probably short of the actual number. The aboriginal absence of well-defined, named political bands could easily account for the discrepancies in lists of Southern Paiute divisions furnished by Lowie's informants (1924, p. 193).

Although information is not now available to show whether the occupants of the smaller band territories mapped by Kelly for southern Utah carried on communal activities as true bands, it is certain that the people in the enormous Las Vegas "band" area were not a band. Where Kelly's map shows a single band, Powell and Ingalls list 8 "tribes," some of which they said comprised several formerly independent "tribes" (1874, pp. 10–11). Each of these was probably a group of encampments, like the Shoshoni villages to the west and north, which wintered at a certain site. These 8 "tribes," including 2 in probable Shoshoni territory (fig. 1), were: 31 Kau-yai'-chits at Ash Meadows under Nu-a'-rung [Coville (1892, p. 358) recorded that the Ash Meadows population was mixed Shoshoni and Southern Paiute. The same is true today and was probably true in aboriginal days]; 68 Ya'gats of Amagrosa under Ni-a-pa'-ga-rats [probably also mixed with Shoshoni]; 18 Kwi-en'-go-mats at Indian Spring under Pats-a'-gu-ruke; No-gwats near Potsi under To-ko'-pur; Pa-room'-pats at Pa-room Spring [probably Pahrump Spring] under Ho-wi-a-gunt (the last two groups total 56); 161 Nu-a'-gun-tits of Las Vegas under Ku-ni'-kai-vets; 57 Mo-vwi'-ats at Cotton-wood Island under Ha-va-rum-up; Mo-quats at Kingston Mountain under Hun-nu'-na-wa; Ho-kwaits near Ivanspaw under Ko-tsi'-an; Tim-pa-shau'-wa-got-sits at Providence Mountain under Wa-gu'-up (the last 3 groups totaled 85).

The total population for Kelly's Las Vegas area, omitting Ash Meadows and Amagrosa, is 332. The total area is about 9,450 square miles; the density, 1 person to 28.5 square miles. Though the population was doubtless somewhat reduced by 1874 and Powell and Ingalls probably overlooked a few Indians, this estimate is reasonable as compared with the Shoshoni area, for the territory is exceptionally infertile. Certainly Wheeler's estimate of 2,000 for this same general area (1875, p. 37) is many times too great.

PAHRUMP AND LAS VEGAS

Detailed information is available only for the Southern Paiute of Pahrump Valley and Ash Meadows. It is from AH and MHo. The natural environment of this region is like that of the neighboring areas of Beatty, Death Valley, and the Kawich Mountains. Its greatest asset was the Spring Mountains to the east, which rising to a great height (Charleston Peak, 11,910 feet), afforded abundant pine nuts, seeds, and considerable game.

Subsistence activities.—Pine nuts, tu:v, were gathered in the Spring Mountains. The village chief announced when the nuts were ripe but had no authority in managing the trip or the gathering. Families traveled alone or in small groups and each gathered on its own tract until snow made it impossible. Most families returned to the winter village in the valley but some remained in the mountains.

The gathering process was like that of the Shoshoni. Women pulled cones from the trees by means of poles 15 to 20 feet long, each having a fire-bent hook on its end. The cones were gathered into conical baskets, a'ʰus, and carried to a pile where they were burned to extract the nuts. Loose nuts which had fallen to the ground were also picked up. All these were carried down to the winter village. Other nuts were left in the cones and stored in the mountains in grass- or brush-lined pits covered with grass, brush, and earth.

Pine-nut tracts were owned by men and inherited by their sons. A woman gathered on her husband's land. Trespass sometimes caused fights but usually resulted merely in verbal exchange. It was generally avoided, however, because owners were believed to practice witchcraft against trespassers. Permission to gather on a tract was readily extended to families which owned tracts in areas where the crop had failed. Thus, Shoshoni at Ash Meadows were often invited to pick on the Spring Mountains, and, when the Spring Mountains crop failed, Paiute were invited to pick in the Shoshoni Mountains. The latter locality was less desirable, however, as it has little water.

Mesquite, hopi^hmp', which ripens in August, was fairly abundant at Ash Meadows, where families owned groves. Screw beans, also ripening in August, were an important food at Ash Meadows but were less plentiful at Pahrump. Both beans were gathered in considerable quantities and stored for future use.

Other wild-seed plants grew more sparsely over wide areas. Perhaps for this reason tracts of them were not family owned. Ash Meadows people went either 30 or 40 miles to the Calico Hills or to Big Dune in the Amagrosa Desert for sand bunch grass seeds (*Oryzopsis hymenoides*), wai'^l. At Big Dune they sometimes met Beatty Shoshoni. As this seed often grows miles from water it was necessary to transport water in a basketry olla. Another important wild seed, ko' (=Shoshoni kuhwa, *Mentzelia* ?), which ripened in early spring grew higher in the hills. Ash Meadows people gathered it in the Funeral Mountains or near Cane Spring, both of which were also visited by Shoshoni.

The northwestern limit of aboriginal horticulture was probably Pahrump Valley and Ash Meadows. Crops grown were corn, squash, beans, and sunflowers. Cultivation, which has been described in detail elsewhere, entailed planting small fields in moist soil near streams and using a little irrigation. The cultivated fields at Manse and Pahrump in Pahrump Valley were scattered in small plots. Apparently there was insufficient arable land for all families to own plots. Those without land traded wild plant foods for cultivated crops. AH seemed to think that these foods were freely distributed rather than actually bartered. If true, the gifts were probably to related families.

There was no question of inheritance of fields, for the crop was destroyed, even if about to bear a harvest, at the death of the owner.

Cultivated, like wild, vegetable foods were nowhere sufficiently abundant to permit permanent attachment to a locality. Crops were harvested and stored during a brief period, after which the family continued its travels in search of wild foods until winter. In late fall, 1849, Manley (1894, pp. 127–133) saw a single Indian family living alone somewhere on the eastern side of the Amagrosa Desert, where they had grown a small amount of corn and apparently some squash near a hot spring.

Hunting seems to have played a very minor role in Southern Paiute economy, as game was scarce. Ash Meadows people usually went to the Spring Mountains for deer, but sometimes took them on the Shoshoni Mountains. Because of the great distance back to the village, they butchered them at once, dried the meat and skins, and carried them home in nets. Mountain sheep, which were formerly very numerous, were taken in the mountains between the Amagrosa River and Pahrump Valley and in the Funeral Mountains. Both deer and sheep were hunted by individuals or small groups of men without formal organization or leaders.

Communal antelope and rabbit drives, both of which were among the most important Shoshoni collective enterprises, were said not to have been practiced. There were few antelopes. Rabbits were taken with traps or surrounded by fire, neither method involving large groups of hunters.

There was no form of ownership of hunting territories.

It was customary if not obligatory for a hunter to share large game with his neighbors.

Festival.—The annual fall festival was probably the outstanding activity which in aboriginal days united several villages. Unfortunately, however, the village alinement is not known. In recent times festivals were held at places where the population had been concentrated, for example, Manse, Pahrump, Las Vegas, or Moapa. AH said that in a given year only one of these places would hold the festival and that visitors came from Beatty, Ash Meadows, Pahrump Valley, Las Vegas, etc., and even from San Bernardino. The long journey from many of these localities could only have been made with the horse and wagon. ChB at Las Vegas said that Pahrump and Las Vegas held independent festivals, each under its own chief, and that Tule Springs people joined the latter.

The festival lasted 3 or 4 days and terminated with mourning rites. It was planned and directed by the local chief, who had it announced 6 or 8 months in advance. While the dances and rites were in progress the chief made speeches from time to time. Amusements included the circle dance, a borrowed form of the Ute bear dance, and two special dances. On the last night buckskins and other property, which had been accumulated, was burned for persons who had died within the year.

The last festival was held about 30 years ago.

Political organization.—As the Southern Paiute appear to have had no communal activities except the annual festival, it is impossible to imagine any true band unity in native times. Warfare was probably unimportant except, perhaps, among people near Las Vegas, who were subject to raids by the Mojave.

The arrival of the white man introduced new factors. Reduction of native wild-food resources led the Paiute to band together somewhat in order to raid and rob the white man. Eventually, horses aided them in extensive travel and in communicating and cooperating with one another. And finally, when the period of struggle was over, the United States Government assembled the people on reservations and dealt with them through their representatives. Consequently, there emerged loosely united aggregates which became known as bands.

Probably Powell and Ingalls' list is comparatively representative of the native period when village members wintered together at a favorable site and, under the advice of a village "chief," foraged the same general terrain. There was, however, little cohesion, except the possible bond of relationship, between families within a village and even less between members of different villages. Though Wheeler named Tercherum as the "principal chief" of this area in 1869, he remarked that he "seemed to have little authority outside his own small number of wick-e-ups" (1887, vol. 2, p. 37).

From informant testimony, Paiute of the Pahrump and Las Vegas regions were never unified in a single band. AH named a succession of three Las Vegas chiefs (towin'dum): Patsadum, who died many years ago; then Tasiü'dum, who also died many years ago; then A:udia', who was recently killed. For the region of Ash Meadows and Pahrump he named Takopa (who was probably born at Las Vegas and died at Pahrump about 1895). Takopa's main function was to direct the festival. ChB added that when Mojave raided Las Vegas people, Takopa might assist them, perhaps even taking command.

Informants from both Pahrump and Las Vegas regarded Takopa as chief of "all the Southern Paiute" but could name no function of his which did not involve dances or transactions with the white man. Benjamin, a veteran scout of the United States Army, who had lived at Tule Springs near Las Vegas, succeeded Takopa in his position.

Marriage.—Marriage was in no way connected with unilineal village groups. There was no rule of post-marital residence nor of village exogamy.

ChB knew of no polyandry, polygyny, nor cross-cousin or pseudo cross-cousin marriage. AH denied avoidance of relatives. He said the levirate and sororate, however, were practiced.

NORTHERN SHOSHONI BANDS

LEMHI AND CENTRAL IDAHO

The great mountain mass of central Idaho rises abruptly on the northern edge of the arid Snake River plains. Although precipitation is sufficient to support coniferous forests on an unusually large portion of this area, the ranges are high and rugged and the canyons deep and narrow, rendering it unfavorable for human occupation, except in the Lemhi Valley.

Shoshoni and possibly some Bannock had penetrated this region and established comparatively large villages on the Lemhi River and several small villages in isolated places in the mountains. Some were even located east of the continental divide—the Bitter Root Mountains—in western Montana. Although the Shoshoni language seems to have been identical throughout central Idaho, there was, prior to the consolidation of the mountain villagers on the Lemhi River, when all of them became known as Lemhi, a marked cultural difference between the inhabitants of the Lemhi River and the mountains. In Lewis and Clark's time, 1806, the former were a loose band possessing many horses, hunting buffalo, and even engaging in some warfare under a true chief. For many years the latter continued to be impoverished, disorganized mountaineers, who, in their isolation, successfully avoided most contacts with the white man and with other tribes. JP, who had lived in one of these villages, said that they were induced to move to the Lemhi Valley only by the promise of rations. A reservation was established there, but in 1907 the entire Lemhi group was moved to Fort Hall.

The distinction between mountain and Lemhi Valley Shoshoni, which is of great importance to the present study, has not, however, always been revealed by terminology applied to these people.

Lewis and Clark, who saw only the Lemhi Valley people, said that they called themselves Cho-sho-nê (vol. 2, pp. 366–367), though JP thought "Shoshoni" to be of white origin. Gass (p. 121) called them Snake. Humfreville (p. 271) calls the "fierce tribe that lived near the headwaters of the Salmon River and in the Upper Snake River Valley" Tukuarika, Mountain Sheep-eaters. Wheeler (1879, p. 410) also applies Tuka-ri'ki to the Salmon River Snakes generally.

Lander says of these people (1860, p. 137): "Chief, Qui-tan-i-wa; in English, Foul Hand,' with 'Old Snag'; and the Bannoch 'Grand Coquin.' Lodges, 50; subsistence, salmon and trout, elk, deer, and antelope; range, on Salmon River and the mountains north of it; horses, a small number. A small band of the Sheep-eaters are very fierce and wild, rarely visiting whites."

Fort Hall Shoshoni designated these people collectively as Agaidüka (salmon eaters) and CT, from the lower Snake River near Bruneau, called them Tukadüka (mountain sheep eaters) or Agaimbagate (agai, salmon + pa, water + gate, belong to). Both the Lemhi and the mountain dwellers called themselves Agaidüka, Shoshoni, or Nü:wə, but the latter distinguished themselves as Tukadüka. These are probably Lewis and Clark's "Broken-moccasins." I shall designate the mountaineers by Tukadüka[22] and the Lemhi River population by Lemhi, though the latter name is not native.

Neighboring tribes were: Flathead, called Da:[ta] sivana (datasiva, something flat), to the northeast in Montana; Nez Percé, called Sowiga'[a] (probably the root or tuber), occupying the lower Snake and Salmon Rivers to the northwest across the mountains[23]; Crow, called A'[a] (horn), northeast of Yellowstone; Shoshoni in Wyoming south of the Crow, called Kogoho'e, and in southern Idaho, called Pohogue'. In western Idaho the Tukadüka had slight contact with the Shoshoni of southwestern Idaho, called Yahandüka (ground-hog eaters), or, sometimes, Tudubiwa.

Although the Tukadüka remained isolated until comparatively recent times, the Lemhi had frequent contact with their various neighbors. They were often visited by the Nez Percé, Flathead, and southern Idaho Shoshoni, who found the Lemhi Valley a refuge from the raiding Blackfeet. Sometimes, also, they joined these tribes on trips for buffalo, or met them at Camas Prairie in western Idaho.

In 1832 Bonneville encountered Nez Percé on the Upper Salmon River. He mentioned 300 lodges of Pend Oreille who wintered on the Racine Amere, eating roots and dried bison, and who traveled from spring until fall on the headwaters of the Missouri River, Henry's Fork of the Snake River and the northern branches of the Salmon River (Irving, 1898, vol. 1, pp. 108–111, 123). In 1833 Work (Lewis and Phillips, pp. 137 ff.) saw Flathead and Nez Percé wintering on the Lemhi River. A few years later Beckwourth encountered Flatheads on the Snake River (p. 112). In 1838 Parker was accompanied by Nez Percé and Flatheads on the upper Salmon River (1842, pp. 107–108). Gottfredsen states that Bannock, Shoshoni, and Nez Percé were fishing in the Lemhi River in 1855, when the Mormon mission was founded at Fort Lemhi (pp. 90–91).

Villages.—Following are the villages listed by JP, the numbers corresponding to those on the map, figure 10:

1. Pasasigwana (pa, water+sasip:, blood+gwana, smell), at a warm spring in the mountains north of Clayton. About 30 families. These wintered together, but in summer groups of two or three families moved together on foot, gathering vegetable foods and hunting small game around the headwaters of the Salmon River, East Fork of the Salmon River, the Lost River Range and the Salmon Range. The head man was Woŋgowütavi, his duties consisting mostly of directing fishing (paŋgwidagwani, fish chief) in the Salmon River.

---

[22] Lowie, 1909, p. 206, mentions Ā'gai-dika at Lemhi and Tuku-rika in the Lemhi district. Kroeber, 1909, p. 268, recorded the Lemhi as Duku-dika-nü.

[23] This location was also given by Bonneville (Irving, vol. 2, p. 4).

Once these people went to Camas Prairie where they procured some horses and subsequently joined other Shoshoni in buffalo expeditions to the east.

2. Sohodai (sohovi, cottonwood+dai, place). On the upper Middle Fork of the Salmon River, near Three Rivers. About six families. Tuŋgwüsü, headman.

3. Bohodai (bohovi, sagebrush). Near the junction of Middle Fork and the Salmon River. About 20 families. Gusawat (gus, "pants"+awat, gone), headman.

4. A site on the upper Salmon River where a few families from Sohodai sometimes wintered.

5. Pagadüt (lake, named from Red Rock Lake), on Red Rock Creek above Lima, Montana. The village was called Unauvump (una, make+uvump, locomotive) after the railroad was built. About 40 families, scattered from the vicinity of Lima to the lake. Dagwocijon (dagwoci, perspiration+John), headman.

6. Possibly a few families lived in the vicinity of Dillon, Montana.

7. Pasïmadai (pasï, "spruce"). Upper Salmon River. About 2 families. No headman.

8. Guembedüka (guembe, "short-tail ground hog.")[24] About 7 miles north of the town of Salmon. About three families who joined the Lemhi River people under Tindoi.

9. Pa:dai (pa, water), the villages or camps scattered along the Lemhi River, centered at Salmon. These people got horses at an early date. JP thought they were procured from a Spaniard who had an adobe house at Fort Hall, and subsequently ate his companions and moved to Dillon, Montana. It was believed that Tündoi's brothers-in-law had somehow procured the horses from him. Lewis and Clark, however, estimated that there were 400 horses (about 4 per man) in the Lemhi Valley in 1806. They were equipped with Spanish bridles and some had Spanish brands (vol. 2, p. 347; vol. 4, p. 74).

JP's estimate of the Lemhi River population for about 1860 or 1870 is 100 camps or about 500 to 600 persons. Lewis and Clark did not see the entire population assembled, but estimated that a group under one "chief" had 100 warriors, 300 women and children, or 400 souls (vol. 2, p. 370), and that another "chief" had 60 warriors, who were augmented from time to time by men from encampments which were strung along the river (vol. 2, p. 338–339). Possibly a third group had 7 lodges (vol. 3, p. 6). Gass mentions 1 village, which perhaps was included in Lewis and Clark's estimate, which had 25 lodges and many horses (p. 123). The grand total would

---

[24] Lowie, 1909, p. 206, places Kuembe-rika in southern Idaho. A different group?

be at least 600 persons. It probably decreased somewhat after the arrival of the white man, but perhaps 100 families were added when the Tukadüka moved down to the valley.

The total Tukadüka and Lemhi population was therefore about 200 families or 1,200 persons in a subsistence area of some 27,000 square miles, or 1 person to 22.5 square miles.

Lewis and Clark (vol. 3, p. 16) and Gass (pp. 124–125) observed that the difficulties of procuring food imposed a hardship upon a large group and that the smaller, isolated encampments seemed to fare better.

Subsistence activities.—Throughout the mountains, subsistence was principally on seeds, roots, mountain sheep, deer, and salmon. Antelope were scarce; there were no buffalo. The fertile and lower Lemhi Valley had some antelope. Moreover, the Lemhi Shoshoni could keep horses with which to make expeditions to the south and east for buffalo and to the west for seeds and roots, especially camass. In fact, many seeds utilized by Lemhi grew along the Snake River but not in the salmon district or were more abundant near the Snake River, so that possession of horses was a great advantage.

At best, however, foods were not plentiful. Gass (p. 123) described the Lemhi as the "poorest and most miserable nation I ever beheld; having scarcely anything to subsist on except berries and a few fish."

The main plant foods listed by JP were:

Seeds which could be stored for winter: Five species or kinds of sunflower (*Helianthus*); a little lamb's quarters (*Chenopodium*), *Sophia* (boi'); rye grass; cattail; wada (unidentified); stickseed (*Lappula*); rose; "white" (?) pine nuts (woŋgoduba). Gass in August 1806 observed Lemhi River people who had gathered quantities of sunflower seeds and lambs quarters, which they pounded and mixed with service berries to make a kind of bread (p. 125).

Plants eaten as greens: tsinambogo (unidentified); onions.

Roots which could be stored for winter: a thistle (tsin꞉); yamp꞉; nəp꞉ (unidentified); *Valeriana* (kuiyu); kan[a] (unidentified); soiga (unidentified); pasigo' (perhaps *Calochortus*), procured only at Camas Prairie; cattail; ha꞉pi (unidentified); bavo (unidentified); stickseed (*Lappula*); winigo (unidentified; Salmon and Snake Rivers); payump꞉ (unidentified); hunib (unidentified).

Roots which could not be preserved: a cactus (müts); pā'wa (*Rumex?*, eaten green); onion (kunk); prickly pear cactus (wogavi); dag꞉[u] (unidentified; procured in Lemhi country); sigo (procured in Lemhi country).

Berries preserved: service berry, chokecherry.

Berries not preserved: elderberry.

This region is far north of the occurrence of *Pinus monophylla*, but nuts of the "white pine" were gathered in some quantity, especially in the mountains bordering the Lemhi Valley on the west. A number of related families usually traveled together and the women picked. Nuts were carried back to the winter village in buckskin bags and, if there were a surplus, it was cached in the mountains to be gotten on future trips. If other foods were plentiful, stored pine nuts might last all winter. There was no ownership of pine-nut or other food areas.

There were few deer. Antelope were surrounded on horseback and shot with bows and arrows. Such surrounds were usually held in midwinter, when the snow was deep. People came down from the Salmon River to near the present town of May. They were usually led by the general hunt chief, dugapavi (duga, hunt+pavi, leader), who was named Yumapai. Shamanistic drives with corrals were unknown.

Rabbits were too scarce for communal hunts, until comparatively recently, when the use of nets was borrowed from people to the south.

Young water fowl were sometimes taken in drives in August, under any leader.

Distribution of game killed by any hunter to all village members was not compulsory unless there was starvation. Ordinarily he shared only with relatives.

Parker (1842, pp. 106–107) recounts a horse surround of buffalo in 1835 somewhere near the upper Snake River.

Fish taken in the Salmon River and its tributaries were: Tahmaagai (tahma, spring+agai, salmon), a variety up to 18 inches long, which could be taken all winter; in March they went into small streams to spawn. Probably *Salmo gairdneri* Richardson.

Aŋgaagai (aŋga, red), redfish?, August.

Agai, Chinook salmon, August.

Tsa: pănk[w1] (tsaund, good+pănk[w1], fish), "trout," occurring in all streams.

Mu: dziwihü' (muvi, nose+dziwihü', pointed), "white fish."

Mu: gada (holding on with mouth), sucker.

Ondamaya (onda, yellow+ma'ᵃ, hand+ya, hanging; i. e., fin), somewhat like a sucker.

Puhiwȧ'ᵈ (puhi, green+wȧᵈ, stripes), about the size of minnows, but are not minnows.

Awito'ᵒ (?), about 6 inches longer; "somewhat like catfish."

Padoɡoa (pa, water+doɡoa, snake), "eels," i. e., lamprey.

Construction of fish weirs involved several families. Weirs were built on the Lemhi River and other tributaries but not in the Salmon

River. Usually three or four families cooperated. Other persons sometimes stole the catch or even parts of the weir, but nothing was done about it. For construction of more ambitious weirs, especially in the Lemhi River, about 20 families cooperated, erecting their tipis on the bank at each end of it. A man was stationed at each end of the weir to watch for the fish while the people danced. When the fish came he requested a number of men to go along the weir and help him remove the fish. They strung the fish on willows and carried them to shore, distributing them among the families. There was no shamanism or ceremony connected with fishing. Any interested men were leaders.

In addition, fish were taken by means of hooks, harpoons, baskets, and dams by individual fishermen.

Many subsistence activities involved all or large portions of the Lemhi population in a way that contributed materially to its solidarity. The following were described by JP for the period following the amalgamation of the Tukadüka with the Lemhi.

During the summer some families went east to hunt buffalo while others went west to Camas Prairie to trade buffalo hides to the Nez Percé for horses. A family preferred to hunt and trade in alternate summers.

As buffalo were extinct in Idaho by 1840, the hunting families crossed the Bitter Root Mountains to Crow territory in the vicinity of Yellowstone, gathering seeds, roots, and berries on the way. Tündoi was the leader. For protection against marauding parties of Blackfeet they often joined forces with Fort Hall Shoshoni and Bannock, Wyoming Shoshoni, Flatheads, and sometimes even Crows. All summer they followed the herds. In hunting all the men set out at the same time, each taking fast horses with which he ran down the animals. They did not surround, impound, or drive them over cliffs. In October these families returned to the Lemhi Valley with their hides and dried meat.

As trips to Camas Prairie involved neither communal hunts nor danger of raids by hostile tribes, they were made by small, independent groups of related families which had no formal chiefs. The main purpose of these trips was to trade buffalo hides for horses.[25] These families generally remained in the same place until October, eating sage hens, grouse, ground hogs, woodchucks, trout from the small streams flowing into the Malad River, and deer and antelope from the mountains. They gathered yamp:, pa: sigo'° ha: p⁽ᵘ yutavo'°, pit:sogo, drying any surplus and transporting it home in

---

[25] Bonneville observed that Nez Percé, Flathead, and Pend d'Oreilles, all of whom occasionally visited Camas Prairie, had many horses in 1833, some individuals owning 40. Lewis and Clark (vol. 3, p. 5) also saw many horses among them.

buckskin bags. Some meat was also preserved. Although some Shoshoni from Fort Hall and from the lower Snake River and Nezperce also spent the summer in this prairie, there was neither competition for food nor ownership of food territories, as there was said to be sufficient for all. Even Shoshoni who wintered in Wyoming under Chief Washakie sometimes visited Camas Prairie.

Families usually returned to the Lemhi River in the fall and remained there all winter. They subsisted largely upon stored foods, supplemented by fowl and deer hunted in the vicinity. Famine was not uncommon.

In early spring and summer salmon could be had from the river while antelope and deer were killed nearby. But Lewis and Clark noted in August that they caught very few salmon (vol. 3, pp. 45–46).

Lewis and Clark's observations shed some light on these activities in 1806. They first met Shoshoni on horseback near Beaver's Head, Wyoming (vol. 2, p. 329). Between Beaver's Head and Dillon they encountered a camp in August digging roots (vol. 2, p. 334). Shortly thereafter they encountered a camp of 60 or more mounted warriors on or near the Lemhi River (vol. 2, pp. 338–339). The 400 persons met later may have included these. Others were scattered along the Lemhi River in small encampments. Although buffalo were still plentiful in Idaho, especially toward the Snake River, they reported that the Indians had only dried cakes of berries to eat, fearing to travel for buffalo because of warring tribes (vol. 2, p. 349). Blackfeet, especially, were raiding west of the Rocky Mountains and the Lemhi were evidently still insufficiently organized or numerous to confront them. They record (vol. 2, pp. 374–375) that from May until the first of September the Indians caught salmon in the Salmon River, then traveled to the headwaters of the Missouri River to join other Shoshoni and Flathead. Together they hunted buffalo and returned home with the meat in the fall.

Warfare.—This was an important factor in amalgamating the Lemhi. By 1806 tribes east of the Rocky Mountains were a serious menace. In August Lewis and Clark found the Lemhi remaining in their own valley for fear of raids (vol. 2, pp. 366–367). Each man kept a horse picketed at night (vol. 2, p. 347). Already warfare was sufficiently important to support systematic boasting of heroic deeds (vol. 2, p. 370).[26] Among the enemy tribes were the "Minnetares, called Pâh'-kees" (vol. 2, p. 341) and the "Chopunnish" (vol. 5, pp. 106–107, 270). Blackfeet were the most persistent enemies. Bonneville observed that Blackfeet raids against Nez Percé, Flatheads, and Pend d'Oreille sometimes prompted these tribes temporarily to join the Shoshoni for protection and that some of the battles were fought on or near the Salmon River (Irving, 1898, vol. 1, pp. 118–123, 144–151, 187–190, 200–209).

---

[26] War equipment and the system of counting coup and boasting are described elsewhere. (See also Lowie, 1909, pp. 191–195.)

Relations between Crow and Shoshoni alternated between peace and war (pp. 207–209).

In early times these fights were carried on by the Lemhi River people, under Tündoi. A varying number participated and sometimes joined forces with the Fort Hall Indians. The small mountain villages of the Salmon River region engaged in no warfare. After they had moved to the Lemhi River JP knew only of raids for horse stealing.

Festivals.—These were probably of little importance in uniting the small mountain villages which were too isolated to assemble advantageously. The few families in each occasionally held various forms of the circle dance.

The Lemhi River people, however, had festivals of some size and importance. The round dance was held normally in the spring and fall, but, as it was thought to bring blessings, it was also held during any period of sickness or other trouble. For the various kinds of dances, leaders with appropriate qualifications were in charge.

Chieftainship.—There was a significant difference in the nature and function of chieftainship between the Tukadüka and the Lemhi. Prior to consolidation with the Lemhi, the mountain dwellers lacked even formal village chiefs. Instead, a man possessing the necessary qualifications and prestige directed those activities which required supervision. Thus, Woygowütavi, the degwani of the village of Pasasigwana, did little more than direct fishing. When several related families camped together during the winter and foraged together during the summer, the oldest man, or, if he were infirm, perhaps his son, directed their movements.

Among the Lemhi, the chief, tegwani (talker), did not hold a formal position, but in the various group activities he had greater scope for authority. The extent of his authority depended in a large measure upon his personality, intelligence, and oratorical ability.

Lewis and Clark state that the chief did not inherit his position in 1806 but one became "chief" merely by prestige and example, everyone being a chief in some degree (vol. 2, p. 370). Thus, one group of about 60 mounted warriors had a chief called Ca-me-âh-watt (vol. 2, pp. 338–339) and another group of about 100 families had a chief called Too-et-te-conl or Black Gun, a war name (vol. 2, pp. 366–367). As warfare increased and as trips across the Rocky Mountains into enemy territory for buffalo became necessary, the importance of centralized control was enhanced. The chief regulated these group activities and, later, dealt with the white man. Lowie (1909, p. 208) states that his tasks were to direct the camp, preside at councils, receive visitors from other tribes, and conduct hunting and fishing excursions.

By the time the Tukadüka had consolidated with the Lemhi, the earliest period known to JP, the need for control of group activities and for a representative to deal with the white man was considerable. The main responsibility fell on Tündo'e (boiling; so called because he was fond of soup), whom Lander (1860, p. 125) stated was half Shoshoni and half Bannock. Lander further represents "Ten-toi's" father, "Old Buonaparte," to have been a noted chief but says that Ten-toi "is not a chief, but has very great influence with the tribe, and has distinguished himself in wars with the Blackfeet."

Tündo'e was succeeded by his son, Tu: pombi (black hair or head), whose interpreter was Na: goda, a man who possibly was not a Lemhi. Tu: pombi did his own speaking. Lowie, however, noted that in 1906, Tu: pombi played an insignificant role at councils (1909, p. 209).

Tu: pombi was succeeded by his brother, Wĭnc, who JP says is still living. Wĭnc needed neither interpreter nor announcer.

Special activities not involving the entire group were directed by various qualified individuals. Thus, fishing was managed by some fishing expert when several families cooperated. Hunting was usually directed by Yumapai. War parties were led by men who possessed dreamed war power. Lowie states (1909, p. 208) that sometimes there were as many as 10 "little chiefs" of war fame in a single community.

The institution of police, dürakone (surrounding something), who were stated by Lowie to have assisted at dances and hunts (1909, p. 208), was, according to JP, introduced comparatively recently.

Property.—There was no property in land or natural resources.

At death, a person's father, mother, or brother disposed of his possessions. His clothes, blankets, and cherished articles were buried with him, a few things being given to his children. His horses were distributed among people not related to him. His relatives received a few horses only if he had owned a great many.

Marriage.—There was no rule of local exogamy, but JP thought that small villages had occasionally been forced to follow it because they had come to consist entirely of related and consequently unmarriageable persons.

Marriage was prohibited with any true first cousin (Lowie's informants, however, denied this; 1909, p. 210) and with pseudo parallel-cousins. One called his father's brothers "father," his mother's sisters, "mother," and their children, including stepchildren, "brother" and "sister." The preferred marriage was with a pseudo cross-cousin, that is, with the mother's brother's stepdaughter or, lacking such a girl, with the stepmother's brother's daughter or father's sister's stepdaughter.

Acquisition of a spouse was accomplished in three ways.

(1) Orthodox marriage was with a pseudo cross-cousin or with a girl whose father sought a good hunter for her. In either case the man often lived with his prospective wife's family for some time in a kind of bride service to demonstrate his hunting ability. There was neither bride purchase nor exchange of presents. Prior to consummation of the marriage, the man visited the girl's camp each night and slept with her, but refrained from intercourse and departed early in the morning. After a while he remained there continuously and openly and they were considered wed. Residence was matrilocal for a time, during which the couple often visited the husband's family. Eventually they moved to permanent patrilocal residence. If the husband's father were dead, however, they might remain in matrilocal residence.

Lewis and Clark's account does not wholly tally with this. They state (vol. 1, pp. 370–371) that infant girls were promised to an older man in return for horses. When grown, that is, 13 or 14 years old, the girl, accompanied by gifts which about equaled those the father had received, were presented to the man. In 1909 Lowie (p. 210) observed that infant betrothals still occurred, but the necessity of gifts to parents was denied by his informants.

(2) *Abduction.*—A man, assisted by a group of friends, went to the camp of a girl who had caught his fancy and attempted to abduct her. Her father or husband sometimes successfully resisted or yielded her only after a fight. If she ran away and returned home, some men let her stay, some attempted to abduct her again. Occasionally her first husband successfully recaptured her.

(3) In the spring, previous to breaking up the winter encampment, a man might court a girl by staying at her camp. Her mother and female relatives might try to drive him away with digging sticks if they disapproved, but sometimes yielded for fear he would kill the girl. He then remained until openly accepted as a son-in-law.

Polygyny was frequently, but not necessarily, with sisters.[27] The sororate might also be followed if the deceased's wife's father liked the young man and wished to have his next daughter take care of the children. But this was not obligatory; nor was the widower obliged to accept the sister.

Polyandry was not a formal marriage arrangement, but rather sex privileges which were sometimes, but not always, extended to a brother. This privilege was rarely extended to cousins and never to unrelated men, because it was said that whereas unrelated women got along well in polygamy, the same did not hold for men. Often,

[27] Lewis and Clark record that it was seldom sororal (vol. 1, p. 370).

when an older brother married a woman, the younger brother occupied the same house and was permitted access to the wife when his brother was away. The younger man, however, always expected to acquire a wife of his own later. Sometimes, however, though the younger brother lived with the married couple, he was required to stay at a friend's house when the older brother was away. Or he might remain at the house merely as a kind of guard, to prevent any sex delinquencies on her part during her husband's absence.

When sex privileges were extended to a cousin it was JP's opinion that they were very temporary. A close friend of the husband had access to the woman only clandestinely, against the husband's will. He was never invited to share her.

It was JP's opinion, however, that any man who would sleep with his older brother's wife was "crazy" and untrustworthy.

The levirate, like the sororate, was often followed if desired but was not required.

A common practice was the marriage of a brother and sister to a sister and brother, who, however, occupied separate houses. This was called navutiyugwin ("sitting opposite one another"). Also, several brothers married several sisters, but each couple occupied a separate house.

JP said that sometimes, when a girl liked one of two intimate friends, but the other wished to marry her, the first might entice her to his house ostensibly to marry him and there turn her over to the other. She could not successfully resist this because they would use force.

It is apparent that despite certain formal aspects of marriage, marital ties frequently shifted and woman's status was insecure and unsupported by any great regard for female chastity. Lewis and Clark reported (vol. 1, p. 371) that a husband would even barter a wife for a night or longer, though he was disgraced if she had a clandestine affair. JP said that retaliation for infidelity depended upon the individual. Some men did nothing. Some beat the paramour, who was supposed to offer no resistance. Lowie adds that the husband might demand a horse as indemnity or shoot one of the lover's horses (1909, p. 210). Apparently outright theft of a wife was more condoned by society than a secret affair. Separation was more likely to follow infidelity by the wife than by the husband. When separating, however, the woman always took the children, her mother helping to rear them.

In all cases the essential feature of matrimony was that the couple should live together with some intention of permanency. The stability of an alliance depended upon personal attachment, age, presence of children, individual attractiveness, the husband's physical strength, and whether the spouses were pseudo cross-cousins.

Family and kinship.—In addition to the usual parent-child relationship, a brother and sister seemed to be unusually close, though how they would ordinarily be thrown together after marriage or through any rule of post-marital residence is not clear. JP said they usually tried to camp close together. If they did not live near each other after marrying more often than chance would allow, it is difficult to see why this bond existed.

At any rate, children were considered particularly close to the mother's brother, ada, between whom there was high regard. While a boy's parents lived he frequently visited with his mother's brother and if his parents died he preferred to live with this uncle. If his father died the ada took some of the responsibility of raising him. Sometimes an additional attraction of the mother's brother was the presence of a stepdaughter, with whom he would anticipate marriage. His mother and uncle preferred this, for it tightened family bonds. Such bonds, of course, were very important in a society lacking any nuclei for the formation of allegiances except the family and the local group.

There was also some intimacy between a young man and his father's sister, baha, who might assume responsibility for him in the event of the death of his mother.

Kinship usages are an intimate part of the family relationships. A man's closest friend and joking relative was his mother's brother's or father's sister's stepson, that is, his probable brother-in-law. To him he was closer than to his real brother, though after marriage his real brother sometimes lived with him, whereas his brother-in-law never did so. As close friends, these pseudo cross-cousins associated together and helped one another. Also, they were joking relatives, called naninuhünt (joking), nanohïnt (teasing) or namasumohugünt (teasing). Jokes concerned sex or something one had done. They might hide each other's clothing or taunt each other about cowardice. Once a man lost his breechclout during a race and his cousin chided him about it. Once a man dressed up like a ghost, waylaid and chased his cousin until he "passed out." A similar freedom existed between a man and his female cross-cousin, even though she were married to another man. These relationships still obtain at Fort Hall.

There was little such joking between a man and his mother's brother, nor could these relatives appropriate each other's property. The uncle might, however, call upon the boy to perform a service for him as, for example, breaking a horse, for which he would perhaps reward him with an unbroken horse.

Between brothers and sisters there was little restraint, though joking was not as extreme as between cousins.

60285—38——14

Prior to marriage a young man's obligations were, of course, to his own family, to whom he supplied game. After marriage it was to his wife's mother and father, especially while residence was matrilocal. At Fort Hall he was required to take game to his mother-in-law, even though she were 20 miles away.

There were no kinship avoidances.

FORT HALL BANNOCK AND SHOSHONI

Two linguistic groups, the Shoshoni and the Northern Paiute-speaking Bannock, seem to have occupied the Fort Hall region since prehistoric times, though prior to their acquisition of horses they were undoubtedly scattered over a wider territory.

The Shoshoni at Fort Hall are distinguished from those in western Idaho by having had some horses and a comparatively high degree of political solidarity at an early period. They called themselves Bohogue (bohovi, sagebrush+gue, butte, i. e., the butte northeast of Fort Hall). This term was sometimes used to include the Bannock. They were called Pohogue' by the Lemhi, Pohoguwe by peoples lower on the Snake River, and Wi: nakwüt (wi:, knife, probably iron knife) by the Bannock.

The Bannock, a horse-owning group living in close association with the Shoshoni, called themselves Bana'kwüt (ba, water+nakwüt, possibly a nominal ending). Fort Hall Shoshoni called them Ba: naite (probably same derivation as Bana'kwüt), translated as "people from below." [28]

The linguistic similarity of the Bannock and Northern Paiute (see vocabularies, pp. 274–275) leaves no doubt that they once formed a single group, though within historic times they have been separated by 200 miles.

Location of Bannock in eastern Oregon by various early writers is susceptible to four explanations: (1) The Fort Hall Bannock actually were located in eastern Oregon in early historic times; (2) groups of Bannock who often ranged on horseback from western Wyoming and from Fort Hall to western Idaho were encountered when on a temporary visit to eastern Oregon; (3) Northern Paiute of eastern Oregon were called Bannock; (4) early travelers and trappers failed to identify the various Shoshonean-speaking people they met in different places. Of these, the first explanation is least probable, the last two most probable. Though historical sources are very little help in locating the tribes of this region, Bannock was

---

[28] Lowie (1909, pp. 206–208) gives Banaite as the Lemhi Shoshoni designation of the Bannock. Wheeler (1889, p. 410) calls them Bannock or Panai'ti, but erroneously classifies them with the Shoshoni linguistically.

frequently applied to Mono-Bannock speaking peoples of eastern Oregon (pp. 269–271).

Most often horse Shoshoni were called Snake and foot Shoshoni were Diggers, Shoshokoes or Shoshonee, though usage was far from consistent. Northern Paiute-speaking groups were rarely distinguished from Shoshoni.

Ross (1855, vol. 1, pp. 249–252), who visited the area about 1820, apparently lumped the scattered Shoshoni families of southern Oregon as "Ban-at-tees," translated as "robbers" (the Shoshoni name for the Bannock) or "Mountain Snake," saying that they lived in small groups in caves and rocks, dressed in skins of rabbits, wolves, and other animals in winter, went naked in summer, and had only bows and arrows. This does not at all describe the Fort Hall Bannock. Ogden, traveling in 1826–27, used neither "Bannock" nor "Paiute" for the people of southern Idaho or eastern Oregon, though Paiute unquestionably were then living at least in Oregon, but designated the people even on the John Day River (vol. 10, p. 349) and in the region of Malheur Lake (vol. 11, p. 208) as "Snakes." The use of "Snake" or "Shoshonee" for any Shoshonean-speaking people in this area was very common. Wyeth, who founded Fort Hall in 1834, recognized that there were Bannock and Shoshoni in the region, but admitted that he could not tell the difference between them (Schoolcraft, 1851). In contrast to others, he seems to have designated all the Fort Hall horse Indians as Bannock. Humfreville, like Ross, thought the Bannock were merely the more backward Shoshoni of the area. He places the Snake "in and around the Snake River Valley, and their hunting ground extended eastward to the foot of the Bitter Root Mountains and as far south as Ute country" (p. 282). Of the Bannock he says (pp. 287–288), "their hunting ground was to the west of the Bitter Root Mountains and south of the Coeur d'Alene River." They were principally Diggers. Their winter habitations were "a hole in the ground large enough to accommodate their families, with an opening at the top to let out the smoke." Farnham (1843, p. 261) says that "Snakes" or "Shoshonies" occupying a considerable portion of country on Snake River above and below Fort Hall "subsist on the fish of the stream, buffalo, deer, and other game."

Forney said "The latter tribe (Ban-acks) I had frequently heard of, but supposed they were part of a tribe by the same name who live in Oregon Territory . . . but upon making inquiry I learned that they were a separate and distinct people . . . In their habits and appearance they are much like the Snakes, with whom they are on terms of greatest intimacy. They number between four and five hundred, and are all under one principal chief, named Horne" (1858, p. 213). Also, he observed that Bridger had said that 30 years earlier they had 1,200 lodges (1859, p. 363).

Doty (1862, p. 211) speaks of "Eastern Bannacks, who hunt with the Shoshones between Raft River, near Fort Hall, and Bear River . . ."

Burton (1862, pp. 473–474) said the greater number of "Panak" occupied eastern Oregon, but about 500 hunted bison and elk to the east. For 30 years prior to 1860 they had traded at Fort Bridger on the Green River and formerly numbered 1,200 lodges. This estimate of 1,200 lodges almost certainly includes Shoshoni.

Danilson (1870, p. 288) and Jones (1870, p. 279) said that Bannock had always claimed the Fort Hall territory. Jones gave the number as 600 and Mann (1870, p. 274) said there were 800 "Northern Bannacks" under Taggie.

There is no means of knowing when the Bannock separated from the other Northern Paiute. WH thought they had come to Fort Hall from the west, but had no idea when. SB thought they had always lived at Fort Hall.

That the historic location of the Bannock is old, in spite of the survival of their language, is indicated by their culture which, in contrast to the foot Shoshoni who lived immediately below them on the Snake River, was strongly stamped with Plains traits. An ethnographic survey by means of an element list revealed no great difference between Fort Hall Shoshoni and Bannock. The two seem to have wintered together and pastured their horses in and near the lush bottomlands of the Snake River since prehistoric times. They usually made hunting expeditions together on horesback, sometimes going east to Wyoming for buffalo, west to Camas Prairie and beyond to trade and gather roots, and down the Snake River below Shoshone Falls for fishing. The foot Shoshoni, along the Snake River gorge below American Falls, especially on the south bank, were, in contrast to the Fort Hall Shoshoni and Bannock, impoverished, primitive in their culture, restricted in their movements, and unorganized. Few of them owned horses.

The environment of the Fort Hall Shoshoni and Bannock is not unlike that to the west and south. It consists largely of arid, sage-covered desert plains which were largely destitute of game. Wyeth (Schoolcraft, 1851, p. 206), who lived at Fort Hall from 1834 to 1836, said it had very few deer and elk except in the mountains, only a small number of mountain sheep, antelope, and bear, and only two kinds of rabbits. The main asset was salmon, which ran up the Snake River only to Shoshone Falls and therefore required a long trip downstream. Buffalo occurred in the eastern part of the area, and there had been many near Fort Hall in 1834 (Wyeth in Schoolcraft, 1851, p. 217). In fact, Ogden (vol. 11, p. 207) saw many buffalo skulls though no living animals at Silver River near Malheur Lake, Oregon, and informants claimed that several generations ago buffalo had occurred in small numbers even in northeastern Nevada. But buffalo were extinct in northern Utah by 1832 and in Idaho by about 1840 (Frémont, 1887, vol. 2, p. 218). No doubt the sage-covered plains were not their optimum environment, so that the arrival of trappers and the acquisition of fire arms and horses by the Indians was sufficient to exterminate them. It is improbable that in pre-horse days the buffalo was sufficiently numerous or means of taking it sufficiently developed to have made it an important feature in the economy. Fragments of evidence indicate that at this time the economy was substantially like that of the Western Shoshoni.

The horse.—The origin of the horse in Idaho is not definitely known, though there is evidence that some horses, at least, were acquired directly from the Spaniards and that Shoshoni were among the first tribes to have them. CT thought that before the arrival of the Americans Shoshoni had possessed a small variety which they called kobai. Thompson recounts a fight between Blackfeet and Shoshoni in 1730, when the latter (probably Wyoming groups) had horses but the former had none (pp. 328–344), but Wissler (1914) believes that both Blackfeet and Shoshoni had horses in about 1750. It is possible that horses came to the Shoshoni through the intermediary of the Ute in western Colorado who were in contact with the Spaniards in the Southwest at an early date.

The horse revolutionized Shoshoni economy by making it possible to use new methods of hunting which yielded greater wealth in foods and hides and enabled people to live in large and comparatively permanent groups. Families which previously had had to live near their cached foods could now transport the foods to a central location. Large aggregates of people, moreover, could travel together in search of foods. Buffalo were taken in Idaho while they lasted. After 1840, and perhaps to some extent earlier, Shoshoni and Bannock, alone or in company with Nez Percé and sometimes with Flathead, Lemhi, and Wyoming Shoshoni, made long excursions across the Rocky Mountains to the buffalo country of the high plains. Lander (1860, pp. 121–122) says "Pannacks" and even "Salt Lake Diggers" joined in trips to the headwaters of the Missouri and Yellowstone Rivers, the latter making trips of 1,200 miles. Those who had horses naturally fared best.

Wyeth (Schoolcraft, 1851, p. 208) observed that "it is a well-established fact that men on foot cannot live, even in the best game countries, in the same camp with those who have horses. The latter reach the game, secure what they want, and drive it beyond the reach of the former. Thus, the Snakes, while they had no horses, would form but one people, because they would be collected once a year, in salmon time; but the organization would be very imperfect, because the remainder of the year would be spent by them in families widely spread apart, to eke out the year's subsistence on the roots and limited game of their country. After a portion of them, who are now called Bonacks [Fort Hall Shoshoni and Bannock], had obtained horses, they would naturally form bands and resort to the buffalo region to gain their subsistence, retiring to the most fertile places in their own, to avoid the snows of the mountains and feed their horses. Having food from the proceeds of the buffalo hunt to enable them to live together, they would annually do so, for the protection of their horses, lodges, etc. These interests have caused an organization among the Banocks which continues the year through, because the interests which produce it continue; and it is more advanced than that of the other Snakes."

But a concomitant factor producing band solidarity was warfare. Horses were a form of wealth which made these people attractive prey to the roving war parties from east of the Rocky Mountains. And, after 1840, when the Shoshoni and Bannock traveled into Wyoming and Montana for buffalo, they were in imminent danger of encounters with hostile tribes. Consequently it was important that such trips be made by large organized groups. In these frequent clashes with warring Plains tribes and almost annual contact with their Wyoming kin, the Idaho Shoshoni acquired a large number of Plains traits as well as the beginnings of band organization.

The amalgamation of scattered families and villages into a band was undoubtedly a gradual process, progressing as people acquired horses. For a long time, however, remnants of foot Indians probably remained in isolation. For example, near the headwaters of the Henry River, a tributary of the upper Snake River, Hunt's Astoria party encountered a poor type of Shoshoni living in the mountains in 1811 (Irving, 1897, vol. 2, pp. 12–13). According to Wyeth (Schoolcraft, 1851, p. 207), the "Bonacks had horses and went to hunt buffalo, while the Shoshonees had no horses and lived on roots and fish." Wyeth, however, did not recognize the linguistic difference between the Bannock and Shoshoni and seems to have designated all Fort Hall Indians "Bonack." His vocabulary (op. cit., p. 215) is of no assistance in identifying them. As late as 1854, in December, Mullan (1855, pp. 333–334) encountered a single lodge of "Banax" on the Snake River about 50 miles above Fort Hall "on their way to the mountains for game" with their horses. Twelve miles downstream he met three or four families of "Root-Digger Indians" with a few horses. The men were fishing, the women digging roots. The Sioux name for Shoshoni, "Those dwelling in grass lodges" (Hoffman, 1886, p. 297) and the Flathead name "Bark lodges" for Bannock (Teit, 1930, p. 301) may be a survival of the pre-horse and pre-tipi period.

Although the Fort Hall Bannock and Shoshoni were probably comparatively well amalgamated into a band by 1840, there is little doubt that a few small groups continued for many years to live in isolation, because they had no horses or for other reasons. Among the remnants of this scattered population were, perhaps, a few Bannock who later were incorporated with the Lemhi.

Even with the advantage of the horse, it was not always expedient for the combined Bannock-Shoshoni band to move as a unit. They frequently split into small subdivisions, each of which traveled independently through southern Idaho to procure different foods, to trade, and occasionally to carry on warfare.

Subsistence activities.—Seasonal movements described by WH, a Bannock who claimed to have been a young man when the Fort Hall agency was founded in 1862, and by SB, a Fort Hall Shoshoni, are as follows:

In winter most of the Bannock and Shoshoni camped in the vicinity of Fort Hall.

When spring came groups of perhaps six related families, which had camped together, set out, under the leadership of an elderly man, in search of various foods. Whether they went east for buffalo, south toward Bear River for berries and for hunting, or west for salmon, camass, and trading depended upon individual circumstances. Also, whether they joined other groups depended upon where and when they traveled and whether they had horses.

Usually families set out first to Camas Prairie or to the Boise, Payette, and even Weiser Rivers to the west. They traveled on the northern side of Snake River, often along the foot of the mountains. As Fort Hall is some distance above the limit of salmon in the Snake River, an important reason for these trips was to procure salmon either directly from the river or by trade from the lower Snake River Shoshoni.

In August 1833 Townsend recorded that a party of mounted "Bannecks" passed somewhere on the Big Wood River on their way to the fisheries (p. 242). He also met "Snakes" returning with dried salmon (p. 245) and, near the Boise River, saw 30 tipis of horse Shoshoni fishing (pp. 257–261). In this vicinity he also saw 30 "willow lodges of Bannecks" (p. 262). Schoolcraft says (1851, p. 202) that the Snake Indians of the Shoshonee or Lewis' Fork of the Columbia River (Snake River) "periodically subsisted on Salmon . . . which are taken abundantly at the Falls [Salmon Falls]; but at other seasons they have little to distinguish them from the mountain bands." Though this observation probably applies to Shoshoni all along the Snake River, the Fort Hall people stopped to fish en route to Camas Prairie.

At Camas Prairie they usually scattered out to gather roots and seeds. Of vegetable foods, camass was most important. Others were pasigo, pak:, yamp:, ak:, kosiak:, yuhauk:, buhuak:, and kuiyu (tobacco root). As many of these as could be preserved were later transported back to Fort Hall. Meanwhile, from time to time the people assembled with one another and with Nez Percé and local Yahandüka Shoshoni to dance and barter. They traded buffalo skins to the Yahandüka for seeds, roots, dried crickets, and salmon, and to the Nez Percé for horses.

A few families remained in this region all summer, but most of them turned east in late summer to seek buffalo.

Formerly buffalo could be had along the Snake River plains, not far from Fort Hall. After they were extinct in Idaho in 1840, large parties of Indians went to near Butte, Mont., and to Wyoming to hunt them, starting about when the leaves were turning in the fall. Even in 1811, however, Hunt's party saw Shoshoni, who were probably from Idaho, hunting buffalo somewhere near the headwaters of the Green River (Irving, 1897, vol. 1, pp. 385–387).

Fear of the Blackfeet as well as the greater efficiency of communal hunting compelled the main body of Fort Hall Shoshoni and Bannock to travel as a unit, often joining Lemhi, Nez Percé, Flathead, and Wyoming Shoshoni. On their way east they usually procured chokecherries and various seeds, roots, and berries in the mountains. In the vicinity of Yellowstone they sometimes stopped briefly to gather nuts of the "white pine," woŋgoduba, which they either ground and carried to the plains in buckskin sacks or cached to provide food for their return trip.

Buffalo hunting was accomplished merely by running down the animals with fleet horses. First, the chief, Tagi, or his hunt leader sent out several young men to find the herd. There were no formal buffalo scouts. Then men on horseback rode after the animals and shot them, each hunter killing three or four. Meanwhile old men butchered the kill and distributed it equally among all the families.

A few families sometimes wintered on the plains, especially if they had few or no horses. But most people returned to Fort Hall late in the fall, transporting the dried buffalo meat and hides on their horses.

The chief or chiefs directed these entire journeys. Semiformal police (p. 211) kept the people in a more or less compact group, especially when in dangerous territory.

Meanwhile some families remained during the summer in the vicinity of Fort Hall or went to the region of Bear Lake for roots, berries, mountain sheep, and other game. In the fall some families went south to the Grouse Creek region for pinyon nuts.

The Bannock and Shoshoni always wintered together at Fort Hall, though a few families remained in the east and, after the agency was founded, some went to "near Yellowstone" to receive rations. There was no segregation of Bannock and Shoshoni in winter encampments, nor any named subdivisions. The distribution of the camps is shown on the map, figure 12. There were a few camps on Lincoln Creek, on the Blackfoot River near its mouth, upstream on Ross Fork Creek, and on the Port Neuf River as far as Lava Hot Spring. But the greatest number stayed along the bottom lands of the Snake River above American Falls. Bannock Creek was formerly occupied by a somewhat distinct group, the Kamudüka (pp. 216–218).

When the various groups arrived home at Fort Hall in the fall, especially if they had broken up into family clusters during the summer, they made a camp circle for 6 or 7 days, during 4 of which they held the grass dance and scalp dance. Then they scattered out to erect their winter houses. Perhaps six related families built their houses in a cluster.

To supplement the food laid up during the summer, small groups, but never the entire band, went into the plains west of the Snake River to hunt antelope. Sometimes they used corrals, though shamanism was much less prominent than farther south. Hunting by horse relays was preferred. Deer were taken by individuals or by small groups of hunters in the mountains near Fort Hall or in the juniper belt to the north or to the west toward Camas Prairie.

A man manifestly could not divide his kill of deer or antelope among all the neighboring families as was customary among Western Shoshoni. But women from the related families which made up his own cluster of camps came to his house to receive shares, close relatives receiving more than others.

Rabbits did not occur in sufficient numbers at this time to justify communal drives.

Waterfowl were taken in small drives, carried on by one or two families.

Fish which could be taken in the tributaries of the Snake River above American Falls were:

Sapaŋwi (sand, good; paŋwi, fish), trout.
Toyapaŋwi (toyavi, mountain), in mountain streams.
Mugada, sucker.
Wizabankwi, perch.
Tasigi (same as Lemhi pahiwa'ª), "like a minnow."

Fish were taken by means of hooks, baskets, dams, weirs, and harpoons. Weirs required a small amount of cooperation between several families, but did not involve stable organization or ceremony.

In October 1811, probably near Fort Hall, Hunt saw a small village of Shoshoni who had small fish about 2 inches long, roots and seeds which they were drying (Irving, 1897, vol. 2, p. 18).

Observations by early travelers and traders in this region in general corroborate informants' accounts.

Ogden, March 20, 1826, found about 400 persons with twice that many horses along the Snake River near Raft River (below Fort Hall) preparing to descend the river to avoid the Blackfeet. This "camp" moved, carrying buffalo meat, to the Malad River (Idaho) to gather roots and salmon, and in the fall would return to winter in the buffalo plain [probably at or near Fort Hall]. They sometimes traveled to the mouth of Burnt River [Oregon] on the Snake River to trade with the Nez Percé. He mentioned another "camp" of 200 Shoshoni who wintered with the Americans at the mouth of Raft River (vol. 10, pp. 356–357). On October 13, 1827, he met 300 tents of Shoshoni at Camas Prairie. He said, "It is from near this point that the Snakes form into a body prior to their starting for buffalo; they collect camasse for the journey across the mountains [Rocky Mountains] . . . In the spring they scatter from this place for the salmon and horse-thieving expeditions" (vol. 11, p. 362). In the plains north of the Snake River several streams emerging from the mountains to the north lose themselves in the desert. Here in November, near Days River, Ogden saw evidence of 300 "Snake" tents, 1,500 people, 3,000 horses. Nearby, on Goddin's River (probably Little Lost River), he observed many antelope and buffalo (vol. 11, p. 364). Near Fort Hall he was visited by The Horse, chief of the Lower Snakes, with 300 followers. And, at Port Neuf River, near Blackfoot Hill, he saw a Snake camp with more than 1,500 persons. Buffalo were numerous at that time (vol. 11, pp. 365–366).

Ross' observations, about 1819, evince confusion and exaggeration. He claimed that all Shoshoni, apparently including both sides of the Rocky Mountains, made a single huge camp of 10,000 persons under 2 chiefs, Pee-eye-em and Ama-qui-em, who were brothers. At their council were 48 Shirry-dikas and 6 War-are-reekas but no Ban-at-tees (1855, vol. 1, pp. 252–254). Pee-eye-em, however, was a Wyoming chief (1855, vol. 2, pp. 91–92). Though different Shoshoni frequently met in large groups, they did not remain together and the number was well short of Ross' estimate.

At a fishing place on the Wuzer [probably Weiser] River Ross estimated a camp of War-are-reekas under Chief Ama-ketsa to have 900 tents, 4,500 persons, and half that many horses. They were gambling, fishing, and sporting; they had few guns (1855, vol. 2, pp. 102–103). This estimate of 4,500 is a great exaggeration.

About 1822 Beckwourth claims to have encountered Pun-naks (Bannocks) encamped with Snakes on Weaver's Fork (probably Weber River) near Salt Lake. If his identification is correct, they were probably on a trip.

Leonard, who observed Bannock between 1831 and 1836, said they "travel in small gangs of from four to five families . . . this they are compelled to do in order to keep from starvation" (p. 124). In August 1834, he "arrived at the huts of some Bawnack Indians. These Indians appear to live very poor and in the most forlorn condition. They generally make but one visit to the buffalo country during the year, where they remain until they jerk as much meat as their females can lug home on their backs. Then they quit the mountains and return to the plains, where they subsist on fish and small game the remainder of the year. They keep no horses, and are always an easy prey for other Indians provided with guns and horses" (p. 148). But Leonard was frequently confused as to time, place, and tribe and these Indians may have been observed farther west.

Bonneville's observations in 1832 and 1833 substantiate Ogden's. In the vicinity of Three Buttes (Fort Hall) he saw about 130 lodges of Bannocks, which in the spring "move down the right [northern] bank of the Snake River and camp at the heads of the Boise and Payette" Rivers, where they found good pasture for their horses and hunted. They continued down the river to trade beaver and buffalo robes to the Nez Percé for horses, later returning to the vicinity of the Port Neuf and Blackfoot Rivers where there were buffalo (Irving, 1898, vol. 1, pp. 177–178). At the mouth of Little Wyes River on the Snake River he also saw Shoshoni who had come up from the Boise River plain with horses and good equipment they had traded from the lower Nez Percé (op. cit., vol. 2, pp. 2–3). On these prairies near the Boise and Payette Rivers he saw Bannock, in late summer, setting fire to the prairies (op. cit., vol. 2, p. 173). In late fall Shoshoni were at their village at the mouth of the Port Neuf with the Bannocks (op. cit., vol. 1, pp. 316–317, 321–322).

In 1846 Palmer met about 600 lodges of "Snake Indians; they were moving from Big Bear River to Lewis' Fork" (1847, p. 247). These were probably either Fort Hall or Wyoming Shoshoni.

About the same time Frémont met a large number of warriors on horseback on the Bear River (1856, p. 237), who may likewise have been from Wyoming. He also saw a small encampment of Shoshoni at Cane Spring, apparently in the Bear River Valley (1856, p. 248).

As late as 1868 a treaty by which the Bannock and Shoshoni agreed to live on the Fort Hall Reservation specifically provided that they should be permitted to make trips to the buffalo country and to Camas Prairie (Bancroft, vol. 31, p. 515).

Doty stated (1864, pp. 174–175) that in their treaty the "Shoshonees . . . fixed their eastern boundary on the crest of the Rocky mountains; but it is certain that they, as well as the Bannacks, hunt the buffalo below the Three Forks of the Missouri, and on the headwaters of the Yellowstone and Wind rivers. As none of the Indians of this country have permanent places of abode, in their hunting excursions they wander over an immense region, extending from the fisheries at and below Salmon Falls, on the Shoshonee [Snake] river, near the Oregon line, to the sources of that stream, and to the buffalo country beyond. The Shoshonees and Bannacks are the only nations which, to my knowledge, hunt together over the same ground."

Hall (1866, p. 200) said the "Shoshones" and "Bannack . . . run together, swap squaws, etc., separating occasionally into small parties for hunting purposes." They range about the headwaters of the Yellowstone, Gallatin, Madison, Snake, and Green rivers, and around Bannack and Boise, frequently in the territory of Utah." When together, they spoke Shoshoni.

Head said that the Shoshoni frequently visited white settlements to trade buffalo robes for guns and other things (1866, pp. 122–123) and that 1,500 Shoshones and 1,000 Bannacks comprised a mixed band, wintering in southern Idaho, but spending 7 or 8 months in northeastern Utah along the Bear River (1867, p. 188).

Piecing together these fragments of information, there is reason to suspect that the Shoshoni-Bannock band at first was very incompletely amalgamated. Perhaps the different groups encountered by Ogden and others represented early local groups of foot Indians. An increased number of horses permitted the band to grow. A larger band afforded greater security against the predatory Blackfeet. Fort Hall came to be the main winter headquarters. Nevertheless, small groups of varying size under different leaders frequently departed on their own food quests or adventures. There was never such centralized political control that all members of the band could be forced to act as a unit.

Warfare.—Warfare was of considerable importance in establishing band solidarity, for, although these people were never at war with their immediate neighbors, raids by Blackfeet and, at certain periods by other tribes, were a constant danger. (See also Lowie, 1909, pp. 171–173.)

Thompson (pp. 328–343, 367) records a fight between Blackfoot and Shoshoni thought to have occurred about 1730 and says enmity continued to 1800 and later.

Lewis and Clark found Blackfoot raiding Lemhi in 1806 (p. 197). The Blackfoot were reported to be the chief enemy of the Shoshoni by Ross in 1820 (1855, vol. 1, pp. 254–260), by Beckwourth, who records a fight at the Port Neuf River near Fort Hall in 1822 (pp. 99–100), by Ogden, who met Blackfoot in pursuit of "Snakes" near American Falls in 1826 (vol. 10, p. 357), by Bonneville in 1832 (Irving, 1898, vol. 1, p. 178), by Simpson in 1859 (p. 34), and by many others. They had raided south to Utah Lake (Russell, 1921, p. 122).

Relationships with Crow seems to have alternated between friendship and enmity.

In 1806 Shoshoni and Crow were at peace, recently having been at war (Lewis and Clark, vol. 5, p. 270). Beckwourth reported peace about 1822 (p. 139) but Ashley-Smith (Dale, 1918, p. 134) recorded Crow raids against Shoshoni in about 1825 and Ogden recorded them in 1826 (vol. 10, p. 362). Frémont said the Crow and Shoshoni were allied in 1842 (1887, vol. 2, p. 220), but Simpson stated that they were enemies about 1859 (p. 34).

Arapaho were also hostile to Shoshoni, but their raiding parties seldom reached Idaho.

There was intermittent strife with Ute (Ogden, vol. 10, p. 362; Simpson, p. 34), though Ute rarely ventured north of Great Salt Lake. Though peace was arranged between Ute and Shoshoni in 1852 (Young, pp. 147–149), strife continued many years (Forney, 1858, p. 212).

WH stated that some non-Shoshonean tribe called Saiduk: a (saip, tule+duk: a, west; so-called because they made houses and clothing of tules) from Oregon formerly traveled as far east as American Falls raiding Shoshoni. Shoshoni sometimes, however, traded with them at Camas Prairie.

With the Nez Percé and Flatheads the Shoshoni were at peace, frequently joining them for defense against the Blackfeet. Ross, however, gives a hint of some strife with the Nez Percé about 1820 (vol. 1, pp. 254–200), and Teit (1930, p. 361) records a fight between Bannock and Flathead.

Although Shoshoni were usually friendly to the white man, the Bannock seem frequently to have considered them fair game for raids (Irving, 1898, vol. 1, p. 184). Lander said (1860, p. 125): "The Pannacks . . . are well-disposed to the whites, but their horse-stealing proclivities prevent amicable arrangements with them to become lasting . . . ." Even Shoshoni sometimes stole horses from or raided the whites.[29]

The most important battles seem to have been defensive and were led by the band chiefs. Many small raiding and horse-stealing excursions, however, were organized and led by different men. Warfare

---

[29] See, for example, Ogden (vol. 11, pp. 213, 370) who recounts that "Snake" (who might, however, have been Bannock), murdered about 40 white men and Irving (1898, vol. 1, p. 257) who describes Shoshoni thefts of horses.

involved considerable ritual, equipment, vision, and war honors. These are described elsewhere.

Political organization.—Political organization was a matter of direction and control of specific activities by individuals of varying force of character. Consequently it varied not only seasonally but over a period of years.

Wyeth (Schoolcraft, 1851, p. 207), speaking probably of the Shoshoni farther down the Snake River, says, "the paucity of game in this region is, I have little doubt, the cause of the almost entire absence of social organization among its inhabitants; no trace of it is ordinarily seen among them, except during salmon-times, when a large number of the Snakes resort to the rivers, chiefly to the Fishing Falls [Salmon Falls], and at such places there seems some little organization; some person called a chief usually opens a trade or talk, and occasionally gives directions as to times and modes of fishing; and the same is the case with the bands who go into the buffalo region. Other than this, I have perceived no vestiges of government among them; I have never known other punishment inflicted than personal satisfaction by murder or theft . . . Previous to the introduction of the horse among them, they could have had no interest of property requiring organization to protect it, except that of the Salmon fisheries, which must have been nearly coeval with their first settlement in the country, and which, naturally would call for some kind of law to render it available . . . It is not probable they would have combined to protect property they did not possess or to secure themselves against enemies who could not penetrate into their country for want of subsistence, and also because themselves could not remain together in any considerable numbers from the same cause.

"These reasons show a want of motive and power of combination except in the single interest of the Salmon fishery, and convince me that prior to the introduction of the horse no other tribal arrangement existed than such as is now seen in the management of the Salmon fishery."

Speaking generally of the "Snakes" or "Sho-sho-nies" of the headwaters of the Green and Bear Rivers and the eastern and southern tributaries of the Snake River between 1834 and 1843, Russell said (1921, pp. 145–146) "The government is a democracy. Deeds of valor promote the chief to the highest points attained, from which he is at any time liable to fall for misdemeanor in office. Their population amounts to between 5,000 and 6,000, about half of which live in small, detached companies comprised of from 2 to 10 families, who subsist upon roots, fish, seeds, and berries. They have but few horses and are much addicted to thieving. From their manner of living they have received the appellation of 'Root Diggers.' They rove about in the mountains in order to seclude themselves from their warlike enemies, the Blackfeet." The mounted, buffalo hunting Shoshoni "seldom stop more than 8 or 10 days in one place . . . In the winter of 1842 the principal chief of the Snakes [probably Wyoming] died in an apoplectic fit and in the following year his brother died . . . These being the two principal pillars that upheld the nation, the loss of them was and is to this day deeply deplored. Immediately after the death of the latter, the tribe scattered into smaller villages over the country in consequence of having no chief who could control and keep them together." Elsewhere (p. 115), Russell mentions a chief, Moh-woom-hah, who was becoming popular, drawing families from his brother's group. Who-sha-kik (Washakie) was at that time one of his supporters.

Bannock and Shoshoni, though closely cooperating and living on terms of equality, were politically distinct in that each had its band chief.

Prior to the extinction of the bison in Idaho, SB and WH agreed that the band chief was relatively unimportant. Most activities were carried on by small groups of related families, each under its own leader, called dagwaniwəp: He had an announcer who served also as messenger. Succession was patrilineal if the son was suitable; otherwise an influential man was selected by a meeting of people interested, that is, by household heads. Disputes about succession, however, were infrequent. A new chief selected a new announcer if he wished (SB).

Duties of the chief largely concerned the material welfare of his followers. While in winter camp he supervised the supply of food and fuel, having his assistant announce a change of location if necessary. During the remainder of the year he directed seasonal movements in search of food. He was not concerned with disputes in camp, which were settled by participants (though there is some evidence that an influential personality might take a hand in these affairs). He had no obligation to entertain visitors, though he might welcome them (SB).

After the bison was extinct in Idaho and when the intercourse with the white man, especially about matters of land, required greater group control with representative spokesmen, band chiefs and councils became more important (SB). Each band depended upon a chief, who appointed an announcer but had no other assistants (WH).

When hunting buffalo the chief had the hunt announced and individuals warned not to frighten the animals. He appointed a capable leader who was called dugatəgwani. He might not even participate if he were old (SB and WH). He sometimes appointed a special man to take charge of any communal hunting of other game (SB) or else any man took charge. Fishing, however, was carried on by individuals or by small groups each having its own leader. Living above the range of the salmon, fishing was relatively unimportant to these people (SB).

One of the main functions of the band chief was to lead war parties, particularly large fights. Upon these occasions he alone wore an eagle-feather bonnet and carried a spear. WH, however, named one man as band chief, another as war leader. Raiding expeditions were led by brave and experienced men who were permitted to organize and lead parties without the chief's permission.

The band council seems to have come into existence or at least acquired importance after the arrival of the white man. It had no special name. It consisted largely of old men, who were household heads. Anyone, however, might attend its meetings, which were called by the chief. Its function was to advise the chief and to take charge of community affairs in his absence. The greatest civil importance of the chief and council concerned contacts with the white man, especially treaties and land deals.

The institution of police, which was obviously borrowed from Wyoming, is of unknown antiquity. It was largely civil and consisted of four or five middle-aged men, Bannock or Shoshoni, who had a civic spirit. They were selected and instructed by the council. The personnel changed frequently. The chief had little authority over them. They were called ö:hamupe (ö:ha, yellow+mupe, the front lock which stood up; other men painted this white), but were not distinguished by dress. Their duties were to keep the band members together while traveling, especially when in danger of enemy raids. They had little authority in policing hunts except to keep people together and none in keeping order within the camp (SB). WH, however, said that police were merely any men caring to take the responsibility and acting on the chief's orders. They were not distinguished by yellow forelocks, for many other men also wore these. Functioning in buffalo hunts, he called them tudako'oni, meaning "hold back."

Each kind of dance was led by a special man whose knowledge of the dance and competence as a director enabled him to achieve leadership through tacit consent. As dances were usually held only by small subdivisions of the band, the band chiefs had little authority in these activities. They served principally to direct the scalp dance and grass dance in the fall. My informants did not agree with Hoebel (1935) that the sun dance is old at Fort Hall. Its introduction is usually placed at about 35 years ago.

Of true band chiefs there seems to have been two: a Bannock and a Shoshoni. Although their authority extended to the activities enumerated, it was never complete. Groups were at liberty to refuse to participate in activities not to their liking and might split off to ally themselves with petty leaders. Consequently, not only did Bannock and Shoshoni frequently pursue independent courses for various reasons, but each division was in danger of disintegrating. Indeed, Lander (1860, p. 125) reports that Bannock sometimes stole horses from the Shoshoni, though it was not a cause of war. Only the most influential leaders were able to produce unanimity of action. Disagreement was particularly evident in warfare against the white man, for the Shoshoni were inclined to be friendly, but the Bannock carried on frequent raids against the whites. To some extent, however, Washakie, chief of the Wyoming Shoshoni, whose unusual personality seems to have welded the Wyoming Shoshoni into a single band, exercised some control over the Fort Hall Shoshoni and Bannock, and induced temporary peace toward the whites. (See, for example, Hebard, 1930; Irish, 1865, p. 143; Mann, 1865, p. 159; Head, 1866, pp. 122–123; and Tourtellotte, 1869, p. 230.) Jones (1890, p. 90) saw 100 lodges of "Snake and Bannock" from the Wind River country who had left their own tribe under a young man named Tabawantooa. Washakie called them bad men.

When Shoshoni and Bannock traveled together leadership was vested in the chief who had initiated the project, though he consulted with the other chief. Thus, if the Bannock had suggested a hunting expedition, the Bannock chief was in authority (SB). WH, himself a Bannock, said that otherwise the Bannock chief was always in authority, and even SB admitted that, except in dealings with the white man, this was so.

WH said the following were chiefs when he was a young man: band chief, Tagi (this is probably the Tygee, who died in 1871, mentioned by Bancroft, vol. 31, pp. 515–516; Mann, 1866, p. 126, called him Tahgay, 1867, p. 189, Tahjee, and 1870, p. 274, Taggie, chief of 800 "Northern Bannacks"; Mann, 1868, p. 157, called him Tag-gee; Danilson, 1870, p. 288, called him Taggee); Tagi's announcer (called tegwaniwavi), Kusa'gaiyu; war chief, usually Kapi'ta (Spanish, capitan ?). Tagi was succeeded by a distant relative, Batsu'gomezo. He was followed by Pago'it, who was related to neither predecessor. Pago'it died about 1900 or earlier. Bancroft (vol. 31, pp. 518 ff.) states that Buffalo Horn was leader of the Bannock in the seventies. This is doubtless Buffalo Horn mentioned by Burton (1862, p. 474) as chief in 1858.

Lander (1860, pp. 123–124) named Mopeah as chief of about 45 "Pannack" lodges and (p. 137) of 60 lodges. This group ranged through Blackfoot Valley, a few miles north of Fort Hall, where they got camass and trout and went east to the buffalo country via South Pass or the headwaters of Marsh Creek (p. 124) or Salt River (p. 137). Some of them remained in Cache Valley with the "Cache Valley or Salt Lake Diggers." Lander said (p. 125) that "many young men among the Pannacks will not acknowledge their chief's authority." Doty (1864, p. 176) said Bannock chiefs were Tosokwauberaht, "commonly known as the Grand Coquin," Tahgee, Matigund, and others.

SB said that his father, Jimmy, had been the representative in transactions with the white man because he possessed the necessary qualifications. Ěŋga (short) was also something of a chief.

The Kamudüka, of Bannock Creek, had only occasionally banded with the Bohogue' before moving to Fort Hall. After this their chief, Pocatello, who was born in Grouse Creek territory and then moved to Biagamugəp:, became a personage of some importance, especially in the eyes of the white man.

A camp circle was used only in time of danger and for major festivals. The chief pitched his tipi first, then others placed theirs to form a circle, leaving an opening on the east, opposite the chief. Bannock and Shoshoni houses were not segregated. When in danger of raids, limbs were placed between the tipis to form a corral and the horses taken inside. Guards (who were said to usually fall asleep by midnight) were posted.

Marriage.—Some slight differences are evident in Shoshoni and Bannock accounts of marriage. These may be partly the greater fullness of information about the first, partly informant differences, and probably to some extent, at least, cultural differences. Both, however, distinguish orthodox and prearranged alliances from capture and abduction.

Bannock and Shoshoni prohibited marriage between any blood relatives. SB affirmed pseudo but not true cross-cousin marriage among Shoshoni. The preferred alliance was between a man and his mother's brother's (ada's) stepdaughter or the daughter of any female relatives of the mother's brother's wife (baha). In view of polygyny, these female relatives (all called baha) frequently became the mother's brother's wife and consequently provided him with a stepdaughter. Likewise, marriage was permitted with the father's sister's (baha's) stepdaughter and with the stepfather's sister's own daughter, etc. In short, all the children of relatives designated ada and baha who were not related by blood could marry. Pseudo parallel-cousin marriage, however, was forbidden because these cousins called one another "brother" and "sister." Also, true cross-cousins called one another "brother" and "sister."

Among Bannock, also, marriage between true cross-cousins and pseudo parallel-cousins, who called one another "brother" and "sister," was prohibited, but pseudo cross-cousin marriage was preferred. The pseudo cross-cousins were: the stepchildren of the mother's brother (ats), or father's sister (bahwa) or children of brothers or sisters of the ats' wife or bahwa's husband.

Shoshoni marriage took three main forms: "ordinary" marriage, marriage by inducement, marriage by abduction. As all were consummated without ceremony and were extremely liable to dissolution, the usual connotation of "marriage" is not wholly applicable. In fact, the distinction between marriage and nonmarriage in some cases depended upon the birth of a child, and even then the alliance held only so long as the couple continued together. The factors making for permanency of an alliance varied with its kind.

The "ordinary" marriage was that in which a man, seeing a girl of his fancy at a dance or some gathering, induced her to accompany him to his father's camp. Her family was not consulted. If she went with him the mating was consummated and continued as long as she remained.

Marriage by inducement occurred when the girl's family solicited a mate for her. There were several motives for this. They might seek a desirable spouse for the girl, desirability being largely his ability to hunt and help support the camp. If the man were fairly old, the girl's mother might at the same time acquire a lover for herself. The last sometimes led to marriage with both the mother and daughter (p. 215). Again, the girl's father might covet the man's property, for example, horses. Or, the young man might be drawn into such an alliance either because he was easily dominated and lacked initiative to find a mate by other means or because he was attracted by certain inducements. Thus, while he had "sowed his wild oats," the girl had stayed quietly at home making clothing and accumulating property. The girl's mother might also have accumulated property, especially if she had designs on the young man. Eventually, he went to the camp, accepted the property with no obligation to give reciprocal presents, and lived with the girl matrilocally until he had enough property for an independent camp. Meanwhile he hunted and helped support the camp. Matrilocal residence usually lasted a year, sometimes several years. When the young couple set up an independent household it was patrilocal or matrilocal, depending upon circumstances, such as the status of their property or whether their parents were still living.

A Bannock family asked someone, usually the girl's uncle, to inform the young man whom they considered a good hunter that they would like him for a son-in-law. They offered him no presents. He went to the girl's house, slept with her a few days, and was thus considered her mate. Such marriages were usually permanently matrilocal.

Marriage by abduction took two forms: capture and rape. If a Shoshoni man noted a desirable woman, married or unmarried, he assembled his friends, that is, usually his male cousins, and set out to steal her. The husband marshaled his friends and relatives in defense and a gang fight ensued. Though not conducted with intent to kill, the fights were tumultuous and sometimes combatants were killed and the woman injured. Any deaths, however, were not avenged as they were regarded as legitimate hazards of abduction. A deprived husband took no step to recover his wife, though she might return of her own accord. Abductions usually occurred when there was a large encampment (SB). Bannock similarly abducted, a man calling upon his relatives through blood or marriage to assist him (WH). Contests by individual combat seem to have been rare.

Rape only incidentally led to marriage, but was sometimes arranged for a man who had had difficulty finding a woman. Four or five men who were friends, but not relatives, planned to seize a girl and take her out at night. Other men might join them. Older men sometimes knew about the plan but did nothing. They covered their faces, took the girl outside the camp, and each raped her. She might finally be given to the man who wished to take her as his wife.

Shoshoni marriage was often polygynous. This took several forms, depending upon circumstances. If the man had gone to the girl's camp to live, polygyny was sororal. He preferably married the oldest daughter. When she was absent, he had access to her younger sisters. If the younger sisters liked him, he might be considered as married to them. But so long as all lived in the same tipi the distinction between marriage and nonmarriage to all the sisters was slight. SB said it was hard to know whether a man was married to more than one unless the others began to have babies. If the man were older and the girl's father dead he might have relations with both the girl and her mother (provided the latter was not his real aunt). Some restraint was ordinarily expected between a man and his mother-in-law, however. This was explained as explicitly to prevent their "falling in love." A corollary of this was that a man might marry his stepdaughter at the death of his wife.

When Shoshoni marriage was not matrilocal the man might take several women, sisters or not, into his tipi. More often, however, unrelated wives lived in separate houses. All women in his own household were definitely his wives.

Bannock polygyny was usually but not necessarily sororal. Sisters got along much better than unrelated women. The first wife might object if the second were not her sister.

Polyandry as a marriage institution was lacking among both Shoshoni and Bannock, though SB heard of an instance among Bannock about 10 years ago in which a woman slept alternately with two brothers, especially sleeping with the younger when the older was away. The man and wife lived in one house and their children and the younger brother lived in another. The older, who was the real husband, granted his own brother these sex privileges but would not have extended them to another man. SB knew of no instance in which brothers granted each other sex privileges among Shoshoni. WH knew of no true polyandry among Bannock but said that a man often permitted his older or younger brother to sleep with his wife while he was away. Even in such cases, however, the wife was sometimes scolded. If any other man, even the husband's cousin, should assume this privilege, the husband beat his wife.

The levirate, though commonly practiced, was not required. Existence of children was strongly in its favor, but otherwise it was solely a question of preference.

To the extent that marriage was a family alliance, a common practice, when convenient, was the marriage of several brothers to several sisters (not shared in common, however) and of a brother and sister to a sister and brother.

Marriage bonds were loose, but the initiative in a separation was usually taken by the husband. A girl leaving her husband would be reprimanded or sent back to him by her family. If she were discovered in adultery, her paramour, though stronger than the husband, permitted himself to be beaten or his horses to be killed. The wife was sometimes also beaten. Should a woman leave her husband, her family sent her back (SB).

Separations occurred, however, because of infidelity, sterility, or incompatibility. The woman took the children because she was better able to care for them but they frequently visited their father (SB).

Established modes of behavior between certain relatives, beyond the immediate family though by no means accurately defined, seem more stereotyped than among Western Shoshoni. At least a condition upon which this rested was the fact that these large camps permitted all relatives to see one another frequently, whereas among Western Shoshoni they were often scattered in remote camps.

A man's closest friends were his cousins, both parallel and cross, especially the father's brother's sons and male cross-cousins who were often also his brothers-in-law. Other cousins, depending upon family circumstances and residence, were also close comrades. These men helped one another, borrowed freely but did not appropriate one another's property, and went on sexual escapades together. Whereas Owens Valley Paiute prohibited a man and his wife's brother from engaging in lewd talk and particularly from indulging in sexual adventures together, Fort Hall Shoshoni and Bannock closed their eyes to this by the simple expedient of their using "friend" instead of the kinship term during such escapades.

BANNOCK CREEK (KAMUDÜKA) SHOSHONI

Shoshoni occupying the area from Bannock Creek on the Fort Hall Reservation in Idaho to the northern shore of Great Salt Lake in the vicinity of Kelton came to form a single band under Chief Pocatello.

Fort Hall Shoshoni called them Hukundüka, Hoebel (1935) called them Hekandika, and they are probably Wheeler's (1879, p. 409) "Hokanti'kara, or Diggers on Salt Lake, Utah." OD, however, called his own people, the Promontory Shoshoni, Hukundüka and their neighbors to the northwest, Kamudüka (jack-rabbit eaters). For convenience, OD's nomenclature is used.

SB said the language in this territory had differed only a little from that at Fort Hall; GCJ, that it was identical with that at Grouse Creek.

Apparently there were several independent villages in this district in aboriginal days, but when the people acquired many horses and the white man entered the country they began to consolidate under Pocatello, whose authority was extended over people at Goose Creek to the west and probably at Grouse Creek.

A list of the early villages or facts permitting an accurate estimate of their solidarity were not available. OD and GCJ named Biagamugəp:, near Kelton (village 6 on fig. 12), as the principal village in the south. It had 12 to 15 families under a headman named Kutsvata, and seems to have been comparatively independent, conducting its own rabbit and antelope drives in the neighboring flats. Later, Pocatello, who had been chief of Kuiya, a village in Tubadüka territory to the west, became chief of Biagamugəp:.

The Kamudüka of Bannock Creek, though close to Fort Hall, seem to have been independent of the Bohogue' and formerly to have possessed few horses. Many of these people were killed in the Bear River massacre of 1863 and only 50 descendants are said to remain today. They formerly occupied scattered winter encampments on Bannock Creek near the Snake River and on the Port Neuf River between the present town of Pocatello and McCammon (WH). Frémont (1887, p. 279) also found many camps at the head of Bannock Creek. SB believed that the Shoshoni on Bannock Creek had come originally from Wyoming. This, however, is improbable, though some Wyoming families may have settled on Bannock Creek later.

The Kamudüka did not remain together as a single band during the summer, but scattered in small groups of families to gather foods, some going to Bear Lake, some to the Malad River in Utah, and some down the Snake River beyond Twin Falls, perhaps to Camas Prairie.

After the Kamudüka acquired a few horses and the immigrant traffic passing around the northern side of Great Salt Lake became heavy, they began to commit depredations on the wagon trains. It was probably not until this time that Pocatello's influence extended over the whole district of the Kamudüka and their neighbors to the west. In 1860 Lander (p. 137) included them with the "Western Snakes" as "Po-ca-ta-ra's band," inhabiting the "Goose Creek Mountains, head of Humboldt, Raft Creek, and Mormon settlements; horses, few." This approximately coincides with Forney's band of 150 to 180 persons along the northern road to California from the Bear and Malad Rivers to the Goose Creek Mountains (1859, p. 363). Powell and Ingalls (1874, p. 11) call them Northwestern Shoshoni, place them at Goose Creek under Pó-ka-tel-lo, and say they numbered 101 persons. Senate Ex. Doc. 42, 1860, pp. 28–29, names them as "Pocatara's" band of mounted Indians.

These people were eventually admitted to the Fort Hall Reservation where Pocatello seems to have been a personality of some importance. The neighboring town of Pocatello, Idaho, was named after him.

CACHE VALLEY (PÄŊGWIDÜKA)

Though the entire Bear River Valley was occupied by Shoshoni, information about the condition and organization of the Cache Valley people is somewhat contradictory.

This fertile valley was long the center of trapping operations by the white man and, as early as 1826, was the site of an annual rendezvous of Indians and trappers. This inevitably disorganized native activities at an early time.

Cache Valley Shoshoni, acording to OD and his sister, comprised a single band which wintered together at a village (5, fig. 12), called Kwa'ªgün: ogwai (kwa'ª, crane + gün:, house + ogwai, river; so-called because there were many cranes) located along the Logan River above its junction with the Little Bear River, Wüdaogwai (wüda, bear) and along Battle Creek. These people were called Päŋgwidüka (fish eaters). OD thought that only 12 families made up this band, but there is no question that previous to the Bear River massacre of Shoshoni in 1863 the population had been more numerous. It may even have occupied more winter villages.

Doty (1864, p. 175) states that all but seven of Bear Hunter's band were killed in the Battle of Bear River. Gottfredson (1919, pp. 111–115) says that Bear Hunter, Sagwitch, Lehi, Pocatello, and Sanpitch were involved in this battle.

Powell and Ingalls (1874, p. 11) lists two Cache Valley "tribes" or bands. One, numbering 124 persons, was under San'-pits. The other, numbering 158, was under Sai'-gwits. They mention a third group, numbering 17 persons, at Bear Lake under Tav-i-wun-shear.

The Cache Valley Shoshoni ranged along the Bear River under the leadership of Bear Hunter and Lehi, according to OD. Having horses, they sometimes traveled to Bear Lake, which was a common meeting place for Shoshoni from various regions, including Wyoming. They drove rabbits in Cache Valley, and no doubt took buffalo and mountain sheep. Wyeth says mountain sheep were very numerous in Cache Valley in 1836 (Schoolcraft, 1851, pp. 220–221). They went sometimes to the Bear River, near Corinne, for fish.

In August 1842 Frémont (1887, vol. 1, p. 206) saw a large village of horse Shoshoni near the head of Bear River. They had come to hunt antelope and to gather service berries and "kooyah," bitterroot or tobacco root (*Valeriana edulis*). These were not necessarily from Cache Valley, however, as Idaho Shoshoni also ranged in this territory. In Cache Valley he visited a village of poor and hungry Shoshoni (p. 217), and observed that they ate principally "yampah (*Anethum graveolens*), tobacco root, and a large root of a species of thistle (*Circium virginianum*)" (p. 221).

Early accounts, some of which are gross exaggerations, depict these people as unexpectedly impoverished. A reason for this may be raids by hostile tribes as well as the effects of white contacts.

Between 1833 and 1836 Wyeth states that he had seen Utahs, Crows, and Blackfeet in this valley, though the true inhabitants were "Shoshonees," who lived "in the caves and mountains, and retire to their inaccessible haunts on the appearance of their enemies" (Schoolcraft, 1851, pp. 220–221). In 1833 they always fled to the mountains at his approach (p. 226).

De Smet's account of the "Sampeetches" (1843, pp. 165–167) may be intended for the Cache Valley Shoshoni under Powell and Ingalls' Chief San'-pits rather than the San Pete Ute some distance to the south. He says: "The Sampeetches are the next neighbors of the Snakes. There is not, perhaps in the whole world, a people in a deeper state of wretchedness and corruption; the French commonly designate them 'the people deserving of pity,' and this appellation is most appropriate. Their lands are uncultivated heaths; their habitations are holes in the rocks, or the natural crevices of the ground, and their only arms, arrows and sharp-pointed sticks. Two, three, or at most four of them may be seen in company, roving over their sterile plains in quest of ants and grasshoppers, on which they feed. When they find some insipid root, or a few nauseous seeds, they make . . . a delicious repast. They are so timid, that it is difficult to get near them; the appearance of a stranger alarms them; and conventional signs quickly spread the news amongst them. Every one, thereupon hides himself in a hole; and in an instant this miserable people disappear and vanish like a shadow. Sometimes, however, they venture out of their hiding places, and offer their newly born infants to the whites in exchange for some trifling articles."

SALT LAKE VALLEY

Although the territory between the eastern shore of Great Salt Lake and the Wasatch Mountains was settled by the Mormons in

1847, surprisingly little information is available concerning its aborigines. Early mentions of bands and band locations are some-what contradictory and even confuse Shoshoni with Bannock and Ute. It is probable that true Shoshoni completely encircled Great Salt Lake, although some nomenclature suggests the contrary, but the identity and location of the groups east of the lake in Salt Lake Valley are very obscure.

Forney (1859, p. 363) states that 5 bands, totaling 1,000 persons, occupied Cache, Malad, Ogden, Weber, and Salt Lake Valleys and adjacent mountains and canyons. Burton (1862, p. 474) mentions the same 5 bands. Two of these bands have already been described. Cache Valley had at least one band. If Powell and Ingalls were correct, it had two. The Malad Valley band has been described as the Promontory band. The distinction between the other 3 bands is not entirely clear.

Ogden is situated near the mouth of the Weber River and it is difficult to see how Ogden and Weber bands could have been distinct. Some writers, moreover, place the Weber band also at Salt Lake City.

It is probable that occupants of the Weber River were Shoshoni. The Ashley-Smith narrative states that in 1825 "Snakes" killed seven of Etiènne Provot's men at the mouth of Weber River. It is entirely possible, of course, that these Snakes were not permanent occupants of this locality. Subsequently, Weber River people are often designated "Weber Ute" which, however, almost certainly does not mean that they were truly Ute.

Hurt (1856, p. 197) said that the "Treaber Utes" at Bingham's Fort included 60 or 70 men under Little Soldier or Showets. Forney (1858, pp. 209–210) said that Little Soldier was chief of Shoshoni of "Salt Lake, Bear River, Weber River, and Cache Valley" but that the arrival of the whites had compelled his people to live in the mountains. Davies (1861, p. 131) located "Weber-Utes, Little Soldier's band, on Weber River." Burton (1862, p. 476) said "Weber-River Yutas are those principally seen in Great Salt Lake City," a "poor and degraded tribe," whose chief settlement was 40 miles north, i. e., at Weber River. "They understand Shoshonee." Irish (1865, pp. 144–145) said the "Cum-umbahs (or Weber Utes)" numbered about 800, were under chiefs Amoosh, Tetich, and To-tads (Little Soldier) with 2 or 3 subchiefs, and occupied the regions of Salt Lake, Weber, and Ogden Valleys. Head (1866, p. 122) gives 600 "Weber-Utes" or "Cum-umbahs" of Chief To-tado or Little Soldier. Tourtellotte (1869, pp. 230–231) said that 300 Weber Ute were in and about Salt Lake City. Simpson (1876, p. 34), quoting Hurt, regarded the "Cum-um-pahs" and Gosiute as hybrid Shoshoni and Ute. Gottfredson (1919, p. 16) said that Little Soldier was a chief near Ogden.

That these people were called Weber Ute is no proof that they actually were Ute. It is comparable to the incorporation of Ute in the word Gosiute. The few definite references to their language states that it was Shoshoni. They were, moreover, linked with the peoples of Cache and Malad Valleys who are known definitely to have been Shoshoni. According to OD, in fact, Promontory (Malad) and Weber River people foraged freely over each other's territory, no ownership of it being claimed. Nevertheless, true Ute from the south undoubtedly ranged over this territory upon occasion. Bryant (1848, pp. 150–155) claimed to have met several Ute families in Ogden Canyon and several Indians he believed to be Ute (p. 161) just south of Weber River in 1846. OD also stated that Gosiute ranged north to Ogden, though this must have been comparatively late, after they acquired horses.

Information about the vicinity of Salt Lake City is indefinite but seems to indicate that Shoshoni also lived there.

Escalante observed in 1776 that the people near Great Salt Lake, which he did not visit, were called Puaguampes or "sorcerers" (the Shoshoni word for shaman is puhagünt) and that they spoke Comance (which is identical with Shoshoni). They were, he said, eating herbs and living in houses of dry grass and earth. They were not enemies of the Ute and Utah Lake people, though there had been some restraint between the two tribes since the former had killed a Ute man.

Gottfredson (1919, p. 16) named Wanship as a Salt Lake Valley chief. He had fought and killed the Utah Lake chief (p. 21). Alter (1934, Dec. 25), quoting an unnamed source, said that war prowess was necessary for chieftainship in Salt Lake Valley. It is probable that warfare, stimulated by the early introduction of the horse, was of some importance among all the groups along the Wasatch Mountains. Alter also states that one of the Salt Lake Valley chiefs had plural wives and 30 sons, each having a "clan" under him. What is meant by clans in not clear. They were certainly not clans in a technical sense.

OD placed Ute at Salt Lake City and Wheeler (1879, pp, 411–412) classified Weber Ute with Ute, locating them northeast of Great Salt Lake. But several Gosiute informants explained that Weber Ute lived also in the vicinity of Salt Lake City and ranged west to Gosiute territory in Skull Valley and that their language was identical with that of the Gosiute, that is, with Shoshoni. Gocip, whom Simpson believed to be a chief of the Gosiute (p. 54), they named as chief of the Weber Ute.

If, however, the vicinity of Salt Lake City lay in Shoshoni territory, it seems to have been frequented by Ute to an extent that amounted almost to occupation of it. In 1846 Bryant (1848, pp. 165–166), traveling west of the Jordan River, probably near Lake Point on the shore of Great Salt Lake, met Indians called "Utah." The brief vocabulary he recorded appears to be Ute. Remy and

Brenchley recorded that upon arriving in Utah in 1847 the Mormons were met by Wakara or Joseph Walker (chief of the Utah Lake Ute). If this meeting occurred in Heber Valley it was in unquestioned Ute territory; if west of the Wasatch Mountains it places Ute at least temporarily at Salt Lake City. Egan, describing the first immigration of Mormons to Utah, identified only 2 of the numerous Indians met near Salt Lake City; these were "Utahs."

Wilson (1849, p. 67) wrote of a band of "Tenpenny Utahs" with 50 lodges residing in Salt Lake Valley. "Tenpenny," however, was a corruption of Tümpánogots, the name of the Utah Lake Ute. This reference suggests, therefore, that these people were merely visitors to Salt Lake Valley.

The entire country east of the Wasatch Mountains and south of the Uintah Mountains was held by Ute within historic times. In 1776 the Shoshoni or Comanche were raiding Ute within the northern portion of it, probably especially in the Uintah Basin, for Escalante remarked that Ute had left the fertile valleys across the mountains (east of Utah Lake) for fear of the Comanches (Harris, p. 172) and that at about 41° north latitude, probably in the Uintah Basin, Comanche had pursued Ute bison hunters (p. 167). The Ashley-Smith narrative, 1822–1829, however, stated that several thousand Indians, thought to be Ute, were wintering in conical, grass-covered lodges at Brown's Hole on the Green River above the Yampa River (Dale, 1918, pp. 143–144) and that Utes were met at the mouth of the Uintah River (ibid, p. 151). These Utes claimed an area 150 miles long, 100 miles wide, the mouth of the Uintah River being its center. These are the Uintah Ute, discussed below.

The region of Utah Lake, Sevier Lake, and central and eastern Utah was unquestionably Ute.

So far as is known, different groups of Shoshoni were never at war with one another. Between Shoshoni and Utah relations were generally peaceable, though warfare broke out occasionally.

WESTERN UTE BANDS

Little information was obtained through field work among the Ute. Nearly all the Ute who formerly lived west of the Colorado River are now on the Uintah Reservation, where they have merged with Ute native to the Uintah Basin and from neighboring regions. Their consciousness of former band affiliation appears to have been overshadowed by present reservation divisions. A small remnant of Pahvant Ute live at Kanosh, Utah, but the people are so young and so intermixed with Southern Paiute that little reliable information is obtainable from them.

In native times the Ute of western Utah seem to have been distinguished from their Southern Paiute neighbors by their failure to practice horticulture. Among the Southern Paiute horticulture was probably not the major subsistence activity, but it was apparently practiced by all groups. In early historic times the Ute were distinguished from both Southern Paiute and Gosiute Shoshoni by their possession of horses and some measure of band organization.

Inadequacies of early accounts leave much to be desired in an attempt to reconstruct Ute political history. It seems permissible, however, to infer that their native organization had once been much like that of the Western Shoshoni and Southern Paiute and that the development of bands followed the introduction of the horse and the increased importance of warfare. A concomitant of this development was the acquisition of certain Plains traits, such as the tipi, and later, the Sun Dance.

Though Escalante, 1776, did not mention horses in western Utah, it is probable that there were at least a few (see below). In 1825 the Ashley-Smith party described an encampment of several thousand Indians, probably Ute, at Brown's Hole on the Green River (Dale, 1918, pp. 143–144). It is inconceivable that Indians without horses could have assembled and supported so large an encampment. There is no question that by 1850 the Ute were well mounted, well organized, and warlike. Chief Walker, of Utah Lake, the "Napoleon of the Desert," was raiding southern California for horses (Jones, 1890, p. 41). Walker and others were traveling east to the Green River to hunt and trade and seem to have been fighting Cheyenne and Arapaho and sometimes Shoshoni.

But the advantages of the horse probably came first to the inhabitants of the Uintah Basin and of the fertile western piedmont of the Wasatch, especially Utah Lake and Sevier Lake Valleys and the northern Sevier River. Ute occupying the great central mountain mass in Utah had a country less suitable for horses, and for some time remained on a subsistence level like that of Western Shoshoni. Thus, Tourtellotte (1870, p. 142) said the "Fish Utes" around Red Lake lived by hunting and fishing, and Irish (1865) that the San Pitches are "exceedingly poor, and live principally upon fish, berries, and roots." De Smet's remarks about the Sanpitches quoted above (p. 219) may have been intended for these rather than Cache Valley Shoshoni.

The portion of southern Utah lying east of the mountains consists largely of arid mesas and almost impassable canyons (pl. 3, c). It probably supported a small Ute population (see, however, "She-be-retches Ute," below) who had little intercourse with their kin either to the east or west.

The following is a summary of some of the more important references to the "bands" of Western Ute.

Name	Location	Number	Chief	Reference and date
(1)				
Tŭmpá nogots	Utah Lake			JPi.
Timpanogotzi or Lagunas.	___do___		See p. 228.	Escalante, 1776.
Timpanogotzis	___do___			Dominguez. 1776.
Tinpannah	___do___			Russell, 1834–43 (1921, p. 121).
Timpanogos	Provo River		Little Chief and Stick-in-the-head.	Gottfredson, 1850 ? (1919, pp. 18–19).
	Spanish Fork, Payson		Peteetnet	Gottfredson (p. 103).
	Utah Lake		Walker, succeeded by Arrapene.	Gottfredson (pp. 46–47).
	Spanish Fork	(¹)	Pe-teet-weet	Armstrong (1855, pp. 205–206).
	Springville		Tanta-buggar or High Forehead.	Do.
	Provo		Tintick	Do.
Timpenaguchya or Tenpenny.	East of Sweetwater or Utah Lake.		Wakara	Burton (1862, p. 475).
Tim-pa-nogs	Utah Valley	300	An-ka-tewest (or Red Bay).	Irish (1865).
Timpanogs		800		Head (1867, pp. 174–176; 1868, pp. 148–149).
Timpanogos	Vicinity Spanish Fork Reservation.	500		Tourtellotte (1869, pp 230–231).
(2)				
Pavandüts	Sevier Lake region			JPi.
Pagambachis				Escalante (Alter, 1929, p. 54).
Pah-vants	1. Corn Creek farm 2. Sevier Lake.			Forney (1859, p. 364).
Pahvant			Kanosh; later, Huncop.	Gottfredson (pp. 83, 288).
Pah-van			Peah-namp	Egan, about 1860 (1917, p. 263).
Pahvants			Kon-nosh	Forney (1860, p. 60).
Pavant	Corn Creek and Sevier Lake.	700		Burton (1862), p. 475).
Pah-Vants	Pahvant and Sevier Valley, west to White Mountains.	1,500	Saw-e-set; later Konosh.	Irish (1865).
Pah Vants		1,500	Hanosh	Head (op. cit.).
Pah-vents		1,200		Tourtellotte (1869, pp. 230–231).
Pah-vants	Corn Creek	134	Ka-nosh	Powell and Ingalls (1874, pp. 1, 2, 11).
Pahvants	South and east of Sevier Lake Desert.		Blackhawk	Wheeler, 1869 (1875, p. 36).
Pah-vants	Corn Creek, Parawan and Beaver Valleys.		Kan-nash	Simpson (1876, p. 35).
(3)				
Sampits	San Pitch Valley and adjoining part of Sevier River Valley.			JPi.
Sanpuchi				Arze, 1813 (Hill, 1930, pp. 17–19).
Sampatch	"Ashley's" (probably Sevier) River.			Ashley-Smith, circa 1825 (Dale, 1918, pp. 186–187).
Sampiches	Deserts, south of Utah Lake.			Wilkes (1845).
Sampitches	Headwater San-Pitch Creek.			Hurt (1860, pp. 92–93).
	San Pete Reservation	(²)	Jo	Hatch (1862, p. 206).
Sampichyā	San Pete Farm			Burton (1862, p. 475).
San-Pitches	San-pitch Valley and Sevier River.	500	Sow-ok-soo-bet (Arrow feather).	Irish (1865).
San Pitches		400		Head (op. cit.).
Do		300		Tourtellotte (op. cit.).
Seuv-a-rits	Between Sanpete and Sevier Valley on west and Green and Colorado River on east.	144	Mer'-i-ka-hats	Powell and Ingalls (1874, p. 11).
Sanpitch	Camp near Nephi		Sanpitch	Gottfredson (1919, p. 181).

¹ 70 lodges.
² 80 warriors.

Name	Location	Number	Chief	Reference and date
(4)				
	Uintah Valley and Green River	------	------------------	Forney (1859, p. 364).
Uinta------------	South of Fort Bridger and Green River.	1,000	------------------	Burton (1862, p. 475).
Uintah-----------	Uintah Basin, 3 groups--	210	1. Sowyett-----------	Hatch (1862, p. 206).
		300	2. Anthrow-----------	
			3. Tabby------------	
Do-----------	Uintah River and Green River.	3,000	Saw-e-set and subchiefs Tabby and To-quo-ne.	Irish (1865).
Uinta------------	------------------	1,000	Sow-i-et succeeded by Tabby.	Head (op. cit.).
Uintahs---------	------------------	1,500	------------------	Tourtellotte (op. cit.).
Uinta-----------	------------------	1,000	------------------	Simpson (1876, pp. 34–35).
(5)				
	Green River-----------	102	White Eye-----------	Hatch (op. cit.).
	Grand and Green Rivers.	3,000	-----do-----------	Vaile (1862, p. 235).
Yampa-----------	White River-----------	-----	------------------	Burton (1862, p. 476).
Yam Pah---------	------------------	500	------------------	Head (1867, pp. 174–176. 1868, pp. 148–149).
Yam Pah-Utes-----	South of Uintah Valley--	270	------------------	Tourtellotte (1870, p. 142).
Tampa Ute--------	Northwest Colorado----	------	------------------	Culin (1907, p. 315).
(6)				
She-be-retches------	East of Wasatch Mountains; south of San Rafael's River.	1,500	------------------	Head (op. cit.)
Sheberetches-------	South of Yam Pah Ute--	300	------------------	Tourtellotte (1870, p. 142).
Shiberetch---------	"On Twelve Mile Creek, Sanpete County".	------	------------------	Gottfredson (1919, pp. 294–296).
(7)				
Pavogogwunsin----	Upper Sevier River and Fish Lake region.	400	------------------	JPi.
Fish Utes---------		400	------------------	Head (op. cit.)
Do------------	South of Sheberetches, around "Red Lake".	210	------------------	Tourtellotte (1870, p. 142).
	Fish Lake-------------	(³)	Old Poganeab ("Fish Captain").	Gottfredson (1919, p. 327).
	Pine Creek, near Marys-vale.	------	Angewetimpi----------	Gottfredson (1919, p. 329).
(8)				
Tah-bah-was-chi---	Elk Mountain and Lake Fork.	------	Si-ree-chi-wap----------	Beckwith (1855, p. 51).
Elk Mountain-----	Elk Mountain----------	6,000	Saviot, Enthorof and others.	Vaile (1862, p. 236).
Do------------	Southeastern Utah Territory.	2,000–3,000	------------------	Burton (1862, pp. 475–476).
Do------------	Elk Mountain----------	2,500	------------------	Head (op. cit.).
Do------------	-----do-----------------	2,000	------------------	Simpson (1876).
(9)				
Tampa Ute--------	LaSalle Mountains and vicinity.	------	Capsium or Charles----	Gottfredson (1919, pp. 84–87).

³ "Small."

Utah Lake.—These people were called Tümpa'nogots (tümpi, rock+panogo, water mouth, i. e., canyon+ots, people) by JPi. Burton calls them Timpenaguchyă (water among stones), Timpana, or "Tenpenny" (1862, p. 475).

Escalante visited Utah Lake in 1776. He called it Timpanogo and the people Lagunas or Timpanogotzis. Dominguez, who accompanied him, called them Timpanogotzis or Timpanocuitzis and the Indians from the Sevier River to Great Salt Lake, Yutas Zaguaganas (Whipple, Eubank and Turner, 1856, pp. 126–127). Though Escalante does not mention horses at Utah Lake, he met visiting "Timpangotzis" among "Yutas" on the San Francisco Javier (or San

Xavier, now probably Gunnison River, Colorado) River (Harris, pp. 146–147), a journey which probably required horses, though at least one person seemed to have traveled it on foot. Ute in western Colorado at that time had horses. Escalante leaves the impression that the Utah Lake people possessed some organization. Though he described them as peaceful and gentle, warfare was clearly of some importance. He said that they dressed in "buckskin jackets, leggings, moccasins, and rabbit skin blankets," lived in "cane huts" and ate mostly fish (being therefore called "Fish Eaters"), supplemented by seeds, rabbits, and fowl. There were buffalo to the northwest, but the Ute feared to hunt them on account of the Comanche. At 41° latitude, perhaps in the Uintah Basin region, "Comanche" on horses had pursued Ute buffalo hunters and Ute had left their camps in the fertile valley on the east side of the Wasatch for fear of Comanche (Harris, pp. 167, 172). Further indication of the importance of warfare was the information given him at American Fork, on the northern side of Utah Lake, that of paintings of 3 chiefs the "figure that had the most red color . . . blood . . . represented the big chief," who had wounded most men in wars with the Comanches, the next had less blood and was inferior, while the third had no blood and was a civil chief. At Utah Lake he met 3 chiefs whom he listed in order of importance: Turuñianchi, Cuitzapununchi, and Panchucumquibiran. The last, whose name meant "spokesman," was not a chief but a brother of the "Big Chief," Pichuchi (Harris, pp. 179–183). Of the distribution of Utah Lake Indians in villages, Escalante gives no information.

Utah Lake was not again visited until trappers entered the region about 1820. By the forties, these Indians were well mounted (Frémont, 1887, vol. 1, p. 387).

By 1849 the vicinity of Provo became the spring gathering place for "all the Ute bands of the valleys for 200 miles, east and south," including those under Old Elk (Pareyarts), Old Battiste, Tintic and his brother Portsorvic, Angatowats, Old Sawiet, Old Petnich, Walker and his brother, Old Uinta and his sons, Tabby, Graspero, and Nicquia, Old Antero, and sometimes Kanosh. They raced, gambled, feasted, traded, and took fish which moved up the rivers in great numbers to spawn. Fish were pahgar (suckers), speckled trout (mpahger), and mullet (Gottfredson, 1919, pp. 20–21).

Various chiefs of the Utah Lake people were named by early writers. Perhaps each had headed a village. Walker, however, seems to have risen rapidly to prominence and exercised influence over neighboring groups of Ute.

Pahvant or Sevier Desert Ute.—Escalante stated that four days travel south of Utah Lake he met a camp of 20 Indians, who spoke the same language as at Utah Lake and who wore nose pins of bone and rabbit-skin blankets. They had Spanish features and wore beards (Harris, pp. 185–186). Dominguez called them Tiransgapui and placed their northern limit at 39° 35′ north latitude (Whipple, Eubank, and Turner, 1856, pp. 126–127), which corresponds with that given by JPi. Escalante called them Tirangupui (Alter, 1929, p. 21, places this near Scipio) and gave the southern limit of the Ute as about 38° 3′ (Harris, p. 193, and note, p. 253), which is a little south of the Beaver River. If Escalante's observation were correct, the southern Pahvant boundary has been pushed northward subsequent to his visit, for several early writers placed "Piedes" (Southern Paiute) on the Beaver River (p. 272), Kelly placed Southern Paiute north to the southern end of Sevier Lake (1934), and JPi gave the Pahvant boundary as roughly at Cove Creek, on Beaver River.

The Pahvant Ute were called Pavandüts (water people), according to JPi. They ranged the deserts surrounding Sevier Lake west of the Wasatch Mountains nearly to the Nevada border, where they were somewhat mixed with Gosiute.

Villages were located in the vicinity of the present towns of Kanosh, Deseret, Black Rock, Holden, Lyndyl, and Scipio, each being the winter headquarters of a division of the band. Burton (1862, p. 475) gave 2 divisions in 1860; one at Sevier Lake and the northeastern part of Fillmore Valley, and one at Corn Creek farm.

Many, though not all of the people, had horses.

Foods were gathered principally within the bounds of the territory. This territory was owned by the band and defended against trespass by other Ute, Paiute, and Gosiute. There were no village or family rights to food areas, however (JPi).

The principal vegetable foods were pine nuts, berries, and roots. Both *Pinus edulis* and *Pinus monophylla* occur in the area but the latter was preferred as the nut is larger and softer than the former. To procure it, trips west to the House range were necessary.

Fish in Sevier River were: kaiva pagu ("mountain trout") and mugwütcagwits, sucker.

Deer could be had in the mountains and water fowl along the Sevier River.

In native times the main function of the chief was to keep informed of the whereabouts of good seed crops and to send a messenger to the different villages with the information. In case of war a special man took charge.

Little information is available about dances or other factors which might have integrated the Pahvant. Gottfredson reported that Kanash and Koosharem (upper Sevier River) Ute joined for a

10-day Bear Dance in the spring. Warfare seems to have effected considerable unity in native times. When the Mormons arrived in Utah they quickly settled the fertile portions of the valleys along the Wasatch, preempting Indian village sites and food areas. The necessary transactions with the white man rapidly elevated the chief to a prominent position. The Pahvant were fortunate in being represented by Kanosh, who seems to have won them important concessions.

Egan (1917, p. 263) mentions Peah-namp, who was married to a Gosiute woman, as "Pah-van" chief about 1860. According to Irish (1865), Kon-osh ("Man of white hair") and several subchiefs succeeded Saw-e-set. Kanosh was succeeded by Hun-cop; Moshoquop was Kanosh's war chief (Gottfredson, 1919, p. 288). Burton (1862, p. 475) said there was "one principal and several subchiefs" in 1860.

Sampits.—(Cane people; so called because much cane grew in their territory, JPi) ; according to Burton (1862, p. 475), Sampichyă corrupted to San Pete.

Gottfredson (1919, p. 32) said that in 1849 the Indians claiming the country around Manti, on San Pitch Creek, wintered in the Sevier River Valley where there was less snow and where they could take deer, rabbits, ducks, and geese and trap beaver and mink. In the spring, they camped west of Manti. They numbered several hundred persons but by 1860 were only 40 to 50 lodges having 4 to 10 persons each. The chiefs were Arrapene (elsewhere said to be the Utah Lake chief), succeeded by Sowiette (elsewhere said to be the Pahvant and also Uintah chief).

Yampah Utes.—Located somewhere south of the Uintah Basin. This country was described to Ashley-Smith (Dale, 1918, p. 151) as a place with little game, where people ate roots, fishes, and horses. But Tourtellotte (1869, pp. 230–231) said the "Yam Pah-Utes" were mounted and lived by hunting.

Pavógowunsiɲ.—This band occupied the upper portion of the Sevier River south of the Salina River. Gottfredson (1919, pp. 327–329) suggests two groups here: one a small group under Old Poganeab or "Fish Captain" at Fish Lake; the other a very different people under Angewetimpi at Pine Creek near Marysvale to the west. He states (p. 343) that Walker Ammon was chief at Koosharem (between these two localities) but this must have been after the general Ute alliance.

Elk Mountain Ute.—Vaile (1862, p. 236) said Elk Mountain Ute were well mounted. Starting in April, they traveled to the Grand River, then to the Bear River, Laramie Plains, and the Snake country, or to the White River and down the Green River to Snake country. After hunting buffalo and fishing they returned home in September. Sometimes they went to the Navajo country to trade.

There were 1,000 under Saviot and Enthorof and a total of 6,000. Burton (1862, pp. 475–476) numbered Elk Mountain Ute at 2,000 to 3,000.

Burton also mentioned Parawat Yutas: ; "the Tabechya, or Sun hunters, about Tete de Biche, near Spanish lands (probably Escalantes' Tabehuachis of the Dolores River, western Colorado); and the Tash Yuta, near the Navajoes." But Beckwith (1855, pp. 53–55) seems to locate Tah-bah-was-chi near Elk Mountain where Escalante located Sabuaguanos, Escalante's Tabehuachis being on the Dolores River.

Post-Caucasian period.—After 1847 white men rapidly settled Ute country and decimated supplies of native foods. The ensuing strife, which culminated in the Black Hawk war in the sixties, provided an opportunity for dominating personalities to extend their political and military influence.

One such personality seems to have been Walker, whom Jones (1890, p. 41) called the "Napoleon of the Desert" and P. P. Pratt in 1848 called a "celebrated chief" (Alter, Dec. 31, 1934). Gottfredson reckons his birth to have occurred in 1815 at Spanish Fork near Utah Lake and says the name means "Yellow," a plausible translation. He became chief not by inheritance but by having accumulated cattle and horses in raids in southern California in 1846 or 1847 (Gottfredson, 1919, pp. 319–320; Alter, quoting Daniel H. Wells, Dec. 31, 1934). He was probably civil rather than war chief. Showan was a war chief under him (Gottfredson, 1919, p. 82). Frémont (1887, vol. 1, p. 386) recorded that during the forties Walker's Ute were well mounted and equipped with rifles. He met them near Fillmore. In 1849 Manley (1894, p. 90) met Walker with his band on Green River. At Walker's death, in 1855 (Burton, 1862, p. 475), a meeting of all the neighboring Ute elected his brother, Arrapeen, chief (Alter, March 30, 1935; also, Lewis, 1855). According to Alter (Dec. 31, 1934), Walker had 6 brothers: Arrapeen, Grocepeen, Sampitch, Ammon, Tabbinaw, and Yankawalkits. Some of these, however, have been named as chiefs of other bands and there may well be question whether they were blood brothers.

Contemporary with Walker, however, was Soweite, whom P. P. Pratt in 1848 called the "king of the whole Utah nation" (Alter, Dec. 31, 1934). This is probably the Saw-e-set whom Irish (1865) named as Pahvant chief and again as Uintah chief. Head (1867) also named Sow-i-et as Uintah chief. Evidently he had moved to the reservation. His subchiefs were Tabby (Sun) and To-quo-ne (Black Mountain Lion) (Irish, 1865).

The Black Hawk war may be said to have started about 1865, raids continuing until 1870. At no time, however, did any chief hold real authority over allied bands of Ute. Some Ute had gone to the

Uintah Basin, others settled peaceably at Spanish Fork and Corn Creek farms. Black Hawk was most obstreperous, raiding between Cedar City and Payson, Ancatowats being his main raider. But in 1867 Black Hawk controlled only 28 lodges. After his death in 1870 Au-a-vor-un and Shenanagon continued his raids (Gottfredson, 1919, esp. pp. 226, 274, 294–296).

ANALYSIS OF DATA

This section will analyze the ecological and social determinants which in complex interaction produced the different kinds of Shoshonean sociopolitical groups.

ECOLOGICAL DETERMINANTS

The natural environment was a constant. Many important features of the social groups inhabiting it depended upon the manner in which it was exploited by special economic devices and by the subsistence habits entailed. These largely predetermined the population density, imposed limitations upon the size, distribution, and mobility of village groups, and affected the nature of economic cooperation, political controls, and certain property rights. Different techniques, of course, had somewhat unlike effects. The present white population, which is about 15 times denser than the native population, utilizes many natural resources of the Great Basin which were ignored by the Indian and has extreme division of labor. Neither individuals nor families are self-sufficient today; even the population as a whole depends upon other areas. Goods not produced locally are transported from elsewhere by facilities far surpassing those of aboriginal days. The Shoshonean exploitation of the same environment was so simple that the biological family was, in most respects, necessarily the independent self-supporting unit. Commerce was virtually unknown and specialization was extremely rare. The only true specialist was the shaman, though information showing the extent to which he was relieved of ordinary subsistence activities and supported himself entirely by his practice is not available.

Under native economy Shoshonean units smaller than the family survived only with difficulty. It is probable that individuals were able to support themselves, but were, according to Shoshonean standards, underprivileged. Units larger than the family were transient in most parts of the area.

The individual family was in most respects necessarily the independent economic unit. Subsistence in most of the area was primarily upon plant foods. When gathering these foods, group endeavor might bring the pleasure of companionship, but it did not increase the per capita harvest. In fact, because few plants other than the pine nut grew in dense and extensive patches, it usually decreased the harvest. As food shortage was always a real danger it was necessary that families harvest alone or in the company of not more than one or two other families. A woman harvested exclusively for her own family. The only collective activity connected with plant foods was irrigation in Owens Valley and occasional sowing of wild seeds in central Nevada.

It is conceivable that had seed yield been extraordinarily great, specialization in industry might have been possible, so that certain women could have devoted full time to harvesting and traded surpluses for goods made by other women who spent most of their time in manufacturing. This was impossible because the techniques utilized by Shoshoneans for exploiting their limited resources did not permit a woman to gather more plant foods than were absolutely required by her family. Surplus for trade was very unusual. She frequently shared seeds with neighbors and especially with relatives, but was not obligated to do so.

Hunting was the complement to harvesting. Game provided not only essential foods but skins for clothing and materials for certain implements. Most hunting was also on a family basis. Small species, such as rodents and insects, were taken by both men and women. Large game was usually taken by men, while women gathered plant foods. A hunter was obligated, however, to share large game with other members of the village. Thus a family was able to provide most of its wants without assistance. But in time of dire need other families came to its aid if possible.

But the family was not always the maximum economic unit in hunting. When taking buffalo, antelope, rabbits, deer, mountain sheep, and, under certain conditions, water fowl, fish, and even insects, collective effort increased manyfold what an individual hunter could have procured. The duration of such hunts and the profitable number of participants depended upon special conditions in each case. Among the Western Shoshoni and many of their neighbors game was so scarce that these hunts usually lasted only 1 to 2 weeks and never more than 6 weeks. Participants rarely numbered more than two dozen families. Salmon runs in the Snake River permitted somewhat larger groups to assemble for slightly longer. Groups which had access to the buffalo were able to remain together for several months. In fact, buffalo hunting so outweighed the advantages of seed gathering that Northern Shoshoni families separated and scattered out to harvest plant foods only during a small portion of the year.

Several plant and animal species occurred in such great quantities in certain localities during short periods that, even when they were not taken cooperatively, they drew large numbers of families to such localities. Outstanding among such species are pine nuts, which were often a major factor in the location of winter villages, and salmon, crickets, and grasshoppers, which were sometimes taken cooperatively as well as by single families.

An economic factor of major importance was the horse, which affected native subsistence activities in several ways. First, it permitted foods gathered over a wide area to be transported to a central location, thus enabling families to congregate in large communities instead of scattering to live near the sources of their food. Second, it permitted a large number of families to move as a unit to different areas where foods were abundant. This was particularly important in hunting buffalo, which had to be taken east of the Continental Divide after they became extinct in Idaho and Utah. Finally, it greatly facilitated slaying such animals as the buffalo.

The effect of these ecological factors varied in the different parts of the area.

Among Western Shoshoni plant harvesting was the main subsistence activity, game being relatively scarce. For the greater part of the year families necessarily traveled alone or in very small groups and harvested a very large area. They ordinarily ranged 20 miles or more in each direction from the winter village. Their itinerary, though usually the same each year, was not always fixed. Seasonal variation in rainfall and consequently in crop growth frequently required that they alter their routine.

The most permanent association of families was at winter encampments. These were sites where certain families habitually remained during the months when vegetable foods could not be had. Necessary conditions for such sites were accessibility to stored seeds, especially pine nuts, water, sufficient wood for house building and fuel, and absence of extremely low winter temperatures. These conditions were most often fulfilled in the mouths of canyons or within the pine nut-juniper belt in the mountains, though sometimes broad valleys near fishing streams were chosen. Encampments tended to cluster with respect to mountain masses rather than valleys. But whether they were scattered at intervals of several hundred yards to a mile along streams, were situated at springs on mountain sides, or were clustered in dense colonies depended upon the quantity of foods which could be gathered and stored within convenient distance of each camp. In some places families had to camp alone; elsewhere as many as 15 or 20 could congregate in a true village.

But another factor affecting population distribution was annual variation in seed occurrence. Though a winter encampment was always located near the greatest amount of stored foods, the natural yield was not everywhere and always the same. In some areas, for example, Owens Valley, crops were fairly reliable and villages consequently stable. Elsewhere, especially in the deserts bordering Death Valley, the Great Salt Desert, most of Nevada, and the Snake River, people had to traverse enormous territories, modifying their itinerary considerably from year to year as local rainfall or other factors affected plant growth. The erratic occurrence of the all-important pine-nut crops, for example, required that a family often remain in different localities in successive years. Along and north of the Humboldt River the pinyon nut is too scarce to have been an important factor, but other plant species also were unreliable and many had a somewhat similar effect. People consequently were not always able to return to the same winter village.

Western Shoshoni cooperative hunts did not permit permanent associations of families or villages for several reasons. First, these hunts lasted only while the quantity of meat taken was sufficient to feed the assembled crowd—a few weeks. There was rarely a surplus which, being stored for winter, would be a factor in the location of winter villages. Second, alinement of families or villages for hunting was often different for each species. Antelope and rabbits, the most important species in this part of the area, often occurred in different parts of a valley. Moreover, the more important hunts were held only where there was an antelope shaman or rabbit drive director; every valley did not have such men. For communal hunts, therefore, families traveled from their village or from where they happened to be gathering seeds to the most convenient location and often cooperated with very different people in successive hunts. They might join families from across their valley for a rabbit drive, go to a neighboring valley to hunt with its residents in an antelope drive, travel in another direction to a marsh to join a waterfowl drive, and associate with immediate neighbors to hunt deer in their own mountains. If their local pine-nut crop failed the next year they might be thrown into association with still other people for these hunts.

Because the territory exploited by different families was variable as well as overlapping, ownership of food areas would have been impractical. It was absent among Western Shoshoni, excepting possibly the Reese River area.

The only exceptions to these generalizations were Owens Valley and possibly other Northern Paiute, the Snake River Shoshoni, and the Southern Paiute.

In Owens Valley natural resources supported a population many times denser than in the remainder of the western area. The villages were comparatively large and closely spaced on Owens River and the Sierran streams. Moreover, extreme geographic diversity provided all essential foods and materials within small territories. Consequently, instead of traveling during the greater part of the year, the Owens Valley Paiute were able to harvest the main foods by traveling only a day or two from their villages and could assemble readily for communal hunts in the valley. Not only were villages stable and inhabited more or less perennially, but the same neighboring villages usually cooperated for communal hunts and for irrigation. Habitual exploitation of the same general terrain gave point to, if it did not account for, the origin of band territory. Ownership of territory and habitual cooperation in irrigation and hunting, therefore, were economic factors which contributed to band cohesion.

Information about other Northern Paiute is insufficient to analyze the ecological factors. Apparently those immediately west of Battle Mountain resembled the Shoshoni. It is possible, however, that unusual fertility in such regions as the Carson and Walker Rivers and possibly the Humboldt Sink provided a condition like that in Owens Valley. Apparently there was ownership of pine-nut areas and perhaps other food areas among some Northern Paiute. Such facts are intelligible only in relationship to the total picture, which is not yet available.

The Snake River is unique in having salmon, but their quantity and quality were somewhat less than nearer the coast. When running, the fish were sufficiently abundant to supply all who could take them. The main limitation upon them was their occasional failure to run and the restricted number of convenient fishing places. Large numbers of families forgathered at the good fishing sites, some cooperating in constructing dams and weirs, others fishing alone with spears, hooks, and other devices. The catch was dried for winter. Though salmon afforded considerable food, all accounts indicate that they were rarely sufficient to keep families in plenty during the remainder of the year. Consequently, subsistence was supplemented by vegetable foods and hunting, which was carried on as among other Western Shoshoni. Communal hunts, however, were unimportant, because game was extraordinarily scarce along the Snake River plains. Both game and vegetable foods required unusually long journeys, either to the camass country to the north or to the highlands to the south. Families returned to their salmon caches along the Snake River to winter if the catch had been good; otherwise they remained where the vegetable harvest had been abundant.

Among the lower Snake River Shoshoni, consequently, economic alliances were minimal in spite of large temporary gatherings permitted by the salmon. Minor cooperation in fishing was the only real collective economic enterprise.

Southern Paiute differed from the Western Shoshoni mainly in the practice of a small amount of horticulture. Among the neighbors of the Death Valley and Beatty Shoshoni this modified their ecology only in minor ways. First, as a family returned to harvest the crops it had planted, the annual foraging itinerary was probably somewhat less variable than among Shoshoni. Second, horticulture probably introduced the concept of land ownership. It is possible that owner-ship of pine-nut, mesquite, and screw-bean groves was an extension of the concept applied first to cultivated lands and was made more practicable by the comparatively fixed subsistence routine.

The Northern Shoshoni and many Ute stood in sharp contrast to the Western Shoshoni. Two outstanding factors were involved, the horse and the buffalo. In their effect upon society these were related to each other and to the environment. Both are grazing animals and find their optimum environment in grasslands. Though the failure of the horse to spread farther west until post-Caucasian times may have been partly the time factor, it was largely environmental. Farther north the horse had spread well down the Columbia River. In Western Shoshoni territory the scarcity of grass made its keep difficult. It would, in fact, have eaten the very plants upon which people depended. Moreover, the absence of game herds restricted its usefulness to transportation, which apparently did not compensate for the cost of its keep. It could have been kept most readily in the more fertile areas where the need for transportataion was least. In the west, therefore, any horses acquired were usually eaten. In eastern Idaho and in northern and eastern Utah, however, there were more grasslands and, what was more important, buffalo. When, in 1840, local buffalo became extinct, herds east of the Rocky Mountains were within reach of mounted Indians.

Buffalo hunting, especially when long journeys were entailed, was essentially cooperative. The herds east of the Rocky Mountains were so large that several hundred persons were not only able to maintain themselves during the hunt but to cure sufficient meat to last through much of the year. The hunts were cooperative because, as among all other buffalo-hunting tribes, the yield of a planned, concerted drive was so much greater than what individuals could procure that indi-viduals were forbidden to hunt alone.

Another result of the combined effect of the horse and buffalo was surplus wealth. This had two consequences. First, it prompted some trade. Long trips to the west were made to trade buffalo skins for horses. After trading posts were introduced, skins were traded for various articles. Second, wealth, especially in horses, made the people desirable prey to raiding tribes from the east, which elevated war-fare to some importance. Warfare in turn affected the social group, as pointed out below.

Most other subsistence activities among these people—hunting deer, antelope, and other game, and harvesting vegetable foods—were

carried on by independent families. The organization which had
been in effect during the several months of the buffalo hunt broke
down and each family governed its own activities. Though individual families traveled great distances for various foods, it was
usually possible for them to return on horseback to a centralized
winter camp, and usually they did so. Consequently, a sense of
allegiance and solidarity if not actual organization persisted throughout the year.

Though information about pre-horse Shoshoni and Ute is not available, it is probable that they were at one time fundamentally similar
to Western Shoshoni. If so, the effect of the horse was to produce
band organization, facilitate the acquisition of many Plains traits,
and largely to bring about the differences between Northern and
Western Shoshoni noted in the historical period.

In summary, ecological factors imposed certain conditions to
which society had to conform and provided limits within which it
could vary.

Among Western Shoshoni and probably Southern Paiute the family was necessarily the economic unit. This family was bilateral
rather than patrilineal or matrilineal, first, because an extended family would frequently have been too large to live together; second,
because the uncertainties of food and consequently of residence made
association with persons other than those of the immediate household uncertain. Under the existing ecology it was physically impossible for groups larger than the village to remain in association
during the winter. Though these villages often comprise related
families, frequent change of residence prevented this always being
so. There was consequently no localized lineage, nor condition for
clan development. Social features dependent upon large and prosperous populations were also prevented, e. g., clubs, rank based upon
wealth, slavery, and others. Likewise, political organization was
minimal. There were no bands.

The Owens Valley Paiute, though culturally and economically
similar to Western Shoshoni, lived in an unusually fertile environment and therefore had a dense population which was clustered in
large villages. Restricted subsistence areas coupled with habitual
cooperation of certain villages permitted the development of land-
owning bands with a variety of political controls.

Northern Shoshoni, though having a sparse population, and Ute
possessed the great advantage of the horse and accessibility to the
bison. The horse made it possible for large groups to live and
travel together, and bison hunting entailed much cooperation.
Therefore, despite seasonal disintegration into family units, bands
with appropriate chiefs existed during the greater part of the year.

But they were not landowning because the territory exploited by each overlapped to too great an extent. These large and comparatively stable bands provided a condition for the development of fixed kinship relations, societies (of which there was a bare suggestion), warfare and prestige derived from warfare.

Social Determinants

The more important social determinants producing cohesion in large groups were festivals, the sweat house, and warfare. Kinship bonds also achieved some group solidarity.

Festivals were made possible in most of the western area by the temporarily increased food supply produced by rabbit drives, pine-nut trips, antelope hunts, or other communal economic affairs. The essential motivation of festivals, however, was noneconomic. People desired social intercourse with friends and relatives rarely seen during the remainder of the year. They wished to dance and gamble, and, in some localities, to hold religious observances. Some of these activities, like the dances, were developed in the area. Others, like the games, were probably introduced from neighboring areas at a remote time.

The size of groups united by festivals rarely exceeded that produced by communal economic undertakings. In the Western Shoshoni area festivals could be held only at times of communal hunts or when many families were gathering pine nuts or other species at a certain locality. They merely provided an additional motive for assembling together. Owens Valley bands seemingly held special gatherings for festivals. In providing an extra occasion for band activity, festivals enhanced band solidarity. But, as neighboring bands were often invited, temporary organization greater than the band was sometimes achieved. Among the Northern Shoshoni there seems to have been no major festival in aboriginal days. The Sun Dance is recent. Round dances served merely to amuse small portions of the bands. Possibly the Bear Dance among the Ute and some mourning ceremonies among Southern Paiute effected some group solidarity, but too little is known of who participated in them.

The sweat house was an integrative factor only in a small portion of the area. Among Owens Valley Paiute and a few of their neighbors each village had a large permanent sweat house which served as a meeting house and men's club and dormitory. When villages were not too widely separated all male band members tended to forgather in a central sweat house. Western Shoshoni were too unsettled and their villages usually too small to make it profitable to construct a large house. The Northern Shoshoni and Ute also lacked a community sweat house or its equivalent.

Warfare on a scale large enough to affect social cohesion was known only in the eastern part of the area. Its occurrence corresponded very largely with that of the horse. There is no evidence of serious and prolonged strife between Shoshonean groups, though Shoshoni and Ute were periodically at grips. Permanent and irreconcilable enemies lived east of the Rocky Mountains, the Blackfeet being pitted against Shoshoni and the Arapaho against Ute. The absence of enemies within Utah and Idaho and among tribes to the west made winter villages comparatively secure, except as Blackfeet parties occasionally crossed the mountains and sometimes harassed small parties. Warfare, consequently, was not a motive for band consolidation in Ute villages; it forced Shoshoni winter encampments to amalgamate only to a minor degree. When, however, Ute or Shoshoni crossed the mountains to bison country, especially when Shoshoni and Bannock visited the vicinity of Yellowstone, raids were a real danger. They traveled in large bands under the direction of chiefs and joined forces with Flathead and Nez Percé when possible. When in hostile territory police kept the party together. Warfare thus increased organization which communal bison hunting had required.

Offensive warfare rarely if ever involved the entire band. Following Plains patterns, it was restricted to raids by small parties conducted to steal horses and acquire war honors. War and victory dances, like festivals, seem not to have involved all band members.

West of the area of bands and the horse, warfare was virtually unknown. Shoshoni never fought one another except in family feuds which somewhat disrupted group unity. Upon rare occasions Shoshoni fought their Paiute neighbors, but no organization was entailed. Southern Paiute seem to have been the victims of Ute slave raids, at least after the arrival of the whites, but the effect of this upon Southern Paiute organization is not known.

Shamanistic performances and funerals drew many visitors, but, being informal, were usually attended only by residents of the local village or by people within a convenient distance.

The relationship of kinship to the composition of the sociopolitical group is conspicuously greater among Western Shoshoni than among Northern Shoshoni. Among the former, organization rarely surpassed the bonds of kinship. Relatives sought one another's proximity. Though exigencies of the food quest often forced related families apart, they wintered together if possible. Very small villages frequently consisted exclusively of related families and large villages had many that were related. Several marriage practices contributed to this condition. Residence was with one parent or the other, rarely independent. And, if there were unrelated families in a village, their children often married one another and remained there. When brothers and sisters married sisters and brothers they all wintered at the same site if possible.

This high degree of relationship between village members naturally enhanced village solidarity, even when village communal economic and social activities were unimportant. A very practical aspect of this solidarity was willingness to share food with relatives. When economically possible, these related families traveled together in the food quest and participated in the same communal activities. The village headman, therefore, was the most vigorous and competent member of the related families which made up the majority of the population.

The importance of kinship in village control decreased in proportion to the village size. When single kin groups did not comprise the majority of the population they ceased to dominate the village. The leaders of communal festivals and hunts served without regard to family ties.

Among the Northern Shoshoni population aggregates were so large that a person inevitably lived in the proximity not only of his relatives but of many unrelated families. The only conspicuous effect of kinship here was to divide the winter encampment into small clusters of perhaps half a dozen related families. These also traveled together in the quest of seeds, roots, berries, and fish when communal band activities were not in progress.

SOCIAL AND POLITICAL PATTERNS

THE FAMILY

Many, though not all, characteristics of the family were produced by the ecological and social determinants previously discussed.

The biological family, that is, parents and children, constituted the household. Among Western Shoshoni the household was very nearly a self-sufficient economic unit and as such an independent social and political unit. With the exception of large game, all foods belonged exclusively to the households of the persons acquiring them. Food-gathering activities were conducted largely by independent households under the leadership of the household head.

But, though the household was the most stable social and economic unit, some factors tended to disrupt it and others to enlarge it or to extend obligations beyond it. The main disruptive factors were divorce, which occurred easily and frequently, and wife abduction. These, however, merely realined households.

The household was often enlarged by the inclusion of relatives, especially grandparents, who had no households of their own. It was also temporarily enlarged by the addition of the spouse of one or more of its children. Up to a year of matrilocal residence as bride service was common and, in any event, a young married couple usually remained with one family or the other until they had children or their own house. A household might also be augmented by polygyny or polyandry. These forms of marriage were probably not produced in this area by economic factors, but unusual individual wealth was a condition upon which they rested. A man could not hold one wife, to say nothing of several, unless he were a diligent hunter and brought home many buckskins. Polyandry was usually an extension of hospitality and sex privileges to the husband's brother, who would eventually acquire a wife of his own. But it meant that one woman had to provide an increased amount of seeds. The average household was about 6 persons, according to census data, but additions might bring it up to 10.

These additions to the household, however, were not permitted to threaten the welfare of the biological family. Those who were able-bodied shared the tasks of food seeking. Old or infirm persons, especially grandparents, cared for the children. But when starvation was imminent or the exertion of long treks for food excessive, infirm persons were abandoned to perish. Necessity thus strictly limited expansion of the household.

There were also responsibilities if not strict obligations to persons outside the household. Whether a village were large or small, several related families usually lived in the proximity of one another. These were usually the households of parents, their married children, brothers and sisters and their spouses, and other close relatives who, in some localities, were further related through cross-cousin and pseudo cross-cousin marriage. These related families traveled together and camped near one another. Though not obligatory, food was freely shared with them. The male members of these households assisted one another in abducting a wife or in defending a wife against abduction and rendered mutual assistance in other ways.

Though the nature and extent of the manifold duties and obligations between kinfolk is a rich field for more extended inquiry, sufficient information is now available to indicate that these duties and obligations had crystallized into very few definite patterns among Western Shoshoni. In order that obligations to a relative shall have significance, there must be assurance that one will see him sufficiently often and under sufficiently well-defined circumstances. In the Western Shoshoni area lack of consistency in post-marital residence and frequent change of residence for practical reasons brought certain

STEWARD] BASIN-PLATEAU ABORIGINAL GROUPS

relatives into close association at some times and widely separated them at other times. There was, for example, no assurance that the maternal or paternal grandparent would be present to care for children, that a sister's son or a brother would be on hand to help build a fish dam, that maternal aunts or uncles would be encamped nearby and require a dole of seeds, or that any particular relatives would be able to help defend one's wife against abduction.

The more stable social conditions of the bands of Northern Shoshoni were more favorable to the development of readily definable patterns of behavior between kin. A person knew when and under what conditions he would see his different relatives. Thus, a man knew that he would be in frequent contact with his father's sister, so that it was possible for him to help support her, to marry her stepdaughter, and to have her sons as his closest companions. The possibility of fulfilling these functions with respect to the father's sister in Western Shoshoni society was too uncertain for them to have meaning. A man would live near his father's sister so that he could help support her and associate with her son only if the father and his sister had decided to remain in the same locality.

But many of these kinship relations must be understood in historical terms. Although a certain minimum of association with individuals may be a condition for the development of duties and attitudes toward them, it cannot account for all such duties and attitudes. Both Owens Valley Paiute and Northern Shoshoni had large and fairly stable population. But the former observed a strict mother-in-law avoidance, whereas among the latter, practicing pseudo cross-cousin marriage, a man and his mother-in-law were close friends and sometimes even married. The former imposed restraint between brothers-in-law, but among the latter, brothers-in-law went on sexual escapades together.

MARRIAGE

In the Basin-Plateau area marriage created an economic unit which insured survival of the individual, a biological unit which somewhat insured certain sex privileges, and a social unit which guaranteed security for children and which united kinship groups. Though none of these was distinctive of the area, it is possible to show that many features of them were delimited and patterned by local conditions.

Marriage was an economic alliance in a very real sense. It has been pointed out previously that the biological or bilateral family formed the core of the household and as such was a union which brought into cooperation the complementary economic activities of the sexes. In a region where the burden of subsistence overshadowed all other activities this was extremely important. Although any particular marriage might be of brief duration, a person could not, in the interest of self-preservation, afford to remain long single. He was generally wed to one person or another during most of his adult life.

Another motivation to marriage was the necessity of caring for children. That a person would acquire a spouse in self-interest was insurance that children would be supported by two parents most of the time, even though one was often a stepparent.

The role of exclusive sex privileges in matrimony seems to have been secondary. Though such privileges were recognized, extramarital affairs were evidently managed readily. Legal rights to a wife, moreover, were often waived temporarily for a consideration. Strong personal, perhaps even monogamous, attachments undoubtedly existed, but cannot have been strong bonds. Explorer's journals are too full of accounts wherein men fled ingloriously at the arrival of strangers, leaving their women to the latters' mercy. Moreover, individual attachments were attenuated by the practice of polygyny and, in many localities, polyandry.

Economic pursuits were not only a reason for marriage but seem to have contributed to certain features of it. The matrimonial status of each sex was, with a few exceptions noted below, substantially equal. If native male dominance was to man's advantage, women's somewhat great economic importance in seed gathering offset it. There were virtually no noneconomic activities which either sex would use as a social lever. The family therefore was a well-balanced bilateral unit, neither sex having appreciable advantage.

One expression of this sex equality appears to have been the practice of both polyandry and polygyny (Steward, 1936). The sororate and levirate were intensified in this area. As sororal polygyny was a simple step from the former, fraternal polyandry was a simple step from the latter. The partial distribution of polyandry in this area indicates, however, that sex equality is probably an incomplete explanation of it. Polygyny, preferably sororal, was universal, but polyandry, though occurring among most Western Shoshoni, some Northern Shoshoni, at least the Panaca Southern Paiute, and some Northern Paiute, was definitely lacking among Owens Valley Paiute and their neighbors, Ash Meadows Southern Paiute, and Shoshoni in the vicinity of Death Valley. Theoretically, moreover, nonfraternal polyandry should have occurred as often as non-sororal polygyny. Apparently it did not. Among Western Shoshoni it was usually fraternal, being essentially an extension of sex privileges to a brother prior to his marriage to some other woman. Less often it was true marriage contracted with the intention of permanency.

Nonfraternal polyandry was rare. Park reports (1937) that polyandry was always fraternal and was conceived as true marriage among Pyramid Lake and Walker River Northern Piaute. O. C. Stewart (1937) reports polyandry among Northern Piaute at Pyramid Lake, Owyhee, McDermit, Winnemucca, and Burns, but states that the first three, at least, practiced the nonfraternal form.

It is probable that several factors which have not yet been ascertained determined the occurrence of the different forms of polyandry. Park has suggested that among Paviotso (Northern Paiute) frequent polygyny left a shortage of marriageable women. This may have been a contributing factor, but among Western Shoshoni the frequency of polygyny seems to have been insufficient to have made a great difference. I would venture now only to state that among Western Shoshoni, sex equality, which was largely the result of economic pursuits, was a condition necessary to the origin and diffusion of polyandry.

Practices respecting post-marital residence, though slightly weighting woman's status, failed materially to alter family balance among Western Shoshoni. Temporarily, residence was almost everywhere matrilocal, the husband often spending a year or more in a kind of bride service during which his general acceptability and hunting prowess were ascertained. Sometimes residence was matrilocal until several children had been born, because the aid of the maternal grandmother was sought in childbirth and infant care. Such temporary residence seems to enhance the status of women. Park (1937) reports matrilocal residence among the Northern Piaute. But permanent residence among Western Shoshoni was determined solely by certain practical and personal circumstances: 1, Abundance of local foods; 2, the whereabouts of relatives; thus, when a brother and sister married a sister and brother, the two families preferred to live near each other; also, proximity to other favorite relatives might be sought; thus, if the parents of only one spouse were living, the couple might settle near them; 3, whether a headman of some kind was in the family; relatives often preferred to live near such men; 4, whether marriage were with a cross-cousin, pseudo cross-cousin, or unrelated person from the same village, none of which required change of residence; 5, whether marriage were by capture, the woman always being brought to the man's village.

Definitely to woman's disadvantage in much of the Western Shoshoni area was marriage by abduction. The Southern Paiute custom described by Hamblin (1881, pp. 34-36) is somewhat similar to that of the Shoshoni. In a dispute about women on the Santa Clara River the men formed two files and the claimant passed between them defending himself. Such men were often aided by their relatives. Hamblin was once requested to assist a man who called him "brother." Sometimes single combatants fought for the woman. More often a man was aided by all possible relatives and friends in fights which might last all day and into the night. One involved more than 100 men who had come out at night to fight by a circle of fires. When the woman for whom they were contending was seriously beaten in the fray, the squaws stopped hostilities by throwing baskets of coals on the fighters.

Obviously, women were given no choice in selection of mates in abduction cases and, although they might run away later, their lot was not exalted.

Furthermore, although there is no clear evidence of recognized claims to hospitality, such as lending wives to visitors, countless stories relate that wives were gambled away to other Indians or were loaned to white men for small presents.

Among Northern Shoshoni, not only was polyandry less common, but the practice of mass raping attests little regard for the status of women. It might be conceived that women's lessened importance in a bison-hunting peoples partly accounted for this.

In the absence of extensive social and political bonds, kinship was extremely important in determining marriages. To a very large extent, one family or a group of related families was the sociopolitical unit, especially among Western Shoshoni and somewhat among Northern Shoshoni. There was, therefore, a definite desire to ally families through multiple marriages. As relationship was a bar to marriage in all but the few localities practicing cross-cousin marriage, several preferred usages permitted multiple interfamily marriages.[30] It was preferred that several brothers should marry several sisters, though never as group marriage, or that a brother and sister should marry a sister and brother. This practice is reflected in kinship terms and appears in several genealogies. The levirate and sororate were strong. Polygyny was preferably sororal and polyandry preferably fraternal.

In some parts of the world the levirate and sororate were inescapable obligations, marriage being essentially a family contract. Owens Valley Paiute and Southern Shoshoni recognized such obligations, avoidance of the levirate and sororate being accomplished only by payment to the deceased spouse's family. In the remainder of the area the levirate and sororate were observed only partly because marriage was a family alliance. They were followed as often because of personal preference. They not only continued the bond uniting two families, but permitted a widowed person to acquire a spouse whom

---

[30] But in some places kinship terms expressly indicate that relationship is believed to cease after 3 generations. The great-great-grandparent is not regarded as a relative.

he knew well and who would take more than a stranger's interest in his children.

In the northern part of the area pseudo cross-cousin marriage and, in a few localities, real cross-cousin marriage also served to strengthen kinship bonds. A person's pseudo cross-cousin (the stepson or stepdaughter of the mother's brother or father's sister) was not, of course, a blood relative. But he was so regarded, being called usually by the same terms as a true cross-cousin. Moreover, pseudo parallel-cousins were ineligible for marriage. No doubt pseudo cross-cousins were often available for marriage because frequent separation and remarriage, previously discussed, often introduced stepaunts, stepuncles, and their children into the family. As brothers and sisters often lived near one another, especially when two families were united by several marriages between their children, a person often found a pseudo cross-cousin in his own village.

In cross-cousin and pseudo cross-cousin marriage it was impossible to discover that either side of the family was given preference, except at Fort Hall where marriage was preferably between a man and his father's sister's stepdaughter.

In summary, it appears that Basin-Plateau conditions had provided a milieu for the development of certain marriage forms. In establishing substantial sex equality they produced an essentially balanced family and provided a condition from which polyandry as well as polygyny might develop. It is difficult to see, however, that conditions necessarily entailed either of these practices. In containing a minimum of social and political activities, society elevated kinship bonds over social and political bonds and thus motivated practices which would strengthen kinship bonds. But it probably did not predetermine the exact nature of those practices. Multiple interfamily marriages are a simple device for strengthening and the sororate and levirate for continuing an alliance between two families, but there is no obvious reason why cross-cousin or pseudo cross-cousin marriage should have been developed in some localities but not in others.

Finally, although the marriage pattern broadly conformed to a condition in which there was comparative sex equality and unusual stress on kinship bonds, elements within it were somewhat contradictory and disturbed its smooth functioning. Among Western Shoshoni, women were economically more important than men, were favored by temporary matrilocal residence, and were privileged often to take a second husband. Yet they were wed polygynously and were liable to abduction. Among Northern Shoshoni there was some matrilocal residence and polyandry, yet women were liable to mass rape as well as abduction. Practices designed to ally kinship groups were similarly often nullified by contrary practices. Despite preference for multiple interfamily marriages, the ease and frequency of separation and marriage by abduction often undid what these marriages had accomplished. Moreover, allied kin groups were often forced by food shortage in the different regions to live widely separated and beyond contact with one another. Thus, despite the importance of kinship, population fluidity prevented crystallization of a fixed set of duties and obligations.

These somewhat contradictory practices were insufficient seriously to endanger group survival. Yet Basin-Plateau patterns had failed to reach perfect internal and external adjustment and were in a state of some unbalance.

POLITICAL ORGANIZATION AND CHIEFTAINSHIP

Political organization and control are commensurate with activities requiring cooperation and management. They must be understood in terms of specific activities. Basic patterns of organization and chieftainship obviously could not be borrowed unless conditions to support them were present. If such conditions were present they would automatically develop without the necessity of borrowing. It is only secondary features—functionally unimportant or potentially variable elements—which are susceptible to diffusion, and even these can vary only within prscribed limits.

Under stable conditions, variation in the fundamental nature and extent of political controls within each region was not great. No doubt periods of instability and change, like the wars with the white man, afforded strong personalities opportunities to achieve unusual authority. Ordinarily, however, a chief's authority was restricted to certain definite activities, such as hunts, dances, war, or ceremonies. Its limits, therefore, were largely predetermined by the factors controlling these activities.

Basin-Plateau political groups and chiefs had no interest in disputes, criminal or civil, between individuals. These were settled by relatives, usually close kin.

The people of different regions in the Basin-Plateau exhibited a remarkable variation in political organization and chief's authority. These ranged from an irreducible minimum in the biological family or household to a maximum in the band. They involved different kinds of activities in different parts of the area.

Among Shoshoni, and probably others, the household was the independent political unit during much of the year and among Western Shoshoni during most of the year. The household head was its leader. When several related families were associated in a winter encampment and traveled together the eldest or most influential man directed activities. He had no title, however.

Small villages, whether or not comprised of related families, had no formal chiefs.

Many larger villages, however, had a single headman. His title, degwani or dagwani, means "talker" and truly designates his most important function. "Chief" usually connotes extensive authority and perhaps should not be applied to these men, though it has been used in this paper. The headman was usually experienced though not necessarily old. Infirmity disqualified him. His task was principally to keep informed about the ripening of plant foods in different localities, to impart his information to the villagers, and, if all the families traveled to the same pine-nut area, to manage the trip and help arrange where each was to harvest. As a "talker," he gave long orations, telling of his information and giving directions to families who cared to cooperate. His authority, however, was not absolute. Any family was at liberty to pursue an independent course at any time.

Each village was named after some salient feature of its locality. As proximity to water was essential to village location, it was most often named after a spring or creek.

Organization superseding the village was only temporary among Western Shoshoni. It involved specific communal endeavors of limited duration and specialized leadership which pertained only to such endeavors. Several of these activities were economic. Rabbit drives brought the members of several adjoining villages to a certain place where they drove under the direction of a skilled rabbit hunter. Antelope drives similarly entailed joint effort, but the leader acquired authority by the accident of having received a vision for the power of antelope shamanism. Festivals, held either at places of abundant foods or at prominent villages, usually required the leadership of a dance specialist. During such communal affairs the headmen of the villages participating usually lent their influence to that of the special director by "talking" from time to time. These talks were harangues, exhorting the people to behave, have a good time, prepare food for feasts, etc. In some instances a village headman was also antelope shaman, dance director, or rabbit-drive leader. But his special authority was restricted to the communal activity and ceased at its conclusion.

There is evidence that some men on the Snake River dreamed powers of leadership in different activities, an example of an accessory feature of chieftainship that could readily have been introduced by diffusion.

Among Shoshoni from the Snake River, Idaho, to Death Valley, California, the largest permanent organization was the village. There is not a single feature which warrants calling any of them a "band."

There are no sharp dialectic, cultural, or political boundaries, nor well-defined named groups larger than the village. Names were sometimes applied to the people of a general but not clearly defined region. Nevada Shoshoni called Idaho Shoshoni "salmon eaters" and were called by them "pine-nut eaters," but neither considered themselves to belong to bands with such names. In fact they rarely used such names for themselves. Nevada Shoshoni never called themselves pine-nut eaters, though some of them occasionally referred to people in another region as eaters of a certain seed. The much publicized Tosawi or White Knife people of the Battle Mountain region are so called because an excellent grade of white flint occurs in that country. But neither informants nor early writers agreed as to the boundaries of people so named. They had no organization and were not a band. Such names had no more political significance than "Digger."

The temporary and shifting intervillage alliances of this region, therefore, instead of consistently allying people of well-defined territories, entailed a linkage of village with village which extended, netlike, throughout the entire area. Political bonds, like subsistence areas, interlocked in all directions.

Factors influencing political organization among Western Shoshoni are brought into relief by a review of developmental stages from the aboriginal period to recent times. Three stages are recognizable, during which military bands temporarily developed, then disintegrated.

1. The native particularistic family and village groups, with temporary alliances for collective enterprises, previously described.

2. The early post-Caucasian period, during which important alterations in native economy began. In northern Nevada this stage subdivides into two phases.

a. This phase began about 1850 and reached a climax in 1860. Horses were acquired in increasing numbers, native foods were reduced by the white man, and warfare, which began with minor clashes between the white men and Indians, reached major proportions. Decreased native foods made it necessary, and horses made it possible to travel widely in the quest of foods. Raids upon immigrant trains and later upon ranches, partly motivated by hunger, brought warfare or the threat of strife. In such regions as Battle Mountain, Steptoe Valley, Gosiute territory, and much of Northern Paiute territory, previously independent villages, now traveling with horses, united into military bands under high commands. Neither the organization nor discipline was strict, and the composition of fighting groups constantly changed.

Throughout most of the Humboldt River region, though people began to amalgamate in groups of increasing size, especially near the growing centers of white population, they remained peaceful.

Political control served to restrain rather than stimulate belligerent tendencies. Tümok, whose history has been previously sketched (pp. 149–150), became the so-called chief of people who had lived along the central part of the Humboldt Valley, South Fork, Huntington, and Ruby Valley and a few neighboring valleys. Headquarters was at Ruby Valley. Tümok's efforts probably more than anything else preserved peace in this area.

At the termination of wars in the early and middle sixties the motivation for joint effort was to win concessions from the white man. Responsible spokesmen were necessary. In 1863 Tümok and other men who were said to represent the Indians of various valleys signed a treaty embracing a huge area. It is doubtful whether the supposed constituents of these signatories had formally chosen them as their representatives or, indeed, if many knew what was occurring. Formal delegation of power to enter agreements binding upon everyone was utterly foreign to native political institutions. After 1863 some of these so-called chiefs continued to speak for the Indians.

The cohesion of the rapidly developed bands was slight. Their territory was not accurately defined, except by fictitious boundaries in the treaty, and they were constantly liable to alteration and dissolution. Remy and Brenchley remarked (1861, p. 128) that there were many groups in this area and that each had a chief, but people had little respect for him except during time of war. The institution of band chief was novel and hence provided opportunity for influential personalities to assert themselves. The office and its duties, having no precedence in native institution and concerning principally warfare and negotiations with the white man, were limited in scope and duration. They survived too briefly to have become institutionalized and to have won respect and general support. When the wars ceased the need for organization largely vanished and chiefs lost authority.

b. This phase began about 1870, when the wars were over, when the white man was well established in the area, and when a profound alteration of native economy had occurred. In southern Nevada, where the Shoshoni had little or no strife with the white man, they passed directly into this phase without the intervening and transient development of military bands.

By 1870 native plants had been so reduced by cattle grazing and native animals by hunting that complete reliance on them was no longer possible. Indians consequently began to attach themselves in small family groups to ranches, where they worked as hands, and in large colonies to ranch towns and to the rapidly booming mining towns where their labor was in demand. Under the new conditions they could establish comparatively permanent residences; it was unnecessary to travel continually in search of foods. There was little need for political control on the ranches. The comparatively large communities at some of these towns, however, became centers for such native communal affairs as festivals and rabbit drives. With improved transportation, people from great distances attended. During several decades certain of these towns were the scenes of festivals whose magnitude surpassed anything known in aboriginal days. For example, people of the general region of Smoky Valley, Ralston Valley, Tonopah, Hot Creek, the Kawich Mountains, and even Lida began to abandon their local festivals to attend the huge festival at the mining town of Belmont, where many families had gone to live. Kawich, a person of evident prestige, become one of the main leaders of the Belmont festival.

But native political control in these colonies did not extend beyond native communal affairs. As members also of the white man's community, they were largely subject to his organization and laws. The only function of headmen, beyond directing native activities, was to deal with the white man, because the Indian was still but slightly assimilated culturally or linguistically.

During this time, of course, many Indians had gone to reservations, where somewhat artificial institutions were at once imposed upon them.

3. The third period was one of a general collapse of all political institutions brought about by accelerated deculturation. Although assimilation is nowhere complete even today, it had progressed sufficiently to destroy most distinctively Indian political institutions. Deculturation was more or less proportionate to intimacy with the white man. In the Humboldt Valley it became effective by 1880; in isolated parts of southern Nevada it was probably unimportant until 1900. As interest in native customs waned, communal hunts were first abandoned. Festivals were next dropped. Festivals now are largely limited to reservations, where deculturation has been slower, where large numbers of people make them more expedient, and where embarrassment because of the white man's criticism of native practices carries less weight.

The present trend of those not on reservations is toward physical and cultural assimilation. To some extent, assimilation is a goal, sought especially by the younger generation who desire to avoid the handicaps imposed by race prejudice. A contrary trend, however, persists from the second stage, when Indian groups had representatives to deal with the white man. In order to win fulfillment of treaty obligations and other advantages, different persons with varying degrees of support have fought the Indian cause. More recently organizations of white people have backed and encouraged such activities.

Though the independent village was the political unit of Western Shoshoni, in some regions certain villages habitually came together for communal hunts and festivals. This occurred where the population was extraordinarily dense and villages consequently either large or closely spaced, or where possession of the horse enabled them to assemble in large aggregates. This repeated association produced a bond among them which, if sufficiently strong, approximated that of a band. When reinforced by ownership and defense of territory against trespass and by a group or territory name it was a true band. This condition existed in Owens Valley, where a communal sweat house and communal irrigation further augmented band esprit.

The functions of the band chief in Owens Valley were commensurate with band affairs. He planned communal affairs, though specialists might actually direct them, sent messengers to the different villages to inform them of his plans, and talked at the affairs.

Northern Shoshoni families remained together for a sufficient portion of the year during the buffalo hunt and winter encampment to warrant designating them as bands. Allegiance to these bands was not, however, absolute. The stable constitutents of a band were the nuclear groups of related families which probably had been independent units in the prehorse period. Upon acquiring horses, they consolidated in larger groups to hunt and camp together under the leadership of influential men. This trend was evidently in progress when the white man arrived in their country. Many families still lacked horses, especially those in the mountains of the Lemhi region, and necessarily carried on subsistence activities in comparative isolation. The consolidated groups varied in size and stability. If desirous of hunting bison in hostile territory, a large number cooperated, submitting to direction by a single chief. Whether families remained associated at the winter encampment depended upon their individual interests, their regard for the chief, and other factors. Dissatisfied with the principal chiefs, groups might pursue an independent course under men more to their liking. This was especially true of those who objected to the usual Shoshoni policy of peace with the white man and who wished to engage in raids.

A chief's authority was consequently of uncertain scope and duration and depended largely upon his persuasiveness. The most remarkable personality seems to have been Washakie, chief of Wyoming Shoshoni, to whose judgment and leadership even Idaho Shoshoni and Bannock often submitted. A chief's main task was supervision of tribal movements when on hunting or trading expeditions. Establishing and enforcing a policy toward the white man augmented his power. Responsibility for hunting and warfare seems often to have been delegated to special men. Visionary powers were an especially important qualification for leadership in war. Leading successful war parties gave men some distinction and, consequently, influence.

Though information about the Southern Paiute and Ute is inadequate, there is some indication that they differed from each other somewhat as the Western Shoshoni differed from the Northern Shoshoni. The Southern Paiute, at least between Death Valley and Las Vegas, were organized only on a village basis. Kelly states (1934) that all Southern Paiute were divided into definite dialectic groups. But these groups rarely had names and seem, in aboriginal times at least, to have had no political significance. The Ute, however, had horses at an early time and, like the Northern Shoshoni, traveled, hunted bison, and fought in large groups under the control of chiefs. These groups habitually returned to certain lands which some persons believe they owned. Moreover, each was named, at least within the historic period. In short, they were bands.

Though these fndamental forms of chieftainship and political organization depended almost entirely upon the activities to which they pertained, and were consequently of unquestioned local origin, certain secondary features were arbitrary, had little functional significance, and seem to have been borrowed embellishments. For example, the formal office of chief's speaker occurred in the northern part of the area but was lacking in Owens Valley. It was obviously a dispensable element and, occurring in some neighboring areas, could readily have been borrowed. The partial dependence of chieftainship upon visions in the north became essential to the effective functioning of chief only after people learned to consider it so. It, too, was undoubtedly borrowed.

Powell and Ingalls take the view that the unorganized condition of many Shoshonean groups in 1872 was the result of the arrival of the white man. This view is contrary to the one held here. They state (1874, p. 3) : "Their hunting grounds have been spoiled, their favorite valleys are occupied by white men, and they are compelled to scatter in small bands in order to obtain subsistence. Formerly, they were organized into nations, or confederacies, under the influence of great chiefs, but such men have lost their power in the presence of white men, and it is no longer possible to treat with these people as nations, but each little tribe must be dealt with separately. The broad territory over which they are scattered has been parceled out among the tribes by common consent, usually determined at general councils, so that each tribe holds a certain district of country as its own." They further state (1874, p. 9) : "The original political organization of the tribes under consideration [Utah, Nevada, and Idaho Shoshoneans] had a territorial basis; that is, the country was divided into districts, and each district was inhabited by a small tribe, which took the name of the land, and had one principal chief. These tribes, or 'land-namods,' as they are called in the Indian idiom, were the only permanent organizations, but sometimes two or more of them would unite in a confederacy under some great chief."

Except among Southern Paiute, however, their ethnographic observances were not extended. Moreover, their own detailed evidence on Southern Paiute, cited on pages 180–185, supports the view advanced here rather than theirs.

PROPERTY

Property concepts, like political organization, are functionally related to and develop from specific conditions and practices. It is difficult to envisage any mechanism for borrowing basic concepts.

The most elementary principle of property occurred among the Western Shoshoni. Objects belonged to persons who expended work on them and used them. All natural resources, with the sole exception of privately owned eagle nests, were free to anyone. This was not communal ownership; it was not ownership at all, because no group whatever claimed natural resources. Water, seed, and hunting areas, mineral and salt deposits, etc., were freely utilized by anyone. But once work had been done upon the products of natural resources they became the property of the person or family doing the work. Willow groves could be used by anyone, but baskets made of willows belonged to their makers. Wild seeds could be gathered by anyone, but once harvested, they belonged strictly to the family doing the task, even though they might be shared with other families. When wild seeds were sowed, the crop but not the land was owned. Egan Canyon Shoshoni, however, stated that even sowed plots could be harvested by anyone.

Community property was rarely held by groups larger than the household. Women owned their baskets, clothes, and other objects used by them, while men owned hunting equipment and things peculiar to their sex. The household owned the house, foods, and general equipment. All this conforms to the work-use-ownership principle. The outstanding exception is large game. A hunter was entitled to keep the skin and some choice portion of the meat for his family but was obliged to share the remainder with village members, first consideration being given to his relatives. The loan of objects to and sharing of other food with members of the community were acts of courtesy and in no sense were recognition of communal claims.

Truly communal property was scant. Often many families cooperated in the construction of a deer or antelope corral and divided the game taken. They jointly prepared and used dance grounds and fish weirs. But once abandoned, anyone was at liberty to use these things in the future. It is significant that the only appurtenances peculiar to communal activities that could be carried home were rabbit nets, which were always made and owned by individual men. There is some evidence, in fact, that men claimed all rabbits caught in their nets during drives.

Some form of land ownership is common among tribes in many parts of the world. Often it is not the land per se but exclusive rights of hunting, fishing, gathering, or agriculture on it that is claimed. It may be postulated that habitual use of the resource in question by the family, village, band, or other group was a necessary condition for the development of claims to it.

The Shoshoni lacked any form of ownership of land or resources on it (except eagle nests). No group habitually and exclusively utilized any clearly defined territory for hunting, fishing, or seed gathering. Their failure to do so has already been tentatively explained in ecological terms. The people were primarily seed gatherers. The sparse and erratic occurrence of vegetable foods required that territories exploited by different families and villages not only should vary from year to year but should greatly overlap. There was no competition for vegetable foods, because good crops, especially of seeds, ripened and fell to the ground so rapidly that people could not possibly gather all of them. When the crop in one locality failed people went elsewhere, usually having been informed of the promising harvest by residents in its vicinity. If crops were poor everywhere, which was not uncommon, everyone went hungry. The pinyon nut appears to have been outstanding in preventing ownership of food areas. Even in a succession of fertile years a grove yielded 1 year but not the next. In good years it afforded far more nuts than could possibly be picked. Families consequently traveled to the locality of a good supply, were welcomed by local residents, and often cached their nuts and remained there during the winter. Under such conditions, ownership of vegetable food resources would have been a disadvantage to everyone.

The annual variation in game was somewhat less extreme. The area lacked both large herd animals and animals trapped extensively for furs. Even deer, antelope, and mountain sheep were comparatively scarce. In areas where hunting was the most important subsistence activity it is understandable that men should prefer to remain in territory known to them and defend it against trespass. In the Western Shoshoni area, however, seed gathering instead of hunting determined the economic routine. Men accompanied their families to seed areas and hunted where they had an opportunity. Areas hunted, therefore, like seed areas, overlapped and could not advantageously have been owned.

Among the Northern Shoshoni the relative importance of hunting and gathering was reversed. But during the period for which information is available hunting was carried on in a kind of no-man's land east of the Rocky Mountains. Though probably hunted principally by different bands of Shoshoni, it was also visited by Flathead, Nez Percé, Blackfeet, Crow, and sometimes other tribes. Probably none of these claimed it. Certainly none had enforced a claim.

It might seem that Snake River Shoshoni, like many tribes in the salmon area, would have developed some kind of ownership of fishing sites. That they did not is probably explainable by the uncertainties of their subsistence. Too often salmon failed to run, or, affording but a meager catch, forced families to make long journeys to search for game and vegetable foods elsewhere. Wyeth (Schoolcraft, 1851, p. 244), who was at Fort Hall from 1834 to 1836, stated of the Shoshoni along the Snake River, "None of the roving tribes . . . claim the ownership of its soil; they visit it only to hunt game [probably referring especially to bison which formerly could be had near Fort Hall] . . ." The inhabitants "exist in small detached bodies and single families, and change their locations so widely that they seem to have no particular claim to any portion . . . No considerable body of these Indians . . . can be found whose lines of wandering have not continually interlocked with those of similar bands." Had salmon afforded ample subsistence such wandering would have been unnecessary.

Owens Valley Paiute were distinctive for their band ownership of hunting and seed territories. There are two possible explanations of such ownership. One, the pattern was borrowed from neighboring California, where it was prevalent. Two, it developed in response to local ecology. Neither is susceptible to positive proof, but the second has several arguments in its favor. First, it is difficult to envisage a means by which a concept which is so interrelated with particular subsistence activities could have been borrowed. Against this, however, is the fact that it appears to occur among other Northern Paiute just west of Reese River whose subsistence is like that of Western Shoshoni who lack land ownership. Second, band ownership of food territories obviously originated somewhere for good reasons. Its repeated occurrence among widely separated groups in different parts of the world suggests that under certain conditions it has developed very readily. Third, conditions for its development appear to have been present in Owens Valley. The population was comparatively dense, stable, and settled in unusually permanent villages. The country was fertile, so that subsistence activities could be carried on according to a comparatively fixed routine within a small territory.

Each territory was only large enough to embrace all the natural resources habitually exploited and included both game and vegetable foods. The disruptive effect of the erratic yield of wild seeds, especially the pine nut, was outweighed by the importance of communally irrigated and therefore comparatively reliable seed patches in the valley, which were communally harvested. A theory of local origin of band ownership of territory then must assume that habitual exploitation of a territory which neighboring groups rarely traversed led to its exclusive exploitation and defense against trespass. The resources owned were irrigated and nonirrigated seed plots, fishing places, and territory for communal hunts. Individual hunters, being less destructive of game and often pursuing animals which ran for miles, were privileged to hunt where they pleased.

Within the framework of Owens Valley communal band ownership there seems to have been some family ownership of land. As a band went always to the same pine-nut groves and as it was customary throughout the pine-nut area for large groups to agree to at least a temporary division of the pine-nut groves, it is understandable that certain families should habitually have picked from the same localities which they regarded as their own and defended.

The Southern Paiute near Death Valley had no band ownership of food territories, but families were said to have owned cultivated land and plots of mesquite, screw beans, and pine nuts. Though an understanding of property rights among Southern Paiute requires more information than is available, it may be suggested that ownership of wild-seed plots was an extension of the ownership concept developed in connection with cultivated land. Areas of other wild seeds and hunting areas were not owned.

It is futile at present to speculate about property rights among the Ute. Fragments of information suggest band ownership of territories. But whether ownership was of seeds, animals, or both, and what relation it bore to subsistence activities can probably be ascertained only by intensive field study. Whatever theory of property the Ute held, however, mounted Ute bands within the historic period traveled widely over one another's territory on hunting excursions.

SUMMARY

The type of sociopolitical groups in the Basin-Plateau area was conditioned to a definable extent by human ecology. Rainfall, soils, topography, and climate determined the nature, quantity, and distribution of plant and animal species which were required for food. The hunting and gathering devices and transportational facilities known in the area allowed only a certain quantity of these to be procured and consequently limited the general population density. The subsistence habits required in each region largely determined the size, nature, and permanency of population aggregates. These, in turn, predetermined many, though not all, features of social structures and political controls. In some regions, as among Western Shoshoni, exigencies of existence permitted little variation in the general sociopolitical pattern. When, however, ecology allowed latitude in subsistence activities, noneconomic factors, such as warfare, festivals, ceremonies, etc., became determinants of the sociopolitical patterns.

Among Western Shoshoni and many of their Northern Paiute and Southern Paiute neighbors it was physically impossible for families either to remain in one place for any considerable time or for more than a few families to remain in permanent association. The outstanding sociopolitical units, consequently, were the biological family and the small winter village, consisting of a loose aggregate of families. Families comprising a village were often related. The village headman or "talker" was little more than family leader or village adviser. Interfamily and intervillage alliances for cooperative enterprises were of limited scope and brief duration, occurring only at communal hunts or festivals, each of which had a special director. Because, however, of the erratic occurrence of wild seeds and the frequent variation of terrain covered, alliance did not always bring together the same families or village members. Habitual cooperation of the same people and therefore the development of fixed if limited political allegiances and controls was impossible. Likewise, habitual and exclusive utilization of particular territories by certain groups could not develop. The families composing villages were frequently unrelated because the lack of a rigid rule of post-marital residence and frequent shift of residence for practical reasons had prevented the formation of unilateral groups or lineages.

Kinship bonds were of great importance in this society. It is probably their importance that motivated married children to live near their parents or near one another and that prompted multiple marriages between two families. Such bonds were probably a condition of, if not the cause of, the development of pseudo cross-cousin marriage and in some localities of true cross-cousin marriage. But families were bilateral; neither side was conspicuously weighted. It was evidently this balance that permitted frequent fraternal polyandry as well as polygyny. Though kinship ties were important, the uncertainties of residence and of assured association with specified relatives prevented the development of an elaborate and nicely fixed set of kinship duties and obligations.

Other ecological factors permitted the growth of more complex sociopolitical forms in certain parts of the Basin-Plateau area. Villages amalgamated into bands when one of two conditions were present. First, they became bands when a fertile environment permitted large and closely spaced villages, obviated the necessity of extensive travel, and allowed certain people habitually to exploit a given territory and associate together in communal activities. This condition was present in Owens Valley, where named, landowning bands lived under the direction of chiefs with well-defined authority. Band unity was reinforced by communal sweat houses and mourning ceremonies.

Second, bands formed when transportation was so improved that large groups could live together and either bring their foods to a central point or travel as a body in search of them. Ecology thus permitted, if it did not cause, band development. Bands were formed in late pre-Caucasian times among Northern Shoshoni and probably among Ute. They were named but were not landowning. Their solidarity was reinforced by need for protection in warfare. In the remainder of the area the horse was introduced late and bands were of brief duration. Political control of mounted bands centered in chiefs whose authority varied somewhat with their personalities, but which was immeasurably increased by circumstances incident to the arrival of the white man. Control of certain activities, however, such as war and hunting, was delegated to special men.

These bands were composed of unrelated families. They were so large, in fact, that even had rules of post-marital residence been fixed they could scarcely have developed into lineages. The fundamental nature of the families comprising them was probably laid down in preband times, at least among Northern Shoshoni. But perennial association with most of one's relatives gave point to fixed kinship duties and obligations which seem to have been much more clearly defined than among Western Shoshoni.

SOME GENERAL IMPLICATIONS OF THE PRESENT STUDY

SOCIOPOLITICAL GROUPS AMONG HUNTERS AND GATHERERS

A previous study (Steward, 1936 c) postulated that certain features of the sociopolitical patterns of many hunting and gathering peoples were produced by definite social and ecological determinants. The generalizations made were:

"All peoples in an area of low population density have some form of politically autonomous, landowning band, which is greater than the bilateral family. The size of the band and the extent of the territory it utilizes are determined by the number of persons who, due largely to ecological factors, habitually cooperate at least during part of the annual round of economic and social activity. Band unity is expressed in a consciousness of common interest and submission to some degree of central control during community enterprises, although such control may be lacking during parts of the year. The authority of the leader is consequently small and temporary and his position is seldom a fixed institution."

It was further found that there are two types of such bands, depending upon special factors. One is unilineal, the other composite. All unilineal bands analyzed in this study were patrilineal and patrilocal, consisted of actual or fictitious relatives, and were consequently exogamous. This type occurred where ecology prevented group size from exceeding fifty to one hundred members and where emphasis upon hunting or other factors tending toward male dominance made it patrilocal. It was found among Northern Bushmen, African Negritos, Semang, Australians, Tasmanians, Fuegians, and in southern California. The theoretical counterpart of the patrilineal band is the exogamous, localized, matrilineal band, the distribution of which has not yet been summarized, but which probably occurred among some primitive horticulturists. For example, archeological evidence suggests that these may have existed among Basket Makers and early Pueblo in the Southwest and provided nuclei for subsequent clan development (Steward, 1937 a).

Composite bands are not unilineal but consist of unrelated families which consequently need not observe band exogamy. In these the enlarged kinship group and political group are thus not coextensive. This type occurs where the group is somewhat larger (usually more than 100 persons) or where for various reasons, such as lack of strict rules of patrilocal or matrilocal residence or presence of cross-cousin marriage, band exogamy is unnecessary. Composite bands occur among Southern Bushmen, Andamanese, many Algonkians and Athabascans of Canada and, no doubt, elsewhere.

When generalizations are made, it must be assumed that further investigations may require supplementary theories to fit facts not previously known. The present investigation has shown that certain Basin-Plateau groups conformed in great detail to the previous generalizations. Other groups exhibited novel cause and effect relationships which do not invalidate previous generalizations but require supplementary hypotheses. No doubt a similar analysis of groups not covered in these studies will indicate other new kinds of cause and effect relationships.

Owens Valley Paiute possessed the typical composite band. The Northern Shoshoni, who acquired horses at an early date, also had composite bands. But in their failure to own territory the latter departed from the usual composite band pattern. This departure, however, has been shown to be a result of the horse-bison economy

which required that the subsistence areas of the different bands overlap. Data on Ute are inadequate but suggest a pattern like that
of the Northern Shoshoni.

Western Shoshoni, probably Southern Paiute, and perhaps some
Northern Paiute fall outside the scope of the previous generalizations, which were too inclusive. They lacked bands and any form
of land ownership. The only stable social and political unit was
the family. Larger groupings for social and economic purposes
were temporary and shifting. The radical departure of these
peoples from the band patterns, however, is explainable by ecological factors not previously encountered. It has been shown that the
unusually great economic importance of seeds largely restricted the
economic unit to the family. Communal enterprises did not always
aline the same families, so that there were no large groups having
political unity. It has also been shown that the peculiar occurrence
of certain foods, especially seed species, entailed interlocking subsistence areas which militated against land ownership.

ECOLOGY IN CULTURAL STUDIES

An "explanation" of human behavior patterns explains in proportion as it traces determinants to ultimate sources. These determinants or factors are necessarily stated in different terms. Some
are innate human drives, which, though overlaid and obscured
by culture patterns, must sometimes be stated in psychological and
even physiological terms. Some are more or less arbitrary behavior
norms to be treated in terms of invention and borrowing. But both
are adapted in varying ways and degrees to the requirements of
existence in a particular natural environment. The adaptation must
be stated in ecological terms. Determinants of culture, therefore,
are interrelated in a complex equation. It is difficult to see how
in any society the extent and force of purely cultural and psychological determinants can be ascertained if the ecology which conditions and delimits them is unknown.

Attention to the role of ecology, however, is neither environmental
determinism nor economic determinism. Extreme environmental
determinism has had ample refutation. Economic determinism,
though resting to an undetermined extent upon substantial truth,
is, especially in such extreme interpretations as the Marxian, primarily a philosophy, not a scientifically demonstrated fact. Emphasis
upon human ecology is not postulation of a general or novel theory.
It is essentially a manner of stating a problem. The problem is
first to ascertain what behavior patterns are required when a certain
environment is exploited by certain economic devices. Second, how,

if at all, such patterns affect other activities and institutions and the latitude allowed them. In short, it entails an equation of culture process involving the interaction and mutual adaptation of both historically and environmentally determined behavior.

It may be argued, of course, that there is danger of taking ecology as the point of departure and that to do so is unwarranted, because any part of the culture might have predetermined ecology instead of the reverse. To this there are two answers. First, it is not claimed a priori that ecology predetermines anything. The extent of its effect is an empirical problem in each instance. Second, ecology involves one unalterable factor, the natural environment. Quite unlike economies may be imposed upon any environment, each comprising a system of activities and each exploiting different resources in the environment—for example, the Pueblo, the recent Indian, and the modern white in the Basin-Plateau area. But any system may vary only within limits, otherwise the people will obviously not survive. These limits may be narrow or great and in turn permit small or large latitude in those cultural activities that depend upon them. If wide latitude is permitted by subsistence patterns, the choice of cultural forms may be determined by purely historical factors. Thus, an ecology might permit a dense population, but whether people lived scattered in many small hamlets or clustered in large towns might depend upon warfare, ceremonies, and other cultural-historical factors. It would be futile, however, to seek historical determinants of village types unless it had been established that ecology had permitted variations in them.

The extent to which ecology conditions and delimits cultures depends, of course, upon the culture. In primitive societies like those described in this paper, it clearly predetermines and delimits certain features of social and political groups. An effort was not made to trace its effect to all the patterns which control an individual's behavior, but it is probable that little behavior could be wholly explained in purely social terms. Even kinship duties and obligations toward different relatives rest ultimately in varying degrees upon ecology. These duties and obligations may not only be partly economic but may well depend upon whether ego lives in the same village with or 50 miles away from certain relatives, upon what occasions he sees them, what kinds of activities they carry on together, and in what manner each fits into the general scheme of property, inheritance, food seeking, government, and other activities. Marriage may rest upon a psychological as well as cultural foundation. But the precise relationship between spouses as well as extensions of kinship groups cannot be understood without adequate reference to their economic functions.

In proportion that societies have adequately solved subsistence problems, the effect of ecology becomes more difficult to ascertain. In complex societies certain components of the social superstructure rather than ecology seem increasingly to be determinants of further developments. With greater cultural complexity analysis becomes increasingly difficult. Who can say today what weight should be attached to industrial progress, to preexisting government and social patterns, or to the propagandistic force of the ideology of democracy or other forms of government as determinants of present and future trends in our sociopolitical system? That certain changes in our own society are explainable in economic terms, however, cannot be denied. The relative growth of urban centers and the concomitant extension of political control over the behavior of individuals cannot be explained by any inherent tendency of human beings to increase in number, to concentrate the population in huge aggregates, and to submit to more and more political control. Concentration of wealth and the crystallization of social classes are not merely psychological peculiarities of human beings. Even the marked changes within the modern family are not purely sociological phenomena. To a very large extent these are all traceable to economic changes.

APPENDICES

Appendix A.—Tribal Distributions

In a previous paper (1937) I gave the general distribution of the main linguistic groups of the Great Basin and adjoining portions of the Columbia and Colorado Plateaus. This was based primarily upon field work. The linguistic groups mapped were Kroeber's 3 branches of "Plateau Shoshonean" (1907, pp. 66–165, 1909)—Shoshoni-Comanche, Mono-Bannock or Northern Paiute, and Ute-Chemehuevi, the last including Southern Paiute—which Whorf (1935) suggests should not be classed together as "Shoshonean." Though Kroeber's map of these divisions (1925, fig. 52) must be modified in some details, it was remarkably accurate in view of the limited information at his command.

It remains to examine early documentary evidence relative to this subject. For the greater part of Nevada south of the Humboldt River source material is almost entirely lacking. For Oregon, Idaho, and northern and western Utah it is abundant but extraordinarily contradictory. In fact it would be valueless to review it had not various authors based classifications of Basin-Plateau groups upon it, thus repeating and even compounding the original errors.

Early writers were liable to several kinds of error. First, the differences between the linguistic divisions are sufficiently slight to have escaped the attention of persons not well versed in these languages. Thus, Wyeth lived two years, 1834–36, at Fort Hall but failed to discover that Bannock and Shoshoni spoke differently. Second, it was often assumed that well-defined, bounded, and named political units would be found everywhere. It was not known that the only grouping in the greater part of the area was the family or village, so that "tribe" had significance only in synonymy with language. As there was little natural geographical grouping, names applied to peoples of localities bore uncertain connotation. Often local names were thought to imply political or "tribal" distinctiveness. Thus the frequent application of Paviotso to Northern Paiute of western Nevada and of Bannock or Snake to their Oregon kin led to the belief that these were three separate tribes. The third and most serious source of error was loose usage. When names were not intended to designate language, they were vaguely descriptive of culture and were applied without respect to locality. Thus "Digger" was used for many groups. Finally, observers did not always distinguish the temporary from the habitual residents of a region. Though mounted Shoshoni and Ute were sometimes encountered several hundred miles from their homes, the fact was not always recognized or stated.

The most common usage was to distinguish mounted from "foot" Indians. Shoshonee or Snake was most often applied to the former, Shoshocoe, Shoshoki, Walker, or Digger to the latter (e. g., Wilson, 1849, p. 66; Hoffman, 1886, pp. 296–298; Burton, 1862, p. 476, even included Washo under Shoshoko or Digger). But these terms were applied inconsistently. Snake was often used also for Indians who lacked horses, who were shy, or who were poor. Shoshonie or Shoshonee was sometimes applied to Kroeber's Shoshonean-speaking peoples, e. g., Schoolcraft (1851, p. 198; 1857, pp. 34–35), Wheeler (1879, pp. 19, 408–413) who included southern California tribes under it, and Simpson (1876, pp. 34–35) who included Snake and Bannock under "Sho-sho-nee." (Latham, 1856, p. 106, following Pike, applied Paduca to all Shoshoneans.) Dennison (1858, p. 262), however, made no distinctions, saying that the "Mountain Snakes, Bonnacks, and Diggers" are "generally known as the Shoshone or Snake Indians and are part of that large tribe." Shoshocoe and Snake, as will be shown below, were also applied to Northern Paiute or Mono-Bannock speaking groups as well as to Shoshoni proper. Bannock, though most often used for the Northern Paiute of Oregon, was frequently applied to various Idaho Shoshoni, mounted or unmounted, as well as to Idaho Bannock proper. Many writers, considering it to mean merely "robbers," applied it to any Indians prone to theft. Ute [31] or Utah was usually restricted to the Ute proper, though it was often applied as Pa-Ute to both Northern and Southern Paiute and as Weber Ute and Gosiute (Gosi-Ute) to two groups of Shoshoni. References to early writers in addition to those cited here will be found in Bancroft (1886, pp. 461–470), whose inferences as to divisions and locations of Shoshoneans are far from helpful.

Wyoming.—Shoshoni of Wyoming were consistently called Shoshoni or Snake and there is little doubt that they all spoke Shoshoni-Comanche. (Gebow's vocabulary of the Rocky Mountains, 1868, for the "Snake or Sho-sho-nay" is Shoshoni-Comanche.)

Montana, Idaho, and northern Utah.—The Shoshoneans of this area were classified in many contradictory ways. Attempts to interpret these sources have led to unwarranted assumptions of tribal movements and to erroneous linguistic and tribal classification. It

---

[31] Harrington, 1911, has suggested that Ute was derived from the Ute-Paiute word nutšĭ, plural nutš ĭ u, meaning "person, people," and that Paiute was probably a corruption of paquatšĭ, plural paquatš ĭ u, Ouray Ute Indian. Paiute had commonly been supposed to be Pa, water+Ute.

must be stressed that reconstruction of events presumed to have occurred two centuries ago requires substantial support, especially when documentary evidence is wanting.

Wilkes (1845) states that according to tradition and general belief Snakes formerly occupied Blackfeet country. Domenech (1860, vol. 2, pp. 60–61) states, without supporting evidence, that several centuries ago "Snakes," "Bannocks," "Comanches," and "some other tribes of Utah" were driven back from their ancient hunting ground on the upper Missouri by the Blackfeet. Hodge (Handbook, vol. 1, pp. 129–130) supposes that Lewis and Clark's "Broken Moccasins" of the Salmon River Mountains and possibly also the Lemhi River people were a northern division of Bannock, who differed linguistically from the Shoshoni and who were driven westward from Montana by the Siksika. Berreman (1937, p. 58) also assumes that Bannock originally occupied the upper Salmon River and part of Wyoming while the Walpapi or Snake, who also spoke Mono-Bannock, lived to "the west, between the Bannock and the Snake River, where they bordered on Sahaptin tribes" and that tribal dislocations, starting with pressure from the Blackfeet, eventually pushed them into Oregon.

Although Blackfeet raids served to concentrate Bannock and Shoshoni in certain localities, slightly narrowing their range, data do not support the hypothesis of important tribal dislocations. Teit, apparently on the authority of Indian informants, states that Shoshoneans held territory in Montana as far east and north as Lewiston and Havre (1930, pp. 304–305, 317–320). This would be difficult to disprove, but it is strange that early documents do not afford some proof of it.

It is not improbable that some Bannock were formerly scattered in the upper Salmon as well as upper Snake River region. But there is no evidence that they were ever the sole occupants of the area or were subsequently driven all the way to Oregon. That Lewis and Clark called the Lemhi River people "Chô-sho-ni" and Gass called them "Snake" is no reason to believe that they were Bannock. The "Broken Moccasins" were, as previously suggested, probably the Tukadüka or Sheep Eater Shoshoni of the mountains. Hodge's difficulty in attaching precise meaning to "Bannock" is indicated by his division of Bannock into five groups: Yambadika or Root Eaters [the name given by informants for western Idaho Shoshoni, who were somewhat intermixed with Northern Paiute], Waradika [who are probably Shoshoni of western Idaho], and the Buffalo-Eaters, Honey-Eaters, and Cottonwood-Eaters, whose location and identity is unknown. (The first, third, and fourth of these were also listed by Hoffman as Bannock bands, 1886, pp. 299–300.) The most numerous references to Bannock in the upper Salmon River region, in fact, are late: Mullan (1855, p. 329), referring to "Banax"; Lander (1860, p. 136), "Bannock"; Sully (1870, pp. 289–290), 500 "Bannock" in southwestern Montana, claiming territory around Boseman and Virginia City; Smith (1871, p. 432), mixed "Bannacks, Shoshones, and Sheep-Eaters" in the Lemhi Valley; and Powell (1891, p. 110), 75 Bannock, 249 Shoshoni, and 109 Sheep-Eaters on the Lemhi Reservation. Bearing in mind the uncertain distinction between Bannock and Shoshoni that long prevailed, even these citations must be regarded with caution. Probably some Bannock were incorporated in the Lemhi Reservation, but this, of course, lends no support to the assumption that they were the sole inhabitants of the region at one time, nor that they were subsequently pushed into Oregon.

As for the Lemhi River and Montana area, one must conclude with Lowie (1909, p. 173) that the "historically recorded westward movements of Shoshone bands driven by Plains tribes thus shrink into purely local migrations and do not affect the tribe as a whole."

Other references to Bannock, Shoshoni, and Snake are further evidence of the contradictory usage. Some have been cited previously (pp. 186–187, 199, 205–207, 218–222). Others are:

Russell, 1834–43 (1921, p. 144), placed "Snake" or "Sho-sho-nies" in the region drained by the head branches of the Green and Bear Rivers and the east and southern head branches of the Snake River. "Snake" was a name used by Crow; the source of "Sho-sho-nie" was not known.

Farnham, 1839, said that the Shoshoni or Snake wandered over the Rocky Mountains between the Colorado and Bear Rivers, "the habitable shores of the Great Salt Lake, a considerable portion of country on Snake River above and below Fort Hall, and a tract extending two or three hundred miles to the west of that post" (1843, pp. 361–362) and were distinguished from the "Bonack" of western Idaho (pp. 318–320).

De Smet, July 1842 met "several families of Shoshonees or Snake Indians and Shoshocos or Uprooters . . ." on the Bear River. They "speak the same language. The only difference we could observe between them was that the latter were by far the poorer" and had few horses (vol. 27, pp. 244–245).

Wilkes (1845) placed Shoshones or Snakes east of Utah Lake, north of the Snake River and north of the Banacks, near Fort Boise with Bonacks between Fort Hall and Fort Boise and from Utah Lake to California.

Hale's (1846, pp. 218–219, map) Shoshoni or Snake vocabulary of Idaho (pp. 569–629) is very similar to Shoshoni-Comanche. He made no local or linguistic distinction between the unmounted Shoshoni and the unmounted Diggers except that the latter lived to the north (p. 219). He failed to identify his "Panasht or Bonaks" to the west of these Shoshoni. Lane (1850, p. 158), quoting Newell, a mountaineer, similarly distinguished the "Shoshonee or Snake," who occupied the Snake River, Bear River, and the region south to Great Salt Lake from the "Ponashta," who lived west and south of the Snake.

Meek (1848, p. 10) mentioned 3,000 Snake and 2,000 "Bonarchs" on the Snake River near Fort Hall.

Wilson (1849, p. 66) distinguished "Shoshonies or Snakes" from "Shoshocoes or Walkers." The former were mounted and extended from Red Buttes on the North Fork of the Platte River, southward to include the "Yan-pa-pa, till it enters the Green or Colorado River," and the Bear River Mountains and "most of the Salt Lake" and Humboldt River. He thus ignored the presence of Bannock. Schoolcraft (1857, pp. 34–35) gave approximately the same boundary for the "Shochonee."

Though Ross (1855) is often cited as an authority, his confusion is evident in his threefold grouping of Shoshoni: (1) Shirry-dikas or Dog-Eaters [the Shoshoni name for the Arapaho; Shoshoni did not eat dogs] living east of the Rocky Mountains; (2) War-are-ree-kas or Fish Eaters [wada is the name of a seed], who were numerous on the rivers west of the Rocky Mountains and were poorly armed and clad, unorganized, and lived by fishing; (3) Ban-at-tees [probably intended for "Banaite," the Fort Hall Shoshoni name for Bannock], Robbers, or Mountain Snakes who "live a predatory and wandering life in the recesses of the mountains and are to be found in small bands, or single wigwams, among the caverns and rocks" and who lived by robbing. This, of course, might describe any of several Shoshonean groups in different States. Ross admitted that classification of Shoshoneans was confused and that his own remarks "cannot be relied upon as entirely correct . . . With all their experience, our friends possessed but a very confused idea of the Snakes, both as to their names and numbers. One would call them Bannocks, and another Wurracks, while a third would have them named Dogs." (1855, vol. 1, pp. 251–252.)

Simpson (1876, p. 34) placed the "fierce and warlike Snakes" in the Snake, Bear, and Green River Valleys east to Wind River.

Doty (1864, p. 173) mentioned "the mixed bands of Shoshonees and Bannacks of the Shoshonee (or Snake) River valley."

Irish (1865, pp. 143–144) related the mixed Shoshoni and Bannock of Idaho to the Wyoming Shoshoni, from whom he distinguished 3 bands of Northwestern Shoshoni in Bear Lake, Cache and Malad Valleys, and the Goose Creek Mountains.

Head (1867, p. 176) placed "mixed bands of Bannacks and Shoshones" in southern Idaho and in the Ogden, Weber, and Bear River valleys, but said they spent much time in the Wind River country since game had become scarce in their own. Another group was the Too-roo-reka or Sheep eater Shoshones "who lived almost entirely in the mountains and very seldom visit the white settlements" (p. 189).

C. F. Powell (1868, pp. 201–203) and Danilson (1869, p. 288) represented the home of the Bannocks to be the region of Fort Hall but the former said there were about 100 in western Idaho.

Wheeler (1879, pp. 19, 408–413) subdivides Shoshoni proper, as distinguished from Snakes of Oregon, into: Wind River or Washakie, Hokan-tikara [my Hukundüka], Go'siats or Goshi-Utes, Tuka-ri'ka (or Mountain-Sheep-eaters or Salmon River Snakes), Tussa'wehe (or White Knives), Paviotso of western Nevada, and Bannock or Panai'ti. The Paviotso actually speak Mono-Bannock and so do the Bannock or Panai'ti if this refers to the Fort Hall group.

Another ambitious but unhelpful classification of Shoshoni or "horse Indians" as distinct from Shoshocoes or foot Indians, is Hoffman's 7 divisions of the former (1886, pp. 296–298): (1) Tukuarika or Mountains Sheep Eaters near the headwaters of the Yellowstone River [my Salmon River group], (2) Tazaaigadika or Salmon Eaters, unlocated [Agaidüka was used by informants for both Salmon River and lower Snake River Shoshoni], (3) Tivatika or Pine

Nut eaters of southern Nevada [Fort Hall Shoshoni applied Tubadüka to Grouse Creek, the Snake River Shoshoni applied it to the Humboldt River Shoshoni, and according to Kroeber (1909, pp. 267–268), Ruby Valley Shoshoni applied Düvedika-nü to Austin Shoshoni], (4) Shonivikidika or Sunflower Eaters, not located, (5) Hokandika or Earth Eaters, not located [my Hukundüka or eaters of huki seeds], (6) Shohoaigadika or Cottonwood Salmon Eaters, unlocated, (7) Yahandika or Ground Hog Eaters, unlocated [my Yahandüka of western Idaho].

Western Idaho.—If the eastern portion of the region was confused by the presence of Bannocks among the Shoshoni, western Idaho was confused by the presence of Northern Paiute adjoining Shoshoni.

Bonneville, 1832–33, used "Shoshokoe" for 100 families met on the Powder River, a tributary of the Snake River in eastern Oregon, whom he described as poor, inoffensive diggers and fish eaters who lacked horses (Irving, 1898, vol. 1, pp. 333–334). Work, 1833 (Lewis and Phillips, 1923, pp. 150–174) used "Snake" for Indians of the Boise, Payette, and Day Rivers. Farnham, 1839, used "Bonack" for mounted Indians inhabiting "the banks of that part of Saptin, or Snake River, which lies between the mouth of Boisais, or Reed's [Boise] River, and the Blue Mountains" and "speak a language peculiar to themselves," that is, different from the Shoshoni or Snake immediately to the east (1843, pp. 261–262, 318–320). Townsend (1839, p. 267) met a "Snake" family on the Brulé (Burnt) River in eastern Oregon.

Hale used "Panasht" or "Bonaks" for the inhabitants of the Snake River above the mouth of the Boise River, who separated the "Winasht" or "Western Shoshoni" of Oregon from Shoshoni or Snake of Idaho (1846, pp. 218–219). "Shoshonees or Snakes" are also distinguished from "Panasht Bannaks" in House Ex. Doc. 76, 1848, pp. 7–8. Domenech (1860, vol. 1, map) locates the "Punashly or Ponacks" on the Snake River in southwestern Idaho. Earlier, in 1839, Leonard (1904, p. 167) had placed Bawnack or Shoshonie on the Willamette River.

Burton (1862, pp. 473–474) said Bannock inhabited the greater part of Oregon, but there were a few to the east who had formerly traded at Fort Bridger, Wyoming.

Kirkpatrick (1862, pp. 267 268) used a novel term, "Winnas," for Indians north of the Snake River on the Bayette (Payette), Boise, and Sickley (Malad ?) Rivers.

Lyon (1865, p. 234) speaks of "Boisé Shoshonees" formerly on the Boise River and of 2,000 Indians of the "Kammas Prairie" tribe. Hough (1866, p. 189) speaks of "Boisé," "Bruneau," and "Kamass" bands of "Shoshonee."

Ballard (1866, p. 190) says "Pi-Utes" lived in southwestern Idaho and Oregon, whereas "Snakes or Shoshonees" lived on the upper Snake River.

Powell and Ingalls (1874, p. 20) class southwestern Oregon under "Western Shoshoni."

Humboldt River and eastern Nevada.—Walker, 1826, called the Indians on the Humboldt River "Shoshokoes" (Irving, 1897, vol. 2, p. 94). Meek (1848, p. 10) used "Bonarch Diggers" for 7,000 Indians west of Great Salt Lake. Humboldt River Indians were called Shoshoni by Holeman (1852, p. 151). Lander (1860, p. 133) said the Indians of the Humboldt River and Goose Creek Mountains were a division of "Western Shoshonee" called "Shoshokoes," and Hurt (1860, pp. 92–93) called the same people Snake Diggers. In 1859 Simpson said there were 500 Bannacks on the "southern border of Oregon, along the Old Humboldt

River emigrant-road" (1876, pp. 34–35). Burton (1862, p. 474) gives 7 bands of "Shoshones" along the Humboldt River and 100 miles south. Doty (1864, p. 175) mentioned two bands of "Western Shoshonees" or "Shoshonee Diggers," the Tosowitch (White Knife) and Unkoahs.

After about 1865 Humboldt River people were called Shoshonee or Western Shoshone, e. g., by: Parker (1866, pp. 114–115), who said there were 2,500 in the whole eastern half of Nevada; Campbell (1866, p. 120); Head, who placed them in western Utah and eastern Nevada (1866, p. 123), including Deep Creek and Ruby Valley (1867, p. 176); Tourtellotte (1869, p. 229); and Douglas (1870, p. 95), who said they were "offshoots of the Shoshonees or Snake Indians of Oregon."

Powell and Ingalls classed them with southeastern Oregon and southwestern Idaho as "Western Shoshones" (1874, pp. 12, 20).

Observations on southern Nevada were more contradictory.

Domenech (1860, vol. 1, map) located Pah-Utah in southern Nevada and southern California, with Apaches in the Death Valley region. Parker (1866, pp. 114–115) included Pahranagat Valley and southern Nevada in Shoshonee territory, while Douglas (1870, p. 95) thought "Shoshonees" did not extend south of the 38th parallel. Powell and Ingalls located "Western Shoshones" south to Duckwater, Hot Creek, and Big Smoky Valley (1874, pp. 12, 20). Wheeler's Shoshoni of Hiko, Nevada (Pahranagat Valley) were, as the vocabulary (1879, pp. 424–465) clearly demonstrates, not Shoshoni but Southern Paiute. This is within the territory allotted by Powell and Ingalls (1874) and Kelly (1934) to Southern Paiute.

Eastern Oregon.—The term Snake was apparently first used by Thompson, 1784–1812, who had heard of "Snake Indians of the Straw Tent Tribe," evidently located in Oregon west of the Blue Mountains (p. 492). Lewis and Clark, 1806–7, used it for a large number of Indians on the Deschutes River (vol. 3, pp. 147–149), who, however, probably did not speak Shoshoni-Comanche as their Lemhi Shoshoni interpreter could not converse with a "Snake" captive woman met below the Cascades of the Columbia River (vol. 3, p. 193). They had previously used Chô-sho-ne (vol. 2, p 366), though Gass, who accompanied them, had used Snake (p. 121) for the Lemhi.

In 1811, while the Astoria party was near the junction of the Boise and Snake Rivers, they were informed that there were no more "Snakes" downstream and they would meet "Sciatogas" (Irving, 1897, vol. 2, p. 46), but several days journey to the west of the Snake River, in Oregon, they met mounted "Shoshoni" (pp. 71–72).

Morse, in 1822 (map and pp. 368–369) placed "Shoshones," which he seems to have identified with "Snake," in all of eastern Oregon and southern Idaho.

Ogden, 1826–28, used "Snake" for Indians of Day's River near the Columbia River (vol. 10, pp. 349–351) and on the headwaters of "Silvie's" (Silver) River (vol. 11, p. 206), and Work (Lewis and Phillips, 1923, pp. 150–174) in 1833, for Indians on Day's River.

Obviously, "Snake" did not have an exact meaning at this time. Then and later it was used indiscriminately for mounted and unmounted Shoshoneans of Idaho, Wyoming, Oregon, and Nevada. Ross' "Snake" vocabulary (1855, vol. 2, pp. 153–154) is of no help in identifying the Snakes for the location from which it is taken is not given. It resembles Shoshoni-Comanche somewhat, but appears mixed. Subsequent use of other names for eastern Oregon Indians is consistent with a change in the ever-confused terminology rather than a shift of tribes.

Wyeth, at Fort Hall, 1834–1836, placed "Snake or Digger Indians" in the valley between the Blue and Cascade Mountains (Schoolcraft, 1851, p. 221), but Wyeth had no idea of the linguistic difference between Northern Paiute and Shoshoni.

Hale's "Western Shoshoni or Winasht," inhabiting what is now eastern Oregon (1846, pp. 218–219 and map) were, from his vocabularies (1846, pp. 569–629; 1848, p. 121), clearly Mono-Bannock. Latham (1856, pp. 106–107) called them "Wihinast."

Lander (1860, pp. 138–139) located 150 lodges of "Warraricas (in English, 'Sun-flower seed eaters') or Diggers or Bannacks, below Fort Boise, west of Blue Mountains," ranging, with very few horses, on the head of John Day's River and west of the Blue Mountains. They subsisted on roots, camas, and plunder. The same year Geary (1860, p. 176) wrote that the "Snakes" of eastern Oregon are to be distinguished from the "Bannacks" and "Sho-sho-nees" of the Rocky Mountains who were well mounted buffalo hunters. Two years later Kirkpatrick (1862, pp. 267–268) placed "Bannacks" from Harney Lake of the Rocky Mountains who were well mounted buffalo hunters. Two years "Mountain Snakes, Bonnacks, and Diggers" are "generally known as the Shoshone or Snake Indians, and are part of that large tribe," and Domenech (1860, vol. 1, map) had located "Bonnack Shoshones or Serpents" in southern Oregon.

Burton (1862, pp. 473–474) said most Bannock were in Oregon.

Huntington (1865, p. 466) listed the following subdivisions of Oregon "Snakes": Yah-hoos-kin, Woll-pah-pe, Wah-tat-kin, I-uke-spi-ule, and Hoo-ne-boo-ey.

Ballard (1866, p. 190) placed "Pi-Ute" in southeastern Idaho and the regions of the Owyhee and Malheur Rivers.

Bancroft (vol. 31, pt. 2, pp. 512–544), using army reports, said that the Indians engaged in the wars in eastern Oregon, especially from Malheur and Warner Lakes, were "Shoshoni." Hoffman (1886, pp. 298–299) placed "Panaiti" in eastern Oregon, western Idaho, and perhaps in Washington.

Huntington (1867, p. 95) applied "Snakes" to middle Oregon, Malheur River, "Pi-Utes and Snakes" to the Owyhee region.

Douglas (1870, p. 95) mentioned "Shoshones or Snake Indians of Oregon"; Meacham (1871, p. 305), "Snake or Shoshoni" near Camp Horney.

Powell and Ingalls included southeastern Oregon under "Western Shoshoni" (1874, p. 20).

Wheeler (1879, p. 410) made a special division of "Snakes" which included the Wi'hinasht at Owyhee River (Hale's "Western Shoshoni" which was Mono-Bannock linguistically) and the Walpa'pi and Yahu'skin of southern and eastern Oregon (whose distinguishing characteristics have never been stated and probably did not exist).

Although archeological and ethnographic evidence may permit the inference that Shoshoneans have expanded northward in recent centuries, pushing the Sahaptins and others toward the Columbia River, there appears to be no means of confirming Teit's hypothesis that this occurred subsequent to 1750 (Teit, 1928, pp. 98–108). Lewis and Clark, 1806–7, left the first documentary evidence describing the Columbia Valley. Ogden, 1826–28, first described eastern Oregon. Their observations indicate that Shoshonean-speaking peoples covered most of Oregon and even reached the mouth of the Deschutes River, where they raided other tribes. Both writers called these peoples "Snakes."

Exact information about the political and linguistic divisions of Oregon Shoshoni must await field work. Meanwhile it is impossible to interpret the available literature in support of Berreman's supposition that although "it seems to be possible to identify the original Mono-Bannock peoples of southeastern Oregon with Northern Paiute of northeastern California," it is also possible to "show that the Snake or Walpapi, of central eastern Oregon in historic times, were late intruders from the east" and that in 1750 only did Northern Paiute as distinct from Snake and Bannock occupy Oregon (1937, pp. 47–54, fig. 1). To the contrary, it seems impossible to avoid believing that early writers loosely applied Snake, Bannock, and Shoshocoe to the same people. There is no evidence that the Shoshoneans of eastern Oregon were divided into readily distinguishable cultural, political, or linguistic groups. Amalgamation of the scattered population into bands undoubtedly occurred only during the Indian wars.

Western Nevada.—CTh, Mill City Paiute, said that in his grandfather's time a people speaking a language different from Paiute had lived in the vicinity of Lovelock. They might, he thought, have been the present Pitt River (Achomawi) Indians. The Paiute were said to have killed many of them and driven the remainder into a large cave where most of them were smoked to death. Other versions of this account have previously been cited (Steward, 1937).

Leonard, 1831–36, called the Indians in the vicinity of Humboldt Lake "Shoshocoes" (p. 167), a term used by other writers for Humboldt River, eastern Oregon, and southern Idaho "Diggers." For example, Wilson (1849, p. 66) used it as synonymous with "Walker or Digger" for any unmounted Shoshoneans, and Hoffman (1886, pp. 296–298) as synonymous with "Shoshoki" for any foot Indian.

Holeman called the Indians near Humboldt Lake "Bannacks" (1853, p. 444), whereas Hurt called them "Py-Ute" (1856, pp. 228–229). Burche (1864, pp. 144–147) said the "Pannakés" lived north of the "Pah-Ute" (under Waw-ne-mucke) in Humboldt County, Nevada, their territory extending "from the Sierras to the Rocky Mountains and from parallels 41° to 45° north latitude." Stony Point on the Humboldt River was the western boundary of the "Shoshonees." Parker (1866, pp. 114–115) placed 1,500 mounted "Bannocks" in Nevada north of the 41st parallel and in the southeastern corner of Idaho. "Pi-Utes," he said, occupied Nevada west of the "Shoshonees" and south of the "Bannock." Campbell (1866, pp. 119–120) agreed with Parker, but used "Snake" as synonymous with "Bannock" of southern Oregon. Douglas (1870, pp. 95 ff.) called the Indians of the Steen's Mountain region "Snake," while Douglas (1870, pp. 94–95) called these together with the McDermit and western Nevada Indians "Pah-Ute." And yet Berreman (1937, p. 57) locates Northern Paiute in southeastern Oregon with Bannock and Snake north of them in 1840 to 1850.

Campbell (1866, pp. 119–120) distinguished "Pi-Ute" of western Nevada [Northern Paiute] from "Pai-Ute" of southern Nevada and Utah [Southern Paiute]. Powell and Ingals (1874, pp. 2, 5, 21) used "Pa-vi-o-tsoes" or "Pah-Utes" for western Nevada and Humfreville (1897, p. 281) used Pah-Ute for northern Nevada.

Simpson (1876, pp. 37–38) placed "Py-Utes" in western Utah from Oregon to New Mexico and in the principal river and lake basins of the Great Basin.

In appraising these references to southern Oregon and western Nevada, the area of the Mono-Bannock speaking peoples, it should be borne in mind that it has not yet been demonstrated that they were natively divided into ethnic groups. Both language and culture appear to have varied so gradually that no locality was truly distinct from others. Bands or other large political groupings existed only after the period of conflict with the white man began, circa 1850 to 1860. Names, few of which were of native origin, were applied by white men to areas much larger than aboriginal ethnic or political groups—Snake or Bannock to Oregon, Paviotso to western Nevada, Mono to eastern California, and Paiute to all.

Southern Utah and southern Nevada.—The main confusion in terminology for Southern Paiute is the designation of the northernmost group of Southern Paiute as "Pi-Edes."

Farnham (1843, pp. 248–249) located Paiutes and Land Pitches (possibly meaning San Pete or Sampits Ute) on the Sevier River.

Hurt (1860, pp. 92–93) mentioned Utah or Piedes under Chief Ammon on Beaver Creek. Irish (1865, pp. 145–46) said the Pi-Edes numbered about 6,000, spoke Utah, and lived "through Beaver and Little Salt Lake Valleys, and on the Rio Virgin and Santa Clara rivers down to the "Muddy" River, under Tut-sey-gub-bets and many subchiefs. They were poor and were often raided by the Utes. The Pah Ute (pp. 146–147) "properly belong in Nevada and Arizona" and were very similar to the Pi-Edes. Head (1866, p. 124) distinguished 600 Pah-Edes under Tut-sey-gub-bets from 1,000 Pah-Utes to their south and 700 Pah Ranagats. (1867, pp. 174–176; 1868, pp. 148–149.) Simpson (1876, p. 35) said the "Pi-eeds" lived south of the Pah-vants, down to Santa Clara. Chiefs were Tatsigobbets and Quanarrah.

Sale (1865, p. 155), in utter confusion, said Pai-Utes numbered 2,000 to 3,000 and claimed the country from Snake Valley to the Colorado River and from the Wasatch Mountains west to Pahranagat Valley.

Wheeler (1875, pp. 36–37) stated that Southern Paiute were called Ute or Piedes while Pah-Utes were the same as Piedes.

Gottfredson (1919, p. 15) placed Piedes at Pinto, Washington County, Utah.

Powell and Ingalls used Pai-Ute for the Southern Paiute, Pah-Ute for the Northern Paiute (1874), and Humfreville used Pi-Ute and Pah-Ute for these two divisions (1897, p. 281).

APPENDIX B.—VOCABULARIES

The following vocabularies were chosen from a large number collected in the field to represent the regional differences in dialect. In many instances, differences in recorded words do not represent absolute local differences, for Shoshonean pronunciation is subject to great variation, especially in the treatment of terminal and whispered syllables. A single informant often pronounced a word very differently upon successive occasions. Individuals sometimes used unlike pronunciation not only because of the characteristic Shoshonean carelessness but because of difference in their ages. There is a noticeable difference which was remarked by the Indians between old and young generations.

ORTHOGRAPHY

a, e, i, o, and u have their continental values.

a:, e:, i:, o:, and u: are prolonged.

ă, ĕ, ĭ, ŏ, and ŭ are short.

å, as in bɪll.

ö, ü, imperfect umlaut.

ã, ẽ, ĩ, õ, and ũ a e nasalize [1].

ə, obscure vowel, often merging with impure u.

c, like English sh.

r, like Spanish r.

v, bilabial.

f, bilabial.

p:, k:, t:, etc., are prolonged. The breath is held for a moment and released explosively, causing a whispered vowel to follow.

ŋ, as in sing.

ǥ, k̄, somewhat fricative.

x, like German ch but farther forward.

θ, like English th. This often approximates t.

s, usually like English, but often slightly blurred like English sh.

', elevated is glottal stop. Occurring at the end of a word, it is almost inevitably followed by a whispered vowel unless the breath be held.

All other consonants are pronounced as in English, except when nasalized.

All elevated letters are whispered or very weakly vocalized.

Accent among the Shoshoni was on the first syllable in all except compound words and is therefore not written in. The only exception is S-LtLk which, like Northern and Southern Paiute, accented various syllables.

There are minor regional differences in pronunciation which did not, however, prevent Shoshoni wherever spoken being intelligible to anyone else speaking it. In general the rate of speaking was much faster in the north. At Fort Hall one or more of the final syllables of a word were entirely inaudible when the word was spoken alone and were vocalized only when the word was spoken in combination with others. Lemhi were the extreme in this respect, speaking with great speed and slurring and whispering the final syllables.

	George's Creek Northern Paiute	Mill City Northern Paiute	Bannock Northern Paiute	Ash Meadows Southern Paiute	Panamint Valley Kawaiisü
One	sümü"ᵃ	suwu't:	süwü'yu	sü':wi	su'yu
Two	wahai'	waha't:	wahai'yu	wai:	waha'yu
Three	pahe'	paihi"	pahi'yu	pai:	pehe'yu
Four	watsiŋ'ʷᵃ	wa'tsukwi	watsü'kwi	watsu'h	watsu'wiyu
Five	manü'gi	ma'nügit	manü'gi	manü'ᶻ	manügi'yu
Six	na':wai	na':fait	na':paihiᶻᵘ	nava'h	navahai'yu
Seven	ta'tsüi	ta':tsui	nata'kwatsu-kwiᶻᵘ	mukwis'	no"ᵒmüzi
Eight	wá'süi	wá':sui	nai'watsukwiᶻᵘ	na:ns	nanüwatsu'wiyu
Nine	kwanu'kⁱ	su'mukadop	suwo'kodoop	yuwip'	su'kumüsa
Ten	su':wano	su'wumanot	su'uwanoyu	masu'h	mu'musu'iyu
Ankle	tsiko'noᵐ	da'wizo'ᵒ	da'wi'tsogo	tumbo'ts	
Arm	bu'ta	buta'	buta'	aŋüv'	nüda'vu
Blood	vai'uŋwa	bü:p:	büü'p:!	pahup'ⁱ	püᵃ'pi
Ear	na'ka	naka'	naka'	naŋgav'	naŋgaviʰ'mi
Eye	vu'si	bui	vui	pu''wi	pu''i
Foot	hu'ka	gügü'	gükü'	na':mp	nambi
Hair	wo:	wöp	wá:	tsopüv'	tsopi'wü
Hand	wãi'ya	mai	mai	mü'ümp'	má''a
Head	wo:	wö:	wá:	tá:ts	tá'tsi
Heart	vi'wü	bi'wᵘ	viwüh'	piümp'	püⁱʰyu
Knee	daŋa'vü	mi'awá	mia'wá	ta:ŋ	tá'na
Mouth	du'p:a	tuba'	dupa'	tump:	tum'bi
Nose	wu'vi	mubi'	muvi'	mu:v	muvito''ᵒ
Teeth	da'wa	da'ma	dama'	tãü'wa	tãü'wa
Tongue	e'go	e'ho	ego'	ãüx	e'go
Liver	nü'wa	nü'wü	nüwü'	nüwümp'	nü'wü
Bone	o'ho	o'ho	oʰo'	há:v	ohá'gwü
Leg	hu'ka	ego'p	gaup:	yugu	yu'u'vü
Antelope	kwaha'du	duna' wadzi'	tuna'	hwa:ns	wan'zi
Badger	hu'na	huna	huna'na	hun	hu'na
Bear	pa'havitci ¹	tokawidja ² padoa ³	wüda'	papau'h	págwi'tc
Coyote	ica''ᵃ	ija''ᵃ	ija''a	cunav'	süna'vi
Crow	kadapü'zi	ada'	ada'	ata'puts	ataka'zi
Deer	tuhi'na	du'itc	duhü'tca	tü:i	tuhu'yu
Eagle	kwi'na'ᵃ	gwina''ᵃ	gwina'	müŋi'puts	mü'ni
Elk	padühi'a	padu'itc	batu'hitc		
Fish	paŋwi	pagwi'ʰ	pakwi'	pagü'idᴢ	pa'güzi
Frog	yagwa'za	pamo'ᶻ	wagotsa':	waxa'tats	waga'ta
Gopher	mü'yu	yua'dzib:ᵃ	yua'dziva	mü':i	mü'ʰyu
Louse	pü'zlavi	pozi''a	posi''a	po':av ⁴ atsüv' ⁵	atsü'vi
Mountain lion	tsoka''ᵃ	kagwi'tuhu	kakwi':doho	tugu'mumunts	tukumü'tsi
Mountain sheep	ko'ipᵃ	koip:	ko'ip:a	na:x	na'gi
Rattlesnake	togo'a	do''okʷ	togo'kwa	kwiyats'	togo'a
Skunk	poni'na	poni't	poŋitc	páʰni'	po'niatsⁱ
Wolf	u'nupi	ica'	ica'	cunav'	cunav'
Jack rabbit	kümᵘ	ka'mü	kame'	ka:m	ka'ʰma
Cottontail	tavotcitci''ⁱ	tavo'	tavü'	ta'vots	tavotsi
Pine nut	tu'ba	tu'ba	tuba'	tuv	tu'ba
Sun flower	pa':xü	akü'	pa':hu	akump'	pa'akutam'ba
Tule	tsai'vü	saib:	sai:b:ᵘ	kovuv'	se'ᵒvüm'ba
Arrow	pa'ga	pő:s	paga'p:ᵘ	hu:	hu'a

¹ Called unu'ᵘ south of Independence.
² Black Bear.
³ Grizzly Bear.
⁴ Head.
⁵ Body.

	George's Creek Northern Paiute	Mill City Northern Paiute	Bannock Northern Paiute	Ash Meadows Southern Paiute	Panamint Valley Kawaiisü
Bow	ai'du	wa''adü	hu:a'dü	a:tc	e'du
Cradle	hu':pa	hup	su'ʰuhup:ᵃ	ká:n	ká'hno
House	no'bi	no'vi	novi'	ka:n	ka'ʰwi
Metate	ma't:a	mata'	mata'	ma:d	ma'da
Muller	tu':su	tusu	düsu':nu	mo:'	tu'su
Pipe	pitci'mu	to'ic	do'i'ca	cüŋwü'p	tsu'ʰnu
Cloud	pagunü'pa	baguna'p:	kumi'va	pagu'nüv	küna'vi
Mountain	toya'vi	kai'va	kai'va	kaiv	te':vi
Night	totsoi'pü	to×an	tu:ga'va	tüwan	tuʰga'no
Rain	pa-ûwa'tü	paüma'b:	pa':umava	u':wad	uwa'da
Rock	tu'pi	tubi'	tupi'	tü'mp	tu'mbi
Water	pa'ya	pa	pa	pa	pá'ᵃ
Bad	tagü'pᵘ	su'ta''ʸᵘ	kapa'	üwü'puwüni	ata'ʰmbü
Good	tsaü'wi	pizai''ʸᵘ	bicai'yu	ha'u'pu	hü'ü'tü
Large	pavai'	pavai''ʸᵘ	pabai'yu	oko'ndum	ive'tü
Small	tü'itcitil	tü':tsi'ⁱ	tu'utsiyu	tsikI'ts	ivepi'tci
Yes	hᾶ'ᵃ	ᾶhᾶ'	ᾶhᾶ'	hü'ü'	hü'ü
No	kadu''ᵘ	kai	kai	ka:tc ᵘ	ke'ǿu
Tobacco	pa'hmu	pahmu'	pahmu'	ko'üp'	ko'o'pi
Hot	ü'dü'üti	üdüt'	kutsü'ŋ:i	tado'i	tado''iǿü
Warm	yuwi'ti	yuwi'	yuʷi'	yua'dai	yuwada'ta
Cold	ü'jü'üti	üzü'ts	özü'ts	tcütu'i	situ''iǿü
Hard	tci'kawüti	üüü'n	önün':ᵘ	tütsi'gai	mü'tsügwiǿü
Soft	yotsoga'ti	yotzok'	yotsok'	yomi'gai	
Nothing	kahi'	kadu'	kadu'	navac'	yuwa't∗
Snow	nuvavi''	nuva'vi	nuva'vi	u:gwi'	nüva'vi
Salt	oŋa'vi	oŋa'vi	ona'vi	owa'v	owa'vi
Sand	paziwa'pᵃ	átu'ba	pasi'wəp:	ota'v	sihwa'mba
Man	na''na	nanu		towa'ts	ta'n'ipüzi
Woman	hu:pi''ⁱ	mo×wo''um	nai'dü	ma:ma'u'	mámá''ᵃ
Fire	ko'so	koso'		ku:n	ku'ʰna
Smoke	kuku'itâte	kwi:p	kwi':dova	kwi:p	kuʰi'pa
Ash	ku'tuzivü	küt:u'zip	koto'niba	hwambip'	kutsa'p:ᵃ
Sun	ta'vaidùadü	ta'va	tava'	tavai'puts	ta'vi
Moon	mü':a	mü'ha	müha'	miyü'dogopits	mü':a
Star	ta𝒹zinu'pa	pa':tuzuᵇᵃ	pa'tusuva	pu':tsiv	putsi'vi
Thunder	to'yagàti	nü'nüava	nünua'va	üwa'diyaxai ᵉ	
Wind	huŋwa'p:	hukwə'p	hukwa'pa	nu:a'dᵘ	ne'ǿu
Sky	tu'gupadàvü	kuwi'b	tugwu'pat	tugu'mp ᶠ	tu'gubaiyavanad
Lake	patsia'ta	paga'düt ᵉ	panu'nad∗		
White	to'savonogitü	toha'gwadjad	teha'kwitcᾰd	tosa'gad ᵘ	ségiǿa
Black	to'tsoagitü	tu'gwadjad	tuhu'kwitcᾰd	topa'gad ᵘ	tu'hukiǿa
Red	a'kavonogitü	atsa'gwadjad	atsa'kwitcᾰd	aŋga'xad ᵘ	a'ŋakiǿa
Blue	puhi'duwatü	huhi'gwadjad	tui'ckwitcᾰd	sagwa'xad ᵘ	pu'huⁱkiǿa
Yellow	oha'vonogitü	ohagwadjad	oha'kwitcᾰd	huvu'ŋgad ᵘ	a'ndokiǿa
North	kwi'wi	kwi'nihanükwüt	kwina'hav	tü:	
South	pi't:a	pa'nakwüt	tava'duhat	tu:va'	
East	si'vi	tavatsewinakwüt	tava'tsivuinakwət	kwa:	
West	pa':mi	tava'iganukwüt	yuŋo'nakwət	kwa:	

ᵉ Literally rain (üwadi), cry (yaxai).

ᶠ Or tuqumpᵃya.

ᵍ Also, panü'n:.

	Fort Hall Shoshoni	Lemhi Shoshoni	Utah Lake Ute	Pahvant Ute	Las Vegas Southern Paiute
One	sum:ə	sum:	su⁻:yʊ	su'wiyus	suwi
Two	wahai't	watü	wa'ene	wae'ne	wai
Three	pait:	pait:ü	pa'ene	pae'ne	pa:i
Four	wa:tsuit	wa:tsuit:ü	waʰtsu'wini	wahtsu'ŋyene	watsu'i
Five	manügit	manügit:ü	ma'nugini	manü'gyene	manü'gi
Six	navait	navaitü	na'vaine	navai'yene	na'vai
Seven	ta:tsuit	ta:tsuitü	na'wikuwine	navai'kavayene	mukw'cª
Eight	naiwatsuit	naiwatsuitü	wahsu'winye	wa'hutsuŋyene	na:nsuwi
Nine	su:wanowomuhünt [1]	su:wanowümihünt	sö'döhsùwinye	sö'dogumsuyene	yuwi'pe
Ten	sü:wáʰ	sü:üwüt	tö'hmsuwinye	tohmsuyene	masu
Ankle	davonts	dawints	taunsuwümp	tªtu'mpitcᵉᵉ	tö'mbotcum [1]
Arm	büdü	büdü	büdü	ä'nav	aŋa'vüm
Blood	bü:p:[1]	bü:p:	paup	paup:[1]	paup:
Ear	nãnk	nãnk:	naŋka'vov	naŋkaf	naŋko'vəm
Eye	bui	bui	pu'iv[1]	pu:ivi	puim
Foot	namp:	namp:	nampü'	namp	nampam
Hair	bambibühüp	bambiʷū	tªtsi'wüv	tªˑtsiwüf	tatsu'vem
Hand	má'ᴀ	má'ᴀ	müv	má'avi	máum
Head	bamp:[1]	bambi	tªtsiv	tª'tsivi	tátsum'
Heart	bix	biˣ	pip:	pi:yü'p:	piüm'
Knee	danəp:	danəp:	daŋu'v	ta':ŋava	taŋəm
Mouth	tümp:	tümp:	tü'mbüv	timpü'vi	tümpam'
Nose	mup:	müüp:	müvi't ūmi	mu:vi'p	muvim'
Teeth	dãü'm:	dauw	dauwu'mb:	tãũwa'mp	tauwə'm
Tongue	e:g:ᵒ	eʰgᵒ	awü'mbi	axö'mp:	augö'm
Liver	nüm:'ū	nü'ʷū	num:	nü'ŋwümp	nüwüm
Bone	dzũhⁿi	zuhⁿi	üv	oo'f	hööv'
Leg	o'ᵐᴀ	doho'ʰ	yuf	yu'u'f	yuü'm
Antelope	kwahadü	kwahadü	wanz	wants	wantsi'
Badger	huna	huna	u'nambuts	u:na'mpüts	hun:
Bear	wüda	wüda'	kwi'yan	kwiya'gant	papa'o
Coyote	izap:ü	izap:ü	yo'gots	yoho'vuts	süna'v
Crow	hai	hai	ota'kunts	ata'kunts	ata'puts
Deer	tuhuya	tuhuya	dui	düu'i	tuhu'i
Eagle	biagwiya'ᴀ	biagwina	kwa'natsüts[i]	kwana'nts	mü.ŋ
Elk	paduhuya	paduhuya	ba'dui	padu'i	paduhu'i
Fish	pĕnkʷi	pãnkʷi	bagü'	pa:ġü'	pagü'ts
Frog	yagwotsa	yagwotsa [2]	po'nuv	paxkwan	woġa'tats
Gopher	yühavite	yuhavite	mi'mbute	mu'iyümpüts	mü'lyü
Louse	po:siᴀ	posia	pü'av	po'avi	atsü'vi
Mountain lion	tökovite	toyuduko	tukw [3]	pia'duk	tukümünts
Mountain sheep	müzəmbia [4]	wasupi [5] müzümbia [6]	na'gat	nax	nax
Rattlesnake	togoa	togoa	to'ġwüv	toxo'avi	kwia'ts
Skunk	ponhiats	ponhiats	poni	pá:ni'	poni':
Wolf	ic	ic	sü'navi	piasina'vi	tuvo'ts
Jack rabbit	kam	kam:	tsü'kamuts	kam:	kam:
Cottontail	dav:	tava [7]	ta'vüts	tavü'ts	tavu'ts
Pine nut	tub:	tuba	tuva'	tuvᴬ	tuv:ᴬ
Sun flower	paak:	pa:k:	akümp	akü'mp	akəmp
Tule	saip:	saip:	pagümp	pagü'mp	to'oi'v
Arrow	ba'k:	hu:pa	u:	u:	hu:
Bow	hu:et	hu:et [8]	ats	atc	ats
Cradle	kohªu		kün	kán	ko:n
House	kahⁿi	kahⁿi	kan	ka'hni	kan
Metate	bot:	bot:	madu'ts	ma:dᴬ	mati

[1] Literally "ten minus one."
[2] Bull frog (pɐyaqwhani).
[3] Or piadukw.
[4] Generic term.
[5] Ram.
[6] Ewe.
[7] A gray rabbit (tump'eitav).
[8] hu: (wood), et (bow).

	Fort Hall Shoshoni	Lemhi Shoshoni	Utah Lake Ute	Pahvant Ute	Las Vegas Southern Paiute
Muller	dus:u	dus:	müts	mu'ᵘ	mu'
Pipe	to'i	do'i	dzunts	tsuŋ	tuwüp
Cloud	to:müp	tomop:⁹	pagu'nüv	paxu'navi	pagunuv:
Mountain	toyavi	toyaᵛⁱ	kaiv	kaiv	kaiv:
Night	tugwanihw	tü:gwaⁿⁱ	tuwü'n	tuhwa'n	tugwa'n
Rain	pa:'yumet	üwaᵈ ü ¹⁰	wánⁱ	pau'ŋwada	üwa'd:
Rock	tümp:	tump:	tumb ¹¹	tump:ⁱ	tump:
Water	pa'	pa	ba	pa	pa
Bad	kedzant ¹²	kezant	kai'yuwü' ü	üvü'püni	üwüpüwüni
Good	sant	sa'ⁱ	a'i	aiyu'du	ha'ü'i
Large	bi:atci	bi:a	pi'adumb' ¹³	pia':vüni	oka'nt
Small	tu:idu	tu:id:	mi''butc	mia'pitc	mi'apüts
Yes	hä'ᵃ	hau'ᵃᵘ	o'wa	ü'mai ¹⁴	hü'ü
No	ke'	ke	kat:	katc	katc
Tobacco	pauhᵐᵘ	pahᵘ	ko'ap	koǝ'p:ⁱ	koap:ⁱ
Hot	üdüint	üdüint	kᵘ'tcuint ü	kw ütsu'ŋi	tadu'i
Warm	yuwaix	yuwaix	yuo'düint	kwiyü'mige	yuwadad ü
Cold	üjuin	üjuint	s:tint	s ütu'i	citu'i
Hard	kut:a''ⁱ	ku:tant	dü'ntsiyud	tü'ntsige	mutcu'int
Soft	yu:naix	yotsogüt:	paiᵛᵘgwǝd	yu:mi'ge	yunigad: ü
Nothing	kehe'wa'ᵃ	kehinimba ¹⁵	kambü'a	nava'stümp	na'vais
Snow	tak:avi	takavi	nuva'ᵛⁱ	nuva'vi	nuvav
Salt	onap:ⁱ	onaᵛⁱ	ö'aᵛⁱ	oa'vi	oa'v
Sand	paziwümp:	pasiwümp:	siwü'mp	siwü'mp	öta'v:ᵃ
Man	----------------	denǝp: ü			
Woman	--------	tambia ¹⁶			
Fire	waihient ¹⁷	gotop	naent	na'ent' ¹⁸	naaint
Smoke	kwip:	kwip:	kwi:kʸᵃ	kwii'p	kwi':kadü
Ash	gutsip	etomb ¹⁹	kuiv	naḳe'v: ²⁰	kutca'p:
Sun	ta'p:ⁱ	taave	tavᵃ	tav:ᵃ	tavo'püts
Moon	müh	mü'ᵃ	mü''tots	mü''togots	mia'dogopüts
Star	ta:dzümp:	ta:dzinümp:	pu'tsiv	pu'tsiv	pu:ts
Thunder	tomoyagait	to:moyagut ²¹	o'nu'nint	ü'nu'nuitc	yaga'nak
Wind	nüet:	nüait:	nu'ᵉᵗ	nua'da	nua'du
Sky	tugumbaᵃᵃ	dugumba	tuwu'ntkiya	tugümpayavi	tugwu'mp
Lake	pagadüt	pagadüt	pagad ᵘᵈ	paǥa'düd	paga'dud
White	tosavit:	tosavit ü	tᵉüso'gᵃᵈ	tᵉsa'gad	to'sad ᵘᵈ
Black	tuhuvit:	tuhuvit ü	tu'kwad ü	tu''kwadu	to'pad ᵘᵈ
Red	äŋgavit:	äŋgavit ü	aŋga'd ᵃᵈ ü	aŋka'gadu	a'ŋkagad ᵘᵈ
Blue	evuhivit:	evuhivit ü	sauwa'dz	sauwá'gadu	sa'wögad ᵘᵈ
Yellow	ohapit:	ohapit ü	eo'k ᵃᵈ ü	oa'kadu	huvüŋkad ᵃᵈ
North	kwiñaha' ²²	weyupunt ²³	tuwa'	kwiyü'm	tandü
South	tavedukw-naŋwa ²⁴	----------------	tu'i	pⁱtu'm	tanduva
East	tavendo i ²⁵	tavendoin	kwa	tavemaŋwis-nankpüts	suvi'amad: ü
West	yuindü ²⁶	yuwindumbi-dunt	mi'tui	taveyaukw-nankpüts	hugato

⁹ baqunap (fog).
¹⁰ wü:id (any precipitation).
¹¹ Also, wikwátnum.
¹² Also niangap:i.
¹³ Also, awut.
¹⁴ Also, ü:.
¹⁵ Also, kehewa or nanatup, all gone.
¹⁶ Literally, the mother
¹⁷ Sometimes, gotob:.

¹⁸ Flame; coals burning, kun:.
¹⁹ Younger generation uses ku:tuzip.
²⁰ Also, kutsa'p:.
²¹ Literally, cloud crying.
²² Also, üjuint (cold).
²³ Literally, sideways.
²⁴ Literally, sun under direction.
²⁵ Literally, sun up, direction.
²⁶ Literally, evening, direction.

	Deep Creek (Gosiute) Shoshoni	Skull Valley (Gosiute) Shoshoni	Grouse Creek Shoshoni	Promontory Point Shoshoni	Lower Snake River Shoshoni
One	sumü	suma	sümütsi	süm:ə	sumə
Two	watu	wat:u	watü	wahatu	wat:
Three	pait ü	pait	pait:	pait:	pait:
Four	waǿ:uit	watsuit	watsuit	watsui⁴	watsuit
Five	manügiǿ	manugit	mana'git	managit	manügit
Six	navait	na:vait	navait	na:vait	navait
Seven	tatsuiǿ	ta:tsuit	tatsuit	ta:tsuit	ta:tsuit
Eight	wásuiǿ	na:watsuwit	namawatsuit	naiyawatsuit	naiwatsuit
Nine	suwumiənt	suudomihunt	sü:wumihünt	sü:wanowumi-hükənt	sü:wanowumi-hünt
Ten	suwat	suuwat	sümat	sü:wat	sü:mat
Ankle	dawivod	daponts	tavota	davonts	datsiŋgono
Arm	budü'	buda	büdü	büd:	büdü
Blood	büpi	büp:	büp:	büp:	büüp:
Ear	nĕnk	nänk	nänk	nänk	nänk:
Eye	bui	bui	bui	bui	bui
Foot	nambe	namp	namba	namp	namp:
Hair	bambiwup	bamp:i	bambiwüp	bambiwü	bambiwüp
Hand	má	má'ⁱ	má	má'	má'ⁱ
Head	bambi	bamp:i	bambi	bamp:	bamp:
Heart	bi:	bi	bix	bixc	bix
Knee	daŋap	danəp	daŋəp	dagəp	danəp:
Mouth	dumbe	dump	dumbi	dümb:	dumbi
Nose	muvi	muijut ¹	muvi	muf:	mup:
Teeth	dãũwa	dau'w⁴	dama	dam'	dam:
Tongue	ego	eǵo	eǵo	ek:ᵒ	ek:
Liver	nüwü	nĩwü' ü	nüwü	nüw ü	nüwü
Bone	duni	zuhⁿⁱ	zuhnip	zuhnip	zuhⁿⁱ
Leg	á:	o'om	o'ma	o'om	áhmá ²
Antelope	kwahadu	kwahadu	kwaadu	kwahadu	kwahad:
Badger	huna	huna'⁴	huna	huna	huna
Bear	wüda	wüda'⁴	kwuda	wüda'	wüda ³
Coyote	ijap:⁴	ijap:ü	izapü	ijap:ü	ijapü'
Crow	hai	kak; hai	kak; hai	kak; hai	hai
Deer	du'huya ⁴	sogoduhuya	(sogo) duhuya	sogoduhuya	tuhuya
Eagle	biagwina	biagwina	biagwina	biagwina	biagwina
Elk	paduhuya	paduhuya	paduhuya	paduhuya	paduhuya
Fish	paŋgwi	pankwⁱ	pankwⁱ	pankwⁱ	pänkwⁱ
Frog	wago	yogwadza	wago; yawats	yagwadza	payagwhani
Gopher	ihavitc	yuavitc	yuabits	yuavitc	yuhavitc
Louse	posiats	pusia	pusia	pusia	puzia
Mountain lion	toyaduko	toyadüko	toyaduko	toyaduko	toyuduka
Mountain sheep	tuku; müzəm-bia	müzambia	müzambia	müzambi'	wasup:
Rattlesnake	togoa	togoa	togoa	togoa	togoa
Skunk	ponhiat	ponhiats	ponhiats	ponhi'	ponhiats
Wolf	biaic	biaica	piaic	biaic	ic; biaais ⁵
Jack rabbit	kamu	kamu'	kam:	kam:	kamu
Cottontail	tavo'	ta:vu''ᵘ	tabo	tab:	davo
Pine nut	tuba	tuba''⁴	tuba	tubⁿ	tuba
Sun flower	iəmbi	iombi	ak:; hiomb	hiomb:	
Tule	tusaip	saip	saip:	saip:	saip:
Arrow	hupaga	baga	hupak	bak:	hua
Bow	uedu	hu:ed:; aiduko	aiduko ⁶	hu:ed	eduko
Cradle	gonu	gohnu	gohnu	gohnu	gohⁿᵘ
House	gaʰni	gahni	kahni	kahni	gahⁿⁱ

¹ Also, muvi.
² Also, düdügua.
³ baduo, shaman's secret name; also, one who transform themselves into bears.
⁴ Or sogo (earth) duhuya, prob. contrasted to pa (water) duhuya, elk.
⁵ icavaip in myths.
⁶ huedu (bow and arrow).

	Deep Creek (Gosiute) Shoshoni	Skull Valley (Gosiute) Shoshoni	Grouse Creek Shoshoni	Promontory Point Shoshoni	Lower Snake River Shoshoni
Metate	bot:o	bot:	bot:	bot:	bot:
Muller	tusu	dusu	tus:	dusᵘ	dus:
Pipe	toi	doi	do'i	to'i	to'i
Cloud	pagunəp	pagunəp	pacüm; toməp	paicüm; toməp:	toop:⁷
Mountain	toyavi	toyavi	toyavi	toyaví	toyavi
Night	tugwani	tugwani	tugwani	tugwani	tu:gwani
Rain	pahuwadu	pa:umet	pa:umət	pa:umət	paumət
Rock	tumbi	tümbi	tumbi	tumbi	tumbi
Water	pa	pa	pa:'	ba:	pa
Bad	kejand:	kejant	kejant	kejant	kejant
Good	tsand:	zant	zant	zant	zant
Large	biand:	biap:	biap:ü; bietci	biap:	biəb:
Small	tuədüt	duondütci	tuündutsi	düidü	tüit
Yes	hä'ᴬ	hä'ᴬ	hä'	hä'ᴬ	hä'ᴬ
No	ke	ǵe	ke	ke	ge
Tobacco	pahu	puipauhmu	pahmu	pauhᵐᵘ	pahᵘ
Hot	üdüint	üdüint	üdüint ⁸	üdüint	üdüint
Warm	yuwaint	yuwaix	yuwənt	yuwaix	kutsuniˣ; yuwaix
Cold	üjüint	üjüint	üjüint	üjüint	üjüint
Hard	kutand:	kutant	kutant	kutan	kütai
Soft	yuniged:	yuwigüt	yunaindutsi ⁹	yotsogait	yonzogayu
Nothing	nanəp	kehimba	kebinimba	kehimba	kehimba; na-natüp
Snow	takavi	takavi	takavi	takavi	takavi
Salt	oavi	onap:ⁱ	onavi	onavi	ohavi
Sand	tuguvi ¹⁰	pasiwümb	pasiwəmbi	pasiwəmp	paziwümbi
Man			dainəp:ᵘ		tenəpu'ᵘ
Woman			waipü		waipü'ᵘ
Fire	kuna	goto	gotohunt ¹¹		kotop:; guna'
Smoke	kwip	kwip:	kwip:	kwip:	kwip:
Ash	gusip	gutsip	gutsip	gutsip	kutuzip
Sun	tave.	tave''nⁱ	tave'	tav	tave
Moon	müa	müa''ᴬ	müa'	müa	mü'ᴬ
Star	tatsiumb	ta:tsiümbi	ta:tsinump:ⁱ	tatsiümp:ⁱ	tazinumbe
Thunder	tombavitc	tombavitc; tomoyagat:	tomoyagait	tomoyagait	tomuyak
Wind	nued:ᵘ	nuait	nüet	nuet	nüaip:
Sky	tugumbⁱ	tugump:	tugump:	tugumbanavi; tugump:	tugump:
Lake	pagadud:	pagadut	pagadut:	paǵadüt	pagadüt:
White	tosagait:	tosagat	tosavit:	tosavit	tosaᵛⁱᵠᵘ
Black	tuhugaid:	tukat	tuuvit:	tuhuvit	tuhuᵛⁱᵠᵘ
Red	aŋgagaid:	aŋgagut	aŋgavit:	aŋgavit	äŋgaᵛⁱᵠᵘ
Blue	puigaid:	puigut	aivuⁱgĕt:	puivit	buhiᵛⁱᵠᵘ
Yellow	oakait:	oakat	o:apit:	ohapit	ohaᵖⁱᵠᵘ
North	gwianait	kwinahwet	kwinahe'	kwinahe'	kwinahenuŋwa
South	tavinait	yuwanaix	yuwahue'	yuwanai'	yuwanainuŋwa ¹²
East	tavendoinuŋwa	tavendoinaŋwat	tavendoinais ¹³	tavendoinaŋwa	tavendoinuŋwa
West	panait	taveyuwinaŋwat	taveyuinuŋwa	taveyuwinaŋwa	taveyuanuŋwa ¹⁴

---

⁷ bagunəp (fog).
⁸ Also, ku:tsiniqunt.
⁹ Also, yotsoquit.
¹⁰ pasiwamp (grave).
¹¹ guna (fire wood).
¹² yuwaix (warm), nais (side), nunwa (direction).
¹³ tave (sun), dloi (up), nais (side).
¹⁴ tave (sun), yua (down), nunwa (direction).

	Little Lake Shoshoni	Panamint-Death Valley Shoshoni	Lida Shoshoni	Kawich Mountains Shoshoni	Morey Shoshoni
One	süwü't:^{ü}	süwü't:	süwü'tü'	süwüt:	sümü'^{ü}
Two	waha't^{ü}	wat:	wa:tü'^{ü}	wa:t	wat^{ü}
Three	pa^{h}i't:^{ü}	pait:	baitü'^{ü}	pai:t:	bait^{ü}
Four	wa'tsũi	watsui$^{d\,ü}$	watsu$^{ɸ\,ü}$	watsũit	watsuit^{ü}
Five	manügi	manigi$^{d\,ü}$	manugit:^{ü}	manugit	manugit^{ü}
Six	navai	navai$^{d\,ü}$	na:vait^{ü}	nahwai	navait^{ü}
Seven	tats:ui	tatsui$^{d\,ü}$	ta:tsuit^{ü}	ta:tsũi	da:tsuit^{ü}
Eight	wásui	wásui$^{d\,ü}$	wá:suit^{ü}	wá:sui	wá:suit^{ü}
Nine	wanik:^{i}	waniki$^{d\,ü}$	kwanukit^{ü}	kwanuk:	suwu:tuwa
Ten	sũwăd^{o}	sũwăd^{ü}	sũũwanat:	sũwano	sü:wad^{ü}
Ankle	dambotsa	datsiŋgono	datsiŋgono	datsiŋgono	dawaigo'^{o}
Arm	budü	budüp	budü'	bü:də	buda'
Blood	pauopi	pawu'pi	pauwupi'^{i}	bü:p:	bü:pi'^{i}
Ear	n:üŋgi	năk:	nank	naŋgi	nănk
Eye	bui	bui	bu:i	bui	bu:i
Foot	n:ambi	nambi	nambe	nambe	nambe
Hair	tsop:ip:^{ü}	tsop:ip:	tsopip:	bambip	bambiwüp
Hand	má'^{a}	má'^{a}	má'^{a}	má'^{a}	má'^{a}
Head	bambi	bambi	pambi	bambi	bambi
Heart	bi^{h}wü	bi^{h}wü	bihwü	bihu	bih:u
Knee	daŋəp:^{ü}	daŋəp	daŋəp	taŋəp:	daŋəp^{i}
Mouth	dümbi	dümbi	tümbi	dümbi	dümbe
Nose	muvi	muvi	muvi	muvi	muvi'
Teeth	dăũwa	dăũwa	dăũwa	dăũwa	dăũwə'^{e}
Tongue	ego	ego	ego	ego	ego'
Liver	n:üwü	nüwü	nũwü	nũwü	nũwü'
Bone	ndzü'hi	^{n}dzüwip	dzuhi	dzuhi	dzü^{h}wi
Leg	n:uŋgwü'p^{ü}	nuŋgwüp	huŋup	huŋgəp	ă:'^{ă}
Antelope	wanzi	wüŋzi	wanzi	wanzitci'^{i}	kwahadü
Badger	huna	huna	hunatsi'^{i}	huna	huna
Bear	paha'witc	pahavitc	pahavitc	wüda	wü:dü'^{ü}
Coyote	icavaip	icavaip	icavaip	ija'p	ija'pü'^{ü}
Crow	kak:^{i}	kak:	kak:	kak:	hai
Deer	tüyü	tuyü	tü:yatsi'^{i}	tuhuya	duhuya
Eagle	kwiyă'^{ă}	kuyă'^{ă}	kwina'^{a}	kwina	(bia) gwina'
Elk	----------------	----------------	paduhuya	paduhuya	baduhuya
Fish	paŋwi	paŋgwi	paŋwitci'^{i}	paŋgwi	baŋgwi
Frog	woga't^{a}	woga't^{a}	pawago''^{o}	yagwatsa	
Gopher	y:avi'tc^{i}	yavitc:	yũa'vitc	yuavitc	iahavitc
Louse	poslats^{i}	poslats^{i}	posiavi	posiats	bosiats
Mountain lion.	tükumuts^{i}------	----------------	tukumüns; toya'doku'^{u}	toyadoku'^{u}	tukuwits
Mountain sheep.	naga; wásupi	wasu'pi	wasupi'^{i}	wasupi'^{i}	wásupi'^{i}
Rattlesnake	togo'a	togo'a	togo'a	togo'a	to'goa
Skunk	pon^{h}i'ats^{i}	poniats	ponhiats	ponhiats	bonhiats
Wolf	to^{h}pi------	----------------	----------------	biais	biaic
Jack rabbit	kamu	kamu	kamu	kamutsi'^{i}	ka^{h}mutsi
Cottontail	tavü'tsi	tabü'tsi	tavu'tsi	tavu'tsi	davotsi'^{i}
Pine nut	tuba	tuba	tuba	tuba	tuba
Sun flower	pa'akü	ak:^{ü}	ak:^{ü}	ak:^{ü}	aku'^{u}
Tule	tsaimbip^{ü}	tsaimbip:	saimimp	sai:p	saip:
Arrow	pagamboza	paga'mbüs	pagamboü'tsa	pagambo'tsa	hua'vi'
Bow	edu	edü	hu:edu	hu:edu	edu:
Cradle	kohno	kwa^{h}ü	gohnu	gohnu	gohnu
House	kahni	kahni	kahni	kahni	ghani
Metate	pot:o	bot:o	bo:to'	bo:to	boto
Muller	tusu	tusu	du:su	tu:su	dusu

[1] Literally, big hawk.

	Little Lake Shoshoni	Panamint-Death Valley Shoshoni	Lida Shoshoni	Kawich Mountains Shoshoni	Morey Shoshoni
Pipe	pahundo'ı	bahu'ndo'ı	pahundo'ı	pahundo'ı	bahundoi
Cloud	pagunəpü	pagu'nəp	pagunəp:	pagunəp:	bagunəp
Mountain	toya'vi	toya'vi	toyavi	toyavi	toyavi
Night	wüˣi	tugwa'ni	tugwa'nip:	tugwa'nip:	dugani
Rain	ūwa'dü	ūwa'dü	ūwadü; paūma'ᵃ	pāūuwəp	bahwavi
Rock	tümbi	tümbi	tumbi	tumbi	dumbi
Water	pa	pa	pa:	pa:	ba
Bad	kedzau'win:ü	tütsüp'u	tütsüpüdü	tütsüpü'dü	adzaitü
Good	tsauwi'nu	tsāūwi'nu	tsauwu'ndü	tsaudu'ndü	tzaundü
Large	piapuyu	piapü̃ʰʸü	pia'puᵈü	biu'nd	bia'ndü'
Small	tutsi'tsiu	tutsitsidü	tü:tcutci'ı	tü:tcutci'ı	dü:duitsi
Yes	hã'ᴬ	hã'ᴬ	hãduᴿº; hagia (?)	hã'ᴬ	hã'ᴬ
No	ke	ke	ke:	ke:	ke
Tobacco	pahu'mbi	pahumbi	pahumbi'	tamba'ho	bahu'
Hot	üdü'ina	üdüiŋdü	u:duina	u:duinᵃ	üdüint
Warm	yuʷina	yuwa'inᵗ	yuwaindü	yuwainᵃ	yuwaiʰ
Cold	iju'ih'ü	üjüiŋdü	üjü'ina	üjü'inᵃ	üjüint
Hard	kuta'mbuᴵ	kuta'mp:	küta'mp	kütam	kutan
Soft	yotso'kait	yotso'kwatsidü	yontsogwandü	yo'nsogonᵃ	yuwivitü
Nothing	kehümba'ı	kehümba'ı	kehi'mba'ı	kehi'nunt	ke'
Snow	taha'bi	taha'bi	taha'vi	taha'vi	dakavi
Salt	üŋwa'bi	ūwabi	ūwavi	üŋavi	uŋgwavi'
Sand	tugu'vi	pa'siŋump:	pasiŋwa'mbi	pasiwambi	basiamb
Man	tãŋwü'mü	taŋwa'mü	tãŋwumu'	tãŋwumu	daŋgwəp
Woman	wa'ipü'ü	wa'i'pü'ü	wai'ipü'ü	wai'ipü'ü	huvitci'ᴵᴵ
Fire	kuna	kuna	kuna	waiantᴵ	guna
Smoke	kukwi'pi	kukʷi'pi	kuki'p:; kuki'kün:ᴬ	(ku)kwip:	gwi:pi'
Ash	kutsa'pᴬ	kutu'sipᴵ	tugutsüp	kutusəp	kutagutsəp
Sun	tabi	tabi	tave	tave	davai
Moon	mü'a	mūa	mūˣa	mūa	mūa
Star	tatziu'mbi	tatsiu'mbi	daziumbi'ı	daziumbi	daziumbi
Thunder	toyagüdü	toyagadu	to:yagadᵃ	to:yagadᵃ	do:mbaij
Wind	nū'aidü	nūaidü	nū:aidü	nü:aipi	nüaipü'ü
Sky	tugu'mbanàbi	tugundu'banabi	tugumbi	tu:gu'mbi	dugu'mbi'ı
Lake	pabün'a	pabü'na	pavu'na	pavu'na	biavaᴵ
White	tosa'bitü	tosabitü	tosavi'tü'ü	tosavitü	tosavitü
Black	tupabitü	tupabitü	tupavi'tü'ü	tuuvitü	tüüvitü
Red	aŋga'pitü	aŋabitü	aŋgavitü'ü	aŋgavitü	ãŋgavitü
Blue	puwi'bitü	puwibitü	bui'vitü'ü	buivitü	buivitü
Yellow	huwümbitü	andupitu	ūa'pitü'	ūa'pitü	owapitü
North	kwia'ˣwipü	kwiaʰmitü	kwina'hipü'ü	kwina'hipu'ᵘ	gwia'haip
South	pita'pü	----------------	pi'tapü'ü	pitapu'ᵘ	bitanüŋgwa
East	tavedukü	tavündukü	tavaidu'kwa	tavaidukwa	tavainüŋgwa
West	panu'ŋgwa	----------------	pana'ŋgwatü	panaŋgwatü	yuwinuŋgwa

ᴵ Also, kutambuiʰyu.
ᴵ Probably "old woman" only, see p. 316.
ᴵ kuna, here and to the north, means firewood.
ᴵ Or kutsap.
ᴵ Literally "big water".

	Smith Creek Shoshoni	Battle Mountain Shoshoni	Elko Shoshoni	Egan Canyon Shoshoni
One	sumü'ä	sumu	sumü	sumu'
Two	watü'ä	wahat:	wat:	watu
Three	paitü'ʋ	paihit:	pait:	pait:
Four	watsuiøü'ä	watsuit:	watsuiø	watsui⁴
Five	manugiøü'ä	manugit:	manügiø	manugi⁴
Six	na:vaiøu	na:vait	nafaiø	navai⁴
Seven	da:sumiøü'ü	ta:tsuit	ta:tsuiø	ta:tsui
Eight	wá:suiøü'ä	wásuit	wásuiø	wásui
Nine	suwumihundü	suuwumihundi	suumin	suwumin⁴
Ten	sü:matü'ü	süümanot	süuwaø	suuma⁴
Ankle	dawinjogo'ᵒ	datsingono	datsingono	datsingono
Arm	buda'	buda	buda	bud:
Blood	pü:pi'⁴	büüp:	bü:p:	bü:p:
Ear	nangi	nang:⁴	nank	nänk
Eye	pu:i	buic	bui	bui
Foot	nambe	nambe	namp:	namp:
Hair	bămbiwup	bambiwüp	bambiwup	bambiwüp
Hand	má'⁴	má'⁴	má	má'⁴
Head	bămbi	bambi	bambi	bambi
Heart	bihyu'	bih•	bihʰ	bih
Knee	dănəp⁴	danəp:	danəp	danəp
Mouth	tumbe	dümbi	dump:	dümp:
Nose	muvi'⁴	muvi	mup:	mup:⁴
Teeth	dauma'•	da:ma	dauwi	daum:
Tongue	ego'ᵒ	ego	egᵒ	ego
Liver	nü'mü'	nümü	nüwü	nüwü
Bone	dzuhni	zuhni	zunh⁴	zunhi
Leg	öhö'ö	á:; düdüguo	áhⁱ	á'á
Antelope	kwahada ¹	kwahadu ¹	kwahadu; wazi ¹	kwahad:ᵘ ²
Badger	huna	huna	huna	huna
Bear	wü:düa ³	wüda	wüdü	wüdü'
Coyote	ija''a	ijapü'ä ⁴	ija' ⁵	ijapu'ᵘ; icavaip
Crow	hai	hai	hai	hai
Deer	duhuya'	duhuyə	duhuyu ⁶	duhuyu ⁶
Eagle	kwina	biagwana:	biägwina	biägwina
Elk	paduhuya	baduhuya	paduhuya	paduhuyu
Fish	pangwi	bankʷⁱ	bănkwⁱ	băngwi
Frog	baiyagwadza ⁷	payagwani	payagwats	payagwats
Gopher	yuhavitc	yuhavitc	iyavitc	iyavitc
Louse	posia	bosia	posia	pasia
Mountain lion		toyaduko	toyaduko	toyaduko
Mountain sheep	wasupi'⁴	wasup: ⁸	wasup:	wasup; muzambia
Rattlesnake	togoa	dogo	dogoa	togoa
Skunk	pohiats	pohiats	ponhiats	ponhiats
Wolf	biaic	biaais ⁹	biaija	biaic
Jack rabbit	kaʰmu	kama	tu:kamu; kamu	kamu
Cottontail	tavü'ü	tavo	tavo	tab:ᵘ
Pine nut	duba	tuba	tuba	tuba
Sun flower	akü'ä		ak:	ak:
Tule	saip:		saip	saip:
Arrow	huavi: hu:paga	hua	hü:ed	hupag; hu:ed ¹⁰

¹ Either term used genetically.
² kwahada (doe); wanzi (buck).
³ Also, padua'•; tambaha.
⁴ Used also in myths.
⁵ icavaip in myths.
⁶ Or sogo duhuyu.
⁷ Also paiyaqwani.
⁸ Ram is wasup: or dukwa; ewe, mütsambia.
⁹ In myths is icavaip (or coyote?).
¹⁰ Also bak:.

	Smith Creek Shoshoni	Battle Mountain Shoshoni	Elko Shoshoni	Egan Canyon Shoshoni
Bow	aiduko'^{o}	ediko [11]	ediko	ed:u
Cradle	gohno'^{o}	kohnu	koh^{ou}	koh^{ou}
House	gahni	kahni	kahni	kahni
Metate	potö'^{ö}	bot:	bot:	bot:
Muller	tusu'	dus:	dus:	tus:
Pipe	to'i	do'i [12]	doi [12]	toi
Cloud	to:p: [13]	to:p [13]	to:p:	bagunəp
Mountain	toyavi	toyavi	toyavi	toyavi
Night	tugə'pi'^{i} [14]	tu:gani	tugwani	tugwani
Rain	paüməpi'	ba'ümat	pahump:	pagumət
Rock	tumbi'	dumbi	tumbi	tumbi
Water	pa	ba	pa	ba
Bad	azanitü'	kejant	kejant	üzüit; kejant
Good	tsa:ndü'	zand:	sauünd	sauünd
Large	pia'püdü'^{ü}	biəp:	biəp:	biand:
Small	tui'dütsi'^{i}	duitutsi	düyu	dühu^{tsi}
Yes	hă'^{ă}	hă'^{ă}	hă'^{ă}	hă'^{ă}
No	ke	ke	ge:	ke
Tobacco	pahö'^{ö}	baho	bah^{u}	bah$^{u.}$
Hot	üdüin:^{a}	uduin	üdüiŋ	üdüin^{t}
Warm	yuwai	yuwai	yuwaix	zaiyuwaix
Cold	üjüina	üjüi	üjüin	üijüin
Hard	kutaiyo	kutand:	gutai	nadiam
Soft	yonzogaiyo	yonsogand:	yotsogai	yotsogi
Nothing	kehi'mbai	kehimba; nonütüp:	kehimba	kehiuŋg^{unt}
Snow	ovida'^{a}	takavi	takavi	takavi
Salt	ohavi'	ohavi	ohavi	onavi
Sand	pasiwambi	pasiwambi	pasiwumb:	pasiamb:
Man	tăŋgwa'^{a}	----------	nüwü	denəpü'^{ü}
Woman	waipü'^{ü}	----------	waip:	waipü'^{ü}
Fire	gu:na	wehüpün:	kuna	kuna
Smoke	hwi:pi'^{i}	gwip	----------	kwip
Ash	kutusəp:	kutuzip	kutsəp	kusip
Sun	tave	dave	tave	tabe
Moon	müa	müa	mua	müa
Star	tatzüümbi	tă:tsinumbi	taziümbi	taziəmb:
Thunder	to:yăgik:	toyagitugi	to:yük	toəmbebito
Wind	nüai'pi'^{i}	nuepuid:	nü'a	nüed:
Sky	tugu'mbi'^{i}	tu:gumbi	tugümp:	tugumb
Lake	paga't:ü	bagadüt	bagat:	babagadüt
White	tosaøü	to:savit	tosaviø	tosaviø
Black	tuhuviøü	tuhuvit	tuuviø	tuuviø
Red	ăŋgaviøü	aŋgavit	ăŋgaviø	ăŋgaviø
Blue	puhiviøü	ebuhivit	buiviø	buiviø
Yellow	o:hapiøü	ohapit:	o:aviø	o:apiø^{ü}
North	kwinahinaŋgwaøü'	kwinahanuŋwat	kwinahan^{ü}	kwinahaipun^{t} [15]
South	panaŋgwaøu'	pa:naŋwat [16]	----------	tunavunt
East	tavenaŋgwaøü'^{ü}	tavendoinuŋwat	davenuŋwa	tavenait
West	yuwinaŋgwaøü'^{ü}	(tave)yuinuŋwat	yuwinuŋwa [17]	yuwinait

[11] Or hu: (wood) ed:.
[12] Or pahu (tobacco) ndoi.
[13] Pagunəp (fog).
[14] dugani (midnight).
[15] kwina (north) hai (side) pun^{t} (direction).
[16] pa: (below) naŋwat (side or direction).
[17] Yuwi (warm).

EXTENSIONS OF KINSHIP TERMS

[Parentheses indicate partial extensions]

	Fraternal polyandry practiced	M=MSs=FBW=StM	F=FB=MSsH=StF	S=StS=MnBS=WmSsS	D=StD=WmSsD=MnBD	H=HB=WmSsH	W=WSs=MnBW	Cross-cousin marriage practiced	Pseudo cross-cousin marriage practiced	MB=WF=HF=FSsH	FSs=WM=HM=MBW	HSs=WmBW=WmSWM=WmDHM	WB=MnSsH=MnSWF=MnDHF	Distinguishing terms for cross-cousins	WmB=WmSWF=WmDHF	MnSs=MnSWM=MnDHM	♂XC=WB=MnSsH=MnSWF=MnDHF	♀XC=HSs=WmBW=WmSWM=WmDHM	B=♂C; Ss=♀C	MB=FSsH only; FSs=MBW only	WB=MnSsH only; HSs=WmBW only
NP-FSp	−	−	−	−	−	−	−	−	−	−	−	−	−	−	−	−	−	−	−	+	+
NP-FLk	−	−	−	−	−	−	−	−	−	−	−	−	−	−	−	−	−	−	−	+	+
NP-GeoCr	−	−	−	−	−	−	−	−	−	−	−	−	−	−	−	−	−	−	+	+?	+
NP-LnPn	−	−	−	−	−	−	−	−	−	−	−	−	−	−	−	−	−	−	+	+?	+
NP-MC	−	−	−	−	−	−	−	−	−	−	−	−	−	−	−	−	−	−	+	+	+
S-LtLk	−?	−	−	−	−	−	−	−	−?	−	−	−	−	−	−	−	−	−	+	+	+
S-Lida	−?	−	−	−	−	−	−	−	−?	−	−	−	−	−	−	−	−	−	+	+	+
S-Belm	−?	−	−	−	−	−	−	−	?	−	−	−	−	−	−	−	−	−	+	+	+
S-GSmV	−?	−	−	−	−	−	−	?	?	−	−	−	−	−	−	−	−	−	+	+	+
S-RsRi	−?	+	−	−	−	+	+	−	+	+	+	−	−	−	−	−	−	−	−	−	+
S-SmCr	?	+	−	−	−	−	+	?	?	+	+	−	−	−	−	−	−	−	+	−	+
S-Mor	+	−	−	−	−	+	+	−	+	+	+	−	−	−	−	−	−	−	−	−	+
S-Hmlt	+	−	−	?	?	+	+	?	?	+	+	?	?	(+)	−	−	−	−	−	−	+
S-Ely	+	−	−	−	−	+	+	+	+	+	−	−	−	−	−	+	−	−	−	+	+
S-SprV	+	−	−	−	−	+	+	−	+	+	+	?	?	+	+	+	−	−	−	−	?
GS-SklV	+	(+)	(+)	−	−	?	?	+	+	(+)	(+)	?	?	−	?	?	?	−	(+)	−	?
GS-DpCr	−	−	−	(+)	+	+	+	+	+	+	+	(+)	−	−	−	−	−	+	−	−	(+)
S-Egan	+	−	−	?	?	+	+	+	+?	+	+	+	+	?	−	−	+	−	−	−	−?
S-RubV	+	(+)	(+)	?	?	?	?	+	+	+?	+?	?	?	+	?	?	?	−	−?	−?	−?
S-Elko	−	+	−	(+)	(+)	+	+	+	+	+	+	+	+	+	+	+	−	−	−	−	−
S-BtlM	+	+	−	+	+	+	+	−	+	+	+	+	+	+	−	−	+	−	−	−	−
S-NthFk	+?	+	−	+	+	+	+	−?	+?	+	+	+	+	?	−	−	−	−	−	−	−
S-SnRv	+	+	+	+	+	+	+	−	+	+	+	+	+	+	−	+	+	−	−	−	−
S-GrsCr	+	+	+	+	+	+	+	−	+	+	+	+	+	−	+	+	−	−	(+)	−	−
S-Prom	(+)	+	+	+	+	+	+	−	−	(+)	(+)	+	+	?	+	+	−	−	(+)	(+)	−
S-FtHl	+	+	+	+	+	+	+	−	+	(+)	(+)	+	+	−	+	+	−	−	(+)	(+)	−
NP-Ban	(+)	−	−	(+)	(+)	+	+	−	+	(+)	(+)	+	+	−	−	−	−	−	(+)	(+)	−
S-Lemhi	+	+	+	+	+	+	+	−	+	−	(+)	+	+	−	+	+	−	−	(+)	(+)	−

APPENDIX C.—KINSHIP TERMS

Though kinship terms may provide clues to the possible presence of certain features of the social structure and of behavior of kin toward one another, the actual correlation of those features with terms is entirely a question of empirical fact. Terms may not be used a priori to deduce those features.

Kinship terms were collected from 31 localities scattered throughout part of the Basin-Plateau area. The schedules, a few of which are incomplete, are given on pages 297–306. Comparison of the terms with the outstanding features of the social groups (accompanying table and fig. 13) demonstrates emphatically that despite certain broad correlations, a cause and effect relationship between the latter and the former which was automatic and inevitable is not indicated. Peculiar features of the terminologies seem to have developed in response to social custom in some localities but not in others and to have spread to groups not possessing those customs. In certain

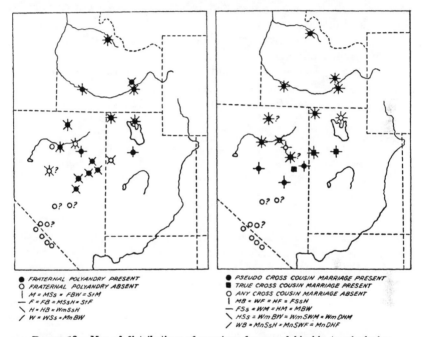

● FRATERNAL POLYANDRY PRESENT
○ FRATERNAL POLYANDRY ABSENT
| M = MSs = FBW = SiM
— F = FB = MSsH = SiF
\ H = HB = WmSsH
/ W = WSs = MnBW

● PSEUDO CROSS COUSIN MARRIAGE PRESENT
■ TRUE CROSS COUSIN MARRIAGE PRESENT
○ ANY CROSS COUSIN MARRIAGE ABSENT
| MB = WF = HF = FSsH
— FSs = WM = HM = MBW
\ HSs = WmBW = WmSWM = WmDHM
/ WB = MnSsH = MnSWF = MnDHF

FIGURE 13.—Map of distributions of marriage forms and kinship terminologies.

instances there was a possible choice of several terminologies, any of which would have been consistent with social usage. And, finally, some features of the terminologies have no relation whatever to social practice. In short, historic, linguistic, and psychological factors as well as functional necessity have obviously combined in different ways to produce the terms.

Several features of kinship terms which seem to rest upon social custom occur throughout the area. These are extensions of terms in accordance with the preference for multiple marriages between two families, wherein brothers marry sisters or a brother and a sister marry a sister and brother of another family. Terminology reflecting this practice may in addition reflect cross-cousin marriage where the latter occurs.

Certain features are limited in distribution and correlate partly with the intensification of the levirate which led to fraternal polyandry and with the intensification of the sororate which led to sororal polygyny. Whereas the latter was universal in the area, however, the correlation of appropriate peculiarities of the terminology with it was not complete. Other features of the terminology are largely limited to those localities practicing cross-cousin or pseudo crosscousin marriage (marriage with the stepchild of a cross aunt or uncle). Each of these is discussed below and the data are summarized in the table.

More extended inquiry into kinship would undoubtedly reveal further correlations and lack of correlations of practices with the terminology. These were beyond the scope of the present study. Only the salient facts are treated here.

Abbreviations used (from Gifford, 1922, p. 14) are as follows:

B	brother	Mn	man	Y	younger
C	cousin	O	older	G	grand
Ch	child	P	parent	Gr G	great grand
D	daughter	S	son	St	step
F	father	Ss	sister	I	in-law
H	husband	W	wife	(ms)	man speaking
M	mother	Wm	woman	(ws)	woman speaking
X	cross				

Grandparent-grandchild terms.—A universal feature of Shoshonean terminology is the segregation of the four grandparents and the use of a reciprocal term between each of them and the grandchild. There is no obvious sociological reason for this. Such terms involve a distinction by sex of the person spoken to when used for the grandparents but a distinction by sex of the person speaking when used for the grandchildren. The same terms are used reciprocally with the great-aunts and great-uncles. These are very similar in all groups.

A single reciprocal term was probably used in most localities between the great-grandparents and great-grandchildren. The term was "dzo, zo, jo," etc., which, appropriately, means "feeble one."

A term for the great-great-grandparent and great-great-grandchild was sought in only a few localities. S–Prom, and GS–DpCr called the Gr Gr G P bia (big) dzo'ᵒ. S–Prom called the Gr Gr G Ch dui (little) jo'ᵒ; GS–DpCr used the diminutive form, dzo'otsi. S–BtlM, S–Lemhi, S–FtHl, and S–GrsCr denied having a term, saying that these relatives were too infrequently contemporary. S–SnRv used geʰ, literally "no," that is, not related.

Most other features of the terminologies accord to some degree
with usages common to the entire area. Especially they reflect preference for the levirate, sororate, and marriage of several children in
one family to several in another. Though marriage with relatives
of any kind was ordinarily prohibited, a few localities practiced
pseudo cross-cousin marriage and true cross-cousin marriage, both
of which somewhat affected the terms. Polyandry also had an
appreciable effect upon them.

Aunts, uncles, nieces, nephews.—All areas distinguished cross and
parallel aunts and uncles. Where polyandry was not practiced
parallel aunts and uncles were also distinguished from parents. In
these localities, however, the father's brother was identified with the
stepfather, which accords with the levirate, and with the mother's
sister's husband, which accords with the marriage of brothers to
sisters, or, perhaps with the combined effect of the levirate and sororate. Similarly, the mother's sister was identified with the stepmother and the father's brother's wife. Some of the Northern Paiute
terms for father's brother, natsugu, may have been descriptive, possibly being na, progenitor + tsugu, old man.

Terms for parallel nieces and nephews are more or less consistent
with the last, though there is some tendency to lump them according
to sex instead of relationship alone. These terms are predominantly
descriptive. Thus, Shoshoni north of Little Lake used duitc or
duivitc (little boy) for any parallel nephew and dogombia (literally,
daughter's child's mother) for any parallel niece. As dogo is extended to mother's father's brothers, dogombia would be literally
correct for a man's brother's daughter, who is his dogo's mother. It
is not correct for a man's sister's daughter, but is nonetheless used.
The use of a reciprocal term between the parallel nieces and nephews
and the aunts and uncles is extremely rare.

Cross aunts and uncles are distinguished from parallel aunts and
uncles and, unlike the latter, are never identified with the parents.
Moreover, among all Shoshoni a reciprocal term is used between
them and the cross niece and nephew. Ada is used reciprocally for
the mother's brother, baha for the father's sister. Though it is difficult to see that there was anything inevitable about such reciprocal
terms, they were expedient in this case as these aunts and uncles
never became one's parents. Parallel aunts and uncles, on the other
hand, frequently became parents through the levirate and sororate,
so that reciprocal terms could not conveniently be used. Paiute,
with no less reason than Shoshoni to use reciprocal terms with cross
aunts and uncles, did not do so.

Cross aunt and uncle terms were extended in all localities in a manner to accord with the marriage of a brother and sister to a sister and

brother. The term for mother's brother was also used for father's sister's husband, whether the latter was actually the mother's brother or not. The term for father's sister was also used for mother's brother's wife, whether she was actually the father's sister or not. Where cross-cousin and pseudo cross-cousin marriage was practiced, these terms were further extended to parents-in-law. It is probable that in all localities the term for a woman's brother's son or daughter was also used for her husband's sister's son or daughter, and that the word for a man's sister's son or daughter was also used for his wife's brother's son or daughter, though conclusive information on this point is lacking.

Two Northern Paiute localities followed unusual usage about which there may be some doubt. NP–MC used huza'ʼⁱ for a man's stepchild and parallel niece and nephew; mido'ʼᵒ for a woman's stepchild and for both parallel and cross niece and nephew; nanakʷᵃ for a man's cross niece and nephew. NP–Ban used mido'ʼᵒ for a woman's parallel or cross niece or nephew; nanak:wa for a man's cross niece or nephew; duwa for a man's parallel niece or nephew.

Brother, sister, and cousin.—All localities distinguished older from younger brother and sister, thus using four terms. Some Shoshoni extended these terms to cousins. Those not practicing cross-cousin or pseudo cross-cousin marriage often extended them to all cousins. Those practicing these types of marriage usually extended them, if at all, only to parallel cousins, and addressed cross cousins with other terms mentioned below. NP–FSp and NP–FLk distinguished all cousins from brothers and sisters, using vua'ʼⁱ for a cousin of the same sex as the speaker and jäü or säü for a cousin of the opposite sex. It is probable that NP–LnPn and NP–GeoCr used these same cousin terms in addition to following the Shoshoni custom of identifying cousins with brothers and sisters.

Several Shoshoni in the central part of the area had special cousin terms which distinguished them by sex but not by relationship. These were S–Lida, S–Belm, S–Mor, and S–RsRi using dăngumbua for a male cousin, though the last also used zugubua. GS–DpCr used daga. S–Lida and S–Belm used niwa for a female cousin. S–Mor, S–RsRi used awasawa' or auwasauwüpü (signifying half sister). GS–DpCr used sauwupu'.

S–GSmV distinguished all cousins from brothers and sisters by bua'ᵃ.

Several Shoshoni localities in addition to extending brother and sister terms to cousins also used separate terms to distinguish cousins by sex. Male cousin: Dui or daga, S–Lemhi; daga, S–FtHl, S–GrsCr, GS–SklV (but F Ss S was called "brother" or bitcogwe, B l at GS–SklV); dui, S–BtlM. Female cousin: Sauwü, S–Lemhi

STEWARD] APPENDICES

(awasauwupu for more distant than first cousin; sau'mo, S–FtHl
(also saumopü) ; saumapu, S–GrsCr ; sauwupu', GS–SklV (but F Ss
D called "wife" or "sister").

Where cross-cousin marriage was not practiced there is no obvious
sociological reason for the fact that some localities extended brother
and sister terms to cousins whereas other localities distinguished
cousins in various ways. The smallness of Western Shoshoni villages, wherein one was unlikely to live in the proximity of many
cousins, may have contributed to their frequent failure to distinguish cousins from brothers and sisters but cannot account for all
the different usages.

Relatives by marriage.—Husband and wife were distinguished
from all other relatives except in those localities practicing polyandry, mentioned below.

Except where real or pseudo cross-cousin marriage or polyandry
were practiced, terms for brother-in-law, sister-in-law, parents-in-law,
and children-in-law followed a simple system. According with the
marriage of a brother and sister to a sister and brother, one term was
used for wife's brother and a man's sister's husband and another
term for husband's sister and a woman's brother's wife. The first term
was usually either distinctive or was the term dej or daitc which was
used in other localities for cousin. The second term was usually
wadapia among Paiute and bahambia among Shoshoni, meaning
literally in both cases a woman's brother's child's mother. According with the marriage of brothers to sisters, one term was used for
wife's sister and a man's brother's wife and another term for husband's brother and a woman's sister's husband. The first term was
usually huza (Paiute) or osa (Shoshoni) the meaning of which is
not known+pia or bia, mother. The second term is huza+na,
father, in Paiute. When it is osambia in Shoshoni it is probably
incorrect.

Terms for the spouses of brothers-in-law and sisters-in-law seem
seldom to have been fixed. They depended largely upon any previous relationship to such persons. If there were no relationship, various words were used and these were sometimes also applied to
cousins. A few examples are:

Wife's sister's husband: Gadavü'a'ᵃ (rival), NP–FSp; kadavüa''ᵃ
NP–FLk; gwadubua (friend), S–LtLk; daŋgombua (cousin), S–
Lida.

Wife's brother's wife and husband's brother's wife: Jãū (cousin),
NP–Fsp; sãu, NP–FLk; gwadubua, S–LtLk; "sister" if actually a
sister, otherwise no term, S–Lida.

Husband's brother's wife: Jãū, NP–FSp; sãū, NP–FLk;· gwadubua, S–LtLk and S–Lida.

Parent-in-law terms were usually one of two types where cross-cousin marriage was not practiced. In the southern part of the area, among both Paiute and Shoshoni, a single term designated any parent-in-law. Farther north, NP–MC, NP–Ban, and S–Ely used also a single term, though NP–Ban also used terms according with cross-cousin marriage. In the region of Great Salt Lake, Shoshoni designated some or all parents-in-law by modified grandparent terms which trace the relationship through the child. S–Prom and S–Lemhi used uduŋdogo (their M F) for W F, uduŋgago (their M M) for W M, uduŋguno (their F F) for H F, and uduhutsi (their F M) for H M. Baha (F Ss) was also used for H M, which accords with cross-cousin marriage. GS–DpCr used gunotsi (F F) for H F and utsi (F M) for H M, but cross aunt for W M and cross uncle for W F. GS–SklV used cross aunt or uncle terms or: numudogo (our M F) for W F; numugago (our M M) for W M; numuhutsi (our F M) for H M. S–GrsCr used guno for H F, and numuhutsi for H M. S–FtHl used numudogo for W F, numungago for W M, numuhutsi or baha (F Ss) for H M; ada (M B) for H F.

Cross-cousin marriage tended to bring about the substitution of cross aunt and uncle terms for parents-in-law.

Terms for the descending generation were less sensitive for the effect of cross-cousin marriage. Even where cross-cousin marriage was practiced, cross niece and nephew terms were rarely extended to children-in-law, in spite of the fact that the frequent reciprocal use of these terms would seem to have made it easy. Instead, children-in-law were usually indicated by a modified grandchild term describing the relationship.

There were several ways of indicating the relationship to the daughter's husband. In the southern part of the area, Northern Paiute used dogona' (a man's daughter's child's father) and Shoshoni used dogonəp (D Ch F, ms). Though literally correct only when used by a man for his son-in-law, women also used it. In the central and northern part of the area, Shoshoni of both sexes used monəp (said to be derived from mununduh, "to get a son-in-law"+ap:, father). In addition, S–SnRv and S–NthFk also called the son-in-law dogoəpü (ms) and gagoəpü (ws).

For son's wife, NP–FSp and NP–FLK used mövi or wövi, the etymology of which is unknown to me. Most other localities designated this relative through her relationship to the grandchild. The most common term was hutsombia (hutsi, a woman's son's child+bia, mother) which is literally correct when used by a woman for her daughter-in-law but, though incorrect for men was used by them nonetheless. Only two Shoshoni localities, S–NthFk and S–SnRv, made the logical distinction, men using gunombia (S Ch M, ms) and women using hutsombia (S Ch M, ws). NP–MC and NP–Ban, on the other hand, used gunupia when either sex was speaking. At S–Egan, only women used hutsombia, men using duaŋgwuh (literally son's wife). GS–SklV also used ada (ms).

In the southern half of the area, including even several localities practicing pseudo cross-cousin marriage, parents of a married couple addressed one another by a single term. These were Mükic'ɪ, NP–FSp and NP–FLk; daiyump, etc., Shoshoni; dai, NP–MC; ta'äū, SP–LV; aivuintc, S–Hmlt and S–Ely. NP–GeoCr apparently used the Paiute term, mukici, for Ch F l and the Shoshoni term, dainup, for Ch M l. Elsewhere, the terms for children's parents accord partly or wholly with cross-cousin marriage and are discussed below.

Effects of polyandry.—Most groups had terms for father, mother, son, daughter, husband, and wife to distinguish them from all other relatives. Where polyandry was practiced, however, parent and child terms were often extended to other relatives. In 6 of the 15 localities practicing polyandry, "father" was extended to father's brother, mother's sister's husband, and stepfather. Sometimes it was qualified as, for example, "little father" or "temporary father." One locality similarly extended "father" but was said by informants not to practice polyandry. There is some possibility, however, that the informant was in error regarding polyandry. Eight groups practicing polyandry, however, did not extend "father."

Though polygyny was preferably sororal everywhere in the 28 localities studied it entailed extension of "mother" to mother's sister, father's brother's wife, and stepmother in only 12 localities. Nine of these 12 localities practiced polyandry; seven of them similarly extended "father." Owens Valley Paiute and Southern Shoshoni, who stressed the sororate and sororal polygyny to the extent of exacting a penalty for their avoidance, did not extend "mother."

Thus it appears that in the area where the intensified levirate led to fraternal polyandry extension of "father" tended to but did not necessarily occur. The extension of "mother," though having a sociological basis everywhere, may have occurred primarily in the localities practicing polyandry as a psychological parallel to the extension of "father" and spread to the 5 localities which did not extend "father." There is no evidence that it was specifically caused in these localities by matrilocal residence or other factors stressing relationship to the maternal relatives in an unusual degree.

Extension of the terms for son and daughter seems to be a similar phenomenon. Of the 15 localities practicing polyandry, 8 extended "son" and "daughter" to include stepchildren and parallel nieces and nephews. Two other localities not practicing polyandry made similar extensions. Five and possibly 8 localities practicing polyandry did not extend them.

All localities practicing polyandry extended "husband" to husband's brother and to a woman's sister's husband and extended "wife" to wife's sister and to a man's brother's wife. In fact, similar extensions were made in 4 other localities, 2 of which were said not to have practiced polyandry and 2 of which were in doubt about it. These localities adjoined those which did practice polyandry, however.

Extension of parent and child terms were:

S–SmCr, S–RsRi, S–BtlM, S–Elko, S–SnRv, and S–NthFk used biatsi (diminutive of bi: 'i or bia, mother) for M Ss, F B W, and St M. S–SnRv used aputsi (diminutive of apu, father) for F B, M Ss H, and St F. The other five localities did not extend "father," but used a different term for F B, M Ss H, and St F.

These six localities did not consistently extend child terms. S–SmCr and S–RsRi did not extend them at all. The others extended them as follows:

S–BtlM used dua (or naduivitci; na in Shoshoni indicates that the child's biological father was another man; na is the common Northern Paiute stem for father; duivitci means boy and also is the diminutive of dua, son, being used commonly for parallel nephews) for S, St S and parallel nephew; bedüpü for D; bedu (or nanaivi; na+naivi, girl) for St D, and parallel niece. Naduivitci and nanaivi were preferred for St S and St D.

S–Elko used dua for S and St S (ms); dua or duivitci for St S (ws) and Ss S (ws); bedu for D and Ss D (ws); bedu or dogombia for St D (ms); bedu or nanaivi for St D (ws). This is a combination of the common parallel niece and nephew terms and extended child terms, women extending farther than men.

S–SnRv and S–NthFk used dua for S and parallel nephew; dua or naduivitc¹ for St S (ws); naduivitc¹ for St S (ms); bedu for D, parallel niece and St D (ws); bedu or nanaivi for St D (ms).

S–Egan, which extended neither parent term, partially extended child terms. It used dua for S and St S (ms); bet (from bedüpü, daughter) for St D (ws) and parallel nephew. These are inconsistent, however, and may be incorrect.

S–Lemhi and S–FtHl extended parent terms as follows: They used bia for M and F B W; biavia (big mother) for M O Ss; nagühavia (nagüha, additional, JPe or temporary, AP) for M Y Ss; ügübia (ügü, new) for St. M; ap:ü for F; biap:ü (big father) for F O B, M O St H; nagühap:ü for F Y B, M Y Ss H; ügüap:ü for St F. In addition, S–FtHl used also bia for F B W, M Ss, and St M; ap:ü for F, F B, M Ss H, and St F.

GS–SklV extended parent terms and also used special terms for parallel aunts and uncles. It used ap:ü for F; dzuguna for F O B; detcuguna for F Y B; probably biap:u for F O B if married to the mother; bia for M; nabiavia for M O Ss; naduivia for M Y Ss; but doka (which is M Ss at GS–DpCr) for F O B W; duidoka for F Y B W. Child terms were not extended.

S–Lemhi extended child terms. It used duadügi for St S; dua for S and parallel nephew; bedudügi for St D; bedu for D and parallel niece.

S–FtHl extended child terms. It used dua for S, St S, and parallel nephew; bedu for D, St D and parallel niece. Though dua is used for the true St S, if a child were adopted or if a man's wife were known to have had a child by another man, the man called this boy duadügi (dügi, to keep).

S–RubV data are incomplete, but it used apüundoi in addition to the usual term, hai, for F B; biatsi in addition to the usual term, dokatsi, for M Ss.

S–Prom used bia for M and St M; biavia for M O Ss and F O B W; duivia for M Y Ss and F Y B W; ap:u (or dzuguna, which was used in Nevada for F B) for St. F; biap:ü for F O B and M O Ss H; nagahuap:u or duap:ü (little father) for F Y B; duap:u for M Y Ss H. Distinguished thus, these correlate with the marriage of several brothers to several sisters rather than with the levirate and sororate. Possibly GS–SklV used similar terms, though the schedule is incomplete and unreliable. GS–DpCr, like southern Nevada, distinguished these relatives by different terms.

S–GrsCr used bia for M, F B W, and St M; biavia for M O Ss; duivia for M Y Ss; dokatsi, which is used elsewhere for M Ss, for St M; ap:ə for F, F B, M Ss H, and St F; also, biap:ə for F O B; dulap:ə for F Y B; dzuguna, which is used elsewhere for F B, for St. F. This combines the usages of both the northern and southern areas.

S–Prom and S–GrsCr extensions of child terms were: Dua for S, St S, and parallel nephew; bedu or bedəpü'ü for D; bedu for St D, and parallel niece. S–Prom also used duivitc interchangeably with dua.

NP–Ban, though not extending parent terms, used duwa' for S, St S, and B S (ms); badü' for D and St D.

GS–DpCr used duəp for S; duanadia for St S and B S (ms); bedəp for D; bedunadia for St D and parallel niece.

SP–LV used ha" muən: (ha", F Y B+muən:, father) for St F; piən:' for M and M Ss; mumpiən:' for St M; tuən:' for S and St S; patciən:' for D and St D.

The terms for husband and wife usually had the prefix nagaha or nani, temporary, when extended. Husband was extended to husband's brother and a woman's sister's husband; wife to wife's sister and a man's brother's wife. The terms for these relatives are arranged in parallel columns on page 304.

Effects of cross-cousin marriage.—True cross-cousin marriage was practiced in five and possibly six localities. Pseudo cross-cousin marriage was practiced in 15 and possibly 16 localities, including the last. Several features of kinship terminology accord with such marriage and have a high though not complete correlation with it.

All localities practicing some form of cross-cousin marriage, except S–Ely, extended the terms for cross aunts and uncles to parents-in-law. Mother's brother was extended not only to father's sister's husband but also to husband's or wife's father. Father's sister was extended not only to mother's brother's wife but to husband's or wife's mother. The only locality making such extensions but practicing no form of cross-cousin marriage was S–Prom. For parents-in-law, it used not only terms tracing relationship through the child, but ada (M B) for wife's father and baha (F Ss) for wife's mother. The extensions in six of the localities practicing cross-cousin marriage were incomplete. That is, in addition to or instead of extending cross aunt and uncle terms to certain parents-in-law, terms traced their relationship through the children. The most common of these terms were: oduŋguno (their, i. e., the children's father's father) for husband's father; odundogo or numudogo (their mother's father) for wife's father; odungago or numugago (their mother's mother) for wife's mother; numuhutsi (their father's mother) for husband's mother. Though not specifically related to cross-cousin marriage, these terms are not inconsistent with it, being, in fact, noncommittal.

Forms of cross-cousin marriage did not entail a similar extension of cross niece and nephew terms to children-in-law, except in two localities. S–SprV used bahatsi (brother's son, ws) for a woman's child-in-law, the terms for a man's child-in-law being in some doubt. S–Elko used cross niece and nephew terms for children-in-law, except that a woman's daughter's husband was called duivitc (son or boy) or monəp: ü and a man's daughter's husband was called monəp: ü in addition to ada. This may be an error in recording.

Another feature according with some form of cross-cousin marriage was the equation of husband's sister with a woman's brother's wife and a woman's son's wife's mother or daughter's husband's mother. This occurred in 10 of the 15 or 16 localities with cross-cousin marriage and in one locality, S–Prom, without it. The Shoshoni term commonly used for these relatives was bahambia (NP–MC, adadzipia), literally woman's brother's child's mother. None used the word for female cross-cousin.

The same localities, with the exception of GS–DpCr, equated wife's brother with a man's sister's husband and a man's son's wife's father or daughter's husband's father. The term commonly used was dej or detc, the primary meaning of which seems to have been wife's brother. But three localities, S–Egan, S–Elko, and S–BtlM, used it also to distinguish male cross-cousins from female cross-cousins and parallel-cousins.

S–SprV extended niwa, a cross-cousin of either sex, to wife's brother, to man's sister's husband and to woman's brother's wife. The term for husband's sister is not known.

Complete consistency with the extensions of the terms for husband's sister and wife's brother would have involved a woman calling her daughter's husband's father or son's wife's father "brother" and a man calling his daughter's husband's mother or son's wife's mother "sister." Only six localities did so. All but one of these practiced some form of cross-cousin marriage and all made the extensions of terms for husband's sister and wife's brother mentioned above. Only two of these six localities completely distinguished cross-cousins from parallel-cousins and from brothers and sisters. The other four extended brother and sister terms to all cousins but used in addition special cousin terms.

At several localities, instead of using brother or sister for a child's parent-in-law of the opposite sex, other terms were used. S–SnRv and S–NthFk used dainump:, the term used south of the area of cross-cousin marriage for any parent-in-law of one's child. S–Egan used sauupü', GS–DpCr used sauwupu and S–Elko probably used sauupa, a term which is used elsewhere for all cousins and sometimes designates siblings collectively. S–Prom used sauwa in addition to "brother" and "sister." S–BtlM used nanadainümp.

It has previously been pointed out that terms for brother and sister were often extended to all cousins. In the region of cross-cousin marriage, however, these tended to be restricted to parallel-cousins. Eight localities, probably all of which practiced some form of cross-cousin marriage, had special terms for cross-cousins, which, however, were usually extended, as previously mentioned, to include certain other relatives. Moreover, the terms varied considerably, having somewhat different meaning in different localities.

S–Ely and S–SprV had a single term, ni"wa or niwa, for cross cousins of both sexes. S–SnRv called male cross cousins dui, female cross cousins, amasau-wə pü (ama, the upper half of the body+sauma, sister or sisters, implying that only the upper half of the body is related to the speaker). S–Hmlt called male parallel cousins dui, the mother's brother's son niwa, the father's sister's son daitc (elsewhere, brother-in-law, etc.), a man's female parallel cousins "sister," and a man's female cross cousins "wife." S–BtlM called female parallel cousins sauwüpü, female cross cousins auwasauwüpü, male parallel cousins "brother" or dui, male cross cousins dui or detc. S–Elko called the father's sister's daughter bahabedu, literally baha's (father's sister's) daughter, and the mother's brother's daughter ada'"bedu. S–Egan used bahabedu for the first, ada for the second.

NOTES TO SCHEDULE OF KINSHIP TERMS

(1) Duəpü, very young son; bedəpü, very young daughter; dua, bedü, older son and daughter.
(2) All cousins called "brother" and "sister." Also, F O B S, daga; F Y B S, haink; F O B D, badzi or nami; F Y B D, sau'mo.
(3) Also, saumopü.
(4) Awasauwüpü, more distant than first cousin.
(5) Ama, upper half of the body.
(6) Or awasauwüpü, ?
(7) Managwa, distant+hai.
(8) Tsi, diminutive ending, meaning in this case, "distant."
(9) Adabu if unmarried.
(10) F O B, dzuguna; F Y B, detcuguna; F O B, if married to mother, biap:u?

(11) Nagahu, temporary or additional+ap:, father. Also, biap: (biap:, big+ap:, father) if F. O. B.; duap: (dui, small+ap:) if F Y B.

(12) Biap:ə, F O B; nagühap:ə, F Y B.

(13) Or biap:ə, F O B; duiap:ə, F Y B.

(14) Biapü, M O Ss H; nagühapü, M Y Ss H.

(15) If father's brother or cousins; otherwise, nauwatup:, "old person."

(16) Gwuh, wife+əpü, father.

(17) Numu, their, i. e., the children's+dogo, mother's father.

(18) Numu, their+gago, mother's mother.

(19) Odun, our.

(20) H M called baha before marriage; numu; their+hutsi, father's mother, after marriage.

(21) Literally, young girl.

(22) Literally, boy.

(23) Literally, daughter's child's mother.

(24) St S, dua; B S, duitc.

(25) St D, bedu or dogombia; B D, naivi, girl.

(26) St S, dua; B S, naduivitc.

(27) St S, naduivitc[1]; B S, dua.

(28) Naivi, girl; na, from some other person.

(29) St S, duanadia; Ss S, duivitc.

(30) St S, duwa'; Ss S, mido'''°.

(31) St D, badü; Ss D, mido'''°.

(32) St S, dua, son+dügi, to keep, i. e., adopt; B S, dua; any young man, naduivitc.

(33) St S, duadügi; Ss S, dua.

(34) St D, bedudügi; Ss D, bedu.

(35) Literally, daughter's child's father.

(36) Literally, son's child's mother.

(37) Literally, son's wife.

(38) B D, bahwa'tsi'[1].

(39) B D, bahatsi.

(40) B S, baha; B D, behunadia.

(41) S W M, nanabahambian; D H M, nanduinu?

(43) W Ss only; B W, no term.

(44) W Ss, naniŋ or nagaha, temporary+gwuh; B W, bavi or dami, brother+aŋgwuh.

(45) Dui, little.

(46) W Ss, vina't:ü or osănəpia; B W, nodu'kwa.

(47) Ss M, nuhuŋ (our) guhəp: (husband); H B, nagaha guhəp: or bia (big) guhəp:.

(48) Or nuhuŋguhəp:.

(49) Same as grandparents and grandchildren.

(50) Ügü, new.

(51) Literally, brother's child's mother.

	Father	Mother	Son	Daughter	Older brother	Younger brother
NP-FSp	nau'a	vi'a	du'a	vai'du	va'vi'ı	waŋa''ₐ
NP-FLk	nau'a	vi'a	du'a	vai'du	va'vi'ı	gwaŋa'ₐ
NP-GeoCr	na'wa	vi'a	du'a	ve'du	vavi'ı	waŋa''ₐ
NP-LnPn	nau'a	vi'a	du'a	pe'dü	bavi'ı	waŋa''ₐ
NP-MC	na	bi'a	dua'	ba'du	bavi'ı	waŋa''ₐ
S-LtLk	nüp:ᵘ	bia	dua	bedu	bavi'ı	dåüi
S-Lida	üp:	bi'ı	dua	baidü'ᵘ	babi'ı	dåüwi
S-Belm	üpütsi'ı	vi:ci	duwütsi	bedü'ᵘ	vavi'ı	daitc
S-GSmV	apu'ᵘ	bi'ı	dua'ₐ	baidü'ᵘ	babi'ı	dåüwi'ı
S-RsRi	apü'ᵘ	bi'ı	dua'ₐ	baidü'	bavi'ı	dawi'ı
S-SmCr	apü'ᵘ	bi:'ı	dua'ₐ	baidü'	bavi'ı	dami'ı
S-Mor	üpü'ᵘ	bi:'ı	?	baidu	bavi'	dåüwi'ı
S-Hmlt	əpü'ᵘ	bia	dua	baidu	bavi	dami (detc)
S-Ely	ápü'ᵘ	bia	duəp:ᵘ	badipü	babi	dami (daitc)
S-SprV	apü'ᵘ	bia	dua'	bedu	bavi	daitc (dami)
GS-SklV	ap:ü	bia	düa	bedu	bavi	dami
GS-DpCr	ap:ü	bia	duəp	bedəp	bavi	da'ı
S-Egan	apü	bia	duəpü	bedəpü	bavi	dami
S-RubV	ăpü'ᵘ	bi	'	baidəp	bavi	dami
S-Elko	ăpü'ᵘ	bi,bia	dua	bedu	bavi	dami
S-BtlM	apü	bi	dua	bedüpü	bavi	dami
S-NthFk	əp:	bia	{duəpü ¹ / dua}	{bedü (¹) / bedəpü}	bavi	dami
S-SnRv	əpü	bia	{duəpü / dua}	{bedü / bedəpü}	bavi	dami
S-GrsCr	apü'ᵘ	bia	dua	{bedu / bedəpü'ᵘ}	bavi	dami
S-Prom	ap:ü	bia	düa	bedu	bavi	dami
S-FtHl	ap:ə	bia	dua	bedü	bavi	dami
NP-Ban	na:	via	duwa'	badü'	pavi''ı	waŋa''ₐ
S-Lemhi	ap:ü	bia	dua	bedü	bavi	dami
SP-Ash	mü:an'	pi:ăn'	tuün'	pateum'	paviʰ'	tsauki:m'
SP-LV	muən':	piən':	tuən:'	patciən:'	bavin:'	tcakin:'

	Older sister	Younger sister	F B S (O)	F B S (Y)	F B D (O)
NP-FSp	hama''ₐ	vuni''ı	vua''ₐ	vua''ₐ	jåü
NP-FLk	ham''ₐ	vuni''ı	vua''ₐ	vua''ₐ	såü
NP-GeoCr	hama''ₐ	buni''ı	vua''?	waŋa''ₐ	hama''ₐ
NP-LnPn	hama''ₐ	vüni''ı	bu'a?	waŋa''ₐ	hama''ₐ
NP-MC	hama''ₐ	vuni''ı	bavi''ı	waŋa''ₐ	hama''ₐ
S-LtLk	batsi'ı	nami'ı	bavi'ı	dåüi'ı	batsi'ı
S-Lida	batsi'ı	nami'ı	daŋgumbu'ᵘ	daŋgumbu'ᵘ	niwa
S-Belm	batcitci	namitci'ı	daŋgumbuatsi	daŋgumbuatsi	niwa
S-GSmV	badzi'ı	nami'ı	{babi'ı / bua'ₐ}	dåüwi'ı	{badzi'ı / bua'ₐ}
S-RsRi	bazi'ı	nami'ı	{dăŋgumbua / zugubua}	dăŋgumbua zugubua	{auwasauwüpü'ᵘ}
S-SmCr	batsi'ı	nami'ı	bavi'ı	dami'ı	batsi'ı
S-Mor	batsi'ı	nami'ı	tăŋgwumbua	tăŋgwumbua	awa'sawa
S-Hmlt	badzi	nami	dui	dui	badzi
S-Ely	badi'ı	nami'ı	babi	{dami / daitc}	{badi'ı}
-SprV	biabadzi	nami'ı	bavi	daitc	badzi
GS-SklV	badzi	nam¹	{daga / bavi}	{daga / dami}	{sauwupu' / badzi}
GS-DpCr	badzi	nami	daga	daga	sauwupu'
S-Egan	badzi	nami	bavi	dami	badzi
S-RubV	badzi	nami	?	?	?
S-Elko	badzi	nami'ı	bavi	badzi	nami'ı

	Older sister	Younger sister	F B S (O)	F B S (Y)	F B D (O)
S-BtlM	badzi	nami	dui / bavi	dui / dami	sauwüpü / badzi
S-NthFk	badzi	nami	bavi	dami	badzi
S-SnRv	badzi	nami	bavi	dami	badzi
S-GrsCr	badzi	nami	daga	daga	badzi / saumapü
S-Prom	(²)	(²)	(²)	(²)	(²)
S-FtHl	badzi	nami	daga / bavi	daga / dami	sau'mo (²) / badzi
NP-Ban	hama'	puni'	pavi"¹ / cia'kwa	waŋa"ᵃ / cia'kwa	hama" / cia'kwa
S-Lemhi	badzi	nami	dui, daga / bavi	dui, daga / dami	sauw ü' / badzi
SP-Ash	patsi:ŋ'	nami:ŋ'	pavihᵇ'	tsauki:m'	patsi:ŋ'
SP-LV	patcin:'	namin:'	bavin:'	tcakin:'	patcin:'

	F B D (Y)	F Ss S (O)	F Ss S (Y)	F Ss D (O)	F Ss D (Y)
NP-FSp	jäü	vua"ᵃ	vua"ᵃ	jäü	jäü
NP-FLk	säü	vua"ᵃ	vua"ᵃ	säü	säü
NP-GeoCr	buni'¹	vavi"¹	waŋa"ᵃ	hama"ᵃ	buni"¹
NP-LnPn	vüni'¹	vavi"¹	waŋa"ᵃ	hama"ᵃ	vüni"¹
NP-MC	vuni"¹	bavi"¹	waŋa"ᵃ	hama"ᵃ	vuni"¹
S-LtLk	nami'¹	bavi"¹	däü'¹	batsi'¹	nami"¹
S-Lida	niwa	däŋgumbu'ᵘ	däŋgumbu'ᵘ	niwa	niwa
S-Belm	niwa	däŋgumbuatsi	däŋgumbuatsi	niwa	niwa
S-GSmV	nami'¹	babi'¹	däüwi'¹	badzi'¹	nami'¹
S-RsRl	auwasauwüpü'ü	däŋgumbua	däŋgumbua	auwasauwüpü'ü	auwasauwüpü'ü
S-SmCr	nami'ʲ	bavi'¹	dami'¹	batsi'¹	nami'¹
S-Mor	awa'sawa'	täŋgwumbua	täŋbwumbua	awa'sawa'	awa'sawa'
S-Hmlt	nami	daitc ?	daitc ?	gwuhu naadu	gwuhu naaduː
S-Ely	nami	niʰwa	niʰwa	niʰwa	niʰwa
S-SprV	nami'¹	niwa	niwa	niwa	niwa
GS-SklV	sauwupu' / nami	bitcogwe / bavi	bitcogwe / dami	gwüp:ü / badzi	gwüp:ü / nami
GS-DpCr	sauwupu	daga	daga	sauwupu'	sauwupu'
S-Egan	nami	detc	detc	bahambedu	bahambedu
S-KübV	?	?	?	?	?
S-Elko	nami'¹	detc	detc	bahambedu	bahambedu
S-BtlM	sauwüpü / nami	detc, dui	detc, dui	auwasauwilpü	auwasauwüpü
S-NthFk	nami	dui	dui	amasaumapü(⁵)	amasaumapü
S-SnRv	nami	dui	dui	amasaumapü	amasaumapü
S-GrsCr	nami / saumapu	daga / bavi	daga / dami	saumapu / badzi	saumapu / nami
S-Prom	(²)	?	?	?	?
S-FtHl	sau'mo(³) / nami	daga / bavi	daga / dami	sau'mo(³) / badzi	sau'mo(³) / nami
NP-Ban	püni" / cia'kwa	pavi"¹ / cia'kwa	waŋa"ᵃ / cia'kwa	hama" / cia'kwa	püni" / cia'kwa
S-Lemhi	sauw ü(⁴) / nami	dui, daga / bavi	dui, daga / dami	sauw ü / badzi	sauw ü / nami
SP-Ash	nami:ŋ'	pavihᵇ'	tsauki:m'	patsi:ŋ'	nami:ŋ'
SP-LV	namin:'	bavin:'	tcakin:'	patcin:'	namin:'

	M B S (O)	M B S (Y)	M B D (O)	M B D (Y)
NP-FSp	vua"ᵃ	vua"ᵃ	jäü	jäü
NP-FLk	vua"ᵃ	vau"ᵃ	jäü	jäü
NP-GeoCr	vavi"ⁱ	waŋa"ᵃ	hama"ᵃ	buni"ⁱ
NP-LnPn	vavi"ⁱ	waŋa'ᵃ	hama"ᵃ	vüni"ⁱ
NP-MC	bavi"ⁱ	waŋa"ᵃ	hama"ᵃ	vuni"ⁱ
S-LtLk	bavi'ⁱ	däüi'ⁱ	batsi'ⁱ	nami'ⁱ
S-Lida	däŋgumbu'ᵘ	däŋgumbu'ᵘ	niwa	niwa
S-Belm	däŋgumbuatsi	däŋgumbuatsi	niwa	niwa
S-GSmV	babi'ⁱ	däüwi'ⁱ	badzi'ⁱ	nami'ⁱ
S-RsRi	däŋgumbua	däŋgumbua	auwasauwüpü'ü	auwasauwüpü'ü
S-SmCr	bavi'ⁱ	dami'ⁱ	batsi'ⁱ	batsi'ⁱ
S-Mor	täŋgwumbua	täŋgwumbua	awasawa'	awasawa'
S-Hmlt	niwa	niwa	gwuhu naadu	gwuhu naadu-
S-Ely	niʰwa	niʰwa	niʰwa	niʰwa
S-SprV	niwa	niwa	niwa	niwa
GS-SklV	taga / bavi	taga / dami	sauwupü / badzi	sauwupü / nami
GS-DpCr	daga	daga	sauwupü	sauwupü
S-Egan	?	?	?	?
S-RubV	?	?	niwa	?
S-Elko	detc	detc	bahambedu / ada'ᵃbedu	bahambedu / ada'ᵃbedu
S-BtlM	detc, dui	detc, dui	auwasauwüpü	auwasauwüpü
S-NthFk	dui	dui	amasauməpü	amasauməpü
S-SnRv	dui	dui	amasauməpü	amasauməpü
S-GrsCr	daga / bavi	daga / dami	badzi / saumupü	nami / saumupü
S-Prom	?	?	?	?
S-FtHl	daga / bavi	daga / dami	sau'mo(ˢ) / badzi	sau'mo / nami
NP-Ban	pavi"ⁱ / cia'kwa	waŋa"ᵃ / cia'kwa	hama"ᵃ / cia'kwa	püni"ⁱ / cia'kwa
S-Lemhi	dui, daga / bavi	dui, daga / dami	sauw ü / badzi	sauw ü / nami
SP-Ash	paviʰ'	tsauki:m'	patsi:ŋ'	nami:ŋ'
SP-LV	bavin:'	tcakin:'	patcin:'	namin:'

	M Ss S (O)	M Ss S (Y)	M Ss D (O)	M Ss D (Y)
NP-FSp	vua"ᵃ	vua"ᵃ	jäü	jäü
NP-FLk	vua"ᵃ	vua"ᵃ	säü	säü
NP-GeoCr	vavi"ⁱ	waŋa"ᵃ	hama"ᵃ	buni"ⁱ
NP-LnPn	vavi"ⁱ	waŋa"ᵃ	hama"ᵃ	vüni"ⁱ
NP-MC	bavi"ⁱ	waŋa"ᵃ	hama"ᵃ	vuni"ⁱ
S-LtLk	bavi'ⁱ	däüi	batsi'ⁱ	nami'ⁱ
S-Lida	däŋgumbu'ᵘ	däŋgumbu'ᵘ	niwa	niwa
S-Belm	däŋgumbuatsi	däŋgumbuatsi	niwa	niwa
S-GSmV	babi'ⁱ	däüwi'ⁱ	badzi'ⁱ	nami'ⁱ
S-RsRi	däŋgumbua	däŋgumbua	sauwupü'ü (6)	sauwupü'ü
S-SmCr	bavi'ⁱ	dami'ⁱ	batsi'ⁱ	nami'ⁱ
S-Mor	täŋgwumbua	täŋgwumbua	awasawa'	awasawa'
S-Hmlt	dui	dui	badzi	nami
S-Ely	babi	dami	badi'ⁱ	nami'ⁱ
S-SprV	bavi	daitc	badzi	nami
GS-SklV	daga / bavi	daga / dami	sauwüpü' / badzi	sauwüpü' / nami
GS-DpCr	daga	daga	sauwüpü'	sauwüpü'
S-Egan	bavi	dami	badzi	nami
S-RubV	bavi ?	dami ?	badzi ?	nami ?
S-Elko	bavi	dami	badzi	nami'ⁱ

	M Ss S (O)	M Ss S (Y)	M Ss D (O)	M Ss D (Y)
S-BtlM	{duí / bavi}	duí / dami	sauwüpü / badzi	sauwüpü / nami
S-NthFk	bavi	dami	badzi	nami
S-SnRv	bavi	dami	badzi	nami
S-GrsCr	{daga / bavi}	daga / dami	badzi / saumopu	nami / saumopu
S-Prom	?	?	?	?
S-FtHl	{daga / bavi}	daga / dami	sau'ma / badzi	sau'ma / nami
NP-Ban	{pavi'¹ / cia'kwa}	waŋa''ᵃ / cia'kwa	hama'' / cia'kwa	püni'' / cia'kwa
S-Lemhl	{dui, daga / bavi}	dui, daga / dami	sauw ü / badzi	sauw ü / nami
SP-Ash	paviʰ'	tsauki:m'	patsi:ŋ'	nami:ŋ'
SP-LV	bavin:'	tcakin:'	patcin:'	namin:'

	St S (ms) / B S (ms)	St D (ms) / B D (ms)	St S (ws) / Ss S (ws)	St D (ws) / Ss D (ws)
NP-FSp	{nanayukwina'ha / duivitc}	sü'adümünüha [31]	{du'yᵃ / nanayukwina'ha}	vatu' / sü'adümünüha
NP-FLk	nanayukina'ha	süa'dümünüha	{nanayukina'ha / du'yᵃ}	süa'dümünüha / vatu'
NP-GeoCr	nanaukinaha	suadü'münaha	du':yü	patu'ᵃ
NP-LnPn	naniukinaha	?	?	?
NP-MC	huza''ᵃ	huza''ᵃ	mido''ᵃ	mido''ᵉ
S-LtLk	duwi'tci	dogombia [33]	doka''¹	doga'tsi'¹
S-Lida	duitc	dogombia	duitc	dokwa'tsi ?
S-Belm	duitc	dogombia	duitc	dokwa'tsi ?
S-GSmV	duivitc	dogombia	duivit	dogombia
S-RsRl	naduitci	dogombia	naduitci	dogombia
S-SmCr	naduivitci'¹	dogombia	?	?
S-Mor	duitc	dogombia	duitc	dogombia
S-Hmlt	?	?	?	?
S-Ely	duivitc	dogombia	duivitc	dogombia
S-SprV	duivitc	dogombia	duivitc	dogombia
GS-SklV	?	?	?	?
Gs-DpCr	duanadia	bedunadia	[39]	bedunadia
O Egan	[36]	bot ?	naduivitci ?	bot ?
S-RubV	?	?	?	?
S-Elko	dua [34]	[35]	{dua / naduivitci}	{bedu / nanaivi}
S-BtlM	{due / naduivitci}	bedu / nanaivi	dua / naduivitci	bedu / nanaivi
S-NthFk	[37]	{nanaivi [38] / bedu}	naduivitci¹ / dua	bedu
S-SnRv	[37]	{nanaivi / bedu}	naduivitci¹ / dua	bedu
S-GrsCr	dua	bedu	dua	bedu
S-Prom	{dua / duivitci}	bedu	dua	bedu
S-FtHl	dua	bedu	dua	bedu
NP-Ban	duwa'	badü'	[30]	[31]
S-Lemhl	[32]	bedu	[33]	[34]
SP-Ash	?	?	?	?
SP-LV	?	?	tuen: ?	patcien:

	M B	F Ss H	Ss S (ms) / Ss D (ms)	H F	W F
NP-FSp	vu'ᵘ	vu'ᵘ	nahaŋ'wa	yahinüp:'	yahinüp:
NP-FLk	vu'ᵘ	vu'ᵘ	naha'gwa	nahinu'pa	nahinu'pa
NP-GeoCr	pu:ᵘ?	?	nahaŋ'wa	?	nahainüpa
NP-LnPn	vu'ᵘ	?	?	?	?
NP-MC	ats:	ats:	nanakwᵃ	yaihi'	yaihi'
S-LtLk	adabu	-------	ada'ᵃ	naipü'ᵘ	naipü'ᵘ
S-Lida	adabu'ᵘ	adabu'ᵘ	ada	yaip:ᵘ	yaip:ᵘ
S-Belm	adabutsi'ⁱ	adabutsi'ⁱ?	ada	yaip:ᵘ	yaip:ᵘ
S-GSmV	adabu'	adabu'	ada	yaipü'ᵘ	yaipü'ᵘ
S-RsRi	adabu	adabuitsiˢ	ada'ᵃ	adabuitsi	adabuitsi
S-SmCr	adabu	adabu	ada'ᵃ	adavo'otsi	adavo'otsi
S-Mor	adabu	?	ada'ᵃ	adavo'otsi	adavo'otsi
S-Hmlt	adabu	adabu	?	adavotsⁱ	adavotsⁱ
S-Ely	adabu	adabu	adabutsi	yaipütsi	yaipütsi
S-SprV	adabu	ada (bu)	ada'	adabu	adabu
GS-SklV	ada	ada	?	ada	numudogo (17)
GS-DpCr	ada	ada	ada	gunotsi	{ ada / ada }
S-Egan	?	ada	ada	gwuhu ada	gwuhuəpü' (16)
S-RubV	ada'	?	?	?	?
S-Elko	ada'ᵃ (9)	ada'ᵃ	ada'ᵃ	ada	ada
S-BtlM	ada	ada	ada	ada	ada
S-NthFk	ada	ada	ada	ada	ada
S-SnRv	ada	ada	ada	ada	ada
S-GrsCr	ada	ada	ada	guno	ada
S-Prom	ada	ada	ada	oduŋguno	{ odundogo (10) / ada }
S-FtHl	ada	ada	ada	ada	numudogo
NP-Ban	ats:	ats:	nana'k:wa	{ yahi' / atsi }	{ yahí }
S-Lemhi	ada	ada	ada	uduŋguno	undundogo
SP-Ash	{ kokim (O) / sunü:m (Y) }	}?	?	?	?
SP-LV	{ k:o'ke'um (O) / suna'əm (Y) }	}?	?	yaihi'tsiim	yaihitsiim

	F Ss	M B W	B S (ws) / B D (ws)	W M	H M
NP-FSp	vaʰwa'	vaʰwa'	yada'ᵃ	yahinüp':	yahinüp:
NP-FLk	vaʰwa'	vaʰwa'	wada'ᵃ	nahinu'pa	nahinu'pa
NP-GeoCr	baʰwa'	baʰwa'	patü'ᵘ?	nahainüpa	?
NP-LnPn	baʰwa'	-------	?	-------	?
NP-MC	bahwa'	bahwa'	mido'ᵉ	yaihi'	yaihi'
S-LtLk	baʰwa	baʰwa	bahwa''ᵃ (18)	naipü'ᵘ	naipü'ᵘ
S-Lida	bahwa'	bahwatsi'ⁱ	bahwa	yaip:ᵘ	yaip:ᵘ
S-Belm	bahatsi'	-------	bahatsi'ⁱ	yaip:ᵘ	yaip:ᵘ
S-GSmV	baha'ᵃ	baha'ᵃ	baha'ᵃ	yaipü'ᵘ	yaipü'ᵘ
S-RsRi	baha'ᵃ	bahatsi	baha'ᵃ	bahatsi'ⁱ	bahatsi'ⁱ
S-SmCr	baha	baha	baha	bahatsi'ⁱ	bahatsi'ⁱ
S-Mor	baha	-------	bahaⁱ	bahatsi'	bahatsi'ⁱ
S-Hmlt	baha	baha	?	bahatsi	bahatsi
S-Ely	baha	baha	baha (19)	yaipütsi	yaipütsi
S-SprV	baha	baha	bahatsi	baha	baha
GS-SklV	baha	baha	?	{ baha / numagago }	{ baha / numuhutsi }
GS-DpCr	baha	baha	(40)	bahatsi	utsi
S-Egan	baha	detc ?	baha ?	baha	baha
S-RubV	baha	-------	?	?	?
S-Elko	baha	baha	baha	baha	baha

	F Ss	M B W	B S (ws) B D (ws)	W M	H M
S–BtlM	baha	baha	baha	baha	baha
S–NthFk	baha	baha	baha	baha	baha
S–SnRv	baha	baha	baha	baha	baha
S–GrsCr	baha	baha	baha	baha	numuhutsi
S–Prom	baha	baha	baha	{odugago baha	numuhutsi (10)
S–FtHl	baha	baha	baha	numugago	{baha numuhutsi
NP–Ban	bahwa'	bahwa'	mido''	yahi'	bahwa
S–Lemhi	baha	baha	baha	udungago	{uduhutsi baha
SP–Ash	pa'a:m	------------	?	?	?
SP–Lv	bahaum	------------	pahatsün	yaigüpütsim	anda'muam

	F B	M Ss H	St F	M Ss	F B W
NP–FSp	natsugu'	natsugu'	natsugu' (15)	bidu''ᵘ	bidu''ᵘ
NP–FLk	natsugu'	natsugu'	nauwatup:	bidu''ᵘ	bidu''ᵃ
NP–GeoCr	natsugu'a	?	natsugu'a	tu:yᵃ ?	bidu''ᵘ
NP–LnPn	{ha'wi'ⁱ natsugu ?	}?	------------	vidu''ᵘ	
NP–MC	hai'i	hai'i	hai'i	bidu'	bidu'
S–LtLk	tsugu'na	?	tsugu'na	doka'vü'ᵘ	doka'vü'ᵘ
S–Lida	juguna	juguna	juguna	dokwatsi'ⁱ	dokwatsi'ⁱ
S–Belm	hai'ⁱ	hai'ⁱ?	hai'ⁱ	dokwa'ᵃ	dokwa'ᵃ
S–GSmV	hai'ⁱ	hai'ⁱ	hai'ⁱ	doka'ᵃ	doka'ᵃ
S–RsRi	hai'	nanagwahai (7)	hai'	biatsi	nanagwabiatsi
S–SmCr	hai'	hai'	hai'	biatsi	biatsi
S–Mor	hai'	?	hai'	dokwatsi	
S–Hmlt	hai	hai	?	doka	doka
S–Ely	hai'	hai'	hai	toka	toka
S–SprV	zuguno''	zuguno''	zuguno''	doka	doka
GS–SklV	(10)	?	?	{biavia (O) duivia (Y)	doka (O) duidoka (Y)
GS–DpCr	duguna	duguna	duguna	doka	doka
S–Egan	hai	hai	hai	doka	doka
S–RubV	{hai aɒüundoi	}?	?	{dokatsi biatsi	
S–Elko	{hai nazugo	hai nazugo	hai nazugo	}biatsi	biatsi
S–BtlM	natsugu	natsugu	natsugu	biatsi	biatsi
S–NthFk	nadzugo	nadzugo	nadzugo	biatsi	biatsi
S–SnRv	aputsi	aputsi	aputsi	biatsi	biatsi
S–GrsCr	ap:ə (11)	ap:ə	{ap:ə dzuguna	biavia (O) duivia (Y)	}bia
S–Prom	{nagahuap:u duap:u	}nagahuap:u (14)	{ap:ü dzuguna	biavia (O) duivia (Y)	biavia (O) duivia (Y)
S–FtHl	ap:ə (12)	ap:ə	{ap:ə ügüap:ə (50)	biavia (O) nagühavia (Y)	}bia
NP–Ban	hai'i	hai'i	hai'i	bidu'	bidu'
S–Lemhi	{biapü (12) nagühapü	biapü (14) nagühapü	}ügüapü	{biavia (O) nagühavia (Y)	}bia
SP–Ash	{koum (O) haiiŋ' (Y)	}?	?	{mawü:m (O) numpiüm (Y)	}?
SP–Lv	{kuum (O) hai (Y)	}?	hai'muən:	piən	?

	St M	D H (ms)	D H (ws)	S W (ms)	S W (ws)
NP-FSp	?	dogona' (36)	dogona'	wövi	wövi
NP-FLk	bidu''ᵘ	dogona'	dogona'	mövi	mövi
NP-GeoCr	bidu''ᵘ	togona'	togona	?	?
NP-LnPn	----	?	?	?	?
NP-MC	bidu'	dogo'na	dogo'na	gunupia	gunupia
S-LtLk	doka'vü'ü	dogo'nüp (36)	dogo'nüp	ütsombia (36)	ütsombia
S-Lida	dokwatsi'ⁱ	dogonǝp	dogonǝp	hutsombia	hutsombia
S-Belm	dokwa'ᵃ	dogonǝp	dogonǝp	hutsombia	hutsombia
S-GSmV	doka'ᵃ	dogonǝp	dogonǝp	hutsombia	hutsombia
S-RsRi	biatsi	monǝpü'ü	monǝpü'ü	hutsombia	hutsombia
S-SmCr	biatsi	monǝpü'ü	monǝpü'ü	hutsombia	hutsombia
S-Mor	dokwatsi'	dogonǝp:	dogonǝp:	hutsombia	hutsombia
S-Hmlt	?	munǝpü	munǝpü	hutsombia	hutsombia
S-Ely	toka	munǝpü	munǝpü	hutsombia	hutsombia
S-SprV	doka	duivitc ?	bahatsi	bedu ?	bahatsi
GS-SklV	?	monǝp:	monǝp:	{hutsombia / ada}	hutsombia
GS-DpCr	doka	monǝp:	monǝp:	utsombia	utsombia
S-Egan	doka	munǝpü'	munǝpü'	duaŋgwuh (37)	hutsombia
S-RubV	?	?	?	?	?
S-Elko	biatsi	{ada / monǝpü}	{duivitc / monǝp: ü}	{ada}	baha
S-BtlM	fiatsi	monǝp:	monǝp:	hutsombia	hutsombia
S-NthFk	biatsi	{monǝpü / dogonǝpü}	{monǝpü' / gagoǝpü}	{gunombia}	hutsombia
S-SnRv	biatsi	{monǝpü / dogonǝpü}	monǝpü	gunombia	hutsombia
S-GrsCr	{bia / dokatsi}	{monǝp:•}	monǝp:•	hutsombia	hutsombia
S-Prom	bia	monǝp:	monǝp:	hutsombia	hutsombia
S-FtHl	{bia / ügübia}	{monǝp:•}	monǝp:•	hutsombia	hutsombia
NP-Ban	bidu'	dogo'na	dogo'na	gunupia	gunupia
S-Lemhi	ügübia	monǝp:	monǝp:	hutsombia	hutsombia
SP-Ash	?	?	?	?	?
SP-LV	maumpiǝn:'	monatsim'	monatsim'	winsim'piǝn	winsim'piǝn

	S W M (ws) / D H M (ws)	S W F (ms) / D H F (ms)	S W M (ms) / D H M (ms)	S W F (ws) / D H F (ws)
NP-FSp	mükici'ⁱ	mükici'ⁱ	mükici'ⁱ	mükici'ⁱ
NP-FLk	mükici'ⁱ	mükici'ⁱ	mükici'ⁱ	mükici'ⁱ
NP-GeoCr	dainup	mukici	dainup ?	?
NP-LnPn	?	?	?	?
NP-MC	dai	dai	dai	dai
S-LtLk	daiyump	daiyump	daiyump	daiyump
S-Lida	daiyump	daiyump	daiyump	daiyump
S-Belm	daiyumbutsi	daiyumbutsi	daiyumbutsi	daiyumbutsi
S-GSmV	dai'yump	dai'yump	dai'yump	dai'yump
S-RsRi	dai'yump	dai'yump	dai'yump	dai'yump
S-SmCr	tainump	tainump	tainump	tainump
S-Mor	taiyump	taiyump	taiyump	taiyump
S-Hmlt	aivuintc	aivuintc	aivuintc	aivuintc
S-Ely	aivuintc	aivuintc	aivuintc	aivuintc
S-SprV	nami ?	?	badzi, nami	bavi, dami
GS-SklV	?	?	?	?
GS-DpCr	(41)	iaip	sauwupu	sauwupu
S-Egan	bahambia	detc	saumupü'	saumupü'
S-RubV	?	?	?	?
S-Elko	bahambia_	detc	badzi, nami?	sauupa bavi, dami
S-BtlM	nanabahambia	nanadej	nanadainümp	nanadainümp
S-NthFk	bahambia	detc	dainump:	dainump:

	S W M (ws) D H M (ws)	S W F (ms) D H F (ms)	S W M (ms) D H M (ms)	S W F (ws) D H F (ws)
S-SnRv	bahambia	detc	dainump:	dainump:
S-GrsCr	bahambia	detc	{badzi nami	bavi dami
S-Prom	nanabahambia	detc	{badzi, nami sauwa	bavi, dami sauwa
S-FtHl	bahambia	detc	badzi	bavi
NP-Ban	adazipia	dai masi	{nami cia'kwa	dami cia'kwa
S-Lemhi	bahambia	detc	{badzi nami	bavi dami
SP-Ash	?	?	?	?
SP-LV	ta'äü	ta'äü	ta'äü	ta'äü

	Husband	H B Ss H (ws)	Wife	W Ss B W (ms)
NP-FSp	gü:a	huzana'	nodüŋ'wa	huzapia
NP-FLk	gü:a	husana'	nodü'gwa	husabia
NP-GeoCr	kuwa	huzana':ai	naduŋ'wa	husapia
NP-LnPn	?	?	?	?
NP-MC	guma'	nunai'i	nodü'kw	osü'nüpia
S-LtLk	guha	usambia	bunahavi'i	usambia
S-Lida	guha	osambia	gwühü	osambia
S-Belm	nazagupa	osambiatsi	gwütsi	osambiatsi
S-GSmV	guha	?	güütsi'i	naiŋgwühü ?
S-RsRi	guhatsi	naiŋgühatsi	gwütsi	naiŋgwühü
S-SmCr	guhatsi	guhatsi	gwühü	nagahagwühü (44)
S-Mor	guhatsi	{guhatsi (Ss H) naiŋguhatsi (H B)	gwühü	nagahagwühü
S-Hmlt	kuwüp:u	?	{gwütsi gwühü	?
S-Ely	küwəp:u	{küpəw:u aiji'i ? (H B)	gu:wüpu	{gu:wüpu naiŋgwühü
S-SprV	guha	{baviguha (H B) aivunzi (Ss H)	gwuha waip	aivunzi (W Ss) nawaip (B W)
GA-SklV	gwuhəp:ü	?	gwüp:ü	?
GS-DpCr	gwuhəp:	{uduai (H B) guhunədiə (Ss H)	gwüh	gwühnadia
S-Egan	guhəpü	{guhəpü (H B) ? (Ss H)	gwuh	gwuh (B W)
S-RubV	guhatsi	?	gwütsi	?
S-Elko	guhəp:	guhanadua	gwüh	{nagagwüh (W Ss) hangwüh (B W)
S-BtlM	guhəp:	{guhəp: (Ss H) nagahaguhəp: (H B)	gwuh ä	{nagahagwüh (W Ss) nuhuŋgwüh (B W)
S-NthFk	kuhəpü	{nuhuŋguhəp: (Ss H) (47) nagahaguhəp: (H B)	gwuh	(44)
S-SnRv	kuhəpü	{nuhuŋguhəp: (Ss H) (47) bagahaguhəp: (H B)	gwuh	(44)
S-GrsCr	guhəp:ü	guhəp:ü	gwüh	{duigwüh (45) gwüh
S-Prom	guhəp:	{dainəp:ü (Ss H) guhəp:ü (H B)	gwüh	{duigwüh(W Ss) (45) gwüh (B W)
S-FtHl	guhəp:	guhəp:	gwuh	{duigwuh (W Ss) gwuh (B W)
NP-Ban	guma'	{guma' (Ss H) nunai'i (H B)	nodü'kwa	(46)
S-Lemhi	guhəp:ü	{guhəp: (48) nagahaguhəp:	gwüh ä	{naiŋgwuh ü (W Ss) nuhuŋgwuh ü (B W)
SP-Ash	?	?		?
SP-LV	kuma''əm	nainkumaəm	piwa''əm	naimbiwaəm

	H Ss / B W (ws)	W B / Ss H (ms)		H Ss / B W (ws)	W B / Ss H (ms)
NP-Fsp	yatapia	yado'	GS-SklV	?	?
NP-FLk	watapia	yado'	GS-DpCr	bahambia	dej:u
NP-GeoCr	atapi'a	datohi'	S-Egan	bahambia	detc
NP-LnPn	?	?	S-RubV	?	?
NP-MC	adatsipia	adatoi	S-Elko	bahambia	detc
S-LtLk	bahambia [31]	nandoi	S-BtlM	nanabahambia	dej
S-Lida	bahwambia	nundoi	S-NthFk	bahambia	detc
S-Belm	bahwambiatsi	andoitci	S-SnRv	bahambia	detc
S-GSmV	zugubüa	adandoi	S-GrsCr	bahambi	detc
S-RsRi	adandoi	adandoi / daitc, niwa	S-Prom	bahambia	detc
S-SmCr	no word	daiitci	S-FtHl	bahambia	detc
S-Mor	zugubua	andoi / niwa	NP-Ban	adadzipia	masi'
S-Hmlt	?	dej ?	S-Lemhi	bahambia	detc
S-Ely	bahambia	deji	SP-Ash	?	?
S-SprV	?	adandoi / niwa	SP-Lv	andamuən	andamuən

	F F / S S (ms) / S D (ms)	F M / S S (ws) / S D (ws)	M F / D S (ms) / D D (ms)	M M / D S (ws) / D D (ws)
NP-FSp	gunu'u	hutsi"i	dogo'	wu'a
NP-FLk	gunu'u	hutsi"i	dogo'	mü'a
NP-GeoCr	gunu'u	hotsi'i	dogo'o	wu'a
NP-LnPn	?	?	?	?
NP-MC	gunu"u	hutsi"i	dogo'o	gago"o
S-LtLk	güno"o	hutsi'i	dogo'o	gago"o
S-Lida	gunu'	hutsi	dogo'	gago'
S-Belm	gunutsi	hutsütsi'i	dogotsi'i	gagotsi'i
S-GSmV	gunu'	hutsi	dogo'	gagu'
S-RsRi	gunü'ü	hutsi'i	dogo'o	gago'o
S-SmCr	gunü'ü	hutsi'i	dogo'o	gago'o
S-Mor	gunü'ü	hutsi'i	dogo'o	gago'a
S-Hmlt	guno	hutsi	dogo	gago
S-Ely	güno	hutsi	dogo	gago
S-SprV	guno (F F) / gunotsi (S S, D)	hutsi'i (F M) / hutcitci (S S, D)	dogo (M F) / dogotsi (D S, D)	kago (M M) / kagotsi (D S, D)
GS-SklV	?	?	?	?
GS-DpCr	guno	utsi	dogo	gago
S-Egan	guno	hutsi	dogo	gago
S-RubV	?	?	?	?
S-Elko	guno (tsi)	hutsi (tsi)	dogo (tsi)	kago (tsi)
S-BtlM	guno	hutsi	dogo	gago
S-NthFk	guno	hutsi	dogo	gago
S-SnRv	guno	hutsi	dogo	gago
S-GrsCr	guno	hutsi	dogo	gago
S-Prom	guno	hutsi	dogo	gago
S-FtHl	guno	hutsi	dogo	gago
NP-Ban	guno'o	hutsi'	dogo''	mua'
S-Lemhi	guno	hutsi	dogo	gago
SP-Ash	?	?	?	?
SP-LV	gunu'um (F F) / gunutsin (S S, D)	hutsi'um	togotsum	gagun

	Gr G P Gr G Ch		Gr G P Gr G Ch			Gr G P Gr G Ch
NP-FSp		S-Mor		S-BtlM		dzo
NP-FLk		S-Hmlt	dá'ᴀ	S-NthFk		dzá'ᴀ
NP-GeoCr		S-Ely	dá'ᴀ	S-SnRv		dzá'ᴀ
NP-LnPn		S-SprV	zó'ŏ	S-GrsCr		jo'
NP-MC	dzo	GS-SklV	?	S-Prom		dzo'o
S-LtLk		GS-DpCr	dzo'o	S-FtHl		dzo'
S-Lida		S-Egan	dzo:	NP-Ban		dzo'o
S-Belm		S-RubV		S-Lemhi		dzo
S-GSmV		S-Elko	{zo'o (Gr G P)	SP-Ash		
S-RsRl			{zotsl (Gr G Ch)	SP-LV		(⁴⁹)
S-SmCr						

APPENDIX D.—NATIVE NAMES OF PLANTS

Abbreviations are: manuf., plants used in manufacturing; med., plants used medicinally.

A: dzin (food), *Amaranthus hybridus.*

Agai suhu, med., *Salix.*

Ă: govi agovi (food), *Opuntia.*

Aiwabok:°, no use, *Cirsium* perhaps *neomexicanum.*

Ăk, food, *Sophia sonnei.*

AK:, food usually *Helianthus;* possibly *Aplopappus* sp.

Aka'vü, food, *Sophia sonnei.*

Akü'ii, aku, food, *Helianthus annus;* also, *H. aridus.*

Ămu, amuh, food, *Allium* sp.

Aŋakwiwi'tum, no use, *Castilleja angustifolia.*

Aŋabauwiya, food and med., *Rumex mexicanus.*

Aŋagwu'p, med., *Enceliopsis argophylla.*

Aŋagawana, manuf., *Apocynum androsaemifolium.*

Anabimotoyump, no use, *Castilleja angustifolia.*

Anatsu, med., *Asclepias crytoceras.*

A: nzi (?), food, *Hookera.*

Atsa, food, *Sophia sonnei.*

Awadaviciwüp, med., *Chrysothamnus tortifolius.*

Awimu, food, unidentified.

Babahovi, med., *Artemisia gnaphalodes.*

Bădusi, food, *Allium.*

Bagonǝp, food, *Ribes aureum.*

Bagwana, food, *Mentha* sp.

Bahmü, food, same as bavo; unidentified root.

Bahunduwaya'a, smoking, *Apocynum cannabinum.*

Ba: k, food, *Helianthus annuus.*

Bambigana, manuf. and food, *Ribes inebrians.*

Bambibogo, food, unidentified greens.

Baugona, food, *Mantha* sp.

Bauwiya, food and med., *Rumex crispus.*

Bauwuŋgop: (?), food, *Holodiscus dumosa.*

Bavo, food, unidentified greens.

Bavogo, bavogo', see bavo.

Bavop, med., *Artemisia gnaphalodes.*

Biadumaya, smoke, *Arctostaphylos platyphylla.*

Biakü, food, *Helianthus.*

Biasonip, food and manuf., *Elymus condensatus.*

Biazonip, see biasonip.

Biawiyümbi, food, *Shepherdia argentea* or *Lepargyrea.*

Bogombi, bo: gumbi, food, *Ribes aureum.* Also, any berry, S-Lemhi.

Bogunǝp:, manuf. and food, *Ribes inebrians.*

Bohombi, food, seed of *Artemisia tridentata.*

Bohovi, food, *Artemisia tridentata.*

Boi', same as Bo: ina.

Bo: ina, food, *Sophia sonnet*.

Bokumbi, no use, *Atriplex confertifolia*.

Bomb:, bombi, food, seed of *Artemisia tridentata*.

Büʰak:, safe Bühüak, *Helianthus*.

Bühü'ak:, food (NP-Ban), *Helianthus*.

Cicəp:, no use, *Eurotia lanata*.

Dagü, dagü, food, unidentified root.

Dagüip, med., unidentified root.

Dasimb:, food, same as tasum, a round cactus.

Do'gohi, food, unidentified tuber.

Doi, food, seed of cattail.

Donambi, food, *Prunus* sp.

Du:, see dui.

Duambi, food and manuf., *Amelanchier glabra* and *A. alnifolia*.

Dubiciwəp:, food, *Chrysothamnus stenophyllus*.

Dübüs', same as tüpüsi'ʰ.

Dubuwi, dubwi', food, any species used as greens.

Dudumbi, food, *Ephedra viridis*.

Duəm, duemb:, food, berry, *Amelanchier glabra* and *A. alnifolia*.

Dugu, food, "wild potatoes", S–RsRi.

Duhavi, food and manuf., *Amelanchier glabra* and *A. alnifolia*.

Duhiyumbü', food, elderberry, *Sambucus*.

Dui, food, unidentified root (?) or seed (?).

Duŋwip (?), manuf. and food, *Ribes inebrians*.

Duna, food, unidentified root, possibly *Cymopterus montanus* (Chamerlin, 1911: 51).

Dünambi, manuf., *Cercocarpus ledifolius*.

Du'u, food, unidentified root.

Dzin:, food, probably cactus, same as tasum (?).

Dzowiga, food, unidentified.

Goiyu, goiyu'u, food, probably *Valeriana edulis*.

Gubanap, manuf., *Sphaeralcea ambigua*.

Guŋga, güŋga, food, same as gunk:

Gunk:, food, *Allium acuminatum*.

Guuuwip, food and manuf., *Sambucus*.

Gwidogomb:, manuf., *Sphaeralcea ambigua*.

Hape, food, see ha: pi.

Ha: pi, ha: pⁿ food, unidentified root.

Hiamb:, food, *Helianthus annuus*.

Hovitc, any flower (S–Elko)

Hugap:, hugapi, manuf., *Phragmites communis* (*Phragmites vulgaris*).

Hugi, food, unidentified seeds, probably as hugwi.

Hugwi, food, "wheat grass".

Huhpiˣya, food, *Lycium andersonii*.

Huhwi, food, unidentified seed, S–LtLk.

Huki, food, probably *Stipa speciosa*.

Hukümbi, food, unidentified seed.

Hunai, med., *Chaenactis nevandensis* (?) or more probably *Artemisia spinescens*.

Hünab', med., *Cowania stansburiana*.

Hunap:, probably same as hünab'.

Hunavi, see hünab'.

Hunatsi, med., *Artemisia spinescens*.

Hunib, hu:nib:, food, unidentified species.

Hunivª, same as hunib.

Hupuhya, food, probably *Lycium andersonii*.

Hüü, hüʻⁿ, food, unidentified.

Hu'u'piva, food, *Lycium andersonii*.

Huvi, food, *Opuntia*.

Ijahua, med., *Symphoricarpos vaccinioides*.

Ijap: wana, manuf., *Symphore carpos vaccinioides*.

Kaibasi' tum, med., *Salvia carnosa*.

Kaiuhava (?), med., *Salvia carnosa*.

Kamac, food, *Quamasia quamash*.

Kaŋgwana, med., *Salvia carnosa*.

Kanª, food, unidentified root.

Kanambi, food, *Artemisia nova*.

Kanapohovi, food, *Artemisia nova*.

Kanikc, food, unidentified root.

Ko: gⁿ, ko: ga, koga, food, *Lepidium texanum*.

Kogi', food, unidentified root.

Kogiha, food, *Calochortus kennedyi*.

Kogwi, food, *Calochortus kennedyi*.

Koiya, food, unidentified; same as koo. yah (?).

Komuta, food, unidentified.

"Kooyah" (Frémont, p. 237), food, *Valeriana edulis*.

Kosbadüp, food, *Atriplex canescens*.

Kosiak:, food, probably *Helianthus*.

Köyo, food, unidentified seed.

Kozidümp:, no use, *Chaenactis nevadensis.*

Kuha, food, *Mentzelia dispersa.*

Kuhwa, food, *Mentzelia dispersa.*

Kuia, kuiyu, kuiya, food, probably *Valeriana edulis.*

Kuŋga, kuŋga'a, food, a small species of *Allium.*

Kunk, same as guŋga.

Kunugi', kunugip, food, *Sambucus.*

Kusiak:, food, *Helianthus annuus.*

Kutcimbogo, *Legume* sp.

Kutcindambono, *Legume* sp.

Kutzu', food, unidentified seed plant.

Ku:", food, *Mentzelia dispersa.*

Küyu, food, see Kuia.

Kwasinab:, food, *Sitamon hystrix.*

Kwasinab:", food, *Poa nevadensis.*

Kwütciani, food, *Holodiscus dumosa.*

Mahavit, food, probably *Eleocharis.*

Mono, food, *Eragrostis secundiflora.*

Mübiep:, no use, *Grayia spinosa.*

Mudunüp, no use, *Atriplex nuttallii.*

Müga'ta, no use, *Chylismia brévipes.*

Mügü'bump, food, *Anisocoma acaulis.*

Muh, same as amuh, food.

Mütä, same as muts, food.

Mutcuki, mutcuk,', unidentified plant used as greens.

Müts, muts:, food, a large round cactus.

Mutwanz, no use, *Erodium cicutarium.*

Nadü'mb:ᵃ, nadu'mp:ᵃ, food, *Poa nevadensis.*

Naha'tap', NP-LnPn, probably same as mahavita.

Nəp:, food, unidentified root.

Neviŋgu'nu, food, unidentified, probably seeds, S-DthV.

Nunsuad, any "weed" (S-Elko).

Nüwünoko, food and med., *Rumex crispus.*

Oakap:, med., *Grindelia squarrosa.*

Osüik:, any leaf (S-Elko).

Ovi, food, *Prosopis glandulosa.*

Ovü'ha, food, *Gilia micromeria.*

Padonzia, med., *Achillea millefolium.*

Padü'z, food, *Allium.*

Pagwiəmp:, same as pagwinump.

Pagwinump, the plant of *Artemisia tridentata.*

Pak:, pàk:, food, *Helianthus annuus.*

Paŋwabuihˣᵃ, food, *Ribes aureum.*

Pa'nodop, food, foxtail.

Pasawi' :jabᵃ, no use, *Chrysothamnus stenophyllus.*

Pasawitümb:, med., *Chrysothamnus* sp.

Pasĭ, food, "spruce."

Pasida, food, *Salvia columbariae.*

Pasigo, food, same as sigo(?).

Pasonip, food, the plant of *Elymus condensatus.*

Paso'pi, food, grass like red top.

Pasowüᵘ, med., unidentified.

Paui'o, food, *Rumex crispus;* also, *Agrostis.*

Pauwiya, food and med., *Rumex crispus.*

Pawaᵗᵃ, food, unidentified seed; NP-FLk.

Pavohop:, med., *Artemisia gnaphalodes.*

Pä'wa, food, same as pauwiya (?).

Pawatsiva, food, *Aster* (?).

Pawa'ziba, med., *Aster canadensis.*

Payamp:, food, unidentified root.

Pazün , food, *Cirsium,* perhaps *neomexicanum.*

Pit :sogo, food, unidentified root.

Pohovi, the plant of *Artemisia tridentata.*

Poia, põia, food, *Sophia sonnei.*

Poina, food, *Sophia sonnei.*

Poovi, food, *Artemisia tridentata.*

Puipahmo, smoke, *Nicotiana attenuata.* (See vocabularies for other names.)

Punib:, see hunib.

Puwiba, puwipa, see Puipahmo.

Sagəp:, manuf., *Salix amygdaloides.*

Saip:, food, *Juncus parous.*

Sawabᵘ, food, *Artemisia tridentata.*

Sawavi, same as sawabᵘ.

Sego, food, *Brodiaea* (?)

Seguyup, no use, *Eriogonum.*

Sicəp, no use, *Kochia vestita.*

Sigo, si :go, food, *Calochortus gunnisonii,* also *Hookcra* sp.

Sihü, food, red-top grass.

Sii, food, *Allium* sp.

Simu, food, see sihu.

Sipümb:, no use, *Chrysothamnus nauseosus* (?).

Siup:, food, *Poa nevadensis.*

Sivəp: sivəp:', no use, *Chrysothamnus* probably *nauseosus; Tetradymia glabrata* and several other species.

Siwəp:, probably chewing gum, *Chry-sothamnus stenophyllus.*

Sobi', food, *Hilaria jamesii.*

Sogodiümb:, no use, *Eriogonum thomasii.*

Sohna, food, *Lappula occidentalis.*

Soiga, food, unidentified root.

Sonebehe (NP-Ban), food, same as huki.

Sonip:, any grass; also, *Hilaria jamesii,* food.

Sowik, probably same as soiga.

Sugəp:, manuf., *Salix amygdaloides.*

Suhuvi, manuf., various sp. of *Salix.*

Suŋgavi, manuf.

Sunü, food, *Lappula occidentalis.*

Sunu, su:na, food, *Lappula occidentalis.*

Sunu, sünu'ᵘ, food seeds, *Atriplex argentea;* also, unidentified root (S-Elko).

Su:wəp;, food, *Chrysothamnus stenophyllus.*

Tagü, food, same as dagu.

Tahonadz', food, unidentified species, like small cattail.

Takü, food, unidentified root.

Täsum, food, a small round cactus.

Tatsip, no use, *Symphoricarpos vaccinioides.*

Täünüp:, no use, *Lupinus kingii.*

Taveciwəp:, med., *Chrysothamnus tortifolius.*

Tavowap, no use, *Tetradymia glabrata.*

Tävwa, any flower (S-Elko).

Tawisiw p, med., *Eriogonum sp.*

Tazüp, med., see dågup.

Tci'wi, food, *Anisocoma acaulis.*

Tiŋgambogo', food, unidentified greens, probably *Cirsium.*

Tiüga, food, unidentified S-Kawich.

To:dzəp, med., unidentified.

Togoa, yuŋgümü, med., unidentified.

Toi', to'i, food, *Typha latifolia.*

Tonumbi, food, *Prunus* sp.

Tonopuda, food, unidentified seed, S-LtLk.

Tonovi, manuf., *Sarcobatus vermiculatus.*

To'ocawi, food, *Prunus* sp.

Töpoi, food, unidentified root.

Tosa'mbi, no use, *Chrysothamnus stenophyllus.*

To:təmb:, to:təmb', food unidentified berry.

Towoiyuŋkha, med., *Achillea millefolium.*

Toyasiwəp, no use, *Tetradymia glabrata.*

Toyaciwəp, toyaziwep:, no use, Chrysothamnus, probably *nauseosus.*

Tsiabi, tsiəmb:, tsiavi, food, *Rosa californica (R. ultramontana).*

Tsin:, food, same as dzin:, probably *Cirsium.*

Tsinambogo, same as tiŋgambogo'; unidentified greens, probably *Cirsium.*

Tsogodzidzina, food, unidentified roots.

Tsowiga, food, same as dzowiga,; unidentified.

Tsün', food, probably *Cirsium.*

Tuba, food, *Pinus monophylla,* the seed.

Tübuwi, food, see dubwi'.

Tuəmbi, tuəmb:, food and manuf., *Amelanchier alnifolia.*

Tuhiumbi, food, *Sambucus,* elderberry.

Tuhuva'p, no use, *Eriogonum.*

Tui, food; unidentified root.

Tü'mü, food and med., *Rumex crispus.*

Tuna, food, see duna.

Tünambe, manuf., *Cercocarpus ledifolius.*

Tüpüsi'', food, *Brodiaea capitata* (?).

Tutumbi, food, *Ephedra viridis.*

Tutemb:, food, *Ephedra* prob., *viridis.*

Tutu'mbip, food and med., *Ephedra nevadensis.*

Tutu'p:'ᵃ, food, *Ephedra nevadensis.*

Tu:uyümba, food, *Sambucus microbotrys.*

Tuvuwap, food, *Pinus monophylla,* the tree.

Tüwi'p:, no use, *Cryptanthe racemosa.*

Tuwüip:', plant or flower.

Üəp: üəpi, food, *Chenopodium album.*

Umbeh, any seed (S-Elko).

Ütcüp, food and manuf., *Rhus trilobata.*

Üyüp:, food, probably same as Üəp:.

Waciip:, food, unidentified seed. S-Lida.

Wada, food, unidentified seed.

Wadunzi, the plant of *Elymus condensatus;* seeds called Wa:vi; possibly same as wadzovi.

Wadzovi, wadzovi'', food, *Dondia erecta.*

Wa:gova, unidentified root.

Wahavi, same as wa: vi.

Wai, food, *Oryzopsis hymenoides.*

Waiya'ᵃ, same as wa: vi.

Wakaba, food, NP-FLk; unidentified berry.

Wana, manuf., *Apocynum cannabinum.*

Wa: vi, vaavi, food, seeds of *Elymus condensatus.*

Waya, see waiya'ᵃ.

Wayabim:, see waiya'ᵃ.

Wayavimp, probably same as wayabim:.

Winigo, food, unidentified roots, perhaps *Fritillaria pudica.*

Wipuda tumbi, no use, *Ephedra nevadensis.*

Wiya, food, acorns, *Quercus*, NP-FLk, NP-Owens Valley, S-LtLk.

Wiyubimp, no use, *Erodium cicutarium.*

Wiyumb:, wi: yumbi, food, unidentified berry, *Shepherdia* or *Lepargyrca.*

Wiyup¹, food, "buck berry."

Woaku, wo: aku, food, *Helianthus annuus;* also, *H. aridus.*

Wogavi, food, *Opuntia.*

Woŋgoduba, food, *Pinus.*

Wotsǝp, manuf., *Symphoricarpus vaccinioides.*

Wüciüp, food, *Sitanion hystrix.*

Wü: sia, food, probably *Sitanion hystrix.*

Wüsiüp:, same as wuciup.

Yampa, yamp:, food, see Yomba.

Yubikua, no use, *Chilismia.*

Yuhu'ak:, food, probably *Helianthus* (NP-Ban).

Yümb:, yümb;, see yomba.

Yomba, food, *Carum gairdneri.*

Yutavo'°, food, unidentified root.

Yurihuva, food, unidentified; s-Bty.

Winünu, food, greens, S-Lida.

Wüps, any tree, S-Elko.

APPENDIX E.—MISCELLANEOUS USES OF PLANTS

MEDICINAL PLANTS

Achillea millefolium, yarrow. Padonzia or towoiyuŋkha (serrate leaf), S-SnRv and Oyhee. Leaf mashed and applied to sores. Root boiled and drunk to cure indigestion, but is not cathartic.

Argemone hispida, pricklepoppy. Artemisia and pinyon belts. S-Lida (PF), seeds ground and boiled for physic. No name or use, S-Elko.

Artemisia gnaphalodes, sage. Throughout area in artemisia to yellow pine belts. Pavohop:, S-Owyhee (CT); whole plant boiled for drink or for bath for small children with fever. Bavop, S-Elko; whole plant except roots boiled and drunk for colds. Babahovi, S-RubV (BM), whole plant boiled with taveciwǝp (rabbitbrush) and drunk for colds. S-Lemhi, pavohop, probably same; root juice used for sore eyes.

Artemisia spinescens, bud sagebrush. In artemisia belt throughout. Hunatsi, S-Hmlt, S-DiaV; fast 5 days, boil whole plant and drink for physic. Hunai, S-Elko; mix with pitch and apply externally or drink for physic, especially for venereal disease; person using this may not eat meat. Unknown, S-Lida (PF) and S-Rubv.

Asclepias cryptoceras, milkweed. Artemisia and pinyon belts, probably throughout area. Ana (translated as "white" but more probably "red") tsu (medicine), S-Elko; roots mashed and applied to major cuts and wounds. Not recognized by BM, S-Elko.

Aster canadensis (*A. canescens?*). Pawa'ziba, NP-LnPn, boil root and drink to facilitate urination with venereal disease.

Chaenactis nevadensis. Spruce and alpine belts; not known in southern part of area. Hunai (?), S-Elko; boiled into tea for physic to stop diarrhea. Not identified, S-RubV. Kozidümp, S-LtLk, not used.

Chrysothamnus sp.　Pasawitümb:, S–Lida; whole plant boiled for liniment. Not identified, S–RubV.

Chrysothamnus tortifolius, rabbitbrush.　Plains, mountain sides, and canyons up to 8,000 feet.　Tave (rabbit) ciwəp: (brush), S–RubV (BM) ; whole plant boiled and drunk for colds, measles, smallpox, and swellings.　Awadaviciwup, S–Elko.

Cowania stansburiana, cliffrose.　Artemisia and pinyon belts throughout. Hünab[1], S–Lida (PF), boil whole brush for physic.　Hunavi (huna, badger), S–DiaV.　S–Elko; boil whole plant and drink for measles and smallpox. Hünabi, S–RubV (BM) ; same use as S–Elko.　This is probably the S–Lemhi hunap:, used for sore eyes.

Enceliopsis agrophylla.　Covillea belt, southern part of area.　Aŋgagwu'p (red brush), S–Lida (JS) ; tea for stomach disorders.

Ephedra nevadensis.　Tutu'mbip, S–LtLk, tea, especially for kidney disorders. See also "Food Plants."

Eriogonum sp.　Tawisiwəp, S–SprV; boil flower and drink for stomach disorder.　S–Elko, also for stomach disorder.　Not recognized, S–RubV (BM).

Grindelia squarrosa, gumweed.　Artemisia to yellow pine belts, throughout. Oakap:, S–RubV (BM) ; used for smallpox.

Helianthus.　A species called pi : akənzïp:, S–Lemhi; root boiled and drunk for physic and emetic.

Helenium montanum, sneezeweed.　Artemisia to yellow pine belts.　S–Elko, roots used for gonorrhea.　S–RubV, not recognized.

Pentstemon palmeri.　S–Lida (PF) ; leaf ground and put on burn.

Rumex crispus, dock.　Around settlements; introduced from Europe.　Nüwü-noko or pauwiya, S–Elko; roots mashed and applied to swellings.　Bauwiya or tümü, S–RsRi (GJ), same use.　Nüwünoko, S–RubV, made into tea.　See also "Food plants."

Rumex mexicanus, dock.　Everywhere, especially in wet places.　Aŋga (red) bauwiya, S–Owyhee (TP) and S–SnRv.　Roots mashed and applied to cuts and sores.

Salix.　A species called agai (salmon) suhu, burned and applied to sore eyes, S–Lemhi.

Salvia carnosa, sage.　Covillea to pinyon belt, throughout.　Kaibasi'tum, S–LtLk; tea for stomach trouble.　S–Lida, same use.　Kaiuhava (?), NP–FLk, use unknown.　Ka (wood rat) ŋgwana (smells), S–Elko; tops boiled into tea for blood tonic.　Not identified, S–RubV.

Symphoricarpos vaccinioides, snowberry.　Yellow pine and aspen belts; north. Ija (ijap, coyote) hua, S–Elko; whole plant boiled for eyes.　Tatsip, S–RubV (BM), no use.　See also "Plants used in manufacturing."

Rumex mexicanus, dock.　Everywhere, especially in wet places.　A ga (red)
Welwitschia diffusa.　Covillea belt; south only.　NP–FLk, boil for tea for emetic.

UNIDENTIFIED MEDICINAL PLANTS

Biji (milk) dubuwi (any greens), S–Elko; roots mashed and applied to minor cuts.

Dágüp, S–SprV; tázüp, S–Elko; a long, whitish root, mixed with tobacco and smoked to cure a cold.

Togoa yuŋgüwü, S–Lemhi; roots used for physic.

PLANTS USED IN MANUFACTURING

Amelanchier glabra and, probably more generally, *A. alnifolia*, service berry. In important quantities only in northern portion of area. Dühavi, S–DiaV, S–Elko, used for bows. Probably used for bows elsewhere. Also, basket rims, digging sticks.

Apocynum androsaemifolium, dogbane. Mountain sides and canyons up to aspen belt. Äŋga (red) wana (string, net), S–Elko, S–RubV. Bark used for string.

Apocynum cannabinum, dogbane. Covillea and artemisia belts. Wana, S–RsRi, S–RubV; bark dried and used for string.

Artemisia tridentata, sagebrush. Throughout area. Bohovi, Shoshoni; sawavi, NP-MC. Wood for fire drill and hearth; bark for tinder. Bark also for twined bags and garments, especially in north.

Cercocarpus ledifolius, mountain mahogany. Upper pinyon, yellow pine, and aspen belts, throughout. Tünambe, dünambi, S–Lida, S–Elko, S–RubV, and elsewhere. Used for digging stick; by S–Lida for arrows; GS-DpCr, for bows.

Echinocactus polycephalus, devil's pincushion. Needles used for awls, southern part of area. (See Coville, 1892.)

Elymus condensatus and probably other species. Used for house thatching and beds, especially in north.

Epicampes rigens, grass. Southern part of area. Foundation for some coiled basketry (Coville, 1802).

Juniperus utahensis juniper or "cedar." Characteristic tree of the pinyon belt. Used for bow. Branches for houses.

Martynia proboscidea, devil's horn, unicorn plant, devil's claw. Used for black in basketry, southern portion of area. (See also Coville, 1892.)

Pinus monphylla, pinyon or pine nut tree. Limbs for houses; boughs for house covering in mountains.

Phragmites communis (*P. vulgaris*), reed or cane. Hugapi, hugapi: Shoshoni. Stems used for arrow shafts.

Rhus trilobata, sumac. S–DthV and S–Pan, used for white in basketry (Coville, 1892.)

Ribes inebrians, currant. Duŋwip, S–DiaV, stems used for arrows. But S–Elko said duŋwip applied to another plant, calling *R. inebrians* bogunəp:. S–RubV, bambigama; not used.

Salix amygdaloides, peachleaf willow. Along streams of the artemisia, pinyon, and yellow pine belts. Sugəp:, S–Elko; sag p:, S–RubV; basketry materials.

Salix lasiandra, willow. Along streams up to yellow pine belt, throughout. Used for basketry in S–DthV (Coville, 1892) and probably elsewhere. This is probably the species generally called suhuvi, Shoshoni.

Sambucus, elder. Used for flutes.

Sarcobatus vermiculatus, greasewood. Abundant in Covillea and artemisia belts. Tonovi, Shoshoni, NP-MC. Used for arrow foreshafts, sometimes for digging sticks and other purposes requiring hardwood.

Sphaeralcea ambigua, desert mallow. Southern portion of area. S–DthV boiled and syrup mixed with potter's clay (Steward, 1933:266, Owens Valley Paiute used *S. fremontii*). Gwidegomb:, LtLk; gubanap, SP-Ash; not used. S–Lida not used.

Symphoricarpos vaccinoides, snow berry. Wotsəp or ijap: (coyote) wana (string or net), S–DiaV; bark used for string.

PLANTS USED IN SMOKING

Apocynum cannabinum, dog bane. Bahunduwaya'*, S–Elko; bark mixed with tobacco. Elsewhere, used for string.

Arctostaphylos platyphylla. In pinyon to aspen belts, throughout. Bia (big) dumaya, S–RsRi, S–Elko, S–RubV. Bark mixed with tobacco. Another plant similarly used called dumaya, S–RsRi.

Cornus, dogwood. Nevada Shoshoni (Remy and Brenchley, 1861, p. 129) used the bark of a species of *Cornus*.

Nicotiana attenuata, wild tobacco. Artemisia to yellow pine belts, throughout. Leaf dried for smoking. Hoffman (1878, p. 467) mentions this species for southern Nevada.

For smoking, see also, Chamberlin, 1911 : 34–35; Steward, 1933 : 319–320.

Vaccinium, blueberry. Nevada Shoshoni used the bark of a species of Vaccinium. (Remy and Brenchley, 1861, pp. 129–130).

NAMES OF SOME PLANTS NOT USED

Adenostegia sp., tuwü'ip: (any plant or flower), S–LtLk.

Amaranthus blitoides.

Atriplex nuttallii, mound saltbrush. Mudunüp, S–Lida (PF).

Atriplex confertifolia, shadscale. Large colonies of the Covillea, artemisia, and pinyon belts. Bokumbi, S–Elko, S–RubV (BM).

Aploppapus linearifolius interior.

Bassia hyssopifolia. Introduced from Asia. Not identified.

Castilleja angustifolia, painted-cup, paintbrush. Aŋa (red) kwiwi'tum, S–LtLk; anabimotoymup, SP-Ash.

Chrysothamnus nauseosus, rabbitbrush. Very common in artemisia belt. Sipümb:, S–Li ɑ (PF); sivəp:[1] or toyaziwəp:, S–Elko; toyaciwəp, S–RubV.

Cryptanthe racemosa. Tüwi'p:, S–LtLk.

Chylismia brevipes. Arid areas in Covillea belt. Müga'ta, S–LtLk.

Chylismia sp. (?), Yubiku'a, S–Tonopah.

Dithyrea wislizeni. Not identified.

Eremalche rotundifolia. Deserts, Covillea belt.

Ephedra nevadensis, jointflr. Wipuda tumbi, S–Lida (PF). *E. viridis*, tutumbi, used by S–Lida for tea. See *Ephedra*, under "Food plants."

Erodium cicutarium, alifileria or storksbill. Introduced from Europe. Mutwanz (from mutuʰmazəp, humming bird), S–LtLk; wiyubimp, SP-Ash.

Eriogonum thomasii. Desert areas of Covillea belt, but collected in artemisia belt. Sogodiümb:, S–SprV, S–RubV.

Eriogonum sp. Tuhuva'p, SP-Ash; segu'yup, S–LtLk.

Eurotia lanata. Plains and arid areas, Covillea to pinyon belts. Cicəp:, S–Elko, S–RubV; good only for stock feed.

Grayia spinosa, hopsage. Pakümbi, S–LtLk.

Kochia vestita, gray molly. Sicəp, S–RubV.

Layia douglasii. Not identified.

Legume sp. Kutcindambono, S–Elko; kutcimbogo, S–RubV.

Lupinus brevicaulis, lupine. Not identified.

Lupinus kingii, lupine. Ta nüp:, S–LtLk.

Mentzelia laevis. Not recognized, S–Elko; S–RubV.

Norta altissima, introduced from Europe. Not identified.

Phacelia crenulata. Mübiəp:, S–LtLk.

Sphaerostigma decorticans. Southern area. Not identified.
Sphaerostigma veitchianum. Southern Area. Not identified.
Syntrichopappus fremontii. Southern area. Not identified.
Tetradymia glabrata. Throughout artemisia belt. Tavowap, S–Lida (PF) ;
toyasiwəp, S–Elko; sivəp:, S–RubV (BM).

APPENDIX F.—MH's BIOGRAPHY

Mary H was born in Hamil Valley at a place called Tepo'siinatü, where her family lived in a grass house. Sometimes her folks visited the villages at Bishop where her grandparents had lived.

When Mary was a small girl her maternal grandfather fell from a cliff and was killed while hunting eagles in the White Mountains. Desiring to go away because of their sorrow at his death, her parents took Mary and her brother to Geroux Ranch (Tu:na'va) in Fish Lake Valley to live. For many years they made this their winter home.

Mary first heard of white men when she was about 6 years old. The report that two white men with pack animals were passing through the country so frightened her people that they fled to the mountains and hid.

When Mary was about 16 or 17 years old she met her husband, Captain Harry, at a festival. The dance was near Pigeon Springs at pine-nut time (tuba, pine nut, nügatü, dance). The Fish Lake Valley chief had announced the time, place, and duration of the dance and had invited Shoshoni from the vicinity of Lida. Captain Harry attended with the Shoshoni. Mary's father (her mother had died) and Captain Harry's parents agreed that they should marry and, after the festival, the requisite exchange of presents was made. Captain Harry's father gave money (netavi) to Mary's father who later reciprocated with pine nuts. Then Harry came to Mary's village bringing deer meat. He remained and the marriage was consummated without ceremony. This was Harry's second marriage. His Shoshoni wife had died.

Ordinarily, a young married couple lived for some time with the wife's family until they learned to provide for themselves. But as Harry was nearly 30 years old and a good hunter, this was unnecessary. They remained at Tu:na'va for about 2 weeks, then went to Oasis where they built their own house.

Mary and Harry lived at Oasis for about 3 years. During the second year their first child, a daughter, was born. Mary was taken to a small house where she remained for five days, cared for by her maternal grandmother who delivered the baby. After the birth her grandmother bathed her and "talked" that Mary should not be a lazy mother. Five days later, before Mary returned to her dwelling, her grandmother bathed her and prayed again, then advised her to refrain from meat for 8 or 10 days. Mary gave all her clothes to her grandmother and received new ones upon returning home. Meanwhile, Harry, who had not gone hunting for 5 days, was bathed on the fifth day after the birth. He gave his old clothes to the man who performed this service. He then went hunting and killed a deer, but gave all of it away.

A child was usually named by its paternal grandfather if it were a boy and by its paternal grandmother if it were a girl. In this case, when she was about a year old, Harry named his daughter Wino'heküwa'[a] after his sister.

White people had now entered Fish Lake Valley and made the Oasis, Patterson, and McFee ranches. While Harry was working at the last and Wino'heküwa'[a] was about 3 years old, their son Rob was born.

Some time after this, they went to Ozaŋwin:[1] to visit Harry's sister for a month, and back to McFee ranch. Another son was born.

Several years later they moved over to Deep Springs, where they were welcome to live, hunt, and gather seeds. When Deep Springs Ranch was founded, Harry worked from time to time, living nearby. After his death in 1919, Mary burned their camp and all of Harry's possessions and moved to Big Pine where she has lived since with her daughter's family.

APPENDIX G.—STATUS TERMS

Very young babies of both sexes are called oha or ohwa in Shoshoni, descriptive of the peculiar cry of a newborn.

Terms for older persons are not definitely fixed with reference to puberty, marriage, or parenthood. Little girl was naivitci, diminutive of naivi. Naivi was used by S–Lemhi for a girl who had begun to menstruate. This is probably the general meaning, though duepüdü (child) naivi was sometimes used for pre-adolescent girls. S–GrsCr's equivalent for little girl, waiputsi duepüdü, means "little woman child." Naivi was sometimes carried over to the married status, though waip, woman, was generally used. S–Lemhi used tambia, "the mother," for a young married woman. Huvijo'° or huvidzo' for old women is a combination of huvijiji, old woman, and dzo'°, great-grandparent, meaning literally, "feeble."

S–SnRv used duinüp:[1] for a very small boy, bihiǝ for one slightly larger, and davici still larger who did not yet dress or wear a breechclout. The term denu: or dainǝp for man is derived from tenǝpü'[1], S–SnRv, any full-grown male. This generally replaced tuivitc, boy, at about the time of his marriage.

	S-BtlM	S-Mor	S-Hmlt	S-SprV	S-GrsCr	S-SnRv	S-Lem	NP-MC
Baby	oha	ōhwatsi	ohwɛ	ohwa	ohna (tsi)	oha (tsi)	ohna	oma'ᵃ
Little girl	naí'vi	naivitc	naivætci	naivite	waiputsi / duepŭdŭ	naí'vi / yagwani	dzidzi	tsua'ᵃ
Young girl	naí'vi	naivite	naivætci	naivite	duepŭdŭnaivi	naivi ?	tŭdepŭdŭnaivi	tsua'ᵃ
Adolescent girl	naivi	naivi	naivi	naivi	naivi	naivi ?	naivi	cuaidum
Young woman	waip:	naivi	naivi	biandunaivi	waipŭ	waip: / waipŭ'ᵘ	tambia / naivi	mosʷo'ᵘum / pia'wabl
Woman	waip:	waip:	waipɛu	nawaip: / waip:	waipŭ	waip: / waipŭ'ᵘ	tambia	pia'wabl
Old woman	huviji	huvijiji	hu:vjiji	huvijo'ᵒ / huvijupŭtsi	huvidzotsi	huviji	huvidzo'	tuvizo'ᵘm
Little boy	duinŭp:ᵘ / bihie	duitcitci	tuhirŭpŭ	duwiyupu'	tuhinŭpŭ'ᵘ / duepŭdŭ	tuinŭp:ᵘ / bihie	tuiñŭp:e / tŭdepŭdŭ	na:tsi
Boy	duivitci	duite	duitcitci	bianduduitci	tuivitci	davici / duivite / tuinuɔpu / duivitci	bihiɔnɛ / tŭdepŭdŭtuivitsi	tuivitci
Young man	duivitci	duhivitci	tɑŋwɔp:ŭ	dɑŋwŭ'ᵘ		den:u / den:ıtci	tuivitsi	nana
Man	den:u	dɑŋwep	tɑŋwɛ	dɑŋwŭ'ᵘ	dainɔp:ᵘ	denɔpŭ'ᵘ	denɔduivitsi	nana
Middle-aged man	den:u	dɑŋwep	tɑŋwɛ	dɑŋwŭ'ᵘ	dainɔp:ᵘ	denɔpŭ'ᵘ	denɔp:ᵘ	nana
Old man	tsugupŭ	dɑŋwep	tɑŋwɛtci / tsug: (tsŭtsi)	duwujupŭtsi	tsŭgŭpŭtsi	tsugupŭ	tsugupŭ'	wa'itc

BIBLIOGRAPHY

[The following list does not purport to be an exhaustive bibliography of the Basin-Plateau area, but does include the more important sources, especially on the Shoshoni.]

ALDOUS, A. E., and SHANTZ, H. L.
1924   Types of Vegetation in the Semiarid Portions of the United States and their Economic Significance. U. S. Dept. Agr., Journ. Agric. Research, vol. 28, No. 2, Washington, 1924.

ALTER, J. CECIL.
1925   James Bridger. Salt Lake City, 1925.
1928   Some Useful Early Utah Indian References. Utah Hist. Quart., 1: 26–32, 52–56.
1928   Father Escalante and the Utah Indians. Utah Hist. Quart., 1: 75–86, 106–113; 2: 18–25, 46–54.
1934–35   In the Beginning. Publ. daily in the Salt Lake Telegram.

ARMSTRONG, GEORGE W.
1856   [Communication in] Rept. Com. Ind. Affairs for 1855, pp. 204–206, Washington, 1856.

ASHLEY-SMITH NARRATIVES. See DALE, HARRISON C.

AVESON, ROBERT.
1854   Eventful Narratives. The Thirteenth Book of the Faith-Promoting Series. Juvenile Instructor Office. Salt Lake City, 1854.

BALLARD, DAVID W.
1886   [Communication in] Rept. Com. Ind. Affairs for 1866, pp. 190–192, Washington, 1866.

BANCROFT, HUBERT HOWE.
1886–1890   The Works of Hubert Howe Bancroft. Vols. I–XXXIX. San Francisco, 1886–90. Vol. I, Native Races, 1886. Vol. XXV, History of Nevada, Colorado, and Wyoming, 1890. Vol. XXVI, History of Utah, 1889. Vols. XXIX–XXX, History of Oregon, 1886–88. Vol. XXXI, History of Washington, Idaho, and Montana, 1890.

BARBER, EDWIN A.
1876   Language and Utensils of the Modern Utes. U. S. Geol. and Geog. Survey of the Territories, 2: 71–76, 1876.
1877   Gaming Among the Utah Indians. Amer. Naturalist, 11: 351–353, 1877.

BARNES, CLAUDE T.
1927   Utah Mammals. Univ. of Utah Bull., vol. 17, no. 12, 1927.

BEALS, RALPH L.
1935   Ethnology of Rocky Mountain National Park. The Ute and Arapaho. U. S. Dept. Interior, Natl. Parks Service, Field Div. of Educ., Berkeley, Calif., 1935.

BECKWITH, E. G.
1855   Report of Explorations for a Route for the Pacific Railroad by Capt. J. W. Gunnison, Topographical Engineers, near the Thirty-eighth and Thirty-ninth Parallels. In Reports Explor. and Surv. . . . for a Railroad . . . to the Pacific. 1853–54. Vol. II, pp. 1g–128. (Sen. Ex. Doc. No. 78, 33d Cong., 2d sess., Washington, 1855.)
1855a   Report of Explorations for a Route for the Pacific Railroad on the line of the Forty-first Parallel. Ibid., pp. 1b–132.

BECKWOURTH, JAMES P. *See* BONNER, T. D.

BERREMAN, JOEL V.
    1937 Tribal Distribution in Oregon. Mem. Amer. Anthrop. Assoc., No. 47, 1937.

BIDWELL, JOHN.
    1928 Echoes of the Past About California. Edited by M. M. Quaife. Chicago, 1928.

BONNER, T. D.
    1856 The Life and Adventures of James P. Beckwourth. Written from his own dictation. New York, 1856.

BONNEVILLE, CAPTAIN. *See* IRVING, WASHINGTON, 1898.

BRYANT, EDWIN.
    1848 What I saw in California. New York and Phila., 1848.

BURCHE, JOHN C.
    1865 [Communication in] Rept. Com. Ind. Affairs for 1864, pp. 144–148, Washington, 1865.

BURTON, RICHARD F.
    1862 The City of the Saints. New York, 1862.

CAMPBELL, FRANKLIN.
    1866 [Communication in] Rept. Com. Ind. Affairs for 1866, pp. 117–120, Washington, 1866.

CHALFANT, W. A.
    1933 The Story of Inyo. 2d edition. Bishop, Calif., 1933.

CHAMBERLIN, RALPH V.
    1908 Animal names and anatomical terms of the Goshute Indians. Acad. Nat. Sci. Phila., Proc., vol. LX, pp. 74–103, Phila., 1908–1909.
    1909 Some Plant Names of the Ute Indians. Amer. Anthrop., n. s. 11: 27–40, 1909.
    1911 The Ethno-botany of the Gosiute Indians. Acad. Nat. Sci. Phila., Proc., vol. LXIII, pp. 24–99, Phila., 1911–1912.

COVILLE, FREDERICK V.
    1892 The Panamint Indians of California. Amer. Anthrop., 5: 351–361, 1892.

CULIN, STEWART.
    1901 A Summer Trip Among the Western Indians. Univ. of Pa. Free Mus. of Sci. and Art, Dept. of Arch., Bull. 3, 1901.
    1907 Games of the North American Indians. Twenty-fourth Ann. Rept. Bur. Amer. Ethn., Washington, 1907.

CURTIS, EDWARD S.
    1926 The North American Indian. Vol. 15. Norwood, Mass., 1926.

DALE, HARRISON, C., *Editor*.
    1918 The Ashley-Smith Explorations and the Discovery of a Central Route to the Pacific, 1822–29, with the original Journals. Cleveland, 1918.

DANILSON, W. H.
    1870 [Communication in] Rept. Com. Ind. Affairs for 1869, pp. 287–288, Washington, 1870.

DAVIES, BENJAMIN.
    1861 [Communication in] Rept. Com. Ind. Affairs for 1861, pp. 129–134, Washington, 1861.

DE ANGULO, JAIME, and FREELAND, L. S.
    1929 Notes on the Northern Paiute of California. Journ. Soc. Amér. de Paris, n. s. 21: 313–335, 1929.

DE SMET, P. J.
  1843 Letters and Sketches: With a Narrative of a Year's Residence among
        the Indian Tribes of the Rocky Mountains. Phila., 1843. Reprinted
        in Thwaite's Early Western Travels, vol. 27: 123–411, Cleveland,
        1906.
DELANO, ALONZO.
  1857 Life on the plains and among the diggings; being scenes and adven-
        tures of an overland journey to California. New York, 1857.
DELLENBAUGH, FREDERICK S.
  1908 A Canyon Voyage. The Narrative of the Second Powell Expedition
        down the Green-Colorado River from Wyoming and the Explora-
        tions on Land in the Years 1871 and 1872. New York, 1908.
DENNISON, A. P.
  1858 [Communication in] Rept. Com. Ind. Affairs for 1858, pp. 262–265,
        Washington, 1858.
DENSMORE, FRANCES.
  1922 Northern Ute Music. Bull. 75, Bur. Amer. Ethn., Washington, 1922.
DOMENECH, ABBÉ EMMANUEL.
  1860 Seven Years' Residence in the Great Deserts of North America.
        2 vols. London, 1860.
DORSEY, GEORGE A.
  1901 The Shoshonean Game of Nă-wa'tă-pi. Journ. Amer. Folk-Lore, 14:
        24–25, 1901.
DOTY, JAMES DUANE.
  1863 [Communication in] Rept. Com. Ind. Affairs for 1862, pp. 210–212,
        Washington, 1863.
  1865 [Communication in] Rept. Com. Ind. Affairs for 1864, pp. 173–176,
        Washington, 1865.
DOUGLAS, F. H.
  1930 The Ute Indians. Denver Art Mus., Leaflet No. 10, 1930.
DOUGLAS, H.
  1870 [Communication in] Rept. Com. Ind. Affairs for 1870, pp. 94–101,
        Washington, 1870.
DUTCHER, B. H.
  1893 Piñon Gathering among the Panamint Indians.   Amer. Anthrop.,
        6: 377–380, 1893.
EGAN, MAJOR HOWARD and HOWARD R.
  1917 Pioneering the West, 1846 to 1878. William M. Egan, Editor. Salt
        Lake City, 1917.
ESCALANTE, FRAY SILVESTRE VELEZ DE. See HARRIS, W. R.
EVERMANN, B. W.
  1896 A Preliminary Report Upon Salmon Investigations in Idaho in 1894.
        Bull. U. S. Fish Comm. for 1895, vol. 15, pp. 253–284, 1896.
  1897 A Report Upon Salmon Investigations in the Headwaters of the
        Columbia River and in the State of Idaho in 1895. Bull. U. S.
        Fish Comm. for 1896, vol. 16, pp. 151–202, 1897.
FARNHAM, THOMAS J.
  1843 Travels in the Great Western Prairies, the Anahuac and Rocky
        Mountains and in the Oregon Territory. 2 vols. London, 1843.
        Reprinted in part in Thwaite's Early Western Travels, vol. 28,
        Cleveland, 1906.
  1849 Life, Adventures, and Travels in California. New York, 1849.

FENTON, R. N.
   1870   [Communication in] Rept. Com. Ind. Affairs for 1869, pp. 203–204, Washington, 1870.
FORNEY, JACOB.
   1858   [Communication in] Rept. Com. Ind. Affairs for 1858, pp. 209–213, Washington, 1858.
   1860a [Communications in] Message of the President of the United States, Communicating . . . Information in Relation to the Massacre at Mountain Meadows, and other Massacres in Utah Territory. Sen. Ex. Doc., 42, 36th Cong., 1st sess., Washington, 1860.
   1860b [Communication in] Rept. Com. Ind. Affairs for 1859, pp. 362–373, Washington, 1860.
FRÉMONT, JOHN CHARLES.
   1845   Report of the Exploring Expedition to the Rocky Mountains in the Year 1842 and to Oregon and North California in the years 1843 and 1844. Washington, 1845.
   1856   Narrative of the Exploring Expedition to Oregon and North California. In the "Life of Colonel John Charles Fremont" by Samuel M. Smucker, A. M., New York.
   1887   Memoirs of my life, including in the narrative five journeys of western exploration, during the years 1842, 1843–44, 1845–46–47, 1848–9, 1853–54. 2 vols. Chicago and New York, 1887.
GASS, PATRICK.
   1811   Journal of the Voyages and Travels of a Corps of Discovery under the command of Capt. Lewis and Capt. Clark . . . 3d edition, Philadelphia, 1811.
GAYTON, A. H.
   1935   Areal Affiliations of California Folktales. Amer. Anthrop., n. s. 37: 582–599, 1935.
GEARY, EDWARD R.
   1860   [Communication in] Rept. Com. Ind. Affairs for 1860, pp. 171–186, Washington, 1860.
GEBOW, JOSEPH A.
   1868   A vocabulary of the Snake or Sho-sho-nay Dialect. 2d edition. Green River City, Wyoming, 1868.
GIFFORD, EDWARD WINSLOW.
   1922   California Kinship Terminologies. Univ. Cal. Publ. Amer, Arch. and Ethn., 18: 1–285, 1922.
GOTTFREDSON, PETER.
   1919   History of Indian Depredations in Utah. Salt Lake City, 1919.
HALE, HORATIO.
   1846   United States Exploring Expedition during the Years 1838, 1839, 1840, 1841, 1842 under the Command of Charles Wilkes, U. S. N. Vol. 6, Ethnography and Philology. Philadelphia, 1846.
   1848   Indians of Northwest America. Amer. Ethn. Soc., Trans., 2: 1–130, 1848.
HALL, NATHANIEL T.
   1866   [Communication in] Rept. Com. Ind. Affairs for 1866, p. 200, Washington, 1866.
HAMBLIN, JACOB.
   1881   A Narrative of his Personal Experiences as Frontiersman, Missionary to the Indians and Explorer. The Faith-Promoting Series, No. 5, Salt Lake City, 1881.

HANDBOOK OF AMERICAN INDIANS. Frederick W. Hodge, *Editor.* Bull. 30, Bur. Amer. Ethn., pt. 1, 1907, pt. 2, 1910.

HARRINGTON, J. P.
    1911 The Origin of the Names Ute and Paiute. Amer. Anthrop. n. s. 13: 173–174, 1911.
    1911a The Phonetic System of the Ute Language. Arch. Inst. of Amer., School Amer. Arch., Papers, 24: 199–222, New Mexico, 1911.

HARRINGTON, M. R.
    1933 Gypsum Cave, Nevada. Southwest Museum Papers, 8, Los Angeles, 1933.

HARRIS, REV. W. R.
    1909 Diary and Travels of Fray Francisco Atanasio Dominguez and Fray Silvestre Velez de Escalante to discover a route from the Presidio of Santa Fe, New Mexico, to Monterey in Southern California. *In* "The Catholic Church in Utah," by W. R. Harris, pp. 125–242, Salt Lake City, 1909.

HATCH, T. W.
    1863 [Communication in] Rept. Com. Ind. Affairs for 1862, pp. 205–210, Washington, 1863.

HEAD, F. H.
    1866 [Communication in] Rept. Com. Ind. Affairs for 1866, pp. 122–126, Washington, 1866.
    1868 [Communication in] Rept. Com. Ind. Affairs for 1867, pp. 173–180, Washington, 1868.

HEBARD, GRACE RAYMOND.
    1930 Washakie. An Account of Indian Resistance to the Covered Wagon and Union Pacific Railroad Invasions of their Territory. Cleveland, 1930.

HILL, JOSEPH J.
    1930 Spanish and Mexican Exploration and Trade Northwest from New Mexico into the Great Basin. Utah Hist. Quart., 3: 3–22, 1930.

HITCHCOCK, A. S.
    1935 Manual of the Grasses of the United States. U. S. Dept. Agr., Miscl. Publ. 200, Washington, 1935.

HOEBEL, E. ADAMSON.
    1935 The Sun Dance of the Hekandika Shoshone. Amer. Anthrop., n. s. 37: 570–381, 1935.

HOFFMAN, W. J.
    1886 Remarks on Indian Tribal Names. Amer. Philos. Soc., Proc., vol. 23, no. 122, pp. 294–303, Phila., 1886.
    1891 Poisoned Arrows. Amer. Anthrop. 4: 67–71, 1891.

HOFFMAN, W. T.
    1878 Miscellaneous Ethnographic Observations on Indians Inhabiting Nevada, California, and Arizona. Tenth Ann. Rept. U. S. Geological and Geodetic Survey (Hayden Survey). Washington, 1878.

HOLEMAN, J. H.
    1852 [Communication in] Rept. Com. Ind. Affairs for 1852, pp. 149–155, Washington, 1852.
    1853 [Communication in] Rept. Com. Ind. Affairs for 1853, pp. 443–447, Washington [n. d.]

HOPKINS, SARAH WINNEMUCCA.
    1883 Life among the Piutes: Their Wrongs and Claims. Boston, 1883.

HORNADAY, WILLIAM T.
1889 The Extermination of the American Bison. U. S. Natl. Mus., Report for 1887, pp. 367–548, Washington, 1889.

HOUGH, GEORGE C.
1866 [Communication in] Rept. Com. Ind. Affairs for 1866, pp. 188–189, Washington, 1866.

HOUGH, WALTER.
1890 Fire-Making Apparatus in the U. S. National Museum. U. S. Natl. Mus., Rept. for 1888, pp. 531–587, Washington, 1890.

HUMFREVILLE, J. LEE.
1897 Tyenty years among Our Savage Indians. Hartford, Conn., 1897.

Huntington, J. W. P.
1865 [Communication in] Rept. Com. Ind. Affairs for 1865, pp. 461–468, Washington, 1865.
1868 [Communication in] Rept. Com. Ind. Affairs for 1867, pp. 95–103, Washington, 1868.

HURT, GARLAND.
1857 [Communication in] Rept. Com. Ind. Affairs for 1856, pp. 227–232, Washington, 1857.
1860 [Communications in] Message of the President of the United States, Communicating . . . Information in Relation to the Massacre at Mountains Meadows, and other Massacres in Utah Territory. Sen. Ex. Doc. 42, 36th Congress, 1st Sess., Washington, 1860.

INGALLS, G. W. See POWELL, J. W., and INGALLS, G. W.

IRISH, O. H.
1865 [Communication in] Rept. Com. Ind. Affairs for 1865, pp. 142–148, Washington, 1865.

IRVING, WASHINGTON.
1897 Astoria. New York and London, 1897.
1898 The Adventures of Captain Bonneville, U. S. A., in the Rocky Mountains and the Far West, Digested from his Journal and Illustrated from Various Other Sources. 2 vols. "Pawnee Edition," New York, 1898.

JACOBS, MELVILLE.
1937 Historic Perspectives in Indian Languages of Oregon and Washington. Pacific Northwest Quart., vol. 28, No. 1, pp. 55–74, Seattle, Wash., 1937.

JAMES, EDWIN.
1823 Account of an Expedition . . . to the Rocky Mountains, etc. 2 vols., atlas. Phila. and London, 1823.

JARVIS, ROBERT B.
1860 [Communication in] Rept. Com. Ind. Affairs for 1859, pp. 377–379, Washington, 1860.

JEPSON, WILLIS LINN.
1925 A Manual of the Flowering Plants of California. University of California, Berkeley, Calif., 1925.

JONES, DANIEL W.
1890 Forty Years Among the Indians. Salt Lake City, 1890.

JONES, DE L. FLOYD.
1870 [Communication in] Rept. Com. Ind. Affairs for 1869, pp. 277–279, Washington, 1870.

KELLY, CHARLES.
1936 Old Greenwood. Salt Lake City, 1936.

KELLY, ISABEL T.
  1932 Ethnography of the Surprise Valley Paiute. Univ. Cal. Publ. Amer.
        Arch. and Ethn., 31: 67–210, 1932.
  1934 Southern Paiute Bands. Amer. Anthrop., n. s. 36: 548–560, 1934.
  1936 Chemehuevi Shamanism. *In* Essays in Anthropology presented to
        A. L. Kroeber, pp. 129–142, Berkeley, Calif., 1936.
KIRKPATRICK, J. M.
  1863 [Communication in] Rept. Com. Ind. Affairs for 1862, pp. 265–268,
        Washington, 1863.
KROEBER, A. L.
  1901 Ute Tales. Journ. Amer. Folk-Lore, 14: 252–285, 1901.
  1907 Shoshonean Dialects of California. Univ. Cal. Publ. Amer. Arch.
        and Ethn., 4: 65–165, 1907.
  1908 Notes on the Ute Language. Amer. Anthrop., n. s. 10: 74–87, 1908.
  1909 The Bannock and Shoshoni Languages. Amer. Anthrop., n. s. 11:
        266–277, 1909.
  1920 Games of the California Indians. Amer. Anthrop., n. s. 22: 272–277,
        1920.
  1922 Elements of Culture in Native California. Univ. Cal. Publ. Amer.
        Arch. and Ethn., 13: 259–328, 1922.
  1925 Handbook of the Indians of California. Bull. 78, Bur. Amer. Ethn.,
        Washington, 1925.
  1934 Native American Population. Amer. Anthrop., n. s. 36: 1–25, 1934.
LANDER, F. W.
  1860 [Communications in] Message of the President of the United States,
        Communicating . . . Information in Relation to the Massacre at
        Mountain Meadows, and other Massacres in Utah Territory. Sen.
        Ex. Doc. 42, 36th Congress, 1st Sess., Washington, 1860.
LANE, JOSEPH.
  1850 [Communication in] Rept. Com. Ind. Affairs for 1850, pp. 156–165,
        Washington, 1850.
LATHAM, R. G.
  1856 On the Languages of Northern, Western, and Central America.
        Trans. Philological Soc. of London, pp. 51–115, London, 1856.
LEONARD, ZENAS.
  1904 Leonard's Narrative. Adventures of Zenas Leonard, Fur Trader
        and Trapper, 1831–36. Ed. by W. F. Wagner, from original edition
        of 1839. Cleveland, 1904.
LEWIS, DAVID.
  1855 Letter to Brigham Young. The Deseret News, Salt Lake City, Thurs.,
        Feb. 8, 1855.
LEWIS, MERIWETHER, and CLARK, WM.
  1904–5 Original Journals of the Lewis and Clark Expedition, 1804–6.
        8 vols. Reuben G. Thwaites, Editor. New York, 1904–1905.
LEWIS, WILLIAM S., and PHILLIPS, PAUL C., *Editors.*
  1923 The Journal of John Work, a Chief-trader of the Hudson's Bay Co.
        during his expedition from Vancouver to the Flatheads and Black-
        feet of the Pacific Northwest. Cleveland, 1923.
LOCKE, S. B.
  1929 Whitefish, Grayling, Trout, and Salmon of the Intermountain Region.
        Dept. of Commerce, Bur. of Fisheries, Doc. 1062, pp. 173–190,
        Washington, 1929.

LOUD, L. L., and HARRINGTON, M. R.
  1929 Lovelock Cave. Univ. Cal. Publ. Amer. Arch. and Ethn., 25: 1–183,
        1929.
LOWIE, ROBERT H.
  1909 The Northern Shoshone. Amer. Mus. Nat. Hist., Anthrop. Papers,
        2: 169–306, 1909.
  1909a Shoshone and Comanche Tales. Collected by H. H. St. Clair. Robert
        H. Lowie, *Editor.* Journ. Amer. Folk-Lore, 22: 1–20, 1909.
  1919 Sun Dance of the Shoshoni, Ute, and Hidatsa. Amer. Mus. Nat.
        Hist., Anthrop. Papers, 16: 387–431, 1919.
  1923 The Cultural Connection of California and Plateau Shoshonean
        Tribes. Univ. Cal. Publ. Amer. Arch. and Ethn., 20: 145–156, 1923.
  1924 Notes on Shoshonean Ethnography. Amer. Mus. Nat. Hist., Anthrop.
        Papers, 20: 187–314, 1924.
  1924a Shoshonean Tales. Journ. Amer. Folk-Lore, 37: 1–242, 1924.
  1933 The Family as a Social Unit. Michigan Acad. Sci., Arts and Letters,
        28: 53–69, 1932.
  1935 The Crow Indians. New York, 1935.
LYMAN, ALBERT R.
  1930 Pahute Biscuits. Utah Hist. Quart., 3: 118–120, 1930.
LYON, CALEB.
  1865 [Communication in] Rept. Com. Ind. Affairs for 1865, pp. 231–235,
        Washington, 1865.
MACK, EFFIE MONA.
  1936 Nevada, a history of the state from the earliest times through the
        Civil War. Glendale, California, 1936.
MANLY, WILLIAM LEWIS.
  1894 Death Valley in '49 . . . the autobiography of a pioneer. San Jose,
        Calif., 1894.
MANN, LUTHER, Jr.
  1865 [Communication in] Rept. Com. Ind. Affairs for 1865, pp. 158–160,
        Washington, 1865.
  1866 [Communication in] Rept. Com. Ind. Affairs for 1866, pp. 126–127,
        Washington, 1866.
  1868a [Communication in] Rept. Com. Ind. Affairs for 1867, p. 189,
        Washington, 1868.
  1868b [Communication in] Rept. Com. Ind. Affairs for 1868, pp. 156–159,
        Washington, 1868.
  1870 [Communication in] Rept. Com. Ind. Affairs for 1869, pp. 273–274,
        Washington, 1870.
MARSDEN, W. L.
  1923 The Northern Paiute Language of Oregon. Univ. Cal. Publ. Amer.
        Arch. and Ethn., 20: 175–191, 1923.
MASON, J. ALDEN.
  1910 Myths of the Uintah Utes. Journ. Amer. Folk-Lore, 23: 299–363, 1910.
MASON, OTIS T.
  1885 Basket-work of the North American aborigines. Smithsonian Ann.
        Rept. for 1884, part 2, pp. 291–306, Washington, 1885.
  1889 Cradles of the American Aborigines. U. S. Natl. Mus., Rept. for
        1887, pp. 161–212, Washington, 1889.
  1889a The Human Beast of Burden. U. S. Natl. Mus., Rept. for 1887, pp.
        237–295, Washington, 1889.

1891 Aboriginal Skin-Dressing. U. S. Natl. Mus., Rept. for 1889, pp. 553–589, Washington, 1891.

1894 North American Bows, Arrows, and Quivers. Smithsonian Ann. Rept. for 1893, pp. 631–679, Washington, 1894.

1901 The Technic of Aboriginal American Basketry. Amer. Anthrop., n. s. 3 : 109–128, 1901.

1902 Traps of the American Indians—A Study in Psychology and Invention. Smithsonian Ann. Rept. for 1901, pp. 461–473, Washington, 1902.

1904 Aboriginal American Basketry: Studies in a Textile Art Without Machinery. U. S. Nat. Mus., Rept. for 1902, pp. 171–548, Washington, 1904.

MEACHAM, A. B.
1872 [Communication in] Rept. Com. Ind. Affairs for 1871, pp. 297–309, Washington, 1872.

MEEK, JOSEPH L.
1848 Indians in the Territory of Oregon. *In* House Rep. Ex. Doc. 76, 30th Cong., 1st sess., p. 10, Washington, 1848.

MERRIAM. C. HART.
1926 The Buffalo in Northeastern California. Journ. Mammalogy, 7 : 211–214, 1926.

MÖLLHAUSEN, BALDWIN.
1860 Diary of a Journey from the Mississippi to the Coasts of the Pacific with a U. S. Exploring Expedition. 2 vols. London, 1860.

MOONEY, JAMES.
1896 The Ghost-Dance Religion and the Sioux Outbreak of 1890. Fourteenth Rept. Bur. Amer. Ethn., Pt. 2, Washington, 1896.

MORSE, Rev. JEDIDIAH.
1822 A Report to the Secretary of War of the United States, on Indian Affairs, Comprising a Narrative of a Tour Performed in the Summer of 1820. New Haven, 1822.

MULLAN, JOHN.
1855 Report of a Reconnaissance from the Bitter Root Valley to Fort Hall, thence to the Head of Hell Gate River, thence to the Bitter Root Valley. *In* Reports of Explorations and Surveys . . . for a Railroad from the Mississippi River to the Pacific Ocean, vol. 1, pp. 322–349. House Rep. Ex. Doc. 91, 33d Cong., 2d sess., Washington. 1855.

NATCHES, GILBERT.
1923 Northern Paiute Verbs. Univ. Calif. Publ. Amer. Arch. and Ethn., 20 : 245–259, 1923.

NELSON, E. W.
1891 The Panamint and Saline Valley Indians. Amer. Anthrop., 4 : 371–372, 1891.

OGDEN, PETER SKENE.
1909–1911 The Peter Skene Ogden Journals, (T. C. Elliott). Snake Expedition of 1825–26. Ogden Hist. Soc. Quart. 10: 331–365, 1909. Expedition of 1826–7, 11: 201–222, Portland, 1911.

PALMER, JOEL.
1847 Journal of Travels over the Rocky Mountains to the mouth of the Columbia River; made during the years 1845 and 1846. Cincinnati, 1847. Reprinted in Thwaites, "Early Western Travels," vol. 30, Cleveland, 1906.

PALMER, WILLIAM R.
1928   Indian Names in Utah Geography. Utah Hist. Quart., 1: 5–26, 1928.
1928a   Utah Indians, Past and Present (an Etymological and Historical Study of Tribes, Tribal Names, and Tribal Lands, from Original Sources). Ibid., 1: 35–52.
1929   Pahute Indian Government and Laws. Ibid., 2: 35–42, 1929.
1933   The Pahute Fire Legend. Utah Hist. Quart., 6, no. 2, pp. 62–64.
1933a   Pahute Indian Homelands. Utah Hist. Quart., 6, no. 3, pp. 88–102.

PARK, WILLARD Z.
1934   Paviotso Shamanism. Amer. Anthrop., n. s. 36: 98–113, 1934.
1937   Paviotso Polyandry. Amer. Anthrop., n. s. 39: 366–368, 1937.

PARKER, H. G.
1866   [Communication in] Rept. Com. Ind. Affairs for 1866, pp. 113–117, Washington, 1866.

PARKER, Rev. SAMUEL
1842   Journal of an Exploring Tour beyond the Rocky Mountains . . . in the Years 1835, '36, and '37. 3d Edition. New York, 1842.

POWELL, CHARLES F.
1868   [Communication in] Rept. Com. Ind. Affairs for 1868, pp. 201–203, Washington, 1868.

POWELL, J. W.
1875   Exploration of the Colorado River of the West and its Tributaries, explored in 1869, 1870, 1871, and 1872, under the direction of the Smithsonian Institution. Washington, 1875. [House Misc. Doc. 300, 43d Cong., 1st sess., 1875.]
1891   Indian Linguistic Families of America North of Mexico. Seventh Ann. Rept. Bur. Ethn., pp. 1–142, Washington, 1891.
1895   Canyons of the Colorado. Meadville, Pa., 1895.

POWELL, J. W., and INGALLS, G. W.
1874   Report on the Condition of the Ute Indians of Utah; the Pai-Utes of Utah, Northern Arizona, Southern Nevada, and Southeastern California; the Go-Si Utes of Utah and Nevada; the Northwestern Shoshones of Idaho and Utah; and the Western Shoshones of Nevada. Washington, 1874. (Also in Rept. Com. Ind. Affairs for 1873, pp. 41–46, Washington, 1874.)

POWERS, STEPHEN.
1876   Centennial Mission to the Indians of Western Nevada and California. Smithsonian Ann. Rept. for 1876, pp. 449–460, Washington, 1877.

REAGAN, ALBERT B.
1917   The Deep Creek Indians. El Palacio, 5: 30–42, Santa Fe, 1917.
1930   The Bear Dance of the Ouray Utes. Wisconsin Arch., 9: 148–150.
1934   Some notes on the History of the Uintah Basin, in northeastern Utah, to 1850. Proc. Utah Acad. Sci., Arts and Letters, 11: 55–64, 1934.
1934a   The Gosiute (Goshute), or Shoshoni-Goship Indians of the Deep Creek Region, in Western Utah. Proc. Utah Acad. Sci., Arts and Letters, 11: 43–54, 1934.
1935   Some Names of the Ute Indians of Utah, Followed by a Selected List of Words used by the Indians of the State. Ibid., 12: 1–45, 1935.
1935a   Ute Myths. Ibid., pp. 47–49.

REAGAN, ALBERT B., and STARK, WALLACE.
    1933   Chipeta, Queen of the Utes, and her Equally Illustrious Husband, Noted Chief Ouray. Utah Hist. Quart., vol. 6, No. 3, pp. 103–110, 1933.

REED, VERNER Z.
    1896   Ute Bear Dance. American Anthrop., 9: 237–244, 1896.

REMY, JULES, and BRENCHLEY, JULIUS.
    1861   A Journey to Great Salt Lake City. London, 1861.

REPORTS OF THE COMMISSIONER OF INDIAN AFFAIRS, Washington, 1849–1872.

ROBERTS, HELEN H.
    1936   Musical Areas in Aboriginal North America. Yale Univ. Publ. in Anthrop., 12: 1–41, 1936.

ROSS, ALEXANDER.
    1849   Adventures of the First Settlers on the Oregon or Columbia River. London, 1849. Reprinted in Thwaites, "Early Western Travels," vol. 7, Cleveland, 1904.
    1855   The Fur Hunters of the Far West; a Narrative of Adventures in the Oregon and Rocky Mountains. 2 vols. London, 1855.

RUSSELL, OSBORNE.
    1921   Journal of a Trapper. Boise, Idaho, 1921.

SALE, THOMAS C. W.
    1866   [Communications in] Rept. Com. Ind. Affairs for 1865, pp. 155–156, Washington, 1866.

SAPIR, EDWARD.
    1910   Two Paiute Myths. Univ. of Penn., The Museum Journal, 1: 15–18, 1910.
    1910a Song Recitative in Paiute Mythology. Journ. Amer. Folk-Lore, 23: 455–472, 1910.
    1930   Southern Paiute, a Shoshonean Language. Amer. Acad. Arts and Sci., Proc., vol. 65 (1) : 1–296.
    1930a Texts of the Kaibab Paiutes and Uintah Utes. Amer. Acad. Arts and Sci., Proc., vol. 65 (2) : 297–535.
    1931   Southern Paiute Dictionary. Amer. Acad. Arts and Sci., vol. 65, no. 3, pp. 536–730, 1931.

SCHOOLCRAFT, HENRY R.
    1851   Historical and Statistical Information Respecting the History, Condition, and Prospects of the Indian Tribes of the United States. Part 1. Philadelphia, 1851.
    1857   Ibid., pt. 6, 1857.

SCHULTZ, LEONARD P.
    1936   Keys to the Fishes of Washington, Oregon and Closely Adjoining Regions. Univ. Wash. Publ. in Biology, 2: 103–228, 1936.

SCRUGHAM, JAMES G., *Editor.*
    1935   Nevada—A Narrative of the Conquest of a Frontier Land. 3 vols. Amer. Hist. Soc. Inc., Chicago and New York, 1935.

SETON, ERNEST THOMPSON.
    1929   Lives of Game Animals. 4 vols. New York, 1929.

SHURTLIFF, LEWIS W.
    1932   The Salmon River Mission. Utah Hist. Quart., 5, no. 1, 1932.

SIMPSON, CAPT. J. H.
    1876 Report of Explorations across the Great Basin of the Territory of
          Utah for a Direct Wagon-Route from Camp Floyd to Genoa, in
          Carson Valley, in 1859. U. S. Army, Engineer. Dept., Washington,
          1876.
SMITH, A. I.
    1872 [Communication in] Rept. Com. Ind. Affairs for 1871, p. 432, Wash-
          ington, 1872.
SNOW, WILLIAM J.
    1929 Utah Indians and Spanish Slave Trade. Utah Hist. Quart., 2:
          67–73, 1929.
SNYDER, J. O.
    1917 The Fishes of the Lahontan System of Nevada and Northeastern
          California. U. S. Bur. Fisheries, Doc. 843, Bull. 35: 31–86, 1915–16,
          Washington, 1917.
    1919 An Account of Some Fishes from Owens River, California. U. S.
          Nat. Mus., Proc., 54 (no. 2233) : 201–205, 1917.
SPIER, LESLIE.
    1928 Havasupai Ethnography. Amer. Mus. Nat. Hist., Anthrop. Papers
          29: 81–392, 1928.
    1935 The Prophet Dance of the Northwest and its Derivatives: The Source
          of the Ghost Dance. Gen. Ser. in Anthrop., 1. Menasha, Wis., 1935.
    1936 Cultural Relations of the Gila and Lower Colorado River Tribes.
          Yale Univ. Publ. in Anthrop., 3: 1–22, 1936.
SPINDEN, HERBERT J.
    1908 The Nez Percé Indians. Mem. Amer. Anthrop. Assoc., 2: 167–328,
          1908.
SPURR, JOSIAH EDWARD.
    1903 Descriptive Geology of Nevada South of the Fortieth Parallel and
          Adjacent Portions of California. U. S. Geol. Surv., Bull. 208,
          ser. B, Descriptive Geology, 27. Washington, 1903.
ST. CLAIR, H. H. (ROBERT H. LOWIE, ED.)
    1909 Shoshone and Comanche Tales. Journ. Amer. Folk-Lore, 22: 265–282,
          1909.
STANSBURY, HOWARD.
    1852 Exploration and Survey of the Valley of the Great Salt Lake of Utah,
          including a Reconnaissance of a New Route through the Rocky
          Mountains. Senate Ex. Doc., No. 3, Special sess., March 1851.
          Philadelphia, 1852.
STEWARD, JULIAN H.
    1930 Irrigation without Agriculture. Mich. Acad. Sci., 12: 149–156, 1930.
    1932 The Uintah Ute Bear Dance, March 21–29, 1931. Amer. Anthrop.,
          n. s. 34: 263–273, 1932.
    1933 Ethnography of the Owens Valley Paiute. Univ. Cal. Publ. Amer.
          Arch. and Ethn., 33: 233–350, 1933.
    1933a Aborigines of Utah. In "Utah—Resources and Activities", pp.
          161–167. Dept. of Public Instruction, Salt Lake City, 1933.
    1934 Two Paiute Autobiographies. Univ. Cal. Publ. Amer. Arch. and
          Ethn., 33: 423–438, 1934.
    1936 Myths of the Owens Valley Paiute. Ibid., 34: 355–440, 1936.
    1936a Shoshoni Polyandry. Amer. Anthrop., n. s. 38: 561–564, 1936.
    1936b Pueblo Material Culture in Western Utah. Univ. New Mex., Bull.
          287 (Anthrop. ser. 1) pp. 1–63, 1936.

1936c The Economic and Social Basis of Primative Bands. *In* Essays in
        Anthropology presented to A. L. Kroeber, pp. 331–350, Berkeley,
        Calif., 1936.

1937   Linguistic Distributions and Political groups of the Great Basin
        Shoshoneans. Amer. Anthrop., n. s. 39: 625–634, 1937.

1937a Ecological Aspects of Southwestern Society. Anthropos, 32: 87–
        104, 1937.

1937b Ancient Caves of the Great Salt Lake Region. Bull. 116, Bur. Amer.
        Ethn., Washington, 1937.

STEWART, OMER C.

1937   Northern Paiute Polyandry. Amer. Anthrop. n. s. 39: 368–369, 1937.

SUDWORTH, GEORGE B.

1917   The Pine Trees of the Rocky Mountain Region. U. S. Dept. Agr.,
        Bull. 460, Washington, 1917.

SULLIVAN MAURICE S.

1934   The Travels of Jedediah Smith. A Documentary Outline including
        the Journal of the Great American Pathfinder. Santa Ana, Calif.,
        1934.

SULLY, ALFRED.

1870   [Communication in] Rept. Com. Ind. Affairs for 1869, pp. 289–293,
        Washington, 1870.

TANNER, VASCO M.

1936   A Study of the Fishes of Utah. Brigham Young Univ. Contr.
        Dept. of Zool. and Ento., No. 39. Also, Proc. Utah Acad. Sci.,
        Arts and Letters, 13: 155–184, Provo, Utah, 1936.

TEIT, JAMES A.

1928   The Middle Columbia Salish. Univ. Wash. Publ. in Anthrop.,
        2: 83–128, 1928.

1930   The Salishan Tribes of the Western Plateaus (Franz Boas, *Editor*).
        Forty-fifth Ann. Rept. Bur. Amer. Ethn., pp. 23–396, Washington,
        1930.

THOMPSON, DAVID.

1916   David Thompson's Narrative of his Explorations in Western America,
        1784–1812. J. B. Tyrell, *Editor*. Toronto, 1916.

TIDESTROM, IVAR.

1925   Flora of Utah and Nevada. U. S. Nat. Mus., Natl. Herbarium, Contr.,
        vol. 25, Washington, 1925.

TOURTELLOTTE, J. E.

1870   [Communication in] Rept. Com. Ind. Affairs for 1869, pp. 229–231,
        Washington, 1870.

TOWNSEND, JOHN K.

1839   Narrative of a Journey across the Rocky Mountains to the Columbia
        River. Phila., 1839. *Reprinted in part in* Thwaites "Early Western
        Travels," vol. 21, pp. 113–369, Cleveland, 1905.

VAILE, H. M.

1863   [Communication in] Rept. Com. Ind. Affairs for 1862, pp. 232–238,
        Washington, 1863.

WASSON, WARREN.

1863   [Communication in] Rept. Com. Ind. Affairs for 1862, pp. 222–227,
        Washington, 1863.

WATERMAN, T. T.
　1911　The Phonetic Elements of the Northern Paiute Language. Univ. Cal.
　　　　Publ. Amer. Arch. and Ethn., 10: 13–44, 1911.
WEAVER, J. E.
　1917　A Study of the vegetation of Southeastern Washington and adjacent
　　　　Idaho. Univ. Nebraska, Univ. Studies, vol. 17, No. 1, 1917.
WHEELER, GEORGE M.
　1875　Preliminary Report upon a Reconnaissance through Southern and
　　　　Southeastern Nevada, 1869. U. S. Army, Engineering Department.
　1879　Report upon United States Geographical Surveys west of the One
　　　　Hundredth Meridian. Vol. 7, Archaeology. Washington, 1879.
WHIPPLE, A. W., EWBANK, THOMAS, and TURNER, WILLIAM M.
　1856　Report upon the Indian Tribes. U. S. War Dept. Repts. of Ex-
　　　　plorations and Surveys . . . for a Railroad from the Mississippi
　　　　River to the Pacific Ocean, 1853–54. Vol. 3, Washington, 1856.
WHORF, B. L.
　1935　The Comparative Linguistics of Uto-Aztecan. Amer. Anthrop., n. s.
　　　　37: 606–608, 1935.
WILKES, CHARLES.
　1845　Narrative of the United States Exploring Expedition, 1838 to 1842.
　　　　Vol. 4, pp. 471–474; Phila., 1845; also in Utah Hist. Quart., 2:
　　　　73–75, 1929.
WILLIAMS, P. L.
　1928　Personal Recollections of Wash-a-kie, Chief of the Shoshones. Utah
　　　　Hist. Quart., 1: 101–106, 1928.
WILSON, E. M.
　1919　The White Indian Boy. The Story of Uncle Nick Among the Sho-
　　　　shones. Revised and edited by Howard R. Driggs, Yonkers-on-
　　　　Hudson, N. Y., 1919.
WILSON, JOHN.
　1850　[Communication in] Rept. Com. Ind. Affairs for 1849–50, pp. 66–68,
　　　　Washington, 1850.
WISSLER, CLARK.
　1914　The Influence of the Horse in the Development of Plains Culture.
　　　　Amer. Anthrop., n. s. 16: 1–25, 1914.
　1922　The American Indian. 2d edition. New York, 1922.
WOODBURY, ANGUS M.
　1931　A Descriptive Catalogue of the Reptiles of Utah. Univ. of Utah,
　　　　Bull. 21, No. 5, 1931.
WOOTON, E. O.
　1932　The Public Domain of Nevada and Factors Affecting its Use. U. S.
　　　　Dept. Agr., Technical Bull. 301. Washington, 1932.
WORK, JOHN. See LEWIS and PHILLIPS.
WYETH, NATHANIEL J.
　1851　Indian Tribes of the South Pass of the Rocky Mountains; the Salt
　　　　Lake Basin; the Valley of the Great Säaptin, or Lewis' River,
　　　　and the Pacific Coasts of Oregon. In Schoolcraft, vol. 1, pp.
　　　　204–228, Phila., 1851.
YOUNG, BRIGHAM.
　1852　[Communication in] Rept. Com. Ind. Affairs for 1852, pp. 147–149,
　　　　Washington, 1852.

INDEX